The Study and Writing of Poetry:

American Women Poets Discuss Their Craft

The Study and Writing of Poetry:

American Women Poets Discuss Their Craft

edited by

Wauneta Hackleman

The Whitston Publishing Company
Troy, New York
1983

TO THEM

Dedicated to the women poets who contributed articles and
poetry in this collection, but especially to the
Editorial Committee:

Wilma Wicklund Burton
Catharine Fieleke
Alfarata Hansel

who not only contributed, but lost count of the hours they
spent in editing the manuscript for grammatical errors, and
attesting that techniques were adhered to and references
were correct.

TABLE OF CONTENTS

Acknowledgments. vi

Introduction xiii

POETIC FORMS

The Acrostic   Wilma W. Burton. 3
The Ballad   Ethel Eikel Harvey 7
The Ballade   Cecilia Parsons Miller. 12
Blank Verse   Jaye Giammarino 19
The Burtonelle   Wilma W. Burton. 24
Poetry and the Child   Libby Stopple. 26
Cinquain   Violette Newton 31
Clerihewing With Clerihews   Frances Tunnell Carter 34
Understanding and Writing
  Couplets   Margaret Honton. 38
The Elegy   Frona Lane 48
Epic: A Comet Among Stars   Ora Pate Stewart. 51
The Epitaph   Donna Shriver Jones 65
Free Verse   Jean R. Jenkins. 70
The Lai Group and
  Other French Forms   Amy Jo Zook 74
Humorous or Light Poetry   Irene Warsaw. 86
Will You All Come Up To
  Limerick!   Vivian M. Meyer 91
Lyric: The Ecstasy
  Experience   Ora Pate Stewart. 97
Dramatic Monolog: Story
  or Poem?   Donna Dickey Guyer. 108
Native American Poetry   Jean Humphrey Chaillie 114
The Ode   Frona Lane 122
Haiku, Senryu and Tanka   Truth Mary Fowler 127
The Orvillette   Wauneta Hackleman 132
The Pantoum   Marel Brown 134
Parody   Jaye Giammarino 136

Persona	Amy Jo Zook	139
Quatrain	donnafred	145
The Quintain	Lois Carden	151
The Rondeau	Marel Brown	155
Rhymed Verse	Clovita Rice	158
Secrets of the Sestina	Anne Marx	166
The Sevenelle	Virginia Noble	175
The Beymorlin Sonnet	Wauneta Hackleman	176
Glorionic Sonnet	Gloria Martin	177
The Mason Sonnet	Jeanne Bonnette	181
Petrarchan Sonnet	Guanetta Gordon	185
Shakespearean Sonnet	Catharine N. Fieleke	187
Terza Rima	Ruth Van Ness Blair	191
The Triolet	Marel Brown	198
The Triplet and the Tercet	Margaret Honton	201
Tuanortsa	Guanetta Gordon	208
Villanelle	Emma S. McLaughlin	210

SYLLABIC FORMS

The Anna	Anna Nash Yarbrough	217
Cameo	Anna Nash Yarbrough	217
Cinquetin	Anna Nash Yarbrough	218
Cinquo	Anna Nash Yarbrough	218
The Diamante	Cecilia Parsons Miller	218
Ercil	Anna Nash Yarbrough	221
Etheree	Jaye Giammarino	221
The Fantasy	Cecilia Parsons Miller	224
Grayette	Anna Nash Yarbrough	226
Hexaduad	Anna Nash Yarbrough	226
Kerf	Anna Nash Yarbrough	227
Kyrielle	Anna Nash Yarbrough	228
Lanterne	Gloria Martin	228
Laurette	Anna Nash Yarbrough	232
The Manardina	Cecilia Parsons Miller	233
Minute	Anna Nash Yarbrough	234
Neville	Anna Nash Yarbrough	235
Octain	Anna Nash Yarbrough	236
Octo	Anna Nash Yarbrough	236
Onda Mel	Anna Nash Yarbrough	237
Oriental Octet	Anna Nash Yarbrough	237
Pensee	Anna Nash Yarbrough	238
Quatern	Anna Nash Yarbrough	238
Rispetto	Anna Nash Yarbrough	239
Sept	Anna Nash Yarbrough	240
Septet	Anna Nash Yarbrough	240

Shadorma   Anna Nash Yarbrough. 241
Tango   Anna Nash Yarbrough. 241
Tripod   Anna Nash Yarbrough. 241

POETIC TECHNIQUES

Alliteration in Poetry   Virginia Bagliore 245
Assonance-Consonance   D. L. Rudy 249
Cadence in Poetry   Dorothea Neale. 254
Clarity   Verna Lee Hinegardner 258
Poetry in the Classroom   Evelyn Amuedo Wade. 263
Contemporary vs Traditional
  Poetry?   Anne Marx 266
"I Enter"   Alice Morrey Bailey. 272
Concrete Diction   Ida Fasel 278
If You Write a Poem   Marel Brown 284
Imagism   Alfarata Hansel 288
The Importance of Imagery   Alice Briley. 292
The Importance of Metaphor   Alfarata Hansel 298
Parallelism in Poetry   Wanda Allender Rider. 303
Preparing the Manuscript   Grace Kirk Wofford. 309
Prosody   Wilma W. Burton. 316
To Market, To Market . . .   Frances Riemer Burt. 322
Translation   Margaret T. Rudd 326
Challenge—Your Tinder!   Vienna Ione Curtiss. 330
One of the Hidden Unicorns
  in Poetry: Therapy   Wilma W. Burton. 333
Variations in Rhyming   Agnes Homan 339

Quick Reference Index 345

Contributors' Notes. 394

ACKNOWLEDGMENTS

Academic American Encyclopedia, P-85, Arete' Publishing Co., Inc., © 1980; Merit Students Encyclopedia, P-38, MacMillan, © 1979; The World Book Encyclopedia, P-26, World Book International, Inc., © 1979; Enclclopedia Americana, P-121, American Corporation, © 1979; Encyclopedia Brittanica, P-103, William Benton Publishers, © 1970; The American Peoples Encyclopedia, P-1-107, The Spenser Press, Inc., © 1953; Hollow Reed by Mary J. J. Wrinn (How To Revise your Own Poems by Anne Hamilton; THE SACK OF ROME, Mercy Otis Watten, published in THE POETRY OF AMERICAN WOMEN 1632-1943; A UNIVERSAL LAW—Jane Giamarino, published in THE VILLAGER 1978; GOOD NEWS PUBLISHERS—sidewalk psalms and SOME COUNTRY LANES BY WILMA BURTON; THE HAUNTING by Reba Terry; Wakebrook House, 1975, 3rd in a 3-part poem from THE INELUCTABLE SEA by Edna Meudt; Haiku Highlights; American Poetry League; Poetry Society of New Hampshire newsletter; OUTCH International Haiku; California Federation of Chaparral Poets; The Nutmeg; Swordsman Review; Poems from A WORD IN EDGEWISE and WARILY WE ROLL ALONG by Golden Quill Press, Francestown, New Hampshire; Baring-Gould, William S. and Cecil Baring-Gould, eds.; The Annotated Mother Goose, New York: Clarkson N. Potter, Inc., 1962; Cerf, Bennet, ed., OUT ON A LIMERICK, New York: Harper and Bros., 1960; UNRIPE FRUIT by Vivan M. Meyer, Isabel Poeltler and Richard K. Wright, eds., New Jersey Poetry Society, Inc., 1973; Perrine, Laurence, SOUND AND SENSE published by Harcourt, Brace and Jovanovich, Inc., 1975; Pennington, Alex., Frank J. Warnke, and O. B. Hardison, Jr., eds. THE PRINCETON ENCYCLOPEDIA of POETRY and POETICS by Princeton University Press, 1974; Untermeyer, Lewis THE PURSUIT OF POETRY, published by Harper and Rowe, 1960; Wells, Catherineed, CAROLINE WELLS BOOK OF AMERICAN LIMERICKS New York and London: Knickerbocker Press, 1925; Wood, Clement, COMPLETE RHYMING DICTIONARY and POETS CRAFT BOOK,

Garden City Press, New York, 1936, The American College Dictionary, Random House, New York, 1961; Poetry by J. D. O'Hara, World Culture Series, Newsweek Books, New York, 1975; Encyclopedia Brittanica, 1976; Sara Teasdale: Woman and Poet, William D. Drake, Harper and Row, 1979, New York, Pages 40-41; Biblical References from King James Bible; Ibid, by William Drake, Harper and Row, 1979; Dictionary of Quotations, Bergen Evans, Delacort Press, New York, 1968; Ireland in Color, by Harold Clarke, © B. T. Batsford, Ltd., London, England, 1970; Imaginary Conversations, Archdeacon Hare and Walter Landor, Collins Gen Dictionary of Quotations, 1961; William Collins Sons and Company, Ltd., London and Glascow, Page 268; Poems by Ora Pate Stewart from Summer Silver-Autumn Gold; The Improvement Era 1968; The California Writer 1968; World Poetry, Madras, India, 1969; York Poetry Anthology, England, 1971; Utah Sings Vol. V, 1974; The Ensign, June 1978; The Brightness of Hope by Ora Stewart; Poem "Moon's Ending" by Sara Teasdale from Strange Victory, published posthumously 1933, The MacMillan Co., New York; The Collected Poems of Sara Teasdale, The MacMillan Co., 1937; The Pen Woman, December issue, 1976, Fernwood Publications, 1978; Three-Generation Bible, published by Relief Society Magazine, August, 1965; Song of the Cradleboard, published by Arizona Highways, 1978 © by The Arizona Department of Transportation, author Jean Chaillie; The Wedding Day by Jean Chaillie, published in Passage 1976 by Triton College Press, River Grove, IL, reprint permission to Arizona Highways Magazine 1978; Walking the Trail published in Sandcutters, Arizona State Poetry Society Publication 1981; Tribesman, Bittersweet Joy and Song of the Grinding Stone by Jean Chaillie; "Lesson Learned in the Orient" by Anne Marx (Pantoum) in her book Face Lift for All Seasons, 1980, published in Voices International and translated in Bahasa Indonisia (Jakarta); "Hope for a Hostage" by Anne Marx (Malayan Pantoum) published in New York Times and Face Life for All Seasons 1980; New Rhyming Dictionary; Poets Handbook by Burges Johnson; Encore; New Laurel Review, Spoon River Quarterly; Cornfield Review; Bluegrass Literary Review; Pivot, Pteranodon, Kentucky Poetry Review, Cumberlands; The Lyric, Great Lakes Review; Amy Jo Schoonover poems from Echoes of England, 1976; A Sonnet Sampler, Spoon River Poetry Press, 1979 and a New Page, 1979-Reviews by Ohioana Quarterly; Emily Dickinson, Collected

Works, Hallmark; Not So Deep As a Well, Dorothy Parker by Viking Press; Edna St. Vincent Millay from the Buck in the Snow by Harper Brothers; Poems from Pocket Piece by donnafred, published by Marizona Press, 1977, AZ; Love Runs Naked by donnafred, published by Word Weavers Press, 1972; SCORE, published Arizona Republic Sunday Magazine; POET LORE; AIKIN'S BY WAY OF PEOPLE, 1970; The Croton Review; Face Life for All Seasons, Golden Quill Press, © 1980 by Anne Marx; poems by Liboria Romano; The Poet Converses with a Mouse by Carlee Swann, Lebanon, S.D.; National Federation of State Poetry Societies, Inc., Anthology 1978; Clement Wood Poets Handbook, 1940; Iowa Poetry Day Assn's. Bicentennial "Brochure of Poems" P. 25, 1976, Parnassas, Spring, 1977; Parnassus, Fall, 1977 (winning Glorionic Sonnets); THE SILENT HARP (Glorionic Sonnet) by Thelma Murphy, published Parnassus, Fall, 1977; Anthology of World Poetry, Mark Van Doren, 1928; Notes on the Sonnet, Madeline Mason, 1971; The Challengers, Ernest Kay, 1975; Sonnets in a New Form, Cronel Lengyel, 1971; Strophes, April, 1977; FIRST LOVE by Guanetta Gordon, American Bard, Under the Rainbow Arch by Windfall Press; RED ARE THE EMBERS by Guanetta Gordon, published Golden Quill Press; Understanding Poetry by Cleanth Brook and Robert Penn Warren, Holt, Rhinehart and Winston, 1963; The Pen Woman (A Message from Dante), 1980; The Collected Poems of Muriel Rukeyser, McGraw Hill Book Co., 1978; The Collected Poems of Edna St. Vincent Millay, Harper and Row Publishers, 1956; The Collected Poems of Babette Deutsch, Doubleday and Company, 1969; Sylvia Plath, New Views in Poetry, edited by Gary Lane, Johns Hopkins University Press, 1979; Creative Writing of Verse by Arthur Moller, American Book Co., 1932; Handbook of English Literature, Homer and William Watt, Barnes, Noble and Co., 1959; Poetry Handbook, Babette Deutsch, Funk and Wagnall's, 1946; Poet's Handbook, Clement Wood, World Publishing Co., 1946; The Poet and the Poem, Judson Jerome, Writer's Digest Press, 1963; TROILET FOR SPRING by Marel Brown, published Georgia Life Magazine; THE SONG OF THE SEA by Marel Brown, published Hearth-Fire; The Woman Poets in English, McGraw Hill Book Company, 1972, PP. 82-84; Philips' Poems (London, printed by J. M. for H. Herrington at the Sign of the BLEW ANCHOR in the Lower Walk of the New Exchange, P. 143, 1667; Patriotic Heart Songs, Grosset and Dunlap, by arrangement with Chapel Publishing Com., P. 6; Isabella

Gardner's THAT WAS THEN, Boa Publishers, 1980 earlier published under "Cock-A-Hoop in Quest of Childhood," Houghton Mifflin, 1965; The Complete Poems of Elizabeth Bishop, published by Strauss & Giroux, PP. 39-45, 1970; Josephine Miles, Poems 1930-1960, Bloomington Indiana University Press, 1960; Margaret Honton's poems from TAKE FIRE, Dawn Valley Press, 1980, Driftwood East; Above Making Waves, Columbus, Ohio, Woodwinds Impress, 1978; The Sandcutters, Arizona State Poetry Society house organ; POET International; TODAY, SOMEWHERE, poem by LaNita Moses, FL; Anonymous Western Wind, © 1500, P-5 from Western Winds, John Frederick Nims, Random House, Inc., 1954; Coleridge, Samuel Taylor, P-189 from Western Wind; de la Mare, Walter, P-13 from Poetry: Elizabeth Drew, A Delta Book Published by Dell Publishing Co., Inc., 1959; Dickinson, Emily, MY LIFE CLOSED TWICE, P-91 from Sound and Sense, Laurence PERRINE: Harcourt, Brace and World, Inc., 1963; Random House, 1954; Highet, Gilbert, THE POWERS OF POETRY, Oxford University Press, 1960; Isaacs, J., THE BACKGROUND OF MODERN POETRY, E. P. Dutton and Co., 1952; "Literature de Quebec," Europe, Revue Mensuelle February/March, 1966; Bergen Poets, VII, Fall, 1980; from books by D. L. Rudy; Quality of Small, American Poets Fellowship Soc., 1971; Psyche Afoot, Golden Quill, 1979; Grace Notes to the Measure of the Heart, Cranford, N. J. Merging Media, 1979; Sixty Plus; Coffman, Stanley K., Jr., "Imagism" Octogan Books, A division of Farrar, Straus and Giroux, 1977; Gould, Jean, "Amy. The World of Amy Lowell and the Imagist Movement," Dodd, Mead and Co., 1975; "The Imagist Poem" by Benet, William Rose and Aiken, Conrad by E. P. Dutton and Co., 1963; Smith, Janet Adam, "The Living Stream," Faber and Faber, London, 1969; "Look Homeward" by Alfarata Hansel, Alpha Publishing Co., 1980; Kaleidograph and Literary Digest published poem GRACE BEFORE BOOKS; CANA published Poets Forum, 1933; CLOVES-Oregonian, reprinted in B. D. Magazine for Xavier Society, Blind and Deaf, in Braille; LATE SPRING in Greenhouse, Commercial Appeal, The Pen Woman; CYNIC in The Mountain Breeze, Book IV; ACHIEVEMENT published in Toward the Stars and the Muse; Rudd's AND THREE SMALL FISHES (translation), McClure Press, 1974; The Healing Power of Poetry by Dr. Smiley Blaton T. Baker, TIME Magazine; The Writer, June, 1980; Sidewalk Psalms by Wilma Burton, 1979; LIFE'S GREAT SHOW and CAPPY, by Vienna

Ione Curtiss; T. E. Sanders, The Discovery of Poetry, published by Scott, Foresman, © 1967; X. L. Kennedy's An Introduction to Poetry, 2nd edition, published by Little, Brown, 1966, 1971; American Peoples Encyclopedia, published by Spencer Press, 1948, Webster's New World Dictionary, published by William Collins, Inc., © 1980; Harper's Dictionary of Contemporary Usage, Harper and Row, © 1975, Webster's Unabridged Dictionary, Dierkes Press, Chicago, © 1953; Palm Beach Sun, 1940; Florzari Rockwood's Notebook, 1939; Chelsea Standard Newspaper, 1968; Blue Ribbon Books, Inc., Encyclopedia Brittanica, 11th edition, 1910-1911; Rostand, Edmond, CYRANO de BERGERAC (Brian Hooker translation) Henry, Holt and Co., © 1926; Robert Penn Warren, UNDERSTANDING POETRY, Henry, Holt, Co., © 1938 and 4th edition, © 1976; Clement Wood's ESSENTIAL HANDBOOK, Doubleday & Co., Inc., © 1936; Glenview Announcements, 1977; Patterns in Poetry, Harry M. Brown and John Milstead, Scott, Foresman and Co., 1968; Types of Poetry, Zeitlin and Rinaker, The MacMillan Co., 1930; Versification in English Poetry, Geo. B. Woods, Scott, Foresman and Co., 1958; Spoon River Anthology, Edgar Lee Masters, Collier Books, MacMillan & Co., 1962; The Columbia-Viking Desk Encyclopedia, 3rd ed. Viking Press, 1968; Interpretation of: Theatre, Scott, Foresman & Co.; A Book of Epitaphs, W. H. Howe; HERE LIES; Leslie M. Thompson, unpublished ms. SEXISM IN THE CEMETERY; TIME Magazine, March 30, 1981; MacMillan Publishing Co., © 1937; Reader's Digest Great Encyclopedia Dictionary, Random House Dictionary of the English Language Unabridged, Random House, 1967; Poetry World of Culture, Newsweek Books; The Revised College Omnibus, Harcourt-Brace, In., The Complete Poems of Robert Frost, Holt-Rhinehard, Winston NY, 12th printing, 1961; TO THE UNBORN published by Illinois State Poetry Society; requested for publication in Right to Life Magazine; American Heritage Dictionary, New Collegiate Dictionary; Encyclopedia of Poetry and Poetics by Clifton Fadiman; Dictionary of World Literature Terms, Jos. and T. Wadell Shipley; The World in Literature, Robert Warnock and George K. Anderson, Scott, Foresman and Co., © 1950; THE OXFORD BOOK OF VERSE, P-306; Elaine Barry, Robert Frost on Writing, P-129, © 1973-originally published in preface to his 1946 Modern Languge Edition; Aristotle's Poetics, translated by S. H. Butcher, P-99, © 1961; May Sarton, "The School of Babylon," from MOMENT IN POETRY, edited by

Don Cameron Allen, P. 38, © 1962; Edna Meudt, NO ONE SINGS FACE DOWN, Wisconsin House, © 1970; Alleghany Press, © 1976; Louisiana State Poetry Society: 1978 Louisiana Showcase; Calkins Handbook, P. 52; Dictionary of Literary Terms, Jos. Shipley and T. Wadel Shipley, THE WRITER, Inc.; The World in Literature, P. 306, Robert Warnock and George K. Anderson, Scott Foresman and Company, from THE OXFORD BOOK OF VERSE 1950; Syllabic poetry patterns: Anna Nash Yarbourgh's Syllabic Poetry Patterns, © 1978 by Quality Printing Company-Arkansas; SEED OF LOVE, published by Poettidings, January, 1972; Arkansas Poets Roundtable, 1979; Jessie Ruhl Miller's HEAVEN AND EARTH from Maybe It's Upside Down; Horizons, house organ of Western Poetry League, 1937; Flozari Rockwood's NOTEBOOK, 1939; Glowing Lanternes, 1969-1976, Chelsea Standard Newspaper, 1963, EARTHWISE by Nel Modglin; INSOMNIA and ONE GREEN LEAF, Verna Lee Hinegardner; VICTIM by Julia Hurd Strong, published in 1980 NFSPS Anthology; Poems by James R. Gray, American Poetry League Magazine, Winter, 1979; Poet's Forum, Benton Courier (newspaper); The Times (newspaper) in LATCHSTRING column; Webster's Dictionary © 1921; Elementary English, May, 1969, P. 588; Poetic Composition, Robert Wolsch, Teachers College Press, Columbia University, © 1970, PP. 156-158; Webster's Third New International Dictionary; Helen Thomas Allison, "Shadows" in PORTALS, edited by Edna Perviance, Billingham, WA., February, 1980; Inez Elliott Andersen, "Lawn Lore" in NEVER SEND TO KNOW, Kingsport Press, 1962, P. 81; Andersen's FROM A SOUTHERN SPOON RIVER ANTHOLOGY, in AND NOW I HAVE TOLD YOU, Riverside Press, 1979, P. 96; Helen Thomas Allison, "My Possessions" in Springfield News, Springfield, MO., and in Tennessee Voices, The Poetry Society of Tennessee, 1970; George Def. Lord, editor, Andrew Marvell, Complete Poetry, New York: The Modern Library, 1968, PP. 48-50; Abraham Lincoln's "Gettysburg Address" in Freedom's Frontier, Edited by Ray Compton, Chicago: Lyons and Carnahan, 1953, P. 85; Patrick Henry's "Speech in the Virginia Convention" in Literature of America, edited by J. N. Hook, Ginn & Company, 1957, P. 59; Calkins, Jean (compiler) HANDBOOK ON HAIKU and other Form Poems, Kanona, New York: J & C Transcripts, 1970; Babette Deutsch, Poetry Handbook: A Dictionary of Terms, 5th edition, New York: Funk and Wagnalls, 1974; Alex Preminger, et al., (editors) Princeton Encyclopedia of Poetry and Poetics, Princeton, 1974; Gerald Sanders, "A Poetry Primer," New York: Holt, Rhinehart and Winston, 1935 (reprint 1963); Joseph T. Shipley DICTIONARY OF WORLD LITERARY TERMS, Boston, The Writer, 1943, Lewis Turco, The Book of Forms: A Handbook of Poetics, New York, Dutton, 1968.

INTRODUCTION

For this book fifty women poets have written essays on all accepted forms. Also, some new forms have been included which we feel will be accepted after studying this book. They have prepared their essays in contemporary form and from a woman's viewpoint but be assured, they have referred to the old masters, most of them men, for research and reference. The poems in this book are theirs or those of well-known women poets of this era.

It is a first of its kind in the marketplace.

While there are many excellent study books on the market today, there are none that compare to the completeness of this volume. It takes a poetry form and gives you the origin, history, how to build the form into a poem and an example(s) to enlighten you. The *techniques* of writing poetry are discussed in articles covering each technique in detail and with example poetry. One section takes up syllabic poetry for exercises in classrooms, seminars, workshops, or for study by the individual poet. Every poet represented in this book has been or is a teacher at college or university level, or is an editor of a poetry magazine, or lecturer.

There are two uses of language—everyday use or its transfiguration into literary art. Language is one essential tool which almost anyone can handle as effortlessly as he uses the limbs and organs of the body. We are not all born poets so we should master the craft. To do it, we must have instruments. *This book is such an instrument.* Use it and become a craftsman of the art of writing poetry that will live on into other centuries. Contemporary poets listen to different drummers. They can write modern or traditional poetry, but the goal of every poet should be to compose a masterpiece in his lifetime.

This book describes techniques with which to become better poets. For teachers, it provides instructional material. And for everyone interested in poetry we have a *glossary of terms.* This is a separate alphabetized section of more than three hundred and seventy poetry terms. It is a quick reference source to the understanding of poetry.

With pride we offer you the works of fifty of America's well-known women poets.

POETIC FORMS

THE ACROSTIC

Wilma W. Burton

The Acrostic is a verse form in which initial letters of each line (or sometimes the final letters, or inner letters) in vertical order comprise a word or phrase or a regular sequence of the alphabet.

It is usually used in light verse, but can be adapted to more serious poetry as in the acrostic formed from the Hebraic alphabet which appears in the last 22 verses of the 31st chapter or Proverbs, known as the "Good Woman of Proverbs," which employs the entire Hebraic alphabet in proper sequence:

A virtuous woman--who can find?
B eyond the price of rubies is her worth.
C onstantly her husband trusts in her;
D oer of good and refrainer from evil,
F amily needs are her concern--
G iving food to her household brings her joy.
H arvest is hers; for she tends her garden well.
K indly, her arms reach out to the poor.
L inen and wool she weaves against winter cold.
M any, too, are the garments she makes of silk and purple.
N ever disgrace, but honor she brings her husband.
P atience is hers awaiting future joy.
Q uick is her tongue to speak wisdom.
R ewards crown her head for her goodness.
S uch kudos arise from her husband and children.
S halom surrounds her house. In
T ruth her household shall sing her praises:
V irtue is in all her ways for she is a
W oman who walks in the fear of the Lord.
X anadu is another name for her dwelling place.
Y ahweh is well pleased with her
Z eal for good works: they follow her wherever she goes.

(Paraphrased by Wilma Burton)

The word acrostic is taken from the words in Greek, *akros* "at the end" and *stichos,* "line or verse." The form is common in antiquity among Greeks of the Alexandrine period as well as with Latin writers. One of the most remarkable acrostics was contained in Greek verses cited by Eusobius in the 4th Century, the initial letters forming "Jesus Christ, the Son of God, the Saviour." The first letter of each word make up the word Ichthys (fish) to which mystical meaning has been attached, the fish being a symbol of Christ in early Christian literature and art.

Writing of acrostics dates back to the Scriptures with well known examples being the *abecedarian* in Psalms 25 and 119.

While most acrostics use initial letters, when the final letters or words of lines are used, a "telestic" is introduced. When the letters of the acrostic run down the center of the poem, it is called the "mesostic" form. In the following Latin verse the acrostic, mesostic and telestic are used (letters "i" and "j" are considered equivalent, as are "u" and "v"):

I nter cuncta micans	I gniti	sidera	coel I
E xpellit tenebras	E toto	Phoebus ut	rob E
S ic caecas removit	I E S U S	caliginis	umbra S
V ivicansque simul	V ero	praecordia	mot U
S olem justitiae	S ese	probat esse	beati S

Some of the best known English acrostics were written by the Elizabethan poet Sir John Davies. His *Hymns of Astraea* consists of 26 acrostic poems each spelling Elisabetha Regina ("Elizabeth the Queen").

One of the earlier acrostics written during the Puritan period was one by Martha Brewster, a love poem to her husband Oliver. included in her book of 19 poems, Poems on Divers Subjects (published in New London, Connecticut, 1757, and then in Boston in 1759):

Oh, may propitious Heaven still extend,
Lasting Delights to solace thee my Friend
Injoying ev'ry lawful Sweet below;
Viewing by Faith, the Fountain whence they Flow,

Erected be his Throne, within thy Heart,
Rule and Replenish there, thy ev'ry Part.

Blest with a Vine, whose Love and Loyalty,
Richest than choicest Wine her Progeny,
Each like an Olive Branch adorn thy House,
With the Fair transcript of thy loving Spouse:
Soft are the Charms inviolable Bands,
Twine round the Lover's Heart, Raptured he stands:
Eternal King that hath these Powers giv'n,
Renew our Love to Thee, and Love us up to Heaven.

Edgar Allen Poe wrote two love poems using a complicated form of acrostic: *A Valentine* and *An Enigma*. Poe employs two names as acrostics: "Francis Sargent Osgood" and "Sarah Anna Lewis." Numerous word games and some crossword puzzles are based on the principle of the acrostic according to Cecil Golann. Poe used the first letter of the first line, the second letter of the second, third letter of the third, etc. in both poems.

Short forms of longer words are commonly used to give names to modern developments such as *radar* for "radio detection and ranging," or CARE (Cooperative for American Remittance to Everywhere). These forms employ the pattern of the acrostic.

The most frequent use of the acrostic form today is in word puzzles. The best known of these is probably Elizabeth Kingsley's invention, the *Double-Crostic*, which appeared in the *Saturday Review* in 1934. The acrostic is a form often used during the Christmas season. People often employ it in their holiday greetings to friends and relatives, usually using the first letters of their names such as *The John Does*.

The acrostic spells out the title of the poem in the following:

GOD IS A POET
Over high hills and low
Daily his rhyme and meter flow. We see

Iambics in winding river path, and count
Spondees, dactyls in his mountain crests

Amphibrach in ocean laps

Pyrrhic in rain yielding to soliloquy
Of snow. His imagery mirrors
Every heart; He wants each daughter/son
Trochees of His truth to know.

(Wilma Burton, 1980)

The following is an example of the abecedarian, or alphabet verse:

ABECEDARIAN
(Alphabet Acrostic)

Acclaim the literature of man,
Ballads and epics of the dead,
Creative acts of stunning plan;
Daedalus used his hands and head.
Evolving still from fish and ape
Fabulous man, dreamer of dreams,
God's metaphor in human shape:
History chronicles his schemes.
Italian Dante placed in hell,
Judas, called Iscariot, whom
Keenest pangs destroyed, so they tell,
Lamenting treachery and doom.
Maid Marian shared Robin's life,
Naomi was beloved of Ruth,
Oberon had a foolish wife;
Poets, like Shakespeare, outshine truth.
Quixotic man tilts at romance,
Relishes tale of ancient king
Stories of strange significance;
Te Deum laudamus, we sing
Unheard of poets daily pray
Virgilian verse ability;
Withhold not Lord their wreath at bay:
Xerxes died and so must we.
Yearning we go from birth to death:
Zenith claims our ultimate breath.

Liboria Romano

BIBLIOGRAPHY

Academic American Encyclopedia. Princeton: Arete Publishing Company, Inc., 1980, p. 85.

The American Peoples Encyclopedia. The Spencer Press, Inc., 1953, p. 107.

Encyclopedia Americana. New York: Americana Coporation, 1970, p. 121.

Encyclopedia Brittanica. William Benton Publishers, 1970, p. 103.

Merit Students Encyclopedia. New York: MacMillan, 1979, p. 38.

The World Book Encyclopedia. Chicago: World Bood International, 1979, p. 26.

THE BALLAD

Ethel Eikel Harvey

While the origin of the Ballad has been subjected to much dispute for many generations, our most reliable sources of information continue to claim that the Ballad originated as a folk song, an unstructured narrative telling dramatic tales of the times. Such stories, orally transmitted, were filled with suspense and concerned feuds, tragedies, murders, lost loves and other depressing events. Usually, there was incoporated a mythical or supernatural element. And because the dramatization could be highlighted by repetition, the chorus usually added a refrain. Such were the earliest ballads that came down to us from the primitive people of England and Scotland. Since this particular form of poetry existed some five hundred years before printing became available, the ballads were handed down orally from generation to generation, and it is natural that in this constant repetition most of the originals wound up with many versions.

Because the favorite form of entertainment in the early

English and Scottish countries was the ballad singing and story telling sessions, the composition of ballads flourished in the fifteenth century. Yet, it was not until the eighteenth century that learned men began to take interest in the preservation of these early folk songs and poems. In 1765 Bishop Percy made a collection of Old English ballads and this was printed. A generation later Walter Scott published a volume of Scotch ballads. Then F. J. Child of Harvard University published the great collection, *English and Scottish Popular Ballads,* which is filled with footnotes tying the various versions to the proper originals. It is interesting to note here that the ballads chosen by the editor for reprinting in the *Norton Anthology of English Literature, Volume 1,* were considered most effective as poetry. In this publication the spelling has been modernized. Also in the encyclopedia is the Middle English *Judas* which was found in a thirteenth century manuscript and is considered the first ballad to be recorded. There are many variations in *Judas* which made it different in form to the true ballad, yet it testifies to the flourishing of that ballad form at a very early time.

The early settlers and immigrants to America naturally brought with them many of the ballads and folk songs from their homelands. However, it was not long before these songs were Americanized. For instance, the early *Lord Randall* became *Johnny Randall* though it followed much of the story and the pattern of the original. Soon the joy of folk singing and ballad making became part of the growing country. Frontiersmen, lumberjacks, cowboys and boatsmen on the Great Lakes and the mighty Mississippi found pleasure in telling stories in ballad form and singing newly created folk songs. The negroes added their versions singing in the cotton fields by day or sitting outside their cabins in the evening hours. The cowboys roped cattle to the tune of a favorite folksong or created a new one. There have been many collections of these ballads and songs; among them are included John Lomax's *Cowboy Songs and Frontier Ballads;* John Cox's *Folk Songs of the South,* and Carl Sandburg's *The American Songbug.* One of the songs included in Lomax's collection is the ever-favorite *Home on the Range.* This is written in true ballad technique yet has always been known as a song—a folk song. It is reprinted in *Poetry—An Interpretation of Life,* edited by E. E. Clark of the State College of Washington and published by Farrar & Rhinehart of New

York. In the chapter titled "American Ballads and Folk Songs," Clark uses the poem and explains with a footnote that when a distinction can be made between ballad and folk song, the former term is given to those songs that tell a story and the latter to those that express the emotions and thoughts of the author or composer.

According to recognized authorities on poetry technique, the true ballad stanza is a quatrain, a four-line verse. The rhyme scheme is abcb. The first and third lines are tetrameter—four feet; the second and fourth lines are trimeter—three feet. There are no definite restrictions for the number of quatrains needed for any ballad. For this reason we have ballads of varying lengths. One of the longest ballads used in anthologies and text books is *The Rime of the Ancient Mariner* by Samuel Taylor Coleridge. This is termed a literary ballad and is written in seven parts. There are numerous variations in the length of the verses changing from the ballad stanza to verses five, six, seven or more lines long. And just as these privileges are taken with regard to verse length, so too, are the rhyme schemes varied. In explaining these variations, Brooks and Warren, authors of *Understanding Poetry,* an anthology for college students published by Henry Holt & Company, New York, in 1938, explains the variations were necessary in a poem of such length because, had the author used only the ballad stanza, it would have become too monotonous. I would not question such authorities as Cleanth Brooks and Robert Penn Warren, but I have to wonder why any author needs to stretch a story to such a length in order to tell the story.

The well-trained poet, with many published works, is certain to have availed himself of every type of help needed to perfect his craft and is familiar with the best publications. However, for the beginner, the eager writer of any age needing help with his work, I would suggest several paths. In every town, city, state, college and university there are libraries with numerous volumes of poetry, techniques for writing, handbooks for students. In addition to the ones mentioned in the article, there are excellent books by Louis Untermeyer, Leigh Hunt, T. E. Sanders and others. There are librarians available to help. There are also copies of current verse journals, writer's markets, publishers lists. While today's writer may learn much by studying poetry of the past, he should also be familiar with what the editors of current publications are using.

To show how the ballad has progressed from the early primitive days to this century, I am using verses from the anonymous to recognized authors:

LORD RANDALL (An Anonymous early English poem)

> O where hae ye been, Lord Randall my son?
> O where hae ye been, my handsome young man?
> "I hae been to the wild wood, mother make my bed soon
> For I'm weary wi hunting and fain would fall down."

A HOME ON THE RANGE (An Anonymous American Folk Song)

> O give me a home where the buffalo roam,
> Where the deer and the antelope play,
> Where seldom is heard a discouraging word
> And the skies are not cloudy all day.

> The refrain: Home, home on the range
> Where the deer and the antelope play
> Where seldom is heard a discouraging word
> And the skies are not cloudy all day.

2 verses from THE RIME OF THE ANCIENT MARINER (by Samuel Taylor Coleridge)

Part VI, First Voice (The Ballad Stanza):

> But tell me, tell me! speak again
> Thy soft response renewing--
> What makes the ship drive on so fast?
> What is the ocean doing?

Part VII:

> The Hermit good lives in that wood   (Note here the var-
> Which slopes down to the sea!   iance in lines-and
> How lowly his sweet voice he rears!   the archaic spelling
> He loves to talk with mariners   plus change in
> That come from far countree.   rhyme scheme.)

LA BELLE DAME SANS MERCI (by John Keats, 1795-1821)

O what can ail thee, knight-at-arms!
Alone and palely loitering!
The sedge has withered from the lake
And no birds sing.

(The Ballad Stanza. Note the age of Keats.)

THE BALLAD OF THE HARP WEAVER (by Edna St. Vincent Millay)

I could not go to school
  Or out of doors to play,
And all the other little boys
  Passed our way.

(The child who had no clothes.)

A smile about her lips
  And a light about her head,
And her hand in the harp-strings
  Frozen dead.

(The mother is frozen to death weaving clothes for the boy.)

BALLAD OF THE BEDOUINS (by Viola Jacobson Berg, 1977)

There once was a father, El-Farid his name
  Who lived far beyond the Red Sea
And he had a daughter, a sweet little daughter
  And a bright little gypsy was she,
They lived in the desert, the great lonely desert
  Where not many nomads passed through
To see that his daughter, his now grown-up daughter
  Had a face that was ugly to view.
    Oh, play the lute sweetly, give ear to my song,
    And blow desert breezes, my story along.

(One of our most modern ballads-actually a double ballad with Ballad Stanza rhyme scheme, with refrain that has musical meter.)

THE BALLADE

Cecilia Parsons Miller

My first acquaintance with a *ballade* came at a performance of *Cyrano de Bergerac* as the hero composes his account of a duel in poetry that follows the rhythms of the sword play-- "Lightly I toss my hat away--". In my late teens, I was impressed. My enthusiasm led to the purchase of a copy of Brian Hooker's translation of Edmund Rostand's famous play.

When I entered college, the ballad, with its echoes of our hill country and our colonial years, plus the strong link to Elizabethan origins, became predominant in my study and affections. The popularity of such folk singers as Susan Reed and Burl Ives, whom we heard during the time we lived in Connecticut, within easy commuting distance of New York City, fostered this interest.

Since coming to live in Pennsylvania, my Scottish heritage has been enriched by membership in the Harrisburg Scottish Society, and by my close friendship with Alice Mackenzie Swaim. The association between Scotland and the French at the time of the Stewarts makes me wonder if there were not more ballades written at that time in Scotland than we have on record.

There exists a definite similarity between the *ballad* and the *ballade* in that both spring from a very personal outlook, and in most cases are built around a narrative. It is true that the more sophisticated ballade was not as readily accepted by the average hearer, for oral distribution, as the simpler ballad, yet the ballades of Villon enjoyed a popularity that certainly did not depend on the printing press.

As for Cyrano, I was not as overwhelmed by his facility in composition as some viewers might have been, since I had a friend who could toss off a rhymed poem almost without thinking. I grant you, they were not ballades, but they were frequent, and for a high school student they attained a good quality.

I note now with considerable amusement that Cyrano's duel poem has some irregularities frowned upon by some judges when dealing with the French forms. He scattered anapests liberally. The refrain, "Then as I end the refrain, thrust home" sets the pattern. (After all, he had other matters on his mind, including footwork.) Since I do not have the French of Rostand before me, and would be almost totally at a loss if I did, these quirks could be in the translation. Each line of the envoi begins with the reversed iamb, though in the salutation, "Prince! Pray God that is Lord of all," the caesura may well save the day.

The ballad and the ballade are about the same age. The ballade originated in France, in Provence, to be exact. I quote Edmund Gosse, "It is in Provencal literature (then spelt balade) that the ballade takes modern form." It began with the *canzone de ballo* of the Italians. "It was in France, however, and not until the reign of Charles V that the ballade as we understand it began to flourish; instantly it became popular and in a few years the output of these poems was incalculable. Machalt, Froissart, Eustace Deschamps and Christine de Pisan cultivated the ballade most abundantly. Later Alain Chartier and Henri Baude were famous, while the form was chosen by Francois Villon for some of the most admirable and extraordinary poems which the Middle Ages have handed down to us."

"Somewhat later Clement Marot composed ballades of great precision and form, and the fashion culminated in the 17th century with those of Mme. Deshoulieres, Sarrazin, Voiture and La Fontaine. Attacked by Moliere and by Boileau, ballades went out of fashion for 200 years."

In 1861 Theodore de Banville (1802-1891) wrote "The Ballade of Enfants Perdus" (which Gosse states is absolutely faultless) and revived the form. Both Louis Untermeyer and Gosse warmly recommend Helen Louise Cohen's "Lyric Forms From France," where the origin and history of the ballade has been traced in detail. Also a complete analysis may be found in Gleeson White's "Ballades and Rondeaus."

From Untermeyer, "de Banville 'Trente-six ballades joyeuses' brought back to French poetry the intricate rhyme schemes."

Brooks and Warren, 4th Edition, page 531, "The ballade was adopted for a poem with the strophe form ababbcbc. In the 14th century it had three strophes, often octosyllabic lines, with an envoi."

Clement Wood: "The poem stanza should carry an un-broken sense, not be split into quatrains. The refrain line must be repeated without any alteration of sound, though punctu-ation, meaning and spelling may be altered. It must be brought in without strain or effort."

Gosse: "If eight-line stanzas are used, the envoi has five lines. The rhyming is: a b a b b c c d c D, the envoi c c d c D. Six words are needed for the *a* rhyme word, *14* for the *b* rhyme words and 5 for the *c* rhyme word." (This means that one does well to begin a ballade's preparation in the same manner as the recipe for rabbit stew--first catch your hare--count to make sure you have chosen a word that has enough requisite forms whose meaning will not have to be wrenched into context. This is a neat accomplishment when brought off with success.)

Edmund Gosse: "The rules for the envoi were laid down by Henri de Croi, *L'Art et Science de rhetorique,* first printed in 1493."   The salutation: Prince, Princess, Sire (chosen be-cause the poet was usually addressing his patron) or Lord, Muse, etc. set the tone "for a dedication and culmination richer in wording and meaning, more stately in imagery, than the preceding lines."

"The ballade is typically French and is extensively em-ployed in no other language except English." It was taken up by English poets in the 15th and 16th centuries, notably by Chau-cer (who did not use the envoi), by Ludgate and Gower; the sur-viving ballades of Gower are only in French."

"The absence of the envoi, as in the example by Chaucer, as in most of the medieval English ballades, points to a relation-ship with the earliest French form." "The envoi, that section whose function is to tie together the rest and complete the whole as a work of art."

Still quoting Gosse: "Rosetti's translation of Villon's

'Ballade of Fair Ladies' may almost be considered an original poem, especially as it entirely disregards the metrical rules." The well-known line of Rosetti's translation "Where are the snows of yesteryear?" comes out, when dealt with by John Payne ("as lax as French rules allow") "What has become of last year's snows?"

Untermeyer: "The popularity of the ballade may be said to date from 1877 when Edmund Gosse and Austin Dobson introduced these involved forms into English verse. Andrew Lang, W. E. Henley and Algernon C. Swinburne followed suit; by 1890 the ballade and the rondeau were almost as firmly established as the sonnet."

Gosse: "With the exception of the sonnet, the ballade is the noblest of the artificial forms of verse cultivated in English literature. It lends itself equally well to pathos and to mockery, and in the hands of a competent poet produces an effect which is rich in melody without seeming fantastic or artificial."

Brooks and Warren (4th Edition): "19th century poems using the rondeau, ballade, sestina, villanelle, seemed academic, overly 'political' or 'romantic.' But these very associations that for a time seemed to disqualify such complicated forms from use by a serious poet have actually been exploited by some modern writers; that is, the irony of the contrast between the literary association of the form and a modern content and realistic language become part of the effect of the poem."

Babette Deutsch in her *Handbook* gives one stanza and the envoy (this is the spelling she uses) of Villon's "Ballade of the Hanged" translation by Swinburne, with a ten-line stanza and a five-line envoy, with salutation. She states: "The eight-line stanza form admits a double refrain, the fourth as well as the final line being repeated in each octave and in the envoy. The scheme for the stanza is then a b a B b c b C, and that for the envoy b B c C." Henley's "Ballade of Youth and Age" is given as illustration, first stanza and the envoy.

Wood: "The meter of a ballade need not be four-foot

iambic. Andrew Lang's 'Ballade of Primitive Man' has a three-foot anapestic movement with the refrain, 'Twas the manner of Primitive Man.' Dactyls may be used also. A recent (this is 1936 copyright) newspaper ballade had only two trochees to the line, with the refrain, 'Life is gay.' Another merely one iambic foot to each line, with the refrain, 'I love'."

Wood prints in full "Ballade of Dead Actors" by William Henley, mentioned above, and "The Ballade of Prose and Rhyme" by Austin Dobson. He mentions Henley's "Double Ballade of the Nothingness of Things" and Swinburne's "Ballade of Swimming."

Untermeyer prints in full "Ballade on the Ballade" by Richard Untermeyer (published in a high school magazine in 1925) and comments on the device of the refrain which asks a question; "One of the most famous is the *ubi sunt* theme. Villon popularized this in 'Mais ou sont les neiges d'antan'." He prints entire, "I Wonder in What Isle of Bliss" by Justin Huntly McCarthy, commenting on the variations in the refrain and the additional refrain in the sixth line. He also comments that Swinburne's "Double Ballade of August" and Henley's "Double Ballade of Life and Fate" continue to be quoted and prints "Double Ballade of the Singers of the Time" by John Payne which, "though it appears rarely . . . is surely as illuminating as the more familiar ones."

Chaucer's poem "The Complaint of Chaucer to His Purse" was sent to Henry IV in 1399 when he was newly crowned King. Henry immediately added 40 marks to Chaucer's annual salary. The poet died in 1400 so he only enjoyed his raise in salary for one year."

Example:

A LADY IS A RARE EVENT, A BALLADE:

> Stereotypes are set awry
> For men now have the civil right
> To keep the house, and primp, and cry
> While women folk go off and fight.
> To men who used to wire the light,

Unplug the drain, and pay the rent,
(Before the women got uptight)
A lady is a rare event.

No longer is the female shy...
She muscles in with main and might.
Now there is neither gal nor guy
(Though I cannot believe it--quite)
These sexless ones confuse the sight;
Their images are strangely blent.
Amid the contrasts they invite,
A lady is a rare event.

Where are the girls who ruffled by
With beaux who waltzed them through the night?
Where is the kiss and lover's sigh
Since sex hath no more troths to plight?
One cannot tell, by brawn and height,
Which gender poured the drive's cement.
I say again (though it sounds trite)
A lady is a rare event.

ENVOY:

Don't think romance has taken flight,
That chivalry and love are spent.
Whenever youth dreams bridal-white,
A lady is a rare event.

Julia Hurd Strong, Houston, Texas

Julia Hurd Strong's prize winner is a delightful example of the modern treatment of the ballade, as mentioned by several authorities in the preceding pages. She has followed the form exactly, with the exception of the beheaded iambic in the first line, to lend variety and diversion. If a purist insists on more than one variation, lines 17 and 19 could be read in the same manner.

Two more comments from Edmund Gosse: "Dobson's 'The Prodigals,' 1876, was one of the earliest examples of a correct English specimen." "In 1880 Mr. Lang published 'Ballades in Blue China' which found innumerable imitators."

One puzzle remains. Villon's *Des Dames du Temps Jadis* is referred to by Brooks and Warren as "Ballade of Bygone Ladies," by Gosse as "Ballade of Fair Ladies" and by George Frisbee Whicher, writing about Villon for the Encyclopedia Britannica, 11th Edition, as "Ballade to Dead Ladies." One wonders, are there two ballades?

Both the historical research and the present day construction of a ballade make an absorbing adventure. How successful the latter has been I will leave for others to judge. "The trackless meadows of yore have shrunk and dwindled away to a few poor acres." (Kenneth Grahame, *The Golden Age*)

Example:

THE SHRINKING DREAMS

> Where are the trackless woods I knew,
>   where are the fields that stretched so wide?
> I roamed from dawn to dusk to view
>   the reaches of the countryside.
>   The grassy slopes where swallows glide:
> At my soft steps the eagle flies,
>   where mystery and space collide
> That now are shrunk to paltry size.
>
> The buntings soared from ancient yew,
>   the eastern wind was friend and guide;
> I let the pasture ways imbue
>   long days of youth with wonders pied.
>   I thought no time could shrink my ride
> Down shaded paths that held such prize--
>   (they gave no clue to change implied)
> That now are shrunk to paltry size.
>
> The years escaped, now troubles hew
>   deep scars that I can never hide;
> I hold sharp debts that soon come due
>   and haunting fears my hours divide.
>   Descent of reckoning defied

Where innocence with comfort hies;
    the scope of dreams when wonder died
That now are shrunk to paltry size.

    Muse, that responds to love, beside
Itself, with cares in altered guise,
    content me with these fields to bide
That now are shrunk to paltry size.

Cecilia Parsons Miller, Lemoyne, Pennsylvania

BIBLIOGRAPHY

Brooks, Cleanth and Robert Penn Warren. *Understanding Poetry.* New York: Henry Holt & Co., 1938.

Encyclopedia Britannica. Article by Edmund Gosse and George Frisbee Whicher. New York: Encyclopedia Britannica Co., 11th Edition, 1910-1911.

Kennedy, X. L. *An Introduction to Poetry.* Boston: Little Brown, 2nd Edition, 1966.

Rostand, Edmond. *Cyrano de Bergerac.* (Brian Hooker translation). New York: Henry Holt & Co., 1923.

Sanders, T. E. *The Discovery of Poetry.* Scott, Foresman & Co., 1967.

Untermeyer, Louis. *The Forms of Poetry.* New York: Harcourt, Brace & Co., 1926.

BLANK VERSE

Jaye Giammarino

Blank verse is a very specific meter: iambic pentameter, unrhymed.

The iambic foot is made up of one unstressed syllable followed by one stressed syllable. Meter is the poetic measurement of the beat of rhythm. One unit of this measurement is called a foot. The poetic line is named by the number of metrical feet in it. If the line contains five rhythmic beats, it is a pentameter line. The iambic pentameter line is te TUM, te TUM, te TUM, te TUM, te TUM.

The word "blank" implies that the end of the line is blank or bare of rhyme. Rhyme, while highly suitable to most short poems, proves a handicap for long and imaginative work. The very absence of rhyme demands that it conform to higher standards than rhymed verse. Rhyme, when skillfully employed covers a multitude of sins, while blank verse must be looked upon as bare and flawless beauty.

Usually blank verse is not divided into stanzas, but if it is, the first line of each stanza may be indented. Like prose, blank verse is paragraphed. These paragraphs are ended and begun somewhere within the line. A period at the end of the last foot in the line or a sentence begun in the first foot of the line are not considred good technique.

The paragraph, in other words, is stopped before the end of the line and begun after the line's beginning. This short paragraph together must make up a line of iambic pentameter.

Lines shorter than pentameter tend to be song-like and not suitable to sustained treatment of serious themes. Lines longer than pentameter tend to break up into shorter units, the hexameter line being read as two, three-foot units and the heptameter as four foot and three foot units.

The iambic foot may be varied with anapests and spondees, just as in the sonnet, but the "rising rhyme" must be maintained at all times. This is a rigid requirement of the form.

Blank verse should not jingle as in very simple verse or pound the stressed accents and never use the words at the ends of two lines in succession which are so much alike in vowel sound that they seem to rhyme. Another rigid rule of blank verse is that it "not be rhymed."

There is still another requirement about the form which makes all the difference between good blank verse and bad; that is the use of the "caesura." This term means a pause in the line.

Unbroken "run-on" lines allow no pause for breathtaking, nor any hesitation for the grasping of the idea. The pause (caesura) must come at different places in succeeding lines and never in the same place in two lines that follow each other. This is to be avoided if at all possible. A caesura cuts every five foot line of verse, requiring the reader to pause while reading. It is usually set off by a comma, period or other mark of punctuation. The caesura must always appear within the line, but never strictly at the same location in two succeeding lines. The pause should come at the end of a foot anywhere within the line, less frequently at the end of the first foot, just before the last foot and least often of all, at the end of the line.

The caesura is almost as essential to the form as the iambic pentameter line.

Furthermore, many lines of five feet all ending on an accented syallable would grow monotonous. The wearisome uniformity of the "end-stopped" lines should be broken by carrying over the sense of the passage from one line to the next, forming what are known as "run-on" lines. This is done by carrying over in thought from one line to the next without pause, but ending the thought with a caesura in punctuation or speech emphasis somewhere within the line. A caesura should occur in nearly every line. Sometimes two or even three appear within a single line.

Blank verse may seem easy to write for anyone who can write an iambic foot, string five of them together and keep from rhyming the lines. But writing good poetry in blank verse is quite another matter.

Strictly speaking, blank verse is any metrical verse, unrhymed. It is generally understood to mean the Heroic Blank Verse of Shakespeare's plays and Milton's epics. It has been used as a medium for much of the great work of Keats, Wordsworth and Browning, and in modern times of Yeats and Robert

Frost. The simplicity of structure, together with the unlimited number of rhythmical effects possible, make it a most pleasing form for the "extension of the poetic idea." It is almost entirely unsuitable for lyric poetry because it has resonance rather than singing quality. The themes generally thought to be appropriate for the form are meditative and dramatic movements. It is used almost exclusively for long poems and for the serious treatment of serious themes. The natural rhythm of the English language tends to be iambic.

The skillful poet when writing blank verse never breaks a hyphenated word at the end of the line, never divides a word at the end of a line, does not have one syllable on line 1 and the rest of the word on line 2. He uses a spread of idea wide enough to carry over from line to line and occasionally substitutes a trochee for an iambus and recovers the iambic meter at once. He sometimes uses feminine endings, completes a sentence within the line or starts a new sentence within the same line. He uses an occasional short line ending and shifts the caesura or pause in keeping with the sweep of thought, so that it may fall at the end of the line or at varying places within it. He maintains iambic pentameter, unrhymed, at all times.

Blank verse seems out of tune with the modern tempo. At least in short and lyric poetry, modern taste demands either both meter and rhyme, or neither. Verse cannot fly on one wing and blank verse has meter, but no rhyme. Yet it would be hard to find many major poets who have not done some work in this challenging form. Heroic Blank Verse is so easy, yet so hard. It shows up the individuality of the poet and this technical skill with great clarity.

Very few women poets have written more than an occasional poem in blank verse, but Mercy Otis Warren (1728-1814) was the Shakespeare of her day. She wrote tragedies and hoped they would surpass Shakespeare's blank verse. The mid and late 18th century was a time of very little poetry, an unproductive period for men, but it was extremely important for women. The dam for women poets was not to burst until after 1800, but the trickle had already begun.

Example:

from THE SACK OF ROME (by Mercy Otis Warren):

> Come, be thyself again; no longer bask
> Upon the silken, downy lap of hope;
> Leave her to sigh, and whisper to the winds—
> Else snatch by force, and bear her o'er the wilds,
> Through growling forests-hideous, broken cliffs,
> And frozen seas-to Scythis's icy banks,
> Where rugged winds pour from the brindled north
> Adown the mountain's brow-a blast may cool
> The transports of thy love.

ALL THINGS UNTO A LAW (by Jaye Giammarino):

> Nor autumn comes with rampant, warming rays
> To light the fields of corn and fading vines
> With tallow-glow of swift decay. A strange
> And mystic silence fills with air, as leaf
> By leaf, October twirls to earth in sad
> Kaleidoscopic death.
>   To wander where
> The woodland hush is deep and tread upon
> The wilted grass; to hear the winding stream
> Flow down to pasture-land and wading cows,
> Is finding peace with barren tree and vine.
> The drops of dew that fall like footsteps here
> And here, the whir of quail in startled flight
> Enshrines the way of beauty in a time
> Of empty nests. In ultimate decline
> Now nature toils among her garnered sheaves
> In preparation for the graceful pause
> When earth is wed to sleep in keeping with
> The universal law sublime, until
> From winter solstice, spring will rise again
> In joyful wakefulness, and stretch across
> The land with tender hue of greening grass
> As if in answer to the trumpet call.

BIBLIOGRAPHY

Hamilton, Anne. *How To Revise Your Own Poems.* Harper Brothers, 1936.

Wrinn, Mary J. J. *Hollow Reed.* Harper Brothers, 1936.

THE BURTONELLE

Wilma W. Burton

The Burtonelle is a two-column free verse poem with a caesura (thought pause) running down the center between the two columns. It is to be read horizontally with a slight pause between the two columns.

Solomon writing in Ecclesiastes cautions us that there is "nothing new under the sun," and while I do not claim to be the originator of this form since others may or may not have experimented with it previously, I claim rather to be the innovator who chose to commemorate this nation's Bicentennial by writing in this form of poetry each day of 1976 in my daily journal. This practice of writing a poem every day in bound record book is one I have observed for over 20 years and one I recommend to young poets in my classes in order not only to keep a record of each poem written, but for ease in keeping track of their poems as well as serving as a catalyst in furthering the habit of consistently writing poetry.

Being a modern type of poetry, the Burtonelle (which name I gave this form in order to indentify it) lends itself to lack of punctuation and both to traditional and newer thought forms.

In addition to commemorating our Bicentennial year, the Burtonelle held a hidden meaning to me as a poet, which poetry often has for the poet. It represented the end of my marriage: my husband was debilitated in 1975 by encephalitis, a disease which destroyed his mind and caused his death four years later.

While the bulk of the Burtonelles I wrote in 1976 and have written since has as yet to be published, several of them appear in my collection, *Sidewalk Psalms and Some From Country Lanes.* I am including two from this collection:

I AM MORE IMPORTANT	THAN A STAR
True, I cannot scintillate	or light a sky at night
or can I be wished	upon by children
or dreamed upon	with wonder eyes
of first-love	But stars burn out
turn cinders	useless meteorites
and I though flesh-drawn	am still the person
with the soul	You made
and gave	Eternal Life

The Burtonelle served as a certain type of poetry therapy that helped me to live with a certain serenity of mind through the trauma of my husband's illness. The following poem is one which brought with it a buoyancy of spirit as I wrote it:

O, FOR THE JOY-TOSSED	THINGS OF SPRING
confetti	on an apple bough
a red bud's flame	tree-caught
a thousand crocus heads	yellow, purple
rioting	in winter beds
jonquils hitchhiking	with golden thumbs
alerting April	on up-down hills
pussy willows	purring in the sun
and lilacs	making every bush
they hold sway on	a royal throne
willows wading	barefoot in a creek
and small stones	hand-thrown, skipping
in heart and feet	renewed by tossing things
clouds on strings	rice at May-June weddings
and a salad bowl	of all the greens
of brown-world yielding	to the reckless lowland
highland flaunting	of Spring

BIBLIOGRAPHY

Burton, Wilma W. *Sidewalk Psalms and Some From Country Lanes.* Good News Publishers, 1979.

POETRY AND THE CHILD

Libby Stopple

There is within all of us, this forsaken child—this very source of poetry itself. What better way can we, then, examine this source than by examining poetry as written for and, I must add, by the child?

Poetry begins—if there is a beginning or an ending—in the spirit or consciousness which is seeking wholeness. In a more paradoxical way, we might state that it begins in the consciousness which is seeking release into a kind of purity or clearness. This is that purity found in the vast potential of silence, or absence itself; and just as the rests or silences found between the notes of a musical composition are inseparable from the sound, so is poetry inseparable from that vast silence out of which it comes. Indeed within that same silence, the reality of the livingness of music and poetry ultimately exist.

Lest all this may appear to be too profound or analytical, let me hasten to share with you a short lyric I wrote a few years ago to illustrate to a class of young students just what poetry might be. And since poetry is something beyond words, beyond language I first suggested to the children that a poem could possibly only be explained by another poem. Thus:

> Like sunlight in an apple-seed,
> or the sea in a drop of rain,
> A poem is the heart turned inside out,
> And then sung back again.

So that I am saying a poem is an inward way of looking at an outward thing. Children are, in a sense, natural poets, because they are closer to their source. Their inner and their outer world are one: shape, sound, color, tone, rhyme rhythm and feeling are all one and are spontaneous. A child simply feels and his or her innate feelings are the poem experienced. Poetry simply is, for the child, yet the child attaches no name to it. Poetry becomes a way of life, only if that child can be encouraged to retain a sense of wonder and awe, of magic and mystery;

only if that child can be inspired to develop a capacity for imagination and awareness—in short, a potential for vision. Sad to say, this is becoming more and more difficult to accomplish in light of today's manufactured entertainment which includes television, movies and other modern media—today's kind of hypnosis over the child's mind and thinking. Here is where the creative artist in all fields, especially in song and poetry, can influence the child and keep alive and well this wonderful sense of closeness with all things, this precious sense of *all things belong,* this sense of oneness with all things. Is this, perhaps, what Jesus meant when He said we must become as little children?

Now as to the actual writing of poetry for children, I must confess at the outset, that I am more concerned with substance and content, than with form and technique. Perhaps this is why, though I do not consider myself a children's poet per se, I do enjoy working with children. Perhaps I am a bit lazy but I do know that the poem existed long before the rules. However, I also know that there must be discipline. There can be neither law nor art without boundaries and limitations—certain laws. Nature herself, is orderly. But the child, being completely unique, is his or her *own* technique. Children go about humming, singing, tapping their toes and talking to the rocks and grass and trees. They even express themselves as though they were the rocks and grass and trees. Metaphysically speaking, they are! They sense this, only alas, to be taught later in life that they are each separate and apart!

The very first thing to bear in mind, I believe, in writing for children, is that children are people, (albeit, not as tall and wrinkled as some!) The world of the child is the world itself, and as I wrote in the Preface of my book, *A Box of Peppermints:* "...children are already older than they think, wiser than they know." This is precisely why what is good for a child to read is also good for the adult. Consider Barbara Cooney's *Jenny Wren* or Marcia Brown's *Once a Mouse.* Whatever appeals to the child within will also appeal to the adult.

Let us think, for a moment, about the poet and the child. It is very important because as I have intimated earlier I believe poetry, more than any of the arts, can reach directly to the heart

of the child. Just think of what Ann Taylor's "Twinkle, twinkle,
little star" has done down through the years to turn the child's
attention toward the greatness, the mystery and the wonder of
the universe. The image in the poet's mind must be turned like
a searchlight toward our children for they are our future. Every
poet worth his or her salt has written for the child, perhaps because the poet has never really outgrown his or her finer child-
like nature. The poet Emily Dickinson, for instance, has spoken
both to the child and to the adult in her poem:

> A bird came down the walk:
> He did not know I saw;
> He bit an angle-worm in halves
> And ate the fellow raw.....

Although she was not known as a juvenile poet, Emily wrote
many poems to children, some to her nieces and nephews, some
to neighbor children. Remember her "the snake, that narrow fellow in the grass"? Other poets, such as Christina Rosseti, have
written poems most appropriate for children. And from my own
book, *A Box of Peppermints,* here is the poet thinking as a child:

> My little turtle died last week,
> And aunt Ella gave me her jewel case
> To bury him in.
> This morning I dug him up
> To see if he was resting in peace.
> He was.

> Last summer
> We visited a mountain.
> I said: hello mountain, here I am—
> This is me.
> And the old mountain
> Just sat there.

In each case we have an essence, a captured experience, a happening: "the heart turned inside out." A poem is something
that happens inside both the poet and the reader—a direct
knowing. And this direct knowing is a quality that all children possess in abundance. This is why we should never write
down to them, only human to human. They are, as we have

said, little people in this world and they respond most heartily when we treat them so. They have the same joys and sorrows, guilts and fears that we have. It is with this attitude and frame of mind that we may create our best poetry and song for children.

The Haiku, an old form of Japanese poetry, is splendid both to write *for* children and to teach them the written word. It is a direct experience, a breath of beauty communicated through the use of just a few limited syllables (no rhyme.) The Haiku poet notices minute bits of life and, through the use of nouns and usually not more than one verb, builds images such as blue dragonflies, bright red roses, a croaking frog to communicate nature. Both poet and reader become part of the image. All unnecessary words are left out. Children like this. They like simplicity. After only a few minutes of explanation about this form at one of my Poet in Residence classes at an elementary school, the students came up with this sample of a Haiku:

> Fly little sparrow
> Because here comes old squirrel—
> Quick! To your sky-home!

This is the way a child thinks and feels. This is how poetry for the child becomes.

Another form of poetry to which children respond is rhyme and rhythm. This is because rhyme and rhythm are quite elemental to the child. It is their way of anticipating and remembering. It is their way of sleeping and waking. Perhaps this is why mothers down through the ages have sung to their little ones, "Rock-a-bye baby" and then awakened them with, "patty-cake." From one of my folk lullabies:

> Ride a wooden pony through the midnight rain,
> My Rock-A-Bye Baby, you'll be riding again.
> Wake up in the morning sing a cow-boy song,
> A thousand little angels will be singing along.

> Strawberry summers, peppermint skies,
> A hobo clown with sorrowful eyes...

Mama's in the kitchen,
Papa's smoking his pipe,
And we'll all go a-pickin'
When the peaches get ripe...peaches get ripe....

Here the words become image, the image flows and begs to be sung. The poem lives. And here again, children are song and laughter. They love sense and nonsense. Perhaps the poem has no message, no special meaning. Never mind! We are having fun with it! As in another of my songs, "Wimbuley, Wambuley, Wum." I am perfectly aware that there actually is no such thing, but there could be. Later in the song when Wimbuley, Wambuley, Wum actually winks at the child, the child accepts this joyfully. Anything that can be imagined, can *be!* And the child, of all people, knows this.

If you would write for the child, put aside most of your logic and lose yourself in that vast land where there is neither space nor time. Then carefully and lovingly find your way back again. You'll find a child standing there waiting for you, all big-eyed and believing.

WIMBULEY, WAMBULEY, WUM

O what is a Wimbuley, Wambuley, Wum?
Does it have a tail, does it have a thumb?
Does it have a mom and a papa too,
And how can I tell if it's really true?

Who made it happen and who's to blame—
And where did it get such a silly name?
If it doesn't bark, can it bend its knees,
And buzz through the air like the bumble bees?

O Wimbuley, Wambuley, Wum,
Wimbuley Wambuley Wum,
Wimbuley,   Wambuley,   Wimbuley,   Wambuley,
Wimbuley, Wambuley, Wum!

If Whip-poor-wills grew whiskers,
And *now* were changed to *then*,
What in the world would the Walrus do,

And how would the day begin?

Now I've never seen a naked giraffe.
If I ever did I would surely laugh,
But look! There's a SOMETHING and what could it be?
It Wimbed and it Wambed and it winked at me!

Libby Stopple

CINQUAIN

Violette Newton

The cinquain, unlike other poetic forms whose origins are lost in antiquity, was invented in the early part of this century by an American woman, Adelaide Crapsey. It is a product of the Imagist movement whose roots are found in classical Greek poetry, Japanese haiku and *vers libre* of French Symbolists. In an attempt to strip away excess wordage of earlier poetry, the Imagists insisted on simplicity and clarity—a clear picture which left an instant impression on the reader and a longer after-image on his mind. Consequently, such distillations made, for the most part, small poems. The cinquain is no exception.

Crafted on five lines—*cinq* means five in French—it contains only twenty-two syllables. Lines consist of two, four, six, eight and two syllables, respectively. While this little poem looks like free verse and feels like free verse, because of its strict syllable count, it is definitely structured, not free. At first glance, it seems to be one of the simplest forms of un-rhymed verse. The beginning writer may think any sentence can be cut up and rearranged in lines of the proper number of syllables to build a cinquain. In doing this, he may achieve the mechanics of the form, but he has not necessarily written a poem, for the cinquain must have cadence, a feeling of music which is the essence of poetry, and it should present a definite image.

Often likened to the haiku or tanka, cinquain's similarity is in its brevity and imagery, as seen here in the single image:

AUGUST:

> August,
> leaves going gold,
> and an old dragonfly
> hovering jewel-like in his last
> of days.

or this:

NIGHT FREIGHT:

> The long
> train whistling
> past dark woods at midnight
> making a tune to keep himself
> awake.

or here, where imagery is more complex:

SUPERSTITION:

> Three times
> the white owl called...
> they whispered it meant death.
> But he was only calling for
> his love.

or here, where a humorous portrait is created:

THE IMAGIST:

> Amy
> Lowell sat down
> and penned poems fragile as
> air, all the while smoking big black
> cigars.

or if one wishes to confine himself to the strictures of

of rhyme, he may rhyme third and fifth lines:

THE BROWN MOTH:

> Now, dusk,
> and the brown moth
> is evening's butterfly.
> each wing, unfolding, opens its
> blind eye.

Why write in this form? In the first place, it makes a delightful little poem. It is also good practice, as it disciplines the poet to be concise, to pare off every unnecessary word and to hone to brilliance what is left. It is also possible to go beyond the five line poem and write a longer piece where each strophe is a complete cinquain which can stand alone, but placed together can build, as it does in the following poem, to the final sadness:

WINTER SONG:

> Again,
> crysanthemums.
> November tilts bronze gongs
> to year's end. The scent wafts memories
> for me.
>
> We two,
> my aunt and I,
> climbed stone steps up the hill
> to lay stiff sprays over a grave,
> old, small.
>
> She helped
> me tenderly,
> her sister's child—she who
> never raised sons or girls. "Up, love,"
> she urged.
>
> Now chill
> enters my bones
> in chrysanthemum hurt.
> I climb alone with flowers for
> two graves.

CLERIHEWING WITH CLERIHEWS

Frances Tunnell Carter

Indubitably, variety is the spice of life, and poetry is no exception.   Perhaps that is why an English writer invented a special brand of poetry and gave it his middle name!

Edmund Clerihew Bentley (1875-1956) was perhaps more famous during his lifetime for his detective stories, featuring the fictitious sleuth Philip Trent. However, the humorous-type double couplet that bears his name may survive long after Trent's startling cases have ceased to attract interest.

Bentley wrote his first clerihew (pronounced kler'-i-hyoo') as a schoolboy of sixteen. It read:

> Sir Humphrey Davy
> Detested gravy.
> He lived in an odium
> Of having invented sodium.

What makes a clerihew?

The *New World Dictionary* says that the clerihew is a rhyming form of poetry named after Edmund Clerihew Bentley, which is humorous, quasi-biographical, with four lines of varying length.

The *American Heritage Dictionary* describes it as a humorous quatrain about a person who is generally named in the first line of the poem.

Webster's New Collegiate Dictionary adds: "a light verse quatrain rhyming *aabb* and usually dealing with a person named in the initial rhyme.

In the *Encyclopedia of Poetry and Poetics* Clifton Fadiman defines the clerihew as a form of comic poetry that consists of two couplets of unequal length, often with complex or somewhat ridiculous rhymes that presents a potted biography of a famous personage or historical character. "The humor consists on concentrating on the trivial, the fantastic, or the ridiculous and presenting it with dead-pan solemnity as the characteristic, the significant, or the essential."

In the introductory remarks to an omnibus volume, *Clerihews Complete,* Bentley states and illustrates the nature of his work thusly:

> The art of biography
> Is different from geography.
> Geography is about maps,
> But biography is about chaps.

Since this is from the pen of the inventor himself, we cannot question its genuineness. But one notes that Bentley violated the principle of including a reference to a person's name in the first couplet!

Obviously, this art form is not unrelated to the limerick, a light humorous or nonsensical verse of five anapestic lines, usually with the rhyme scheme *aabba.* A clerihew and a limerick on similar subjects might be compared through the following illustrations by Carter:

> Wilbur and Orville Wright
> Invented and made a new flight.
> It flew like a bird,
> And swallows chirped, "How absurd!"

> A pilot went up on a bet;
> His altimeter never was set.
> He thought he was high
> But a mountain was nigh
> And St. Peter he's already met.

It has been pointed out by Fadiman that the clerihew is very British and quite Old School Tie; but nonetheless, it has attracted many practitioners in America as well as England. Among those who like clerihewology are W. H. Auden, Clifton Fadiman, Ellen Evans and Diana Menuhin.

Alice Mackenzie Swaim and Cecilia Parsons Miller, in study-ing the clerihew, have found that the syllable certainly varies. For example, Bentley's "Davey" has a 5-5-7-9 syllabication, while his "Biography" has a 7-9-8-9 pattern.

The two following clerihews, one by Bentley on Stuart Mill and one by Babette Deutsch on Bentley, show 4-8-10-14, and 7-7-11-8 syllables per line.

John Stuart Mill
By a mighty effort of will
Overcame his natural bonhommie
And wrote 'Principles of Political Economy.'

Edmund Clerihew Bentley

Edmund Clerihew Bentley
Worked swiftly if not gently
Tracking down murderers by a hidden clew
In whodunit and clerihew.

Babette Deutsch, from *Poetry Handbook*

Harper's Dictionary of Contemporary Usage illustrates the clerihew with this example:

It was a weakness of Voltaire's
To forget to say his prayers
And one which, to his shame
He never overcame.

Wauneta Hackleman, author and poet has written this clerihew:

GEORGE ELIOT:

Mary Ann Evans: pseudo man
Contrived to fool the Master's plan.
The masculine was quite permissible
Before she joined the choir invisible.

Edmund Clerihew Bentley died on March 30, 1956. Articles about his life appeared in the *Wilson Library Bulletin, Time,* and *Newsweek.* The example of his work quoted in *Time* was:

> Sir Christopher Wren
> Said, "I'm going to dine with some men.
> If anyone calls
> Say I'm designing St. Paul's.

The May 5, 1956 issue of *New Yorker* published nine clerihews by Clifton Fadiman in memory of Bentley. The following were among them:

TERMINILOGICAL

> Andrew Jackson
> Was given to Anglo-Saxon.
> He addressed words unmailable
> To any person available.

SARTORIAL

> Samuel Gompers
> Found the labor movement in rompers.
> After many changes and chances,
> He left it in long pantses.

To conclude this article on the clerihew, this author submits her example poem:

> Bentley's clerihewology
> Tickles my biology.
> I have a good day
> With its humor and play.

Frances Tunnell Carter

BIBLIOGRAPHY

American Heritage Dictionary of the English Language. Boston: American Heritage Publishing Co., 1978.

Deutsch, Babette. *Poetry Handbook.* Universal Library, 1957 and 1962.

Harper's *Dictionary of Contemporary Usage.* New York: Harper and Row Publishing Co., 1975.

Fadiman, Clifton. "Clerihews." *The New Yorker,* Volume 32, May 5, 1956.

New World Dictionary. World Publising Company, 1978.

Newsweek. Vol. 47, p. 89, April, 1956.

Preminger, Alex. *Encyclopedia of Poetry and Poetics.* Princeton: Princeton University Press, 1965.

Time. Vol. 67, p. 110, April 9, 1956.

Webster's New Collegiate Dictionary. Springfield: G. and C. Merriam Co., 1979.

Wilson Library Bulletin. Vol. 30, p. 670, May 1956.

UNDERSTANDING AND WRITING COUPLETS

Margaret Honton

The rhymed couplet has, over the centuries, proved itself as a basic form, one from which other forms can be generated, economical, and adaptable to lyric lines as well as pithy statements. My goals are to convey that (1) the English language has a rich heritage of women poets who have utilized the rhymed couplet in poems about real people in recognizable situations, often occupied necessarily with mundane things, sometimes with survival in a hostile world; (2) some of our finest contemporary poets utilize couplets in striking ways; (3) students of poetry can use couplet forms to practice rhythmic and rhyming skills, and can build poems with couplets if they avoid courting weaknesses.

The couplet, two lines linked, usually rhythmically the same, has been a basic poetic unit since ancient times, developing along with drama and dance. Its rhythmical stresses were an aid for memorizing thousands of lines and transmitting them orally to subsequent generations. Alliteration, the repetition of initial consonants or any vowel in a given line, was another ancient rhetorical aid to aural recall, especially when 6-foot and 7-foot lines prevailed:

> Rhyming couplets, however, come historically   (6-foot line, a-rhyme)
> As a rather recent adaptation in English poetry. (7-foot line, a-rhyme)

In the 16th century, Queen Elizabeth I uses in her poem, "The Doubt of Future Foes," both alliteration within the lines and end-rhymes.[1] This poem, expressing the queen's anxiety about the possibility of rebellions, and announcing her determination not to brook seditious acts or sects, begins:

> The doubt of future foes exiles my present joy,   (6 a)
> And wit me warns to shun such snares as threaten my annoy   (6 a)

The closed couplet is logically or grammatically complete in itself, with both lines end-stopped. Used by Elizabeth I in "The Doubt of Future Foes," the closed couplet is an excellent vehicle for authoritative and oracular statements. Another example of the closed couplet is by the 17th century poet Lucy Harrington, Countess of Bedford, in "Elegy."[2] These stunning lines, long attributed to Donne (who was born eight years after her death), are the first of the heroic couplets used throughout the poem:

> Death be not proud, thy hand gave not this blow,   (5 a)
> Sin was her captive, whence thy power doth flow;   (5 a)

In the open couplet, the sense of the second line needs for completion the first line of the next couplet. This is called enjambment, and allows a free flow of ideas and speech. The 17th century American poet Anne Bradstreet adapts open couplets in "Another Letter to Her Husband Absent on Public Employment."[3] In an extended metaphor, the speaker first compares herself to a loving Hind and her husband to the longed-for Hart/Deer/Dear/Heart:

As loving Hind that (Hartless) wants her Deer,	(5 a)
Scuds through the woods and fern with hark'ning ear,	(5 a)
Perplexed, in every bush and nook doth pry,	(5 b)
Her dearest Deer, might answer ear or eye;	(5 b)
So doth my anxious soul, which now doth miss,	(5 c)
A dearer Dear (far dearer Heart) than this,	(5 c)
Still wait with doubts, and hopes, and failing eye,	(5 d)
His voice to hear, or person to descry.	(5 d)

Notice that the poet builds a dependent clause of four lines before coming to the subject of the independent clause, "my anxious soul." Doing this, Bradstreet matches poetic form to content. The speaker is in some ways dependent for joy on her husband's presence, his voice and person, yet she is independent in house, in pasture, and by streams, managing a household while he is gone for long periods. Three couplets ensue before the main verb, "(doth) still wait" is heard, Bradstreet again matching form to content. In the body of this poem the poet uses iambic pentameter couplets (a classical form), but for the closing she sets one couplet alone in iambic tetrameter (the line often used in romantic and/or light verse.) This emphasizes loneliness and separation, conveys seriousness and playfulness, and functions as her signature:

| Thy loving Love and Dearest Dear, | (4 q) |
| At home, abroad, and every where. | (4 q) |

This poem leaves no doubt that open couplets can embody a greater range of emotions than can the precisely balanced, strongly punctuated, epigrammatic closed couplet. Acquaintance and practice with open couplets can help even the beginner to avoid sounding mushy, preachy, or pedantic.

An 18th century example of the embodiment of feelings with couplets is the advice offered by Mary Lee, Lady Chudleigh, in "To the Ladies."[4] The opening and closing couplets are statements: a wife is the same as a servant, and a woman who values herself will despise men and marriage. The technique in these framework lines is *telling*, not *showing*, and if the rest of the poem were to read the same, it would be more polemical than poetic. By alternating closed with open couplets (the design is 2 lines, 6, 2, 4, 2, 2, 8, 2) the poet creates inner lines that are emotive and persuasive, for example:

> Then but to look, to laugh, or speak,   (4 f)
> Will the nuptial contract break.   (4 f)

The entire poem carries well an individual's protest against established norms of love and marriage.

Couplets have also been utilized in group protest against collective social injustices, as in the 19th century ballad, "Hard Times Cotton Mill Girls."[5] Here the grammar and vocabulary, however unknowingly, help carry feelings:

> Us girls work twelve hours a day
> For fourteen cents of measly pay.

Another 19th century protest ballad recounts "The Avondale Mine Disaster" in which 110 men smothered underground while their women cried:

> "Get out our husbands and our sons, for death is going to steal
> Their lives away, without delay, in the mines of Avondale!"[6]

Ballads concerning injustices against women and the denial of women's rights are prominent in the categories of Domestic Tragedies, Tabloid Crime, Accidents and Disasters, and Criminals' Goodnights.[7]

Some of the preceding poems suggest the gradual and simultaneous development of the rhymed couplet into several ballad stanzas (not to mention Mother Goose rhymes, many of which originated as political poems—you might like to read several that begin with "There was an old woman" for social implications) and hymn stanzas. I could illustrate with a ditty:

> There might be a rhyme within the line of a 6-foot
> or 7-foot couplet;   (8 a)
> Eventually the reader would see   (4 x)
>   Lines broken in half when typeset.   (3 a)

Regarding the influence of hymn stanzas on women poets, I refer you to the finest exemplar, Emily Dickinson. Read a hundred pages or so of her poems, not just the few allotted in anthologies.[8]

An example of couplet and quatrain development of the same ballad is "Frankie and Johnny," published in the 19th century in various forms.[9]   Here are the stanzas parallel in meaning, different in form, the first by a witness:

(St. 26)   Now it was not murder in the second degree,
            and was not murder in the third,
            The woman simply dropped her man, like a hunter drops a bird.
            He was her man, but he done her wrong, so wrong.

In the second, we hear from the accused:

(St. 14)   Frankie walked out on the scaffold   (4 x)
            As brave as she could be: (3 h)
            "When I shot the man I loved,   (4 x)
            I murdered in the first degree;   (3 h)
            He is my man and I loved him so."   (4 refrain)

This discussion of popular songs leads us into the 20th century. Yes, the rhymed couplet is the basis of many contemporary songs: romantic lyrics, folk, jazz, blues, and rock. Most listeners have learned to expect off-rhymes pushed to far-out limits, assonance (with stressed vowels agreeing) and consonance (with final consonants agreeing), as well as alliteration and true rhymes. Any given week's "Top Twenty" songs will provide examples.

Couplets, especially 4-foot iambics, can collapse into doggerel—notably in songs and Valentines, in advertising slogans and political propaganda, in the kind of religious verse categorized by editors as "conversations with God," but also in pieces of nostalgia.

When writing couplets, take very great care to exploit strengths, not weaknesses: (1) Say it with feeling. Do not rely on rhymes alone to convey feeling; make other sensory appeals as well. Include specifics—a sense of time and place, tastes, smells—and details so your poem does not rely on the generalities of greeting card verse. (2) Use the heroic couplet (iambic pentameter closed couplet) sparingly, in epigrams, epitaphs, or mock-heroic stanzas. (3) Avoid all 4-foot rhymed couplets except in satire or parody, or perhaps a lullaby. (4) Play with the classical 5-foot open couplet, as Mona Van Duyn does in "Sentimental Education":

> Now she is grown, and in what winter weather!
> She longs for History, or some such feathers.[10]

(5) Develop a couplet rhythm suitable to the content of your poem. Gwendolyn Brooks, in "obituary for a living lady," uses a conversational tone with long, run-on lines that convey the long drawn-out affair of a friend who, jilted in early womanhood, eventually gets religion,

> And I can't get her to take a touch of the best cream cologne.
> However even without lipstick she is lovely and it is no wonder
> that the preacher (at present) is almost a synonym for her telephone.

Marianne Moore is famous for her unusual stanzas; one she developed for/in her lengthy poem, "The Jerboa," is couplets in 3a, 3a, 3x, 5x, 5b, 3b pattern.[12] One of the stanzas ends with this couplet:

> mongooses, storks, anoas, Nile geese,   (5 b)
> and there were gardens for these—   (3 b)

(6) While expanding awareness with open couplets, expand your concept of rhyming to include consonance and assonance. For instance, working against the cliche *moon/June*, you might use *sun/June* or *park/March*. (7) Build an entire stanza or poem with the rhyme (assonance, consonance) of the first couplet. In one stanza of Mona Van Duyn's "Recovery," the end-words are: old, afraid, hid, cried, mailed, need, kid, good, did.[13] in my poem "Wedding March" the ending words of its 13 lines are aisle, seal, female, candle, male, inflammable, aisle, veil, loyal, all, hypothetical, aisle, real.[14] (8) When rhyming an unusual word, have it in the first line of the couplet so the effect with the second line is freshness, not forcing. Anne Sexton, in "December 16th," varies lines from 3-foot to 9-foot.[15] Her closing couplet also contains the unexpected:

We turned the stove on twice. Oh my love, oh my louse,   (7 g)
We make our own electricity while we play house.   (7 g)

If the end-rhymes had been placed in the reverse order, neither
Anne Sexton nor this love poem could have carried it off.

Although many 20th century poets avoid altogether the
rhymed couplet, some choose to end an otherwise unrhymed
poem with a rhymed couplet, and others use couplets as building
blocks for stanzas and poems. A few highly skilled contemporary poets, including some already cited, have built with couplets memorable poems. I urge you to read, analyze, and emulate
couplets to be found in the writing of Isabella Gardner, Marilyn
Hacker, Josephine Jacobsen, and Josephine Miles.

The writing of couplets today I consider an act of daring.
Occasionally, when a poem of mine evolves with frequent
rhymes, I accept this as a challenge to write couplets, but do
try to vary them rhythmically and/or visually. "The Beginning
Conductor," for example, has a heavily stressed trochaic beat—
quite obvious when the poem is read aloud—the conductor
trying to maintain a very strict pattern and beat, but occasionally allowing the artist to break through. Here is the part of
the first movement:

Upbeat, downbeat, one two three four,   (4 c)
watch dynamics, calm this uproar,   (4 c)
keep eye contact, cue the cornets;   (4 d)
must the bassoons sound like hornets?   (4 d)
Sound on sound on sound surrounds me;   (4 e)
Lord, I lost the timpani!   (4 e)
Watch syncopation balk beat but   (4 f)
concentration keep this neat.
                            Cut!   (4 f)

By contrast, in my "Song and Trio" the rhythm is freer, the
verses lyrical, and the couplets are set in quatrains to reinforce
the idea of song.[16] Here are the opening stanzas:

John, I like to make poems with you,   (a)
to swim through the swirling deja vu   (a)
and burst to the surface singing—   (b)

ears ringing, eyes smarting, flesh tingling.   (b)
                                            (stanza break)
But what should chant glory and laud   (c)
builds to a crying out loud;   (c)
what might recite love in eclipse   (d)
breaks to a tremolo aching from hiccups.   (d)

The several internal rhymes in these lines help break any regularity of rhythm, underscoring the idea of a through-composed song.

In one of my hospital poems, "All Strung Out," the lines are strung all over the page, as in the first stanza:

My psyche sustains the crash   (3 a)
                of cold steel and then the flash   (4 a)
                    of a 22-caliber beadpan;   (3 b)
        the radiator's ceaseless bon-ban;   (4 b)
        call and response of robins at midnight   (4 c)
            somewhere in the fluorescent light.[17]   (4 c)

In one of my back-to-college poems, "Day of Rest," the run-on couplets give an indication of how unrestful the day is, long before the speaker's allusion to Hopkins' *sprung rhythm*.[18] The lengthy introduction, beginning with visual and aural perceptions, continues with a bombardment of other senses while the speaker is trying to write a take-home final:

On Sunday, following disruptions by   (5 a)
the neighbors' lawn mowers and dogs that try   (5 a)
to exceed rash motorbikes in noise and speed;   (5 b)
distractions from a tearful child who pleads   (5 b)
innocence in crashing a borrowed kite;   (5 c)
explanations about the "friendly flight,"   (5 c)
black eye, and bloody nose; after my dizz-   (rhyme delayed)
iness from summonses of telephone   (5 e)
and doorbell asking, "Is anybody home?"   (5 e)
and discouragement from bubbled-over pie   (5 f)
carbon-coating the oven; then's when I   (5 f)
return to the take-home final...

By way of contrast, I will share a poem-away-from-home,

a pastoral love poem, "Disclosures."[19] In this I work against a Valentine rhyme and a rhythm that might deaden sensibilities. The rhymes are separated, aurally and visually, and indicate the separation between the speaker and the loved one. The rhyme for the first line is not disclosed until the final line; this emphasizes the distancing of the couplet and of the couple, and illustrates a kind of circular thinking often experienced in love-lorn situations. I hope you will find in this poem what I value in couplets: the embodiment of feelings conveyed mostly through appeals to the senses, the use of enjambment, some unexpected rhymes, and an overall matching of form to content:

DISCLOSURES

> A meadow lark in camouflage
> does not disguise its trills and turns.
>
> A hidden honeysuckle burns
> its incense on the sultry air.
>
> A field mouse rustles, unaware
> of woodchucks tunneling nearby.
>
> A raccoon family sleeps. Geese fly
> at such great height that I am not
>
> a part of their landscape. A spot
> of butterfly unwarily
>
> lights on my wrist, as near to me
> as you are far. I bite my lip,
>
> and—tasting blood—find that this trip
> and every jolt out of the blue
>
> refers to my sixth sense: to you,
> to you, infrangible mirage.

FOOTNOTES

[1] Poems of this vintage are theoretically in the public domain; practically, though, they are not readily available to the layman. This may be the rationale some scholars have in copyrighting such poems today. "The Doubt of Future Foes" is the opening poem in the collection edited by Louise Bernikow, *The World Split Open: Four Centuries of Women Poets in England and America, 1552-1950* (New York, Vintage Books, Random House, 1974) p. 51, and is included in the compendium edited by Ann Stanford, *The Women Poets in English* (New York, A Herder & Herder Book, McGraw-Hill Book Company, 1972), p. 22. These are excellent collections providing an historical view.

[2] Stanford, pp. 34-35.

[3] Anne Bradstreet, *Several Poems Compiled by a Gentlewoman in New England...Corrected by the Author* (Published posthumously, 1678.) See also John H. Ellis' definitive edition of Anne Bradstreet's works (Charlestown, Massachusetts, 1867, reprinted New York, 1932.)

[4] Stanford, pp. 71-72.

[5] Berkinow, p. 300.

[6] Albert B. Friedman, ed., *The Viking Book of Folk Ballads of the English-Speaking World* (New York, The Viking Press, 1969), p. 308.

[7] These are appropriate chapter headings in Friedman's edition.

[8] Thomas H. Johnson, ed., *Final Harvest; Emily Dickinson's Poems* (Boston, Little, Brown & Company, Inc., 1961.)

[9] The source of the couplet stanza is Carl Sandburg, *American Songbag* (New York, Harcourt, Brace, Jovanich, 1927), p. 81. The quatrain stanza cited by Albert B. Friedman is from *Journal of American Folklore*, 42: 287.

[10] Mona Van Duyn, *Merciful Disguises:* Published and Unpublished Poems (New York, Atheneum, 1973), p. 8.

[11] Gwendolyn Brooks, *The World of Gwendolyn Brooks* (New York,

Harper & Row, Publishers, 1971), p. 19.

[12]Marianne Moore, *The Complete Poems of Marianne Moore* (New York, The Macmillan Company/Viking Press, fourth printing, 1969), p. 10.

[13]*Merciful Disguises,* p. 48.

[14]Margaret Honton, *Take Fire* (New Wilmington Pennsylvania, Dawn Valley Press, 1980), p. 15.

[15]Anne Sexton, *Love Poems* (Boston, Houghton Mifflin, 1969), p. 65.

[16]Margaret Honton, ed., *Righting: Poems and Process* (Columbus, Ohio, Argus Press, 1977), p. 112.

[17]Margaret Honton, ed., *A Golden Asterisk in Time* (Columbus, Ohio, Avonelle Associates, 1978), p. 113.

[18]Margaret Honton, *College Bound* (Self-published, limited edition, 1975), p. 43.

[19]Margaret Honton, First published in *They Came to School Dressed Like Flowers,* an anthology of poets' and students' works during residencies (Cols., OH, Published by the Ohio Foundation on the Arts, Inc. for the Ohio Arts Council, 1978), p. 89; later included in *Take Fire,* p. 9.

THE ELEGY

Frona Lane

The elegy is a nostalgic, melancholy song of mourning (lamentation) or memorial to the dead.

Elegiac meter, or couplet, which is rarely used now, consists of a dactylic hexameter line (6 feet), followed by a dactylic pentameter line (5 feet.) The pentameter is composed of two sections of two and a half feet each: two whole feet, then a single long syllable, followed by a long syllable. When written in English it is usually in accent feet, used often by Gerard Manley Hopkins.

The caesura, literally meaning division, or pause, in the middle of a line in classic verse falls at the end of a word, but usually in the middle of a foot. In English verse it should fall at the end of both feet and word, also employed by Hopkins in his so-called sprung rhythm. An example of elegaic meter is my imitation of Schiller and Coleridge:

> All my friends come to me, take my hand, lift me lovingly up.
> There I'll sleep, there I'll wait aye wait for you, welcome you home.

Notice the caesura following the long syllable "aye," as it is so advantageously used in blank verse.

Although Goldsmith's "Elegy on the Death of a Mad Dog" is considered a pun, it assumes the iambic measure of the elegy, except that it falls short in measure of the line length of four-three syllables, likewise Longfellow's "Psalms of Life," which is an ode in feeling rather than an elegy.

There are very few spondees (two long or stressed syllables) in the English language. Therefore there is a preponderance of dactyls in hexameters, making the meter lighter and more tripping than in the original, and trochees (a long syllable followed by a short one) are often substituted for spondees. In dactylic hexameter, the first four feet are either dactyl or spondee, the fifth usually a dactyl, but occasionally a spondee, when the line is called spondaic verse, and the sixth and last is always a spondee or trochee. Clement Wood says:

> The Greek and Roman classical hexameter was a far more complicated line than the English iambic pentameter. First of all, the syllables were long or short, not accented or accented. The rules for determining whether a syllable was long or short were complicated, and can best be learned from some textbook on classical scansion... Classical meters based on the length of duration of syllables, have never been effectively acclimatized in English verse.

the Greek dactylic hexameter later used by the Romans, had six feet. It's first four must be either dactyls or spondees; the fifth must be a dactyl, the sixth must be a trochee or a spondee.

In English, such hexameters are most effectively written in accent verse; that is, accent dactyls, spondees and trochees replace the durational ones. This was the method used by Longfellow in "Evangeline"; beginning "This is the forest primeval, the murmuring pines and hemlocks."

It should be noted that the classic hexameter also has a break or caesura midway of the line.

Gray's familiar "Elegy Written in a Country Churchyard" is acclaimed the most perfect example in English of classic Greek syllabic verse. It is written in regular iambic pentameter. My imitation is as follows:

> The curfew tolls for me at parting day.
> Think you this is my final resting place?
> My friends are weeping as they stoop to lay
> the lid upon my quiet sleeping face.

To scan the first line, an unaccented syllable is followed by an accented one (iambic); ten syllables of five feet make it a pentameter, or iambic pentameter.

But scanning his verse as a whole, it is not a true elegy, since every line is five feet (pentameter) and none the required six feet (hexameter), although an uneven line now and then approaches a half attempt, if such were meant, which I doubt.

ELEGY ON THIS MACHINE AGE

> And all the gears began to rattle, not
> a man to hear...aye! machines milled on
> and on and on with none, not one man near.
> And hour by hour they ground out meal for bread
> until their meal turned into weevil. This
> is what the weevil said, "Now which is great-
> er evil? Man to eat his weevil bread
> or weevil grow fast, fast as he can

into a monstrous devil, turn and make
a meal of man?"...And all the gears began
to rattle—not a man, no none to hear.
Now one by one the mill machines mill on
and on and on with none, not one, man near.

Frona Lane

EPIC: A COMET AMONG STARS

Ora Pate Stewart

It is said that the cultures of the Western World derive from twin sources: the culture of the Hebrews as has come down to us in the Bible, and the culture of the arts as they have descended from ancient Greece.[1]

Literary coments, with long, long "tales" have streaked across our poet-sky from time to time. They brighten our way with flashes of excitment—leaving in their wake chronicles for our archives, beacons from times past; beacons that search us out with the urgency of kliegs, hunting us down from where our separate deltas have carried us—like fingers of the hand, going in their different ways—each river opening a new mouth to the sea—reminding us that somewhere up stream we all come together, finding our common beginnings.

Webster's states:

> Epic: A long narrative poem about the deeds of a traditional or historical hero or heroes of high station; typically a poem like the *Iliad* and *Odyssey*, with a background of warfare and the supernatural, a dignified syle, and certain formal characteristics of structure, beginning in catalogue passages, invocations of the muse etc.; classical epic, a poem like Milton's *Paradise Lost,* or Tasso's *Jerusalem Delivered*, in which structure and convention are applied to later or different materials. Art epic; literary epic—a poem like *Beowulf,* the *Niblungenlied,* and the *Chanson de Roland*, considered as expressing the early ideals, character, and traditions of a people or nation as the *Iliad* and *Odyssey*

expressed those of the Greeks; folk epic; national epic. (2) Any long narrative poem regarded as having the style, structure, and importance of the epic: Dante's *Divine Comedy* is the epic of the Ages of Faith.[2]

Other definitions of Epic Poetry include, "the names given to the most dignified and elaborate forms of narrative poetry. . ."[3] J. D. O'Hara states, "Almost every culture developed forms of the epic early in its existence." The cultural epic provides a central storehouse for that society's beliefs, values, history and ideals. "The earliest epics are quite literally compendiums of culture. The Babylonian epic *Gilgamesh*, which may be four thousand years old, is now only about half of what we imagine it to have been at one time."[4]

In point of chronology, the *Legend of Gilgamesh* may be the most ancient epic discovered so far (nearly 30,000 tablets and fragments, in three different languages, pieced together to form what could be half the original.) But this is not to say that earlier ones may not still turn up. Gilgamesh being the Babylonian symbol of Noah, the legend comes close to reporting things as they seemed to the early Babylonians (considering the Confusion of Tongues; names were changed. Noah might have been Gilgamesh to them.)

On the other side of the Indus another epic began to grow together, in India. (Although it did not achieve its Sanscrit form until around 400 A.D., it is thought to have been in the making 1500 years.) "*The Mahabharata* is not only the longest epic poem in Sanscrit, it is the longest poem in any language— eight times as long as the *Iliad* and *Odyssey* combined. It is by far the longest poem ever composed—some 100,000 couplets—this massive encyclopedia of Hindu life."[6]

A lesser Indian epic—only twice as long as the combined *Iliad* and *Odyssey*—was the *Ramayana*. (The Teutonic equivalent of the legend of Rama is *The Niblungenlied*, written in the late twelfth century by an unknown German poet. The story has often been retold, especially by Richard Wagner in his four-opera, *The Ring of the Niblungs.*)

As the *Encyclopedia Britannica* states:

The earliest epic poets, Lesches, Linus, Orpheus, Arctinus, Eugammon, are the veriest shadows, whose names often betray their symbols and fabulous character. The *Iliad* and *Odyssey* form for us the type of the ancient epic; when we speak of epic poetry, we unconsciously measure it by the example of the *Idiad* and *Odyssey*. . .[7]

Among a cluster of poets of the seventh century B.C., we come upon this, ". . . And Anyte, (Anita) of whom we only know that she was an epic poetess, and was called 'the female Homer.' "

In the sixth and fifth centuries B.C., there was a school of philosophical epic, Xenophones, Parmenides and Empedocles being the leaders.

It is worth a re-reading of the *Iliad* and *Odyssey*, since these are by all accounts the grandest of all epics. Even though the author was centuries further down stream from the happenings, he has collected and preserved all the right textures, flavors, sensitivities of episodic material. *The Iliad* reads as if Homer were there on the battleground, visualizing all that took place. See how he manages taste, delicacy; he does not over-tell, yet he shows us the trends of their thoughts, and clues us in on their private grudges and slights, their wisdom, their loves and their infidelities. We have tremendous respect and appreciation for his scope and style. His epics *define* the category.

The Homeric genius was duly acknowledged in ancient time. It is thought that he lived and sang in times contemporary with the Hebrew prophet Isaiah, late eighth century B.C., and by his time two or three more Troys had been built upon the *Iliad* ruins. Seven cities claimed Homer' birth—not always the same seven—and six centuries have put in their bid for his life span. And one of his modern translators insists that a woman wrote the Odyssey. Samuel Butler considers that this epic was written from a woman's point of view.[8]

All other epic writers since Homer pale into faded copyists. No other epic has ever been created to stand beside his. But from his generous genius, the thirsty imitators may drink. He is the fount itself.

After half a millennium in the hands of singers, the Homer Treasury was housed for a few centuries in the great library at Alexandria—where it was enjoyed by the greatest scholars of the world—until that repository was senselessly burned. (391 A.D.) This bigoted vandalism has to be one of the greatest tragedies in history—certainly in cultural history.

Octavian (Augustus Caesar, 63 B.C.-A.D. 14) was to boast that he found Rome brick and left if marble. It was his epic poets who were selected to make this hope come true. August-us commissioned Publius Vergilius Maro (70-19 B.C.) to write an epic to excite and unify his people. Vergil turned immediately to Homer for his model, and proceeded to create the *Aeneid.*

Vergil took a sudden illness and died before he was ready; his masterpiece was not yet completed to his liking. He gave explicit instructions that the unfinished manuscripts be burned after his death. We are grateful to Augustus for saving the work. From where we stand it is difficult to see how greater length could improve it. "The *Aeneid* is the most refined and most emotional of epics."[9]

Publius Ovidius Naso (43 B.C.-A.D. 17) did not stand so well as poet-successor to Vergil. His lusty epic was considered a personal braggadocio. His *Art of Love* was less than artistic, and was blamed by Augustus for his daughter's adulteries, and her daughter's. The poet was banished for a time, and condemned by the church for several centuries. His name was finally re-entered into graces; but Ovid is not much read today.

Epic excerpts emerged during the Dark Ages; but it was a bad night for bright stars. *Beowulf* is the only one which exists in anything like complete form, and it is of all Teutonic epics the most important. It is written, like all old Teutonic work of the kind, in *alliterative unrhymed rhythm.* (A modern version by Duncan Spaeth appears in *English Literature*, Vol. I.)[10]

"There exists no clue in Old English literature to the time, the place, the authorship, or the circumstance of the composition of *Beowulf*,"[11] says one text book author. "The manuscript dates from about 1,000 A.D. (Cottonian Collection, British Museum.) How much earlier is a matter of conjecture."[12]

Through research or conjecture another author-of-text says:

> In England the eighth-century Anglo-Saxon author of *Beowulf* seems to have had the *Aeneid* in mind. . . (because of plot and behavior of characters.) As the fragmentary plot suggests, the difficulties of the epic form troubled the author of *Beowulf*, who found himself in a culture different in many ways from those of early times when the epic sense of existence first developed. Such difficulties led to lessenings of the epic, especially in the mediaval *chanson de geste*, a verse narrative of military action and heroic deeds represented by the Russian *Song of Igor's Campaign*, the French *Song of Roland*, the Spanish *Poem of the Cid*—all written in the twelfth century. . ."[13]

The manuscript of Beowulf, this "oldest extant written composition in English,"[14] exists in beautifully calligraphed pages, expertly executed—a literary monument to its unknown author.

There is a category listed—but unqualified—in the dictionaries as *Art Epic*. I believe we have an epic that qualifies to fill this gap.[15]

In ages when women were not expected to be readers and writers, they satisfied their creative compulsions and artistic ambitions with sewing up a story, a poem—a picture. In *Proverbs* 31: 10-31, Solomon celebrates such a woman:

> . . . She seeketh wool, and flax, and worketh willingly with her hands. . . She layeth her hands to the spindle, and her hands hold the distaff. . . She is not afraid of the snow for her household: for all her household are clothed in scarlet. . .[16] She maketh fine linen, and selleth it; and delivereth girdles unto the merchant. Strength and honor are her clothing; and she shall rejoice in time to come. . ."

Solomon was writing in 1000 B.C.

2100 years after Solomon such a woman appeared. An

epic embroidered on a long strip of linen, seems an elegantly impressive example. This epic is 231 feet long and 20 inches wide (high.) It presents 79 episodes in the life of the "greatest hero of his day (from the Norman standpoint)—William the Conqueror;" and the work is traditionally ascribed to his devoted and industrious wife, Matilda.

Matilda was the daughter of the Duke of Florence, who traced ancestry from Alfred the Great (849-899.) Duke William married Matilda in 1053.

As William Fleming states:

> This large-scale example of pictorial art is the so-called *Bayeux Tapestry*, one of the most elegant documents of this or any other time. Here, in visual form, is the story of the Conquest of England by William the Conqueror, recounted from the Norman point of view, in the course of which a vivid picture of life and attitudes of feudal man unfolds. . .

> . . . The design is applied in woolen yarn to a coarse linen surface rather than woven into the cloth itself; it is more accurately described as an embroidery. It was probably intended to cover the plain strip of masonry over the nave arcade of the Bayeux Cathedral. It was apparently completed about twenty years after the great battle it describes.[17]

The colorful pictures are not caricatures or cartoons. They are believable likenesses of her hero in progress; as you walk by the scenes, you simulate the motion picture of his actions, and interactions with friends, foes and accomplices. You come to recognize the characters, his half brother, Odo, Bishop of Bayeux, and others. It can be read and understood, enjoyed in any language (even though the succinct text is embroidered in Latin above the action, under the top border.)

Britannica says:

> . . . More than seventy scenes of the Conquest, beginning with Harold's visit to France and ending with English flight from the the Battle of Hastings (1066.) Displayed in the nave of the Bayeux Cathedral from the end of the 15th century, it was 'discovered'

there by Bernard de Montfaucon in the early 18th century. As a historical source the tapestry is especially valuable for its detail of military equipment and tactics.[18]

The priceless original manuscript—this epic—is housed in the museum at Bayeux, a town in Northwestern France. It has been cherished and preserved since 1100 A.D.—a masterpiece of communication—on-the-spot-reporting—now almost 900 years old. What other book, roll, or scroll—one original print, one edition—can boast such a long life and popularity? There is nothing else like it in the whole world.

In Spanish poetry the *Poem of the Cid* takes first place, as the great national epic of the middle ages; it is supposed to have been written between 1135 and 1175.[19]

In Italy, Dante Alighieri (1265-1321) presented the generation with a masterpiece of a different kind. It would be difficult to find anything comic or humorous in his *Commedia, The Divine Comedy*. (Word meanings get warped and changed with use and age.) By Dante's time:

> people had learned to think primarily of types and groups: pagans and Christians, the damned and the saved. A fresco in Florence Cathedral commissioned in 1465 to celebrate the two-hundredth anniversary of Dante's birth, shows the poet holding an open copy of *The Divine Comedy* and bidding his city embark with him on a journey through Hell. In his book he had honored Homer, Horace, and Ovid by placing them among the great pagan dead in Limbo, and he made Vergil his guide through Hell and Purgatory.[20]

Dante is in a world totally separate from his ordinary experience, and yet his testimony is so vivid and unified that even the non-Italian, non-Christian reader finds the journey through the *Commedia* hauntingly persuasive.

"At the same time it must be admitted that comparatively few readers make the whole trip." T. S. Eliot offers one ironic reason, "It is apparently easier to accept damnation as poetic material than purgation or beatitude; less is involved that is strange to the modern mind."[21]

The sixteenth century experienced a sudden surge with the literary epic. Italy's Torquarto Tasso's *Gerusalemme Liberata* deals with the First Crusade under Godfrey of Bouvillon; Portugal's Luiz vas de Camoes' *The Lucidias* (1572)—a celebration of Vasco da Gama's expedition to Calicut (India) in 1497-98—(and others.)

The most splendid of all epics of Italy however, was, and remains the *Jersalem Delivered,* of Torquarto Tasso (1544-1595). Tasso's epic is in *ottava rima* (an Italian stanza of eight lines, eleven syllables to each line.)   His subject is the First Crusade (which recovered Jerusalem from the Turks in 1099.) The manuscript went through numerous drafts, and at one stage Tasso admitted that he "succeeded in reconciling invention with historical truth by adding a number of romantic and even supernatural episodes to the firm groundwork of the principal historical action."[2 2]

Portuguese literature is rich in epic poems; but all others are obscured by the glory of Camoës, whose magnificent *Lusaids* had been printed in 1572, and forms the summit of Portuguese literature.

Edmund Spenser, England, (1552-1599?) produced the next comet of importance.   "His literary career was that of court poet, striving to please Elizabeth's cultured courtiers." (With Raleigh's advice he had taken the first three volumes of his *Faerie Queen* to show her—which won him a small pension from Elizabeth.)   He produced three more books, continuing his ambitious tribute, but was largely disappointed in his hopes.

> Spenser has been called 'the poets' poet,' for no other poet has furnished inspiration to so many of our great singers. They have gone to him, to catch, or try if they could, some part of the secret of his unequalled gift for making deep and harmonied melodious music out of words. And he has earned the title of 'poets' poet' by giving impetus to great poets, from Milton through Keats and Tennyson down to our own day."[2 3]

His epic, *The Faerie Queen,* was his masterpiece:

> No work is more typically Elizabethan than *The Faerie Queen.*

Of the twelve books he planned only six books and two cantos of the seventh were completed. Each book is divided into twelve cantos. The stanza form which Spenser originated for *The Faerie Queen* is made up of eight lines in iambic pentameter and a ninth line in iambic hexameter, rhyming *a b a b b c b c c* (closely resembling Chaucer's *rime royal*.) The stanza, admirably suited for the long poem, is a favorite of later poets, among them Thomson in *The Castle of Indolence,* Burns in *The Cotter's Saturday Night,* Byron in *Childe Harold's Pilgrimage,* Shelley in *Adonais*—all of which are major works of their authors. . . Indeed, no poem of our language has been more loved by the great poets than *The Faerie Queen.* . . once the ear is trained to his musical wizardry, he is not likely to suffer neglect.[24]

Edmund Spenser was the last of the world's Court Bards. And much of the demand for epics passed away with him.

John Milton (1608-1674) said: "My father destined me, while yet a little boy, for the study of Humane Letters." Grammar school, private studies with home teachers, and six years at Cambridge prepared him for his chosen career. With a Master of Arts degree in 1632 he abandoned his early plans for the clergy for literature.

Milton's life, after a glorious childhood in Buckinghamshire with his father who loved him and worked with him, was later beset with a catalogue of troubles that he had not ordered.[25]

In 1643, when Milton was thirty-five, he married a seventeen year-old girl, Mary Powell—who left after only a few weeks. When Mary was nineteen, she reconsidered her status and returned to resume the marriage. To this union three daughters were born, and one son (who died in infancy.) In 1654 Mary died in childbirth.

By this time Milton was totally blind. For a time he was helplessly dependent upon the whim and temperament of his motherless daughters, (who grew up resenting him and careless of his comforts and wishes.) A brief respite from this bleak loneliness came in 1656 when he married Katharine Woodcock. But in less than a year Katharine also died in childbirth.

In his middle years Milton was busy with speeches and pamphlets supporting Cromwell's Commonwealth; and the wonder (and the blessing) of it is that he somehow escaped the execution that other prominent participants suffered—for less rigorous activities. The Restoration of the Monarchy put an end to his public life. He was forced to go into hiding. But this circumstance made time and privacy for his greatest poetic achievements.

This—but especially his marriage in 1663 to Elizabeth Minshull, who was twenty-five years old—gave him a decade of peace. He produced *Paradise Lost* (1667) and its sequel *Paradise Regained* (1671.) He spent the last years in study, tempered with music and the company of friends. He died of a multitude of maladies on November 8, 1674. His work is an example of what can be accomplished in a life beset with vicissitudes.

Henry Wadsworth Longfellow (1807-82) drew upon New World legends for his narrative verse—*Evangeline, Hiawatha,* and *The Courtship of Miles Standish;* these have several of the requirements of the epic, and served the American populace to fill that need. He became the best loved and most widely translated poet of his day.

As the sun appeared to be going down for the last time on Epic poetry, Alfred, Lord Tennyson (1809-1892), poet Laureate of England, author of *Idylls of the King, Enoch Arden,* and *In Memoriam*, told a friend, "I soon found that if I meant to make any mark at all it must be by shortness, for all the men before me had been so diffuse, and the big things had been done." By shortness he meant simply to refuse the challenge of epic in favor of brief, highly polished poems. "To get the workmanship as nearly perfect as possible," he said, "is the best chance for going down the stream of time, A small vessel on fine lines is likely to float further than a great raft."[2 7]

> The epic formula is, then, an exaltation of heroic narrative, with the addition of philosophic meanings and moral observations. The epic has provided poets with material for millions of lyric poems.[2 8]

Poet after poet has made poetry from this yardage. Our
epic legacy is still at work for us—to explore and refashion
these heirlooms.

After all is said, we could count all the truly great epics
on our fingers between the first and the last. (Amazing that
both these authors should be blind.) Our fiery comet has taken
us for a splendid ride. The very length and power of the epic
have pushed it into an eclipse of fashion—as knights in iron
greaves are to our astronauts. Today we write our epics in
the sky. Who will be our chroniclers?

BITTER SEED OF FREEDOM

The woman called before the bench was small
and old, in a calico dress with mutton sleeves,
she lifted her larkspur eyes and clutched her shawl
with trembling hands before the judge, she spoke
in firm and level voice. "I thank you sir
for giving me this chance to state my views,
that the Supreme Court of this fair land, will concur
to listen to one so charged as Common Scold
because I use my pen to reveal the graft
of men in church and state. My accusers say
my books of Pen Portraits are devilish craft,
as poison mixed to kill with ridicule. . .
though the script is filled with praise as well, I claim
a few as gentlemen of valiant deeds,
though often wrapped in caustic wit which became
the seeds of laughter for my following,
yet crown my subject with lasting fame. My foes
have stoned my house and called me godless old
Anne Royall, age sixty years, who now expose
my hecklers. They found this thirteenth century law
of English text, and built a ducking pool
out at the Navy Yard where they expect
to punish me for printing truth. They drool
at the thought of humiliating a woman scorned.

Your honor, before the last witness is called
to prove me a nuisance, I who have been guest
of politicians, of socialites enthralled

to be my friend, while the President's Mansion bids
me ever welcome, may I advocate
this scene be painted and hung in the Capitol's
Rotunda with our National murals to equate
this year of eighteen twenty nine. Depict
    ANNE ROYALL versus THE UNITED STATES.

But there will be a change of wind when men
shall cherish free speech, free press, and none deny
that corrupt officials be exposed, and one day
equality for men AND women. . . while I
shall go down in history, which alone must prove
the injustice of this trial, and now I await
the decision of the jurors who have heard my plea."

The crowd stood up to cheer or catcall, as fate
sat with the jury, eyes blindfold, while hours
ticked past like the beating of a tired old heart
until all was ready; then Anne was asked to stand
to hear the verdict, "guilty", the vicious dart
so thrown to shame this woman of radical words.

The judge demanded order then declared
the sentence would be a fine and she required
to keep the peace for one year. Anne Royall squared
her shoulders behind hurt pride though her spirit
    soared free.

(Note: Anne Royall was the only woman ever tried as a Common Scold in the history of the United States.)

Guanetta Gordon, from *Red Are the Embers*

FOOTNOTES

[1]J. D. O'Hara, *Poetry*, World of Culture, Newsweek Books, New York, 1975.

[2]*Webster's New World Dictionary of the American Language. Vol. 8,* Chicago: Encyclopedia Britannica, 1956 Edition.

[3] *Ibid.*

[4] O'Hara, *Poetry.*

[5] Nimrod, founder of Babylon (and builder of the Tower from which it took its name) had a grandfater, Ham who had been a participant in the Flood experience; and he had a grandfather who was Noah himself, Captain of *The Ark.* The generations were still long—men's lives had not as yet been "shortened," and Noah was still around for 350 years after the Flood. So Nimrod had been made acquainted with the "Legends." The Gilgamesh legend's greatest value to us is that it is a second witness that there truly was a flood, and that our ancestors—their Ham our Shem, came out of the ark together. (*Genesis.*)

[6] O'Hara, *Poetry.*

[7] *Britannica.*

[8] *The Iliad of Homer—The Odyssey,* (Rendered into English by Samuel Butler) Chicago: William Penton, Publisher, Britannica, Inc., 1952.

[9] O'Hara, *Poetry* ⁻

[10] *English Literature and its Backgrounds,* Vol. I, New York: The Dryden Press.

[11] "Beowulf was a Geat, and his people lived in what is now the southern part of Sweden. (Professor Spaeth's otherwise splendid version of the poem erroneously assumes that the Geats were Jutes.) Hygelac, Beowulf's uncle, is a historical person known to us;. . . and we are able to date his raid on the Frisian coast, referred to in the epic, as having occurred about 516 A.D. . . The hero would have been born about 490, visited the Danes to rid them of Grendel in 510, and ascended the throne in 530. . . We are told he reigned for fifty years. . . Scholars have proved, by linguistic and other tests, tht *Beowulf* was composed some time around 720. (*English Literature and its Backgrounds, Vol. I,* Grenbanier, Middlebrooke, Thompson, Watt, New York: Dryden Press, Sixth Edition, 1957;

[12] *Ibid.*

[13] O'Hara, *Poetry.*

[14]Photograph of page, one page 22, *Poetry.*

[15]*Webster's.*

[16]Read flannels? Interesting.

[17]*Arts and Ideas,* Third Edition, New York: Holt-Rinehart-Winston.

[18]*Britannica,* 1975 Edition.

[19]O'Hara, *Poetry.*

[20]*Ibid.*

[21]*Ibid.*

[22]*Britannica.*

[23]*English Literature and its Backgrounds, Vol. I,* Dryden Press.

[24]*Ibid.*

[25]See Biographical note, *Milton,* Great Books, Vol. 32, Britannica. University of Chicago, 1952.

[26]O'Hara. *Poetry.*

[27]*Ibid.*

[28]*Ibid.*

Grateful appreciation is expressed to Professor J. D. O'Hara, The University of Connecticut, College of Liberal Arts and Sciences, Department of English, for his generous permission to quote from his delightful book, *Poetry.*

THE EPITAPH

Donna Shriver Jones

Anyone who has ever scrawled "Here Lies Chicken" on a torn piece of paper, attached it to a broken twig, and staked it into the ground over the remains of a departed "loved one," has created an epitaph and erected a tombstone.

Just as there is infinite variety in the size, shape, and locale of markers, so there is an assortment of messages on them. An epitaph may be as simple as to indicate only name, year of birth, and year of death (true for such notables as Charles Dickens, John Dryden, Charles Darwin and Robert Browning); it might feature merely a small figure in relief (such as is frequently used to set off the tombs of pets and infants) with pertinent but limited data; or it might be as detailed as to virtually chronicle an individual's entire life.

Example of the last type are the elaborate tombs of the Pharoahs of Egypt, and indeed these are probably the earliest, still extant, epitaphs. They date some 2,000 years B.C. and, with a moving finger that seems to have moved on, and on, denote, describe, and comment on its occupants' every deed and dream. Conversely, Greek epitaphs were less fact than fancy, often bearing epigrams and being frequently in verse, slanted perhaps as much as the Egyptian ones, but distinctly more terse.

Americans interested in genealogy often trace their heraldry to the escutcheons appearing on the early tombstones of their English forbears. The epitaphs on these markers tended not only to fit the solemnity of the occasion but also to mirror the social and religious atmosphere of the era as well. The medieval times therefore featured pious, tender prayer on stones; the Elizabethan and Jacobean period focused on a person's history and occupation: flowery, poetic phrases decorated tombs until the Civil War; and since that period, the conglomerata that has characterized the world in general is reflected on grave inscriptions.

In an earlier era, tombs were placed in the south section of agraveyard, a practice dictated by the belief that the Devil rode in from the north. The north part then, appropriately to the theological tenet of the day, was reserved for suicides. All the occupants' heads faced east towards the rising sun and, presumably, a brighter tomorrow. Currently, of course, since space is a premium, subjects are buried almost anywhere in almost any position; no less care is taken, to be sure, but there is a view towards exigency.

Emblems on headstones might include a person's trade (an unopened lock adorns this one):

> A zealous locksmith dy'd of late
> And did arrive at Heaven's gate,
> He stood without and would not knock
> Because he meant to pick the lock;

or be imbued with a rose or torch or animal, symbolizing the object of the mourner's focus (so noted a personage as William Hogarth, for example, erected for his pet bullfinch, Dick, a stone bearing two cross-bones of birds and featuring the singular inscription:

> Alas poor Dick! Aged eleven.

Then there are the traditional symbols of death, such as the scythe, hour glass, or torch, right alongside the present do-it-yourself-first-designs (such as the insignia of four aces and a fish a presumably Christian gambler ordered to be sand-blasted on her tomb-to-be.)

Latin has always been the preferred language for the dead, and today we may still see such glossolalia as Deo Volente (God willing), Dei Gratia (by the grace of God), Gloria Patri (Glory be to the Father), In Perpetuum (for ever), R.I.P. (for Requiescat in Pace, or Rest in Peace.)

Most epitaphs are serious in nature and are composed or commissioned by family members to another family member. But in addition to these (and the aforementioned pets), deceased friends, slaves, and unknown parties have also been honored.

Unfortunately for veracity, those composed by family members sometimes have a tendency to reflect their donor's need for expiation of conscience, giving to their departed:

> A reputation he had no mind to,
> And a course of life he was not intended to.

We are, furthermore, perennially reminded of loved ones since departed one, ten, twenty or more years, by those who annually memorialize them through the "Gone but not forgotten" poems which frequently appear in our newspapers.

Occasionally a person has left his own epitaph, such as the clergyman Dr. Fuller whose one-liner was:

> Here lies Fuller's earth,

or Ben Franklin's famous de-personification of his dead body as an old, stripped and torn book which hopefully one day would appear:

> in a new and more perfect edition
> corrected and amended by the Author.

And we are familiar with Edgar Lee Masters' fictional town of Spoon River in which the dead seem to speak from the grave their *real* as opposed to their apparent message (an actual, if not literary, practice which incidentally antedates Masters by hundreds of years), such as Serepta Mason crying for understanding as she explains that her life was "bloomless" because

> a bitter wind stunted my petals
> on the side of me which you in the village could see
> . . . (but) my flowering side you never saw!

Humorous, witty, sarcastic, or "gotcha" ones are perhaps most intriguing to those of us who do not care to remain overly long past the witching hour, however. Since many of these that are now legend were once fabricated (such as the hypochondriac's epitaph "See there, I told you I was sick" surely must be), we cannot easily separate fact from fancy. But we can speculate that a long-suffering companion would *want*, whether he actually did or not, to vocalize this sentiment:

> Here lies in silent clay
> Miss Arabella Young,
> Who on the 21st of May
> Began to hold her tongue;

or that a curiosity seeker who:

> scraped away the mossy spray,
> and scratched amid the lichen green
> until he read:
> 'Kate Kelly, dead
> aged 27, Kerosene.'

would rather this have been a nightmare than a real experience; or that the weary mother of four who wrote "Embarkation" which accompanies this article would not dare let it accompany her to her final rest after reading this epitaph which is authentic:

> Here lies the mother of 28,
> It might have been more,
> But now it's too late.

Finally, one pithy example of the "gotcha" variety will do, the one composed by the husband who bemused,

> This spot is the sweetest I've seen in my life,
> For it raises my flowers and covers my wife.

One will do, because with sentiment such as this and those sentiments already expressed, and with tempus fugiting as it will, we had better pause while there is yet time to give some thought as to who we want to say our last words for us and what adornment would be most fitting on our headstone.

Now, let's see, what about beginning with an insignia of two crossed Venus pencils above an IMB Selectric. . .

EMBARKATION

Leaving life's great mausoleum,

Must the soul at once inhabit
Stamen cupped to clasp a spirit?
Talon grasping more than tissue?
Unborn butterfly's soul socket?
Might instead the weary spirit,
Now relieved of mortal burdens,
Merit permanent retirement?

Donna Shriver Jones, appeared in *Modern Images*

DESTINATION: ELEVATION

Forbear to detain me from plunging
off this Cliff of Not Knowing!
. . . a Fixed Foot is a Cemented Step.
Before the rocks beneath can break me,
I may grow me Wings of Wonder
that bear me aloft
to the Region of Perception.

Do not chide me as I plummet
from this ledge of Something Beyond!
. . . Cruising is but Aimless Motion.
Before me the stones below could crush me,
supported by Pinions of Perhaps,
I may rise cloudward
to the Realm of Illumination
. . . and alight at Arrival!

Donna Shriver Jones, First Place, 1976 New York Poetry Forum contest

BIBLIOGRAPHY

Brown, Raymond Lamont. *A Book of Epitaphs.*

Howe, W. H. *Here Lies.*

Masters, Edgar Lee. *Spoon River Anthology.*

Thompson, Leslie M. "Sexism in the Cemetery." Unpub. ms.

Time Magazine. March 30, 1981.

FREE VERSE

Jean R. Jenkins

"Free verse is like playing tennis with the net down."
That statement of Robert Frost's is one of my earliest recollections of poetry. Today I am unsure whether it is a favor-
able or an unfavorable comment. The way I play tennis it makes
a lot of sense. There are still other rules to follow, and net up
or down, it is still a difficult game.

There has been a great deal of controversy about free
verse, and some of the things said on both sides have been
exaggerated and ridiculous. Some people think that free verse
is a final insult to poetry and call it "chopped prose"; others
think that it is the final liberation of poetry; some suspect
that the writers of free verse use it because of inability to use
the conventional forms. Some "new" poets undoubtedly have
tried to write free verse out of laziness or a misconception
of its nature, but some of the best writers of free verse have
used traditional forms with dexterity and success.

Free verse is considered a recent addition to the realm of
poetry. The genre has developed during the last hundred years
or less, though it is possible to find examples in earlier writing.
Writers such as Milton, Dryden, Blake, Arnold, Henley, and
Whitman had not heard of free verse. The "modern" poetry
movement began about 1912 and gained impetus and definition
during and after World War I. Many poets revolted against
some fairly general tendencies of the Victorian era. It was felt
that, with few exceptions, poets had lost contact with reality,
had failed to find ways to sing of the world of the twentieth
century. The "new" poets objected to the sentimental, the
pretty, the merely agreeable. Life, they believed, was not
so simple. They wanted to use expressions which had not only
more impact upon the reader but also more truth in them. They
were dubious about the organization of poetry and the traditional rhythmic forms, so sought ways of avoiding logical or chrono-
logical organizations of poems, and of escaping from the use of
regular rhythms, after the manner of Walt Whitman who had
explained that he used such verse to connect his songs "in a

loose and free metre of his own, of an irregular length of lines, apparently lawless at first perusal, although on closer examination a certain regularity appears, like the recurrence of lesser and larger waves on the seashore, rolling in without intermission, and fitfully rising and falling."

Free verse is often defined as unrhymed verse without a traditional metrical form; but the term "free verse" is modern, adopted from the French *vers libre*. *Vers* in French refers to a line of poetry; hence *vers libre* actually means a "free line." It is from the varying lengths of the lines and the arrangements of stresses within them that we get the best indication that a poem is in free verse.

Free verse does not follow the rules of metrical verse, differing in many ways from conventional poetry. It may or may not be divided into stanzaic units. There may be quite regular stanzaic division, but they are often irregular in length. The line may vary in length from s single syllable to fifty or more. The writer of free verse often uses long sentences so that the flow of sense may be technically uninterrupted for an entire unit. Critically, it has been said that a line of free verse ends where it is convenient to take a breath.

Free verse often makes no use of rhyme, but it may be used to achieve some special effect. It may be used more or less inconsistently thoughout a poem, but the technique is not common. It is more often used in brief units for the purpose of intensifying certain aspects of content. Sidney said, ". . .it is not riming and versing that maketh a Poet. . ."It has never been avowed that a poem achieves greatness because every other line rhymes. Free verse grants the choice of that specific word or phrase to give expression to thought. It allows the "fresh tongue," a special joining of words free of the bonds of rhyme and meter. Words put together are sensations. The business of poetry is to use words to give quality and feeling to those abstract notions and in so doing to put them beyond words.

Good free verse is not at all easy to write. Some say it is the most difficult of all, because there is no repetitive beat to lull the reader's critical faculty, and the slightest intellectual, psychological, or aesthetic failure stands mercilessly exposed. It is also probably the most demanding to read aloud because of the subtlety of rhythmic pattern. T. S. Eliot said, "Even in the 'freest' of free verse there should lurk the ghost of some simple meter 'which should advance menacingly as we doze, and withdraw as we arouse.' " Free verse has a rhythm based on cadence rather than meter. It demands a sensitiveness to cadence, a symmetry which approaches that of a musical composition. The cadence may be found in the number of syllables in the speech phrases within the lines, or in the number of heavier stresses within those phrases. Couperin said that cadence is "properly the spirit, the soul must be added." The writer of free verse must read his poetry aloud. He must listen to it, hear it a number of times over in order that he does not break the rhythm.

A poem is, among other things, an instrument of verbal, and sometimes visual, communication. Those proponents of free verse feel that neither music nor stucture needs to be confining. What a poem communicates is something more than a prose passage, not because of a special language of poetry but because poetry exploits more consistently the full potentialities of language, and in free verse it often communicates through the structure of the poem, the placement on the page. Space betweeen sounds has meaning. Muriel Rukeyser says, ". . . I care very much about the air and the silence let into a poem." Denise Levertov, who considers a poem to be a sonic entity apart from its meaning, determines the physical shape of a poem partly by the clusters of perceptions which break the stanza. Thinking and feeling work together in a poem as a single thing. It may be indicated by lengths of lines, choice of words, punctuation or lack of it, and by the free structrure. In free verse one can pick up the rhythm of feeling in ways that prose (though good prose is rhythmic, too) and conventional poetry with its typographically indicated intonation cannot offer. What happens visually produces a certain psychological effect. With free verse there is an eye/ear coordination. The way a poem looks on a page, however, should not dominate. The poem still needs to say something. A poet must be an architect of poems, if only because a fine line may become finer by benefit of context and imply more by the placement on the page.

Ezra Pound felt that the language of poetry and its rhythms must be those of the speaking voice, with no book-words, no periphrases, no inversions. And free verse was D. H. Lawrence's answer to the kind of verse in which the immediate present could flower. However, he made the qualification that free verse was not a *kind* of verse at all. "It is no use inventing fancy laws for free verse, no use drawing a melodic line which all free verse must toe." Free verse is not lacking in form and discipline. Free verse must be spontaneous—but spontaneity is only achieved with difficulty. Free verse is really only *freed* verse.

BREAKDOWN

3.

I who have lain in discard of forced bulbs
that seldom bloom again must not forget:
My mother had a lily bed,
a riddle in the round that every spring
we watched for, waiting galanthus and harebell
in the snow.
          Would narcissus fade before hyacinth
bloomed? Hyacinths last till tulips made bowls?
Which next, allium, iris, or buttercup?

When greenery of amaryllis and Turk's cap grew
we guessed again as if this were a racetrack.
(We knew rooted bulbs had only Up to go.)
It was mystery that infused us,
healing winter.

O
why
in this
self-knowledge
are deeps that hold
inviolate bird whispers,
moods of wind, all mysteries
foreboding as ineluctable seas?

Edna Meudt from *The Ineluctable Sea*

A MOST PRIVATE NOTE

I have listened to them
over their needles
cackle and complain
about the shattering sounds of their men
and I smile at my happy place in your life

often in my own corner
I wait for the
purring   popping   whistling content
indicative of the depth of your sleeping
                    a most private note
                    belonging to our dark togetherness
                    rather like your whiskers growing
and I have found
that the apparatus is attached to the arm
for when I move into position
and your strength encircles
the breathing softens
to the feathery feel of love
                    upon my cheek

oh   my thimbled friends
I hope you never try
a   w i d e   white bed
with no one to sleep crosswise
or break the sound barrier with snores
and find
            how   unsleepable
                    silence is

Jean R. Jenkins, Brigham Young University

THE LAI GROUP AND OTHER FRENCH FORMS

Amy Jo Zook

In the last several years there has been a modest revival of interest in the so-called French forms, partly because of the return to an emphasis on craft and control, and partly because these forms have a certain charm and usefulness of their own. The idea of strict set forms, especially those which make use of demanding rhyme schemes and/or refrains, makes them "a natural" for writing workshops. The sizes of most of these forms, like that of the sonnet, fit them especially for lyric or other compressed themes. None of them is cumbersome. There is also the freeing-up of ideas that results when form is pre-determined and no longer need be decided, and the happy accidents which occur are a result of the necessity of making the idea fit the frame.

The simplest of all French forms (despite its Greek-derived name) is the *kyrielle*, which is a form commonly used in hymns, and instinctively sought by beginning writers of prescribed form with repeated lines. It employs only two rhymes per four-line stanza, and actually the last line of the first stanza becomes the refrain and determines the rhymes of all the rest of the third and fourth lines of the poem. (Ballad-writers, take note.) This could be simple and charming, or in heavy hands become deadly dull by the third or fourth repetition:

EVEN SO

Your eyes may rove, your words be brief,	(a)
Your moods as changeful as the leaf,	(a)
Your promises be few and slow	(b)
And I will love you even so.	(b)
Long after pleasures fade away,	(c)
Through weary night and blazing day	(c)
I'll follow where the wild winds blow	(b)
And I will love you even so.	(b)
The years may whirl in joy and pain	(d)
Erasing hopes we held in vain,	(d)
Stars may recede and lose their glow	(b)
And I will love you even so.	(b)

Perhaps the most neglected group of French forms is the Lai group, and for good reason: the syllabic structure of one

two-syllable line in each tercet is demanding and can easily become awkward. The very attempt to work smoothly through
these one-foot, usually feminine-rhyme, lines is a challenge
the serious poet will welcome. The *Lai* itself consists of any
number (no specific requirement) of stanzas, each composed
of any number of tercets, in each of which groups there are two
five-syllable lines and one two-syllable line, rhymed aab. Within
a stanza, only the two rhymes are allowed, though each succeeding stanza, if there are more, gets its own two rhymes.

SCHEHERAZADE

E'er she went to bed	(a)
her husband-king said	(a)
ever	(b)
"Dawn you shall be dead."	(a)
She spoke without dread,	(a)
clever,	(b)
cliff-hung him instead,	(a)
lost her pretty head	(a)
never.	(b)

Sharon E. Rusbuldt

This must have seemed too easy for the inventive minds in
that period of French literature, because two more forms evolved. The *virelai ancien* (drawing its name from *vivere*—to turn,
and *lai)* follows the same plan of long and short lines with
their respective rhymes, but makes them also chain rhymes
from one stanza to the next, completing a circle in however
many lines or stanzas the poem includes. One source follows
the history of the *lai* or *virelai* back to early bourgettes, with one
repeated refrain at the end of the last stanza:

GREEN NEIGHBORHOOD BLUES

While I overeat	(a)
my neighbor, that fleet	(a)
meany,	(b)
mows grass flat and neat	(a)
clad in her petite	(a)
weeny	(b)

well-filled bikini	(b)
(pale green and teeny)	(b)
she would	(c)
inspire Cellini	(b)
(where's my martini?);	(b)
she could	(c)

(must she look so good?)	(c)
change my neighborhood;	(c)
I'm shook:	(d)
have I understood?	(c)
is all sisterhood	(c)
forsook?	(d)

Here's what I can't brook:	(d)
I could overlook	(d)
defeat	(a)
if she could not cook	(d)
or if she did not look	(d)
so sweet!	(a)

Sharon E. Rusbuldt

Again, someone must have felt that changing rhymes for each stanza was too easy, for the *virelai nouveau* uses only two rhymes which repeat through the (usually three) eight-line stanzas, re-using some of them as refrains in the manner of the *villanelle* or *rondeau redoublé*. There are no short lines used, nor is any particular metric line prescribed. Note the reversal of lines 1 and 2 in lines 23 and 24:

BY ME

"By me his life was saved"—	(A1)
it should have been engraved	(A2)
in gold since I behaved	(a)
like God the way I waved	(a)
about the fact I'd staved	(a)
off death—he'd swallowed drugs,	(b)
I called the squad then raved	(a)
"By me his life was saved."	(A1)

Months afterward he waved   (a)
a gun: his girl behaved;   (a)
but still he drilled three slugs   (b)
into her chest, then caved   (a)
his head with one. "I saved   (a)
his life:" it taunts and tugs,   (b)
it's kept my mind enslaved—   (a)
it should have been engraved.   (A2)

They tell me I behaved   (a)
correctly when I saved   (a)
his life: they give me hugs,   (b)
(the issue then is waived: (a)
the road to hell is paved   (a)
with good intentions) shrugs.   (b)
It should have been engraved: (A2)
by me his life was saved.   (A1)

Sharon E. Rusbuldt

While the *Rondeau* in its classical pure form is familiar enough to need little introduction, it has several variations and near cousins which bear closer examination. There are, for instance, the *Rondeau in the* style of Charles d'Orleans and the *Rondeau a la Villon,* both of them using refrains which are usually exact but may be incremental, interlocked rhymes, and strict metrical feet. Interestingly, none of the Rondeau variations require a specific foot or metric line, but only that they be consistent throughout the poem. Most of them in English are in iambic tetrameter or pentameter:

UN-LOVE SONG (in the style of d'Orleans)

Among the other things that do not matter   (A)
I hear you boasting your unending love.   (B)
That trap, at least, I know to rise above   (b)
as quicksand lie or envy's brittle patter.   (a)

While dreams decay and lifetime idols shatter (a)
what in the world can you be thinking of?   (b)
Among the other things that do not matter   (A)
I hear you boasting your unending love.   (B)

I watch the rosy petals fall and scatter	(a)
and listen for the melancholy dove:	(b)
HE does not mourn his poor rejected love!	(b)
You mimic now the squirrel's antic chatter	(a)
among the other things that do not matter.	(A)

Amy Jo Zook

FAIR WARNING

Beware, my love, of love's demands	(a)R
that come as sudden as the night	(b)
bringing their beacon-kindling light.	(b)
Those ardent eyes and subtle hands	(a)
of all-embracing robber bands	(a)
you won't escape by sudden flight:	(b)
Beware.	(R)

But if you choose to give commands	(a)
and make yourself the judge of right	(b)
forgetting love's unhappy plight,	(b)
ah, when your heart so haughty stands,	(a)
beware!	(R)

Amy Jo Zook

A very close relative of the *Rondeau* is the *Rondel*, which is in fact only the English spelling of the French form, and many texts call these poems interchangeable. The *Rondel* is generally a fourteen line version of the *Rondeau* type, with division into three stanzas and repeated (refrain) lines. It repeats the second refrain line at the end, making it one line longer than the type used by Charles d'Orleans. There is also an old requirement, usually ignored in English poetry, that the two rhymes be one masculine, one feminine.

FAITHLESS APRIL

Faithless April draws our wonder	(A)
painting endless skies of blue	(B)
where an early darker hue	(b)
spoke of cold and wind and thunder.	(a)

Every diamond she could plunder (a)
now parades before our view: (b)
faithless April draws our wonder (A)
painting endless skies of blue. (B)

Even rainbows we are under (a)
cannot match with colors true (b)
spring's amourns forever new, (b)
breaking winter gloom asunder. (a)
Faithless April draws our wonder (A)
painting endless skies of blue. (B)

Amy Jo Zook

The *Chaucerian Rondel* is a mere ten or eleven lines long, with the usual constraint of two rhymes for the entire poem and the first line used as a refrain for the second and third stanzas of the poem:

COMPLAINT

So summer's gone. How come I never heard (A)
about the parties and the swims? For hours (b)
I just stayed home and weeded all the flowers, (b)

focused binoculars on one brown bird (a)
and dreamed of song. The ice cream freezer whirred (a)
and summer's gone. How come I never heard? (A)

The days so much alike they're getting blurred, (a)
of greeny-grey from weeks of quiet showers: (b)
no fun! The straw is stacked in golden towers, (b)
and summer's gone, somewhere I never heard. (A)

Amy Jo Zook

Swinburnian Roundels have eleven lines in three stanzas, two rhymes, and use a portion of the first line as the refrain, using also to determine the second rhyme of the poem:

HAS SUCH SMAI L HANDS

The rain must fall as night comes near	(a)R
in sweet persuasion fine and small;	(b)
to wash the sky and leave it clear	(a)
the rain must fall.	(b)R
When migratory stragglers call,	(b)
we watch the darker clouds appear	(a)
as patterns looming over all.	(b)
If sun has left the meadows sere	(a)
between the maples gold and tall,	(b)
or at the turning of the year,	(a)
the rain must fall.	(b)R

Amy Jo Zook

A very short form not as much used as the *Triolet* is the *Rondelet,* sometimes (probably mistakenly) called *Rondelay.* In this miniatured form, as with the *Lai,* the most serious inherent problem lies in the short lines which tend to break the flow of the idea. Note that the repeated line is only four syllables long, whereas the rest of the lines are eight syllables, an easier length in English-language poetry:

NEGLIGEE

Soft winter swirl	(A)
wraps old December with pale hands;	(b)
soft winter swirl	(A)
when white-haired ringlets catch and curl	(a)
on every naked tree that stands	(b)
alone. Bare modesty demands	(b)
soft winter swirl.	(A)

Amy Jo Zook

Finally, the grand dame of all these relatives is the *Rondeau Redoublé,* which is lengthy almost as the *Sestina,* and uses repeated lines for refrain in much the same manner as the *Villa-nelle.* Because the poem is so much longer, it should have more

weight of content, or be very witty, so as not to bore the reader.
Here, the lines of the first stanza are each repeated as the refrain
line of succeeding stanzas until all have been used, after which
a last stanza repeats the rhymes (but not actual lines) and concludes with a refrain made from a part of the first line, in the
style of the classic *Rondeau:*

BEANVILLE ACQUIRES A STATUE OF DAVID

Pss-t, David, don your pants! Too much you show!   (A1)R
Our village puritans are stiff with shock,   (B1)
Our lewd folk leer, our kids run to and fro   (A2)
To see your frank anatomy of rock!   (B2)

Now Michelangelo I should not knock   (b)
But he has caused us city fathers woe;   (a)
It rubs us when townspeople glare or mock—   (b)
Pss-t, David, don your pants! Too much you show!   (A1)

The mayor and ourselves would have folks know   (a)
We didn't buy you, boy (you laughing-stock!)   (b)
A wealthy man the statue did bestow—   (a)
Our village puritans are stiff with shock!   (B1)

We used to promenade along this block,   (b)
Old folks and every girl that had a beau;   (a)
But now maids blush and watch the courthouse clock—   (b)
Our lewd folk leer, our kids run to and fro!   (A2)

Though senior citizens could crack a toe,   (a)
Though Ladies' Aid might better darn a smock,   (b)
They all run out as fast as they can go   (a)
To see your frank anatomy of rock!   (B2)

There some, averting eyes, adjust a sock,   (b)
And three their righteous noses loudly blow   (a)
(Though six with grins have joined the gawking flock,   (b)
Four hoot, and kids their rotten apples throw)—   (a)
Pss-t, David, don your pants!   (R)

Audrae Visser

The *Chant Royal* is another French form so sparingly used that its appearance in a contest almost assures a prize. It is not more difficult that the *Sestina* or *Rondeau Redoublé*, but belongs to that class of old forms not yet redeemed from obscurity. Perhaps its length is against it, since it runs to 60 lines, consisting as it does of five eleven-line stanzas and a five-line envoi, all turning on a demanding five rhymes including the refrain line of the fifth rhyme. It resembles a sort of extended *Ballade*; however, the *envoi* of a *Ballade* is addressed to a ruler (Prince) or by extension to God, and the *Chant Royal*, though originally written to the Virgin Mary, has no such requirement in later times. Like the *Ballade*, there is no strict requirement of a particular metric line, but usually it works in tetrameter or pentameter, held constant throughout the poem. There is a shorter version of *Chant Royal*, using ten-line stanzas and a six-line refrain, but its restriction of only four rhymes makes it somewhat more intricate though four lines briefer overall. Even so, almost no one writes either of the strictly-rhymed forms. The unity gained by doing so might well be less effective than the difficulty of finding hackneyed rhymes. The basic rhyme scheme is ababccddedE for each of the five stanzas, and ddedE for the envoi:

CHANT ROYAL WRITTEN UNDER PRESSURE

After all this hard work, I hate to mar
my pristine pages with these muddy feet
that stumble into rhymes my Muses are
ashamed of, awkward and most indiscreet.
But if the editor says "you should try"
then that's the final word, and who am I
to be a coward? But I didn't know
where I should look for answers to my woe,
where sweet mellifluous words would fall like rain
across my pages. There's the fatal blow,
for rhymes like these are any poet's bane.

I spent one evening wishing on a star.
I prayed to all the gods for wit to meet
this challenge; but, about my earthwise par,
they didn't answer—all gone out to eat
or party. That's enough to make my cry,

when all the help I find to get me by
will hardly be sufficient. Any toe—
hold will be good, if you can somehow show
me where the next one is, even explain
its pattern. Ah! a plan began to grow,
though rhymes like these are any poet's bane.

I thought of angels: surely not too far
above our mortal pains? but Gabe and Pete
and all the others took the trolley-car
and went a-picnicking, and so I'm beat
at that game too. You could have heard me sigh
from here to Timbuctoo. And I defy
you to do better. Three strings to my bow,
all broken. Where will I find rhymes a-row
just waiting to be used? Or could I feign
some foreign language that would make them flow?
Ach! rhymes like these are any poet's bane.

Well, then; the textbooks surely ought to har-
bor answers, and I only need to heat
my brain to simmer. Wrong again! This scar
is where they landed on my head, so neat
we had them stacked. I thought I'd merely die
and get it over, but this piece of my
despair was not done yet. And I am slow
to entertain defeat. What if I go
get drunk? It isn't really very sane
to let it run my life and irk me so,
when rhymes like these are any poet's bane.

Before my reputation's turned to char—
coal and grey ash, I think I'm gonna cheat
and not write one at all, and who can bar
my not-verse from the book? The judgment-seat
for poets is still vacant; no one's high
enough to sit there, though they'll often lie
and say they are. But proof will always mow
'em down: nobody else wants to bestow
the laurel-crown-with-diamonds. So I gain
no notoriety, but keep my glow,
since rhymes like these are any poet's bane.

If any Inky-thumb or Holy Joe
thinks he could do it better—worthy foe,
I challenge him! For I've had plenty pain
in working out the conundrum, and lo!
Still, rhymes like these are any poet's bane.

Amy Jo Zook

These do not exhaust all the possibilities of French forms,
but serve as a fair overview of some poems that deserve to have
a wider currency than they do.

BIBLIOGRAPHY

Calkins, Jean. *Handbook on Haiku and other Form Poems*. Kanona, New York: J & C Transcripts, 1970.

Deutsch, Babette. *Poetry Handbook: A Dictionary of Terms*, 4th Ed. New York: Funk & Wagnalls, 1974.

Preminger, Alex, et al., editors. *Princeton Encyclopedia of Poetry and Poetics*. Princeton, 1974.

Sanders, Gerald. *A Poetry Primer*. New York: Holt, Rinehart & Winston, 1935.

Shipley, Joseph T. *Dictionary of World Literary Terms*. Boston: The Writer, 1943.

Turco, Lewis. *The Book of Forms: a Handbook of Poetics*. New York: Dutton, 1968.

All poems used for illustration are my own unless they are otherwise designated, and grateful acknowledgement is made to David Pichaske
of Spoon River Poetry Press and to Esther Weakley of the Columbus, Ohio,
Citizen Journal for the use of poems first printed by them. My other illustrations are previously unpublished work by the poets involved.

HUMOROUS OR LIGHT POETRY

Irene Warsaw

It has been suggested that this article deal primarily with the genesis and development of a few individual poems rather than with poetics and theory, but a few general comments about humorous poetry seem in order.

Humorous poetry is subject to the same rules and the same judgment as serious poetry, with the emphasis shifted here and there to heighten humor. The poet should deviate from the laws governing grammar, sentence structure and punctuation only when it is done consciously and for effect. If the poet can manage it, the humor in a poem should break gleefully upon the reader, who shouldn't have to go back and figure out what's being said or where a sentence ends. This does not mean that the humor should be of the sledgehammer variety but means merely that the point of the poem should be discernible to the intelligent reader without distractive search for clues.

The writer of humorous poetry has the right and even the happy obligation to be very precise in meter and rhyme. Sprightly rhythm and unexpected, outrageous rhymes add to the enjoyment. It is a good idea to establish the rhythm firmly in the first line or two so that it will be fixed in the reader's ear and carry along the occasional unaccented syllable or variable pronunciation.

There is no rule that says humorous poetry must employ rhyme and good rhythm, but most of it is short and a free-verse humorous poem is likely to bear a close resemblance to a prose quip. Espousing the cause of rhyme and rhythm probably brings Ogden Nash to mind. Nash was unique, and that settles that!

A conversational flow of language is best always—well, unless something else works out better. In the following eight-liner, the departure from the normal spoken word order in the last four lines seemed to add to the wryness and saltiness of the tone:

LEND ME YOUR EAR (WITH PRIME INTEREST)

> One picture, an old Chinese proverb maintains,
>   Is better than ten thousand words,
> But I'm not in line for pictorial gains
>   And view this as all for the birds.
> Photography skills I am strictly without;
>   To laughter my art would impel you;
> So what I have done or am thinking about
>   In ten thousand words I will tell you.

Writing in the first person is a propitious device. It is more graceful and engaging to say, "I am peculiar (or foolish) in this respect" in the hope that your reader will say, "Me too!" than to blatantly say, "You are peculiar. . ." These lines illustrate the benevolence of the first-person approach:

> I wish I could forget today
> My quips, which seemed to me so arty,
> So witty, so supremely gay,
> At last night's plushy cocktail party.

Titles are an important element of humorous poetry. By means of serious thought, a lovely brainstorm occasionally blows in and one is rewarded with a pun, double meaning, or whatever (than which few things are more fun.) Changing one word of a familiar expression will do it sometimes, as will breaking a word in two: PERPETUAL COMMOTION, GO TO THE AUNT, THOU SLUGGARD, MISS APPREHENSION.

The hardest part of this fascinating undertaking, for me at least, is finding the next idea. We all scrounge around in the same areas: human foibles, frailties and incongruities; life's problems; giving a proverb or old saw a new twist; getting old; getting fat (or being too skinny); the battle of the sexes; news items; insomnia; animals; weather. Sitting very still with pencil and paper, long enough, eventually bears fruit, however unripe it appears at first. Some subjects, good in themselves, have been used so much that it's hard to score a hit with them. It is as difficult to say something fresh and new about dieting as it is to evoke a spontaneous laughter about the telephone ringing when one is in the shower.

Sometimes an idea falls from heaven conveyed by something someone says or something one reads. In a casual conversation a friend said that their mail carrier was a young woman and that she was pregnant. The idea for this leapt to mind:

> Our mailperson lately is cause for concern.
> She's pregnant, as any observer can learn
> By merely a glance at her contour and size.
> A short leave of absence would seem very wise.
> When I see her coming I'm nudged by the fear
> A Special Delivery may happen right here.

I adopted the mailperson as "ours" because it would have made a longer, clumsier piece to explain about my friend. . .

Revise, revise. Going over your poems almost word by word pays dividends. Some words have a "cuter" sound or a more humorous connotation than others, and a fine play of words just might be found in your mental carrying case. I once had Class B hysterics after I had gone to bed when I found a better word to use in a quatrain—a quatrain and word, by the way, that I'm afraid do not amuse others as much as they did (and do) amuse me. I was working on the not-startlingly-fresh thought we must all inevitably get old or die. My quatrain went along something like this:

> I'm leery of stints I've not tackled before,
> And so getting old is a fate I deplore.
> What's more, the alternative holds no appeal—
> That too is a totally untested deal.

My sleep was delayed a little when it occurred to me to say, in the last line, "That too is an untried (and breathtaking) deal." I had never heard or read of death as a "breathtaking" experience and I think that's funny. I called that one *Proceed at Your Own Risk.*

This quatrain raises the question of whether it's all right to write about death in a humorous vein. Every poet—every *person*—must contemplate death, and I feel one can contemplate one's own death humorously and still be in good taste.

One of my light poems that audiences seem to like serves to illustrate two or three facets of technique:

> There was a time when I could dress
> In garments sweetly labelled S.
> Alas, I had to switch from them
> To somewhat ampler ones, marked M,
> And now it isn't hard to tell
> I'm inching toward that demon L.
> No longer do I dare refuse
> To mind my diet's P's and Q's
> Or some day I am apt to be
> What's so bluntly known as F-A-T.

To carry out the alphabet motif, I called this *O. G. I. C. It Coming.* Note that every pair of rhyme sounds has a letter of the alphabet as the second one. It would be easier, often, in a situation like this, to put the letter in the middle of the line if a rhyme proves troublesome, but it makes a better poem if one is consistent in the placement. Ordinarily I would avoid adamantly having even two similar vowel sounds in the rhymes of so short a poem—vowel variation is always to be sought. However, it seemed to me that using S, M and L as rhyme sounds was desirable and effective enough to justify an overage of short "e" rhymes. I submit that "inching" is a good verb as used here.

Writing in the health areas requires rumination about such matters as doctors, remedies, human relationships, and the parts and functioning (or malfunctioning) of the body for an assailable target. The content of the poems must of course be accurate even though the presentation may follow byways. Some of them necessitate a bit of research. This one did:

> Man's liver is a brownish blob
> That does a most prodigious job.
> It manufactures gall, or bile,
> And normally keeps some on file
> Stored neatly in a pear shaped sack.
> From there the liver's yields attack
> The food man eats, to change its state
> By methods man can't duplicate
> Or even halfway understand.

He ought to treat this outsize gland
With due respect and loving care
To keep it in topnotch repair,
Because to get along at all
Man needs an awful lot of gall.

Clichés may become one's friends, in the building of a humorous or light verse, if they can be given a new turn or a meaning not inherent in them. A little effusion of mine worked out rather well by using a reversed cliché in the second rhyme of each couplet ("less or more", "fro and to").

Now if someone will please say something that will strike the spark for the next poem. . .

YOU AND YOURS—THE WRAP-UP

The human owns a bag, called skin,
To carry his components in.
It's fairly smooth, with here and there
Outcroppings such as nails and hair.
Of varied lengths and color tones,
It houses muscles, organs, bones,
Blood cells, and all that other stuff
That keeps man going well enough.
Without this comprehensive casing
He might forever be misplacing
Some vital part, or losing juices
From unprotected streams and sluices.
Though skin would make quite puny leather,
It helps man keep things all together.

Irene Warsaw

GOOD MEASURE

The talk that occurs
    As she strolls down the beach
Shows clearly that hers
    Is a figure of speech.

Irene Warsaw

UNEARTHLY SENTIMENTS

It may be absurd, but I don't like to fly.
The earth doesn't wobble as much as the sky.
I've looked down on clouds of rare beauty and form
But view LOOKING UP to see clouds as the norm.
My faith in the engines transcends silly doubt.
Still, if they should falter I'd like to peer out
At good, solid concrete my feet can explore
Six inches below, if I open a door.
A city looks strange when I'm high in the air
And muster the courage to see if it's there.
It's certainly true that I get somewhere fast
By flying, and once the brave venture is past
A wonderful smugness pervades flesh and bone.
I don't like to fly, but I love *having flown.*

Irene Warsaw

The poems quoted are reprinted from the author's volumes, *A Word in Edgewise* and *Warily We Roll Along.* Copyright, The Golden Quill Press, Francetown, New Hampshire.

WILL YOU ALL COME UP TO LIMERICK!

Vivian M. Meyer

The origin of the limerick is lost somewhere in time and legend. One theory is that it was a French form brought back to Ireland by war veterans in 1700. Another hypothesis is that it became popular with *Mother Goose's Melodies for Children,* published by her son-in-law in 1719 in an effort to discredit the old lady for her repetition of the "silly" rhymes, many of which were corruptions of English satirical verses which had existed for years. (The unfortunate Mr. Thomas Fleet only succeeded in plummeting his mother-in-law into fame.) Then there is the theory that the limerick began with an alleged old Irish habit of party-goers or pub-crawlers shouting out a line in turn.   After four lines were completed everyone present yelled, "Will you all come up to Limerick!" It has been suggested that as the glasses emptied the lines became spicier and the fame of the Irish for holding their liquor (well or otherwise) became greater.   But the fact remains that no one is sure how the limerick started.

We know, however, that the form appeared in *The History of Sixteen Women,* published by Jay Harris in 1821.   Edward Lear, whose name remains synonymous with the limerick, claimed to have received his inspiration from *Anecdotes and Adventures of Sixteen Gentlemen,* edited and published by John Marshall in 1822 in England.   The author is thought to have been R. S. Sharpe.

Edward Lear, a Londoner, wrote his verses, which he never called limericks, for the children of a friend, the Earl of Derby.   His *Book of Nonsense* was published in 1846.   When it finally dawned on the author that he had become famous for his simple, little rhymes he is said to have been utterly dismayed.   His portfolio of bird pictures has been favorably compared to Audubon's.   He was also a landscape artist, a member of the Royal Academy of Art and Queen Victoria's drawing master.   He was, in addition to all that, a writer of serious tomes, especially travelogues.

Anxious to establish the fact that he wasn't responsible for the limerick, Lear went so far as to point out that Shakespeare had used its form in *Othello*, Act II, Sc. 3:

> And let the canakin clink
> And let the canakin clink
>   A soldier's a man
>   A man's life a span
> Why then, let a soldier drink.

Langdon Reed in *The Complete Limerick Book* used the form to lampoon Lear's plight at the hands of fickle fame:

> A goddess capricious is Fame;
> You may strive to make noted your name
>   But she will neglect you

Or cooly select you
For Laurels distinct from your aim.

Clement Wood in *The Complete Rhyming Dictionary and Poet's Craft Book* stated that the limerick went through three stages. The well-known nursery rhyme "Hickory Dickory Dock" was of the first type. The last line is identical to the first. Edward Lear tended to use the second form which doubles up on the end rhyme of lines one and five:

There was a young lady whose chin
Resembled the point of a pin;
    So she had it made sharp
    And purchased a harp
And played several tunes with her chin.

The third and most widely used form is similar to the following which introduced a new rhyming word into the fifth line:

There was an old soldier of Blister
Went walking one day with his sister
    When a cow, at one poke,
    Tossed her into an oak
Before the old gentleman missed her.

Nursery Rhymes, Mother Goose

One of the hazards of writing an exceptionally good limerick is that you, the writer, will almost certainly be forgotten in time and your delightful limerick will be accredited to that prolific writer, Anonymous. Certainly no one believes Mother Goose wrote the above limerick.

Said to be the only light verse form indigenous to the English language, the limerick reached its peak of popularity in 1907-1908 when newspapers ran contests for winning last lines. By then the punch line had firmly been established as the fifth one. A favorite winning line came in response to:

There was a young lady of Ryde
Whose locks were considerably dyed.
    The hue of her hair

Made everyone stare. . . .

And the winning line read, "She's piebald, she'll die bald, they cried."

Bennet Cerf, the humorist, tells in his book *Out on a Limerick* that the editor of the Limerick Times of that era hated the form, feeling it denigrated his beloved city on the banks of the beautiful River Shannon. On one occasion a young man delivered a sheaf of offensive things to said editor who so rudely rejected the writer's offerings that the latter screeched threatenly, "I'll have you know I'm the featherweight champion of of the Emerald Isle."

"Be you now?" snapped the irritated editor, "Well, one more limerick, my lad, and I'll throw you out, feathers and all!"

Fortunately, we don't all have the bias of the editor in question, so we, like so many famous writers such as Swinburne, Kipling, Tennyson, Robert Louis Stevenson, W. S. Gilbert and many more, want to have a try at the limerick. The rhyme scheme is obviously *aabba*. The meter is anapestic. In general the third and fourth lines, being short, are indented.

In addition to the above rather obvious rules, the limerick often has a story line. It may contain (atrocious or otherwise), abbreviations or deliberate misspellings. And some limericks are slightly naughty or even downright obscene. And there is another type referred to as the puzzle-it-out-yourself style. The following fall into the latter category; it is necessary to read the time as eight-eight and to pronounce the French words as the Americans are prone to do, not as the French would:

> There was a young fellow of Tate
> Who dined with his girl at 8:08,
> > But I hate to relate
> > What that fellow named Tate
> And his tête-a-tête ate at 8:08.

Anonymous

Anonymous didn't use the common rhyme scheme. But he showed no originality when he used the clichéd, "There was a ..."

There is such a thing as a four line limerick. When that formula is used the short lines are simply written as one, and the fourth line is what we'd normally think of as the fifth (punch line).

Howard R. Reeves, of the New Jersey Poetry Society, deviated from that, however, and wrote the following:

> A limerick writer from Brielle
> Wrote verses we all thought were swell.
> But he failed at the sport
> 'Cause he wrote them too short.

Unripe Fruit

During the NJPS banquet seventy-seven persons waited several seconds in utter silence for the fifth line until it dawned on them that they'd missed the point. Then the room exploded in laughter. Another amusing incident came as a result of the publication of the limerick in the above-mentioned NJPS anthology (1973). A self-styled limerick expert wrote to Howard and expressed his disappointment and amazement at such a serious "blunder." He then carefully delineated the "rules" of the limerick.. Some writers feel that all poetic verse forms are carved in rock for all time. As corny as Howard's limerick is, its impact on others holds the hilarious double-take he intended. And don't all creative writers try to make an impact on the readers?

> A baker of bagels one day
> found his bagels were rolling away.
>   But since baking them square
>   he has bagels to spare,
> and, what's more, he cuts corners that way.

Cosmic Cadence

> Since Adam and Eve, by God's grace
> had started the whole human race
>   before there was glue
>   I question (Don't you?)

how they kept those first fig leaves in place.

Starborne

A well-meaning woman named Tooze
was convinced that all bottles of booze
  should carry a warning
  of dangers a-borning,
but who'd care to read that bad nooze?

Boonton Times-Bulletin

In England there lived a recluse
whose molars and canines were loose.
  They rocked with each bite
  so it took him all night
just to eat a small portion of goose.

Swordsman Review

"That statue, though carved by a genius
is entirely too short in the penis."
  But the speaker blushed red
  when the curator said,
"How *many* real ones have you seen, Miss?"

Vivian M. Meyer

BIBLIOGRAPHY

Baring-Gould, William S. and Cecil Baring-Gould, eds. *The Annotated MOther Goose,* New York: Clarkson N. Potter, Inc. 1962.

Cerf, Bennet, ed. *Out on a Limerick,* New York: Harper and Bros., 1960.

Meyer, Vivian M., Isabel Poeltler and Richard K. Wright, eds. *Unripe Fruit,* Dover: New Jersy Poetry Society, Inc., 1973.

Perrine, Laurence. *Sound and Sense,* New York: Harcourt, Brace and Jovanovich, Inc., 1975.

Pennington, Alex, Frank J. Warnke and O. B. Hardison, Jr., eds. *The Princeton Encyclopedia of Poetry and Poetics,* Princeton: Princeton University Press, 1974.

Untermeyer, Lewis. *The Pursuit of Poetry,* New York: Harper and Rowe, 1960.

Wells, Catherine, ed. Caroline *Wells Book of American Limericks*, New York and London: Knickerbocker Press, 1925.

Wood, Clement, ed. *Complete Rhyming Dictionary and Poets Craft Book*, Garden City: Garden City Press, 1936.

LYRIC: THE ECSTASY EXPERIENCE

Ora Pate Stewart

Derivation of Lyric

The word lyric comes from lyre, a musical instrument of the harp family, popularized in ancient Greece.[1] But the harp is first mentioned in the antedeluvian culture of the eighth generation after Adam—the seventh generation of the family of Cain (Genesis 4:21). Jubal Cain, son of Lamech and his first wife Adah—"was the father of all such as handle the harp and organ." This talented musician-inventor lived, in point of time, in the same generation as his celebrated (sixth) cousin, the prophet Enoch. The lyre has been long with us.

What is a Lyric?

The American College Dictionary offers this:

> Lyric—Having the form and musical quality of a song, and especially of a songlike outpouring of the poet's own thoughts and feelings (as distinguished from epic and dramatic poetry, with their more extended and set forms and their presentation of external subjects.) Characterized by or indulged in spontaneous, ardent expression of feeling—to be sung to the lyre.
> Lyricist—one who writes the words for songs.[2]

J. D. O'Hara says, "And finally, there is the form now so popular as almost to eclipse the others—the lyric. . . Even the lyric cannot be pinned down to fixed shapes, meters, and materials." Does not "conform to strict or even clear rules. . .Repeatedly eludes our definition."[3]

Poets for centuries past have tried to capture and define the lyric. It cannot be confined to size and limited to shape. It cannot be sustained through endless couplets of heroic verse, or epic cantos of narrative poetry. It can surface throughout in peaks and pinnacles of excitement. It can settle and distill in placid pockets—reason for writing it down, preserving it—to be brought up and savored again and again—condiments of comfort and peace. But ecstasy cannot level off, extended, stretched like taffy through vast plateaux of expansion. It is an eagle soaring, a skylark singing out-of-sight, a hummingbird at hold. The lyric is the ecstasy experience.

History of the Lyric

In many of the chapters on lyric poetry Sappho is listed as the first great lyricist, and the finest.[4] This greatest poet of Greece was born about 612 B.C., in Lesbos[5] (Mytilene—a Greek island in the Aegean.) She left eight books—some authorities now say ten—of lyric poetry, much of it in "Sapphic stanza," her own metric pattern.[6] (Of these only a few fragments have been pieced together in our times, mended by such twentieth century poets as Dr. Wharton, Yeats, Symons, O'Hara, others.) But I would list a few women, earlier than Sappho, who left lyrical deposits in the chronology of ancient literature.

From the days of the Judges, Deborah the prophetess, Judge of Israel has left us a stirring and powerful lyric for military victory where women played the decisive roles.[7] (Judges 5) Hannah, near the end of the era left lyrics for the birth of her long-awaited Samuel, who was to become the last of the Judges. (I Samuel 1:2-10) And I shall not be surprised if the scholars discover this art form goes all the way back to Mother Eve. It would be the natural beginning.

The most famous lyricist in Biblical times was David, (1085-1015 B. C.) He was expert with the harp, and a splendid composer and performer of lyrics. Before him Job[8] had written (born about 1700 B. C.) and after him (contemporary with Homer) there was Isaiah. Many others in Biblical times qualify.

In Elizabethan times there was a great lyrical awakening, which came to full flower in the nineteenth century.[9] Wordsworth, Shelley, Keats in England, Emily Dickinson in New England. The greatest lyricist of the twentieth century was Robert Frost, and greatest of women lyricists were Edna St. Vincent Millay, Sara Teasdale, Sylvia Plath, Anne Sexton.[10] (These are the ones who have shown the most mastery of "the form.")

What makes a Lyric?

J. D. O'Hara states, "But lyrics do not pretend to deal with the great issues of life or to take us too deeply into truth; at most they provide what Robert Frost was to call 'a momentary stay against confusion.' "[11] Yet Milton, Shakespeare, Frost have all gone beyond this.

Not all ideas can be made into lyrics. "You can't make a silk purse out of a sow's ear."[12] (How old is that one?) Poetic words do not a lyric make—in many cases.

Cardinal Wolsey had a magnificent palace built for himself— at tremendous cost—at a lyrical spot, Hampton-on-Thames. Henry VIII craved to acquire this—for a gift to his second wife, Anne Boleyn. Wolsey was smart enough to see the danger in quoting a price to his sovereign, and decided, with feigned intrepidation, to make the palace a present to Henry—the most costly gift ever presented by a subject to his king—"a gift tinged with a pinch of royal compulsion." While this freshet is cute and original, precocious to its mother, and terrifyingly true, it has not changed my prose into a lyric.

From a delightful little book[13] I picked up in Ireland comes another example:

> Brandon Peak—County Kerry. . . is rich in association with one of the most colourful of Irish Saints—Brendon the Navigator. Mount Brandon was named for him. . . Brendon was born in this district about 486. His life and the story of his voyage is told in *Navigations Brendani,* which was a medieval best seller, translated into all important European languages. In 551 he set out with his companions to find Hy-Brasil, the paradise of the west, where it is said

the sun shone all year round, and fruit and flowers were as plentiful as the Garden of Eden. Brendon's hopeful travelling was as exciting as his arrival. He met "a floating mountain—the colour of silver, harder than marble, of a substance of the clearest silver"— later Atlantic sailors were to be less lyrical about icebergs.[14]

Lyric poetry is as far away from prose as words can go. Walter Savage Landor (1775-1864) has said: "Prose on certain occasions can bear a great deal of poetry: On the other hand, poetry sinks and swoons under a moderate weight of prose."[15]

This is the area where most would-be lyricists flounder. It is worth the extra effort to learn the difference.

Cream churned is butter; cream whipped is something else. (Notice the importance is in what we do to the cream.) The difference is in treatment. Texture and taste are the results.

To get to the meat of it: Satisfying prose is a good old-fashioned beef stew. Poor verse is hash, made out of left-overs warmed up. Good verse is a ham sandwich with a dash of mustard. Good poetry is prime rib. But lyric poetry is fillet mignon.

The lyric is the most loved of all poetic forms.[16]   It is capable of the greatest beauty. Its capsule message is succinct. It is refined. It has no lumps or coarse fibers. It is lean and spare.

Where are Lyrics found?

Lyric is the sun leveling with the sea in early morning, spawning iridescent rainbows that dance before our eyes, tiptoeing through the tops of waves in a moving, sensitive ballet: Color in Motion. The sun rises and it is over.

MORNING MATINEE: RAINBOWS AT ROSARITO BEACH

> Gossamer-clad in psychedelic shades,
> A technicolor troupe, these sun-sea maids,
> Dancing their hearts out—glistening, fire-kist—
> Ballet of cherubim in mull of mist—

Elusive spirit children of the dawn,
Perform their chorus, encore, and are gone.

So sensitive a gift from sun and ocean.
Who can describe—portray—*rainbows in motion?*[17]

Now for an experience on the East Coast:

DAWN—OFF KITTERY POINT

We know that it must fall apart,
Yet something clutches at the heart;
How can a beauty, transient, fleeting,
Set a numbed heart to throbbing, *beating?*
Much as a harp long laid aside
Remembers the song when sound has died—
Waits for the fingers to return,
A heart will wait; a heart will yearn.

The great waves rise to meet the sun—
One moment sea and sky are one.
Sighting a prey, a lone gull swings
Swift to the catch. Dawn-burnished wings—
A bird-brooch, perfect in form and feather—
Pinning the sea and sky together!

Heart, brace yourself! Lean on the wind!
Best not to watch it come unpinned.[18]

No one standing on the east coast of Maine can see an
ocean—sunrise ballet in waves; but neither can a Baja Californ-
ian watch the "sun coming up out of the water," or catch a
seagull pinning the sea and sky together in its first rays. It
is God's way of dividing, distributing his splendors among his
children.

A lyricist should really get around.

Nature of the Calling

It was a lyricist who soothed the madness in a disturbed
king.[19] Lyricists have led misguided youth to turn from drugs

and crime to useful pursuits (state hospital and correctional institution workshops.)[20]   They have been known to bring would-be suicides back to God's realities; to give spark and purpose to the elderly and the abandoned (in rest homes and to shut-ins.) They have even been called upon to tenderize harsh attitudes and prevent riots (in state and federal prisons); to bring comfort and hope to the bereaved and suffering (at funerals and at home.)   One of the important callings is to help the dying to understand and accept the experience of death:

> Death is no sudden, dismal, rude surprise.
> I shall lie down—and shall as surely rise.[21]

One of the most rewarding functions of this gift is to bring order and renewed faith, uplift and comfort to the lyricist's family and self.

The lyricist has a holy calling—a divine responsibility. Especially the woman lyricist—because she has an added ingredient—*tenderness* that gives her extra advantage. (Men sometimes apologize for tenderness.) The world feels warmer, safer, at her fireside. She has to keep her fires burning and control her flame. It is a sacred fire, but if it is allowed to go ingrown and smolder in despond, or flare out of bounds, it is capable of consuming.

Sappho discovered this; and within our times, the gentle, sensitive Sara Teasdale, turbulent Sylvia Plath, compulsive Anne Sexton.[22]   These gifted, talented, famous lyricists went through their shortened lives—wooing death—coaxing it to come closer, pleading for oblivion:

MOON'S ENDING

> Moon, worn thin to the width of a quill,
>   In the dawn clouds flying,
> How good to go, light into light, and still
>   Giving light, dying.[23]

Sara Teasdale

And her own favorite of all her collected lyrics:

LET IT BE FORGOTTEN

Let it be forgotten, as a flower is forgotten,
　　Forgotten as a fire that once was singing gold,
Let it be forgotten for ever and ever,
　　Time is a kind friend, he will make us old.

If anyone asks, say it was forgotten
　　Long and long ago,
As a flower, as a fire, as a hushed footfall
　　In a long forgotten snow.[24]

Others went similar ways (Vachel Lindsay, John Berryman, Orrick Johns, still others)—not because they were lyricists, but because they did not know the broader meaning of life—did not know what all was in the package God had given them. What they had not learned, (or failed to remember) is that there is no such dominion as *oblivion*. What would it profit one to plunge bodily into a barrel of coaltar just to escape a smudge of creosote in a thimble? Surprise: There is no sleep, no death, no oblivion for the human spirit. It is the offspring of God. We are not illegitimate: He owns up to being our Father. We are all responsible to *Him*. David's lyrics captured this, and Job's before him. We all need to keep this truth before us, and to tend to our own forges with controlled and loving care. This lifting power is the true mission of the lyricist.

Inspiration

I served as adjudicator for a series of poetry competitions in Michigan, 1979 and 1980. A non-winner, a woman in her late middle age brought me a sheaf of verse and asked for an evaluation and critique. She concluded, "Of course, I wouldn't want you to change anything. I have no right to alter a word, because these poems were pure inspiration. They came straight from God."

I told her that I would not be able to top that. He is always the Giver of pure inspiration, and he is the ultimate Adjudicator. (Impure inspiration always comes from an opposite source—and thank the Lord, that one is not our judge!)

"In all thy ways acknowledge him, and he shall direct thy paths." (Proverbs 3:5-6) The proverb pleased her, but she was not content. "O, I want you to read them and help me. Advise me. . ."

The thoughts were good basic inspirations. I circled surplus words, made suggestions for more expressive ones, corrected spellings, called her attention to grammar. I named magazines, mentioned books to be read, told her about libraries and workshops, a few competitions so that she could measure her progress, and returned the lot with these comments: "Our lyric babies are born naked. (They even require labor pains to bring them into the world!) They have to be housed, fed and clothed—disciplined. (Don't be surprised—or offended—if there is excrement to be dealt with occasionally.) It is a great responsibility to be the mother of inspirations."

"Even lyrics that come straight from heaven have to be cared for, brought together—composed. The Lord must not be asked to carry the blame for our poor mistakes—our ignorance of grammar, our innocence of rules, our pitiful unlearnedness of what he has provided as means for improving our vessels to contain his sacred oil. I will give the Lord all praise, respect and appreciation for giving me ideas. But I know I'm the one who has to do the work."

The Challenge

The greatest dimension of the lyric is that it can excite and motivate—it can refine and comfort the human spirit. In order to accomplish this the lyricist must surpass Mary-had-a-little lamb; reach for twinkle-twinkle-little-star—(but not stop there)—break through—make a hole in the sky and soar—go-for-the-sun!

Do not be satisfied with a poem that will do. Make it the best you can make it. Then get into highest gear—pray about it—wake-up-in-the-night and think about it. Then make it the best that can be done. As a poet, it is my most expensive secret. It is bought with labor. And I shall never tire of—or retire from the challenge.

"Hail to thee, blithe spirit. . ." Capture exquisiteness
around you, write it up. Smelt it out. Throw away the slag.
Work it over. Craft it. Rub it to its highest shine. Preserve
it. Share it. Set it in the sun where it cannot be ignored. It
is your reason for being. Do not worship it. It is no idol. It
is God's gift to you. Happy Lyric-ing! See you at the mountain top!

COMPOSERS' PRAYER

Who has released mild winds among soft grasses?
Set crickets free to skirl their evening tune?
Our spirits rise with every flock that passes
When wild geese silhouette against the moon.

Frogs chorus deep percussion out from under
The mellow reeds' slim-willow elegance.
Fierce lightnings and the somber voice of thunder
Combine their timbre-strength for resonance.

Trilled meadowlark solfeggio, serenading,
Re-sounds our pitches for divergent parts.
In liquid silver waterfalls, cascading,
Ablutions pour to lave our singing hearts.

Not *without-form-and-void;* but with sudden rejoicing;
Created—organized—for all to share!
Arrange in us these harmonies, new-voicing
These ancient gifts. This, our composers' prayer.

Ora Pate Stewart

THREE-GENERATION BIBLE

I touch it now with fondest heart—
Loosed pages—ancient leather—
That grand old Book that fell apart
Holding us together.

Ora Pate Stewart

FOOTNOTES

[1] All general dictionaries agree.

[2] *The American College Dictionary.* (New York: Random House, 1961)

[3] J. D. O'Hara. *Poetry*, World Culture Series. (New York: Newsweek Books, 1975), p. 14.

[4] Britannica gives good notes on Sappho (although different editions vary the number of her books.)

[5] *Encyclopedia Brittanica.* (1976)

[6] William D. Drake. *Sara Teasdale: Woman and Poet.* (New York: Harper & Row, 1979), pp. 40-41.

[7] All Biblical references herein are from *King James Bible.*

[8] Job was the third son of Isachar and grandson of Jacob, great-grandson of Isaac, great-great-grandson of Abraham. Job was born prior to 1706 B. C. in Canaan and matured in Egypt. The text of *Job* was an Egyptian contribution to our Bible. (Genesis 46:13 for genealogy.) The year 1706 B. C. is listed as year of Jacob's family move into Egypt, (Bible Dictionary, Chronical Tables) and Job is numbered as one of the family who made the journey.

[9] J. D. O'Hara. *Poetry.*

[10] *Ibid.*

[11] J. D. O'Hara. *Poetry*, p. 75.

[12] Bergen Evans. *Dictionary of Quotations.* (New York: Delacorte Press, 1968), p. 631. "The appearance of the expression in *Polite Conversation* (Jonathan Swift) means that it was hackneyed by 1738. Yet not earlier version of this exact form is known. Earlier it had appeared as a satin purse (1659) and a cheverill purse (1611)—both of them plainly proverbial by those dates."

[13]Harold Clarke. *Ireland in Color.* (B. T. Batsford, Ltd., 1970.)

[14]As we can see, Brendon was too far north for Brazil, heading for New England. I must not leave him floating toward a Titanic situation: He did arrive and got as far inland as the Mississippi—which he could see was too wide to cross (he had not brought his ship overland)—and he returned to Country Kerry. "Certain Christian relics found on the eastern seaboard of the United States have been linked with the Irish tradition because of their Celtic appearance." *Ibid.,* p. 92.

[15]Archdeacon Hare and Walter Landor. *Collins Gem Dictionary of Quotations.* (London and Glasgow: William Collins Sons & Co., Ltd., 1961), p. 268.

[16]J. D. O'Hara. *Poetry.*

[17]Ora Pate Stewart. from *Summer Silver—Autumn Gold,* book in process.

[18]Ora Pate Stewart. This Lyric was published by *The Improvement Era,* (1968), *The California Writer,* (1968). *World Poetry,* (1969) where it won Magna Cum Laude (annual) award, (1970) Madras, India. It was reprinted in *York Poetry Anthology,* England, (1971), *Utah Sings,* Vol. V, (1974), and has been used in numerous texts for High Schools and Universities in U. S. A., England and South Africa. It has also appeared in numerous newspapers.

[19]The young David. (I Samuel 16:14-23.)

[20]With the exception of soothing a maddened king, I have personally participated in all the situations expressed here, have taught classes, presented programs and obtained results. (Lists available upon request.) Ora Pate Stewart.

[21]Last lines of sonnet, "Homecoming," by Ora Pate Stewart. This poem was published in *The Ensign,* June, 1978. It will appear as the final lyric in author's book, *The Brightness of hope.*

[22]J. D. O'Hara. *Poetry.*

[23]Sara Teasdale. *Strange Victory.* (Published posthumously, New York: The Macmillan Company, 1933)

[25]Opening line of "To a Skylark," by Percy Bysshe Shelley (1792-1822.)

[26]Ora Pate Stewart. (*Pen Woman,* December 1976; Fernwood Publications, 1978.)

[27]*Relief Society Magazine,* August 1965.

DRAMATIC MONOLOG: STORY OR POEM?

Donna Dickey Guyer

Poets who are basically either story tellers, students of psychology or even frustrated actors, find their natural expression in the dramatic monolog. What is this kind of monolog really—story, play or poem? A few hints indicate that it is a story in verse, a character sketch, or perhaps a part to be dramatised; but most clues point to it as *poetry,* a challenge to create and a deep pleasure to read and listen to as literature and drama.

Ever since the mid-19th century, when Robert Browning burst upon the literary scene with *My Last Duchess* (which he himself called a dramatic lyric) clever writers have been hailed for years for their original varieties of monolog, some dramatic, others less so. Whatever can be said about this literary conformation, it is as poetry the dramatic monolog is popular today, in a continuing magnetic field of creativity and participation that goes undiminished.

What makes a dramatic monolog a poem? Its natural environment is, first of all, drama—the transliteration of emotional experience into action primarily through the musings of a chief character talking to another who never directly responds. The speaker reveals himself, subtly or otherwise, in a sort of organized ramble constructed on a narrative incident. The reader "comes upon" the story problem or the psychological aberration, through a series of little discoveries building to a climax which itself often remains in the reader's own psyche rather than being a denouement in fictional plot.

In other words, the emotional experience on which every poem should be firmly established, is the raison d'etre for the writing of a monolog. The poem is the justification. While emotional experience is projected differently in various types of poems, in a dramatic monolog it is accomplished through the revelations of a single person in the dramatis personae. This factor is what pinpoints our attention and lingers in memory as a genuine happening—provided the poet is a skillful technician with complete mastery of the mechanics of writing.

What else makes the dramatic monolog a poem? Use of figures of comparison (metaphor and simile) heighten the emotional experience and strengthen the statement into the permanent mold of poetry. What the character says in monolog can be implied as in metaphor, or stated as in simile. The comparison is what is important.

Amy Lowell in *Patterns* describes how patterned her garden is with daffodils blowing and blue squills, going on to say that she too in her powdered hair and jewelled fan is a "rare Pattern. As I wander down the garden paths." She says she *is* a pattern, not like a pattern, so this is metaphor. Technique of this sort spells the main difference between good poetry and bad, or even between poetry and prose.

Another important factor in a dramatic monolog as a poem is the immense compression of events and emotional states into a tight and complex work. A lifetime may be covered in twenty lines. To do this takes a thorough understanding of the "how" of poetry writing. While dramatic monologs appear to move in an easy narrative flow, and a characterization seems to come about in an effortless way, these are not simple fashionings of a facile talent. It is easy for amateurs to move one inch too far or to stop an inch too short of dramatic effect.

Choice of language, that is, selection of words for their quality of connotation as well as denotation, goes into the making of a good dramatic monolog. Cliches have no place in any poem. While it is vital for the writer to communicate with the reader, this cannot be done well by using ordinary phasings or even street jargon, except by a skillful touch at the precise and relative moment in a poem's incident. Using language in an abusing way, uncaringly and with indifference to words, will never produce a living piece of poetry, let alone a dramatic monolog.

In Spoon River Anthology, Edgar Lee Maters demonstrates superstar status with expert manipulation of words. In the poem *Rutherford McDowell*, we find, "When giant hands from the womb of the world/Tore the republic." And in *Edmund Pollard*, "I would I had thrust my hands of flesh/into the disk-flowers, bee-infested,/Into the mirror-like core of fire." In *Samuel Gardner*, "I. . . saw this umbrageous elm,/Measuring its generous branches with my eye,/And listened to its rejoicing leaves/Lovingly patting each other With sweet aeolian whisper."

Greatly heightened emotional impact is another device necessary for poetry. Perhaps this trait is more important in a dramatic monolog than in any other form. Each word, every line must contribute to a mounting emotional state of shock, commencing with the first line, even with the title. Space in a poem is at a premium, and writers must begin on the run, without much preamble. If background must be filled in, the speaker in the monolog can refer to it briefly in flashback. But the white heat of feeling has to be maintained as a fire is constantly refueled to be kept burning.

Imagery for the senses is another device that maintains a good poem's forward movement. Readers caught up in an intense character revelation or an exciting story plot can be infinitely more involved when their ears, eyes, fingers, tongues, even their noses can participate in the poem's unfolding inventiveness.

T. S. Eliot in *Journey of the Magi* provides an enormously vivid picture with "camels galled, sore-footed, refractory." And note how the interlocking of the "s" sounds in "silken girls bringing sherbet" never degenerates into mere sibilance but adds a dimension of music.

Grammar and syntax, careful phrasings, a good relation of content to form, even the tie-in of title of poem to the lines that follow, are prime considerations for a dramatic monolog. Nothing must interfere with the action, no flaw must distract. The Columbia Viking Desk Encyclopedia says a dramatic monolog is "a literary form for psychological portraits in verse." If this is true, then a writer's whole fund of wisdom must be brought into play. An innate knowledge of human behavior acquired through study and experience, goes into the structuring of a viable character in a dramatic monolog. One must keep in mind that verse is being created, using the ways and means of rhythm, varying line lengths for different monologs, even rhyme, if desired.

In *The Haunting*, Reba Terry, a contemporary American poet, couples a subtle nuance of rhythm to a salt taste of universal sorrow in her lines, "too lonely to do anything but flail the moon with sad petards of sound."

Another quote from *The Haunting* demonstrates the person-to-person intimacy and impact of understatement which are both inherent in a dramatic monolog:

> I could have told him about the leavetaking and
> wing and claw of chicken on roof he wondered
> about or rusty spots on doors and window panes and
> last four steps of porch he complained about
> wondering loudly what it was but, he doesn't know
> that blood will spray an omen for good as well as
> for the devil and evil can be kept beyond the
> door. He will rest content and only the witch
> and I need know.

To summarize, a dramatic monolog does "tell a story." It does develop character in somewhat the manner of fiction. When read aloud, particularly in public, it does give the impression of a play-on-stage, practically a performance if done well. But above all else, a dramatic monolog is a poem. It is not even a soliloquy, which Clement Wood defines in his *The Complete Rhyming Dictionary and Poet's Craft Book* as "a speech revealing the thought processes of a character in a play out of hearing of the other characters."

A genuine dramatic monolog has been produced only when

intense emotion carefully compressed is called forth by gritty labor in the hard craft known as writing a poem.

TREASURE OF THE SLAVE TRADE

Mugo said one night while we sat close,
though I pretended that I didn't hear.
We had been resting by our cabin door,
shelling pecans. I couldn't sit up straight
from bending in the field all day,
so he supported me, his kind, strong arm
secure upon my back. It was his arm
restrained me when we watched our children sold.
The pain of that was always in my face.
I saw it in the pond behind the patch
when I go there to bathe. Sometimes, to cry.
His eyes grew wild the times white master came
and pushed me roughly through the cabin door,
claiming to have his rights. Yes, it was bad.
But afterwards, when Mugo sobbed, I held
his head against my breast and kissed his hair.
My flesh got thin, and sometimes Mugo drank,
stealing the whiskey out of master's house.
I began to look old, the wrinkles deep.
But we were lucky, for we had a roof
and fish and watermelon from the patch.
Did Mugo ever think how it had been
at home, the African moon, the healing rains?
And later, how the chains gnawed at our wrists,
the dust, the whips, and then the ship's dark hold?
We never learned to read, or write our names
and never got beyond the fields. But when
the night came down we had each other, none
to see or hear. Nykobar, he'd sigh,
loving with love. Then we would go to sleep.
And though I acted like I hadn't heard,
I will remember 'til the day I die
that Mugo told me I was beautiful.

This poem won Grand Prize (Ella Kracke Award) donated by Clement Stone in the 1976 Poets and Patrons contests, Chicago, Illinois.

THE HAUNTING

There were crying sounds in my sleep   Not the weeping
kind   but one long drawn out self-sustaining wail   that
haunts me nightly after lights are out.   He has heard it
too   he sleeping lightly by my side   and after fruitless
searching in the house   would ponder what it was   owl
or wolf or coyote creeping down dark trails   too lonely
to do anything but flail the moon with sad petards of sound.

But   we both knew   it was more persistent than that. Some
ghost it was the way it rattled slender cracks in walls and left
smudged footprints in the flowers   tramping all beneath the
ledge of windows   and I grew afraid   afraid it came for me
and ashamed of that   spoke of my fear for him.

It would go sometimes   for quite a spell   then some dark
night when everything was right and moon hid slivered behind
thick clouds   it would come again   howling as a way-lost
soul.   Close it came with sound so near a person only had
to set his hand upon it   then faded far below the pasture
and the barns.

One night when he and I lay waiting   for the sound and it
to come   the silence stayed till rooster woke the morning
and day was saved for waiting through another night. It didn't
come that night nor the next and we later learned not to watch
the sky for slivered moon and thickening clouds.   He said
it went because it died   and it lies buried in some deep rut
of rock   broken and covered with leaves and roots of new grown
weeds.   I could have told him about the leavetaking   and wing
and claw of chicken on roof he wondered about   or rusty spots
on doors and window panes   and last four steps of porch he
complained about   wondering loudly what it was   but, he doesn't
know that blood will spray an omen for good as well as for the
devil and evil can be kept beyond the door.   He will rest content
and only the witch and I need know.

Reba Terry

BIBLIOGRAPHY

Brown, Harry M. and John Milstead. *Patterns in Poetry.* Glenview: Scott, Foresman and Co., 1967.

The Columbia-Viking Desk Encyclopedia, Third Edition, New York; The Viking Press, 1968.

Interpretation of Theatre. Glenview: Scott, Foresman & Co.

Masters, Edgar Lee. *Spoon River Anthology.* New York: Macmillan Co., 1962.

Sanders, Thomas E. *The Discovery of Poetry.* Glenview: Scott, Foresman & Co., 1967.

Wood, Clement. *The Complete Rhyming Dictionary and Poet's Craft Book,* Garden City Books, 1936.

Wood, Clement. *Poet's Handbook.* The World Publishing Co., 1940.

Woods, George B. *Versification in English Poetry.* Glenview: Scott, Foresman & Co., 1958.

Zeitlin and Rinaker. *Types of Poetry.* New York: The Macmillan Co., 1931.

NATIVE AMERICAN POETRY

Jean Humphrey Chaillie

Native American poetry goes back to the basic need for dance, or body movement, accompanied by song or chant, to commemorate a tribal custom or ceremonial event.

Sometimes the words have since become obsolete, especially if the original need for the song or chant no longer exists.

An example could be the preparation for war; either against another tribe or the attempt to control the advancement of the white man. Each tribe had certain rites and ceremonies that must take place before going into battle. These preparations were varied in length of time and amount of attention given to minute details according to custom. Each warrior must prepare himself as to the war ceremony of his tribe. Perhaps he might have repeated this song or chant in silent preparation for battle.

TRIBESMAN

> I am a tribesman!
>
> I turn not
> From winged darts,
> Or fall down
> From bended bows.
> I tremble not
> In enemy country;
> Nor cry out
> When death approaches.
>
> I am a tribesman!

The only way of preserving a song or chant was to pass it on by word of mouth or by a ritual sequence which represented a special ceremony.

Repetition of certain words or phrases appear in most songs and chants. Four-fold repetition is believed to be a sacred number, especially in the Navajo tribe.

To the non-Indian, much of Indian poetry seems without meaning. This of course is not true, many of the songs or chants have 'Indian meaning,' or a hidden meaning, sometimes referred to as the "speech of the spirit."

Native American poetry is without a 'fixed' form, each tribe controlled the form used in their ceremonies, dictated by the type of ritual. The poetry is seldom rhymed, more closely resembling the free verse form.

With the advancement of white man's culture many of the 'old ways' are not being passed on to the present generation of Native Americans.

My primary interest is the preservation of many of the customs, ceremonies, spiritual rituals, and crafts unique to many of the tribes.

After approximately a quarter century of research, study, personal contacts, and interviews, I feel my most expressive and meaningful contribution to the preservation of Native American culture is through the writing of poetry and prose.

"Bittersweet Joy," exemplifies my dedication to preserve the everlasting "Path of the Rainbow":

BITTERSWEET JOY

    Are you a blue corn-colored song
      carried on the wind of memory
   That lingers over the land
     weeping
       weeping,
   For the hollow voices
  Of your vanished ancestors?
  O sister of the Earth!
  O daughter of the Sun!

I am your earth mother, my spirit cries out to you in your generation of cultural despair.

The human heart cannot be split into two parts. One half left with the descendants of your heritage, to carry on the spiritual ceremonies and tribal customs that began long before the white man set foot on Native American soil. Nor will the other half serenely and guiltlessly carve a career out of a world of cement and connivance; sometimes more brutal than your ancestors ever encountered.

Listen my daughters!

Close your minds as the sun closed her eye when she sleeps;

Come ride with me along the river-of-time-passed; as our canoe passes scenes on the river bank your spiritual minds will be opened.

Have you forgotten the sound of summer rain softly falling on growing corn blades in fields below the mesa?

Do you hear the women singing joyfully together at the grinding stone?

SONG OF THE GRINDING STONE

> Child of the corn!
> Child of the green blades!
> Leave your digging stick,
>   Come to the singing!
>
> Daughter of the Earth!
> Walk the pollen path
> Now prepared for you,
>   Come to the singing!
>
> Sister to the fields!
> Wear virgin corn blossoms
> Hanging from your hair,
>   Come to the singing!
>
> O woman of the Dawn!
> Garment yourself in sunlight
> Greet the new day,
>   Come to the singing!

This song will echo forever along the canyons of your memory. For you are of the earth, the sun, the sky, and the water!

Deep in your heart you will recall the animal stories your great grandmother told you on cold winter nights around the fire. Perhaps one night you will share them with your daughter.

Do not turn your eyes away! Yes, there were times of sorrow, bitterness and struggle, as there is now and will forever be. And yet joy fell on you as sunshine slipped through patches in treetops above your heads, warm and summer-sweet.

Remember, my daughters, from the time of your birthing to the day on which you die, you will not change; for you are of the earth, the sun, the sky, and the water!

Count the days of your ancestors, for they are numbered on the calendar of the Great Spirit!

Keep you spirit free, wherever your body takes you, your spirit is also there. You must not lose your dignity or pride; keep it as a looking glass, be proud of the reflection you see each morning as you meet the day.

My sisters, neglected and dead fields do not regenerate themselves; only rains of remembrance will keep safe the germination of generations of grace, humility, pride, religious spirituality, and the dignity of your race—Native American.

Listen, speak, and remember!

WALKING THE TRAIL

O Father Sky!

My spirit
is a wounded bird
Hovering in the underbrush
Of despair.
I reach out to you
That once again
I may know
The courage of eagles.

O Mother Earth!

With my digging stick
I place corn kernels
In the brown wrinkles
Of your ancient face.
Nourish the lean blades

Into stalks of maturity
That my people
Do not hold empty bowls.

O Great Spirit!

Before me sprinkle wisdom
That I may follow wisely
In the footsteps
Of my ancestors.
In gratitude
I shall quietly walk
The Trail-of-Old-Age
In-Everlasting-Beauty.

THE WEDDING DAY

I come to you
In the season of falling leaves
To become your bride
I sit on your left
Facing east.
After we have washed our hands
From the same bowl
We eat with our fingers
The cornmeal
From the ceremonial basket.
Now is the day
Our spirits make sacred pilgrimage
In four directions
We shall go out standing in beauty
Our spirits embracing.
My heart is full
As a spring river
At second thaw
Rising and pounding against
The banks of my being.
I will walk beside you
On the path
Of your choosing
Though at times the summit
By clouds may be hidden

Beside me
May you fall asleep
Always smiling
Folded in the warm wings
Of my womanhood.
Fill the hollow of my heart
With the laughter
Of children
That we
May know sweet joy together.
Let my body bend as grass
To thy leaning
And straight as a reed
Before
The great wind of sorrow.
May I wear
The long feathers of swiftness
At my death
That I
Leave with you no grief.

(According to the custom of the Navajo)
Jean Humphrey Chaillie

SONG OF THE CRADLEBOARD

In the beginning
The Great Spirit
Scattered stars
Along the trail
Of the universe.
Last evening
At moonrise
A single star
Fell into my
Waiting cradleboard.

O son of my blood!
O child of my bones!

I lay you down
On sun-colored clouds

Drifting in the east
And rainbow ravelings
Of falling light.
Sleep new born baby
As the unopened buds
Of the wild cherry sleeps,
In the cradle
Of unchanging joy.

O child of earth!
O son of sky!

There is a singing
Round-about-you
Tiny bird,
O frail thing,
O seeker of life!
May the white threads
Of happiness
Be woven
Into the weaving
Of all your dreams.

O flesh of 'the people'
O soul of 'changing woman!'
Like startled quail
My joy leaps up,
It is greater
Than the needles
Numbered on the pine.
I make an offering
Of Sweet Smoke
And plant squash
For this gift
Of great joy.

O child of my blood!
O son of my bones!

In the hushed silence
Of unwakened dawn
I gather you

To my brown bosom.

O shining star!
O pendant of bone!

Jean Humphrey Chaillie

ACKNOWLEDGMENTS

"Song of the Cradleboard" was originally published in *Arizona High-ways Magazine,* 1978 by the Arizona Department of Transportation. "The Wedding Day" was originally published in *Passage II,* 1976 by Triton College, Triton College Press, River Grove, Illinois. Reprint permission given by *Arizona Highways Magazine* from *Holding Files* purchased in 1978 by the Arizona Department of Transportation. "Walking the Trail" was originally published in *The Sandcutters,* Arizona State Poetry Society Publication, 1981, Phoenix, Arizona. "Tribesman," "Bittersweet Joy," and "Song of the Grinding Stone," are unpublished poems by Jean Humphrey Chaillie.

THE ODE

Frona Lane

The ode is a lyric poem of exaltation in feeling and style, varying in length and stanza. It should be noble, stately, beautiful and sustain thought in its highest flight; a dignified, intellectual lyric, with purpose to denote intense emotion.

Ode derives from the Greek *odos* (song) and the French *hodox* (to sing). It is kin to the Greek *aude* (voice). Other derivations and literary references are Odin, chief god of Scandinavian and Germanic mythology; Wodin, the Anglo-Saxon name for Odin; *odeum* (song in Greek, Latin and French), meaning a small roofed theater or concert hall of ancient Greece and Rome, used mainly for competition in music and poetry. The Scandinavian reference is to *Valhalla,* from the French *vair* (the slain) and *holl* (hall); the Hall of Odin to which the souls of heroes slain in battle were brought by the Valkyries to spend eternity in joy and fasting. Modern non literary derivations include such words as odograph and odometer.

Odin/Wodin was the god of wisdom and poetry. He became the legendary All-wise by drinking at Mirmir's fountain at the cost of one eye. He is often represented as a one-eyed man wearing a hat and carrying a staff. His other eye is the Sun.

To a Norseman the Promise, or Vow, of Odin (matrimonial or other) is the most binding of all oaths. While making it, the hand is passed through a silver ring or a sacrificial stone. Anyone who violates the oath is disgraced.

Edmund Grosse, who says the ode is "any strain of enthusiastic and exalted lyric verse directed to a final purpose and theme," initiated the choral odes of the Greek drama. The meter is iambic, of varying length, and the "likeness to rhyme at varying intervals of the same rhyme," he continues, "is counterbalanced by the unusual frequency in the recurrence of that rhyme." The varying length dictates changes in feeling; i.e., the longer lines expressing deep feelings and shorter ones light.

Wordworth's "Ode on "Ode on Intimations of Immortality" is the best example of irregular form. Other examples are Dryden's "Song for St. Cecelia's Day," and "Alexander's Feast," also Tennyson's "Ode on the Death of the Duke of Wellington."

Many so-called English odes are but regular stanzaic lofty lyrics; i.e., Wordsworth's "Ode to Duty," Shelley's "Ode to the Nightingale," Shelley adapted the quintain in "To a Skylark."

Coventry Patmore said, however, in his prefatory note to "The Unknown Eros":

> From the time of Drummond of Nawthornden to our own, some of the noblest flights of English poetry have been taken on the wings of this verse (the ode); but with ordinary readers it has been more or less discredited by the far greater number of abor-

tive efforts, on the part of sometimes considerable poets, to adapt it to purposes with which it has no expressional correspondence; or to vary it by rhythmical movements which are destructive of its character.

Ben Jonson (1629) introduced Pindaric Ode, made famous by Pindar, into England. His is the truest imitation of this classical form. The best example is his Pindaric Ode on the Death of Sir H. Morison. It was written to be accompanied by music and dance. The poet usually wrote both. It was divided into *strophe* (turn), *antistrophe* (counter-turn) and *epode* (stand). The strophe and antistrophe were identical in structure and sung and danced to the same tune. In the strophe the chorus moved to the right from a given point; then antistrophe to the left. The epode, or after-song, was the third section of a Greek ode. It differed in meter from the strophe and antistrophe and varied in choral movement and music. It was sung or recited by the chorus standing still.

An interesting reference to Odin in the Golden Bough, which could be subject of a Pindaric Ode, is in the verses of the *Havamal* where Odin says he acquired divine power by learning the magic runes:

> I know that I hung on the windy tree
> For nine whole nights,
> Wounded with the spear, dedicated to Odin,
> Myself to myself.

In Bohemia the ceremony of Burying Death is turned from what could be an Elegy to Death to an Ode to Death in the strophe and an Ode to Life in the antistrophe. In this ritual the children go singing and dancing from their village to the end of it carrying Strawman Death, where they burn the effigy in an Ode to Death, then return to the village singing and dancing as they celebrate Spring, the forerunner of Summer, in an Ode to Life.

STRAWMAN

(A parody on Ben Jonson's Pindaric Ode on the Death of Sir H. Morison)

We carry Death, a man of straw,
   That from our village must withdraw.
He took his stand upon our village square
And left our greening grass and orchards bare.
   Death swam our freezing shores;
   Knocked at unwelcome doors;
Slept in our fields, our churches, homes.
No sunlight warmed our shaking bones.
In large delight we carry Death afar
Before we turn toward home, our brightest star.

We welcome Summer to our town,
   But first comes Spring, dear little clown.
We carried Death away; now bring back life.
We sing and dance and play upon the fife.
   Dear Sun, come back to stay.
   For wheat and corn we pray.
For flowers and grass and open doors
And happy children on our floors.
Dear Spring, bring Summer's pure and vernal light.
Bring love and hope. May all our days be bright.

Children who sing at this festive time
      Of Strawman Death
Or taste a part of Life's full joy sublime
      Do know that breath
   Is sweet in Spring's fresh air
   And love is everywhere.
They know that Summer will come to them tomorrow
   If they but dance and sing—
   Sing and dance with Spring.
They know they have no heart for sorrow
If they sing to welcome Summer; thank Spring
And give to Odin their gladsome offering.

                                        Frona Lane

ODE TO THE SACRED CEIBA

I. Jaguar Prophecy

At that time no Song of Jaguar will shake sacred ceiba.

At that time no language of ancestors will pictograph
halidom looms of ancient Maya in once fertile forest.
At that time no opalescent islands in cerulean sea
or fern, or orchid, or street will panoply farmer or noble.
Nothing will be left of plazas to mark holy passage of time
and days of Chac and his twin Chac Mai. Nor priest crested
with feathers of Quetzal will move slowly up steps of the Temple.

At that time no gulp of greed will seize the land and lacerate
lace of leaves and grasses. All lids of earth
will be closed and Lacadonians of the falling forest
will follow with obsidian eyes the day by day heaving of hills
and ashes of memory.

II. Lost Mayan Heritage

Invaders are locusts devouring the land.
Zapote beetles are tattering the testimony of time.
Ribs of hillocks are gulled and gullied and mud-slung ground.
is shaped hooves of horses and boots of conquering hordes.
Chac the Rain God smiles no more on once-vernal valley.
A young warrior on bare feet stumbles,
as the petral staggers in a storm under rustle of birds
songless under branchless beams of sky.

Summer floods have gouged empy sockets through stone eyes
of headless statue in doorway of Hachakyum. The sun is leaching
the leafmold and the mother doe decries her lost heritage.

An old man croaks in the lobster night, in skeleton shade
of now-leafless ceiba: "I'm weary. I seek a fallen tree
to enter and sleep." . . . No voice of ancestors answer.
No Song of Jaguar echoes from time-worn hill
across once-sweet valley.

Frona Lane

(Note: In Mayan Theology, the sacred ceiba was believed to be the Tree
of Life.)

HAIKU, SENRYU AND TANKA

Truth Mary Fowler

A haiku is a three-line poem of Japanese ancestry that contains seventeen syllables divided into groups of five-seven-five. (One translation of the word "haiku" is "syllable-count.")

A haiku is a poem of perception and awareness of the miracles that surround us in everyday living. It is a nature poem linked with human nature.

The season of the year must be indicated by name or implication.

The haiku must not rhyme, use alliteration, simile, metaphor or other poetic devices. The thinking behind this rule is that in so short a poem, poetic contrivances detract from the meaning of the poem in the same way that gesturing toward the moon with a hand that wears a jewelled bracelet takes away the attention from the beauty and symbolism of the moon.

A haiku must be untitled as a title imposes the interpretation of the author upon the reader instead of leaving him free to interpret the meaning himself.

Haiku are written in the present tense. The time is now.

A haiku does not have to be grammatically correct. Just as we do not have thoughts in complete sentence, so the haiku consists of fragments, making use of spaces in the same way that Japanese art does. Each individual reader fills in the blanks himself, making the haiku "happening" his own, according to his particular background or experience. These poems are not for "skimmers." They are to be read, re-read and pondered. Haiku need creative readers as well as creative writers. Let us take two examples:

1. On Easter morning
   the cicada's outgrown suit
   cast off for the new.

2. White chrysanthemums
   shine against black lacquered hair
   lighting his way home.

1. Did you ever watch a cicada struggle out of his old outgrown suit? This haiku can be appreciated as one of Spring's annual miracles, it can represent rebirth to the born-again Christian or it can renew faith in the resurrection of the body and the life everlasting. The season word, Easter, enhances the symbolism. 2. I see a beautiful Japanese girl dressed in a pink silk kimono, with two white chrysanthemums pinned to her shining black hair. She stands on a little arched bridge waiting for her husband to come home from his day's toil. His white cloth shoes slap little puffs of dust up as he walks swiftly toward her. The warm glow of their love. The season word is, of course, chrysanthemums.

Haiku are non violent because of the Zen influence. The entire culture of Japan owes its uniqueness to Zen. Some haiku-Zen qualities are simplicity. . .naturalness. . .stillness. . . tranquility. There is often a quality of sadness or loneliness in haiku. Following are two such examples:

Tears at mother's grave	Through its hollow stem
salty in my open mouth...	into the vase that holds it
the scent of roses.	this lily's life bleeds.
(American Poetry League)	(Poetry Society of New Hampshire)

SENRYU

The senryu is exactly like the haiku pattern: a three-line poem containing seventeen syllables divided into groups of five-seven-five, except that the haiku is an objective nature poem linked with man, the observer, while the senryu ignores nature and depicts man as he is. Haiku are emotional; senryu are intellectual and get right down to the nitty gritty pointing out weaknesses, vices and human foibles. Sometimes humorous, ironical, unflatteringly personal as they reveal humanity with all of his imperfections:

You touch me. . .I cringe	His "I told you so"
like running into cobwebs	increasing one hundred fold
at scary midnight.	the throb of her hurt.
Programmer checking	Boy plows rice paddy
electronic computor	astride water buffalo
with Dad's abacus.	transitor to ear.
	(Outch International Haiku)

Double injuries:
their cruel laughter hurting
more than losing you.

(Cal. Fed. of Chaparral Poets)

TANKA

The tanka is a five-line poem containing thirty-one syllables divided into groups of five-seven-five-seven-seven. Another definition is that a tanka is a haiku with a comment containing two seven-syllable lines added.

Like the haiku, the empty spaces are as carefully wrought as the expressed words. For example, the full beauty of a Spring day is told in the opening of a single blossom and the reader imagines the whole from the few (perhaps ungrammatical) frag- ʼents.

The writing of tanka was game often played at court, called *renga* or *linked verse*. The first player composed three lines. The second player wrote two lines not as a continuation but as a sort of commentary, which could stand independently as an unrhymed couplet. The third person wrote a related haiku, the fourth added a two-line comment and thus the link poem (or renga) evolved, the number of links sometimes reaching ten thousand or more. (Remember there was no television in the seventeenth century during Basho's lifetime.)

Today's tanka may be more lyrical than the disciplined haiku or senryu. It may also have a title. Examples follow:

SEA FOOD DINNER

> White seagull hovers;
> ocean swells in slow motion;
> silently we wait. . .
> Splash! Fish squirms in a closed beak!
> Blue waves swallow my bare feet!

DEATH WATCH

Old cypress staggers
knee-deep in stagnant waters
of poisonous green—
round-shouldered black vulture waits
on the one remaining limb.

HANDY DEFINITIONS

haibun: a travelogue interspersing haiku and prose
haigu: small sketches expressing in pictures what haiku do with
    words
haijin: a person who composes haiku
hokku: a haiku (obsolete)
jion: symbol sounds
kigo: a season word
nagauta: a long poem
onji: sound symbols
sabi: sadness due to the passage of time
satori: the Zen moment of enlightenment

BOOK HELPS FOR READING AND WRITING HAIKU

Blythe, R. H. *Haiku* 4 Volumes, Hokuseido Press, Tokyo (the Bible of
    haikuists; relates Japanese poetry with American, according to the
    four seasons)

Blythe, R. H., *History of Haiku* 2 Volumes, Hokuseido Press, Tokyo (in-
    valuable background material)

Drevniok, Betty, *Aware—A Haiku Primer*, Portals Publications, 4431 Al-
    drich Road, Bellingham, WA 98225 $7.50 postpaid first class, (valu-
    able collection of haiku information)

Henderson, Harold E., *Haiku in English*, Anchor Books, Doubleday & Co.

Hyers, Conrad, *Zen and the Comic Spirit*, Westminster Press, Philadelphia,
    (a delightful explanation of "the small smile of recognition that
    glistens in Eastern religion)

Keene, Donald, *Japanese Literature, An Introduction For Western Readers*,

Evergreen Books, New York (a brief introduction to an understanding of Japanese poetry, theater, the novel, and an explanation of Japanese words used in literature)

Morris, Iva, *Madly Singing in the Mountains,* a biography of Arthur Wayley.

Sei, Showagon, *The Pillow Book* (translated by Arthur Wayley) written by a lady-in-waiting in the 10th century; witty, sophisticated, excellent translation, Grove Books

Skikilin, Muraski, *The Tale of Gengi,* 2 Volumes, translated by Arthur Wayley from a book written by a court lady in 100 A. D. (Prince Gengi is the Japanese Don Juan, a sort of "Forever Amber" Oriental Style)

Watts, Alan W., *The Way of Zen,* a Mentor Book, The New American Library

Watts, Alan W., *The Spirit of Zen—a Way of Life,* Evergreen Books, New York

Watts, Alan W., *Eastern Wisdom and Modern Life,* Evergreen Books, New York

Watts, Alan W., *On the Taboo Against Knowing Who You Are*

Yasuda, Kenneth, *The Japanese Haiku,* Charles Tuttle Co.

HAIKU MAGAZINES FOR ENJOYMENT OR MARKETING

Dragonfly: Lorraine Ellis Harr, 4102 NE 130th Place, Portland, OR 97230

Frogpond: Lilli Tanzer, Box 265, RD7, Hopewell Jct., NY 12522

Geppo Haiku Journal: C. Joy Hass, ed., 201 Douglane Ave. San Jose, CA 95117

High/Coo: Randy and Shirley Brooks, editors, 26-11 Hilltop Dr., W. Lafayette, IN 47906

Modern Haiku: Robert Speiss ed., Box 1752, Madison, WI 53701

Outch International Haiku Magazine: Nobuo Frank Hirasawa, ed., 2-19-30 Fujimoto, Kokobunji-Shi, Tokyo 185, Japan

P.O.E.T.S.: Happy Publishers, 28627 Aspen Drive, Green Valley Ranch Subdiv. Rt 1, Box 11, Conifer, CO   80433

Portals: Edna Purviance, ed., 4431 Aldrich Road, Bellingham, WA 98225

HAIKU SOCIETIES

Haiku Appreciation Club, 4431 Aldrich Road, Bellingham, WA 98225

Haiku Society of America, Cor van den Heuvel, Japan House, 333 E. 47th St., New York, NY   10017

Haiku Society of Canada, Betty Drevniok, Box 43, Combermere, Ontario, KOJ ILO Canada

Western World Haiku Society, Lorraine E. Harr, 4102 NE 130th Place, Portland, OR   97230

BIBLIOGRAPHY

Haiku Highlights, American Poetry League Magazine, Poetry Society of New Hampshire Newsletter, Outch International Haiku, California Federation of Chaparral Poets, The Nutmeg, Swordsman Review

THE ORVILLETTE

Wauneta Hackleman

The author of the *Orvillette* is Virginia Noble of Sacramento, California. It is her tribute to her son, Orville, who is a disabled veteran. He was a paratrouper in World War II.

The form consists of four stanzas in iambic tetrameter (four feet to the line); has alternate rhyming with rhyme scheme of abcb, adcd, aece, afgf; the author uses *right* rhyme. The first line of each stanza must be identical and the first three beats in the final line of each stanza must be identical.

In the example poem, Mrs. Noble has honored Philip Menard, a poet and artist. Mr. Menard was the founder and first president of the Sacramento Poetry Club. He is also an executive of the Crocker Art Gallery in Sacramento.

On the twenty-fifth anniversary of the poetry club, the members were asked to submit a poem for the occasion. Mrs. Noble wrote the example poem which is the orvillette form:

PHILIP MENARD

> I have not heard him read one poem
> For silence seems to be his choice,
> But when he spoke on art I read
> A thousand poems in his voice.
>
> I have not heard him read one poem
> Yet every slighted verse demands
> That I should tell how I have read
> A thousand poems in his hands.
>
> I have not heard him read one poem
> Yet poetry pleads to eulogize
> This friend and tell how I have read
> A thousand poems in his eyes.
>
> I have not heard him read one poem
> Yet poems that sleep within his heart
> Awake as paintings and I see
> A thousand poems in his art.

Virginia Noble

THE PANTOUM

Marel Brown

While English-speaking poets borrow the French forms from the French people, we learn that the French borrowed the Pantoum from the Malayan Peninsula, where it was used as a song. Victor Hugo is credited with being the first French poet to use and popularize the Pantoum.

Though the Pantoum is not as widely used as some of the other French forms, it has a special charm. Especially for the reader. It can be dramatic, or mind-spurring, even soul-searching.

The Pantoum may be of any number of four-line stanzas, in either three-foot or four-foot lines. It is a fixed form. The second and fourth lines of each stanza become the first and third lines of the next stanza. That pattern is continued for as many stanzas as the poem requires. But the poem always ends with the repetition of the first line of the first stanza as the last line of the poem. With this pattern, each line must be a complete thought. There can be no run-over lines.

Writing a Pantoum isn't as difficult as that rule sounds. It is a matter of poetic discipline. Yet discipline of line repetition does not mean a Pantoum is any less "inspired" than a lyric or a sonnet. It may be rhymed or unrhymed.

When the Pantoum pattern becomes a part of ready knowledge it is like learning to drive a car. You learn by saying: "I push this button, I shift this lever, I press down on the brake at a stop sign." By the time the license is granted, the driver does those things automatically.

Of course, no poem is the result of an automatic preference. Not even a Pantoum. But the "saying" of it—to use a Robert Frost expression—can become so ingrained that it seems automatic, or natural, in the writing.

The Pantoum may not become your favorite French form,

but there is a keen dimension or achievement in being able to write a poem in the Pantoum pattern. The following are two fine examples of the Pantoum form:

LESSON LEARNED IN THE ORIENT

Encircling the world on a wing
we went West until West became East
where morning met evening
when clocks of compulsion ceased.

We went West until West became East
in a land wrapped in smiles and flowers
when clocks of compulsion ceased
as we learned not to count any hours.

In a land wrapped in smiles and flowers
we won wisdom from ways of new friends
as we learned not to count any hours—
though aware that each journey ends.

Flying wiser from East to the West
where morning met evening,
we returned to the start of our quest
encircling the world on a wing.

Anne Marx

(This Malayan Pantoum is included in *Face Lifts for All Seasons*, 1980 and has been translated into Bahasa Indonesia, 1980 (Jakarta). Published in *Voices International.*

HOPE FOR A HOSTAGE

Another day and night
from limits of this room
I keep my inner sight
in landscape without gloom.

From limits of this room
I seek a sacred space
in landscapes without gloom
by blotting out this place.

I seek a sacred space
where loved ones long for me;
by blotting out this place,
doubts turn to certainty.

Time oozing day by day—
I keep my inner sight
on candles far away
another day and night. . .

                                                        Anne Marx

(Published in *The New York Times* and included in the author's book *Face Lifts for All Seasons*.)

PARODY

Jaye Giammarino

Parody is the comic imitation of a serious poem. The poet mimics another poem, usually a well known one, by emulating its style and contrasting thoughtful subject matter with humor. Good parody consists of mimicry and not mere imitation; its purpose being good-natured ridicule of the poem parodied.

Parody is not a poetic form in itself, but one that plays with all forms. The writing of parody, even though the serious-minded poet may look upon it as an unworthy practice, has been handed down to us through the years, and has been engaged in by poets and versifiers of great esteem. A parody, written in ancient Greek, is ascribed to Homer. Shakespeare was parodied by Marston, and Dryden by Buckingham, and so on down to modern times. Among poets, Swinburne has been parodied more widely and successfully than any other poet.

It is good practice for the poet, for it forces him to fit his thoughts into a recognized pattern of rhyme and rhythm, and like light verse, is an exercise in virtuosity; the writer striving to stay close to the model, yet distant; remaining plausible, yet entertaining.

Successful parody depends on the closeness of its resemblance to the original which it mimics, its skill is judged by the extent to which it makes use of the exact words of the original, yet completely changing their meaning. It can twist a serious poem so completely and do it so cleverly, that one may find it difficult, ever again to read the original without smiling at the memory of the parodied version.

When well done, it gives pleasure even to those not acquainted with the original. However, being familiar with the poem being mimicked, makes for greater appreciation of the poet's skill. Many of the verses in Alice's Adventures in Wonderland are parodies of serious British poetry.

Examples:

THE POET'S HOUR (Parody of the *Children's Hour* by Henry Wadsworth Longfellow)

> Between the dawn and the twilight
> When the mind is beginning to sour,
> Comes a pause in the day's stagnation
> That is known as the Poet's Hour.
>
> From my hangups I see in the hazelight
> Invading my pastoral lair,
> Knave Cliche and Grinning Ad-jective
> And pronouns with matted hair.
>
> I mutter Haiku and Tanka, tricked
> By Oriental disguise.
> They sound chiseled and jadelike together
> But take no judge by surprise.
>
> A sudden rush to Thesaurus,
> A hurried raid to my file;
> I must leave to aid uncovered
> No source undisturbed for my style.

Tradition continues to circle
My pen and the gray of my brains.
Villanelles only confound me
And Sonnets flow out through my veins.

I have Free Verse in my bloodstream,
And I will not let it depart,
Though Teasdale and Emily are imbedded
In the Avalon of my heart.

Blank Verse and meter will ever
Remind me of the neoclassic day,
But my rhyme scheming hour is ended
And I have prosed the time away.

                                        Wauneta Hackleman

ME FEVER (Parody of *Sea Fever* by John Masefield)

I must go back on that diet again
To the sugarless tea and no pie,
And all I ask is a salad bar
And a scale to steer me by;
And the carrot sticks and the celery hearts
And jello-molds shaking;
And a happy look on my hubby's face
To see ugly fat breaking.

I must go back on that diet again
For the sight of expanding hide
Is a pitfall of the banquet hall
That cannot be denied.
And all I ask is a winning day
When the extra pounds go flying,
With the chocolate cake and the french fries
I'll be no more a-buying.

I must go back on that diet again
To the vagrant dieters life,
To the starlet's way, and the model's way
Where the shape's like a skinny fife;
And all I ask are encouraging words

To keep me high in clover;
Till the new me, is a glamorous me
And the long diet's over.

Jaye Giammarino

BIBLIOGRAPHY

Johnson, Burges. *New Rhyming Dictionary and Poets Handbook.*

PERSONA

Amy Jo Zook

One of the most useful and intriguing types of poetry to write is the *persona poem.* It lends itself equally well to any form of verse, or even to prose styles, and can be found in almost any length.

Its particular genius lies in the freedom it gives the writer to say what might otherwise seem uncharacteristic or selfconscious, and in the excercise of imagination required to do it well.

Persona is taken from the Greek word for "mask," and refers to the poet taking the personality and speaking with the voice of someone far other than herself. The chosen character may be historic, literary, completely imaginary, or the poet in an earlier or later moment of life. It may involve gender change, or even change of life-form to the fantastical or surreal, a species of personification. It is actually self-revelatory monologue, though it need not be as dramatic as that term suggests. The poet enters into the mind of and actually becomes the new character. Examples might include Jeanne Bonnette's "Jeanne D'Arc Talks to Herself" (in *Leaf Change,* Golden Quill Press, 1979):

They needn't bind me; I am on my way
already to God in His appointed place.
I would not fight my captors or my judges
who sent me to this waiting funeral pyre.

I watch the bustle and I hear the cries
of people in the courtyard crowding close. . . .
close as they dare, for flames might blow
                         their way.

I am leaving all to go to Life
Eternal. Know this: I am not afraid.

or Hilda Doolittle's "Evadne" (in *Love's Aspects,* ed. by Jean
Garrigue, Doubleday, 1975) speaking as a numph loved by Apollo, or Alice Briley's similar celebration of pagan love, "Nymph
and Satyr," spoken from the persona of the satyr (in *A Weaver's
Shuttle,* New Mexico State Poetry Society, 1977):

Through meadow sun and forest shade
I frolicked with my woodland maid.
She looped my horns with a flower crown
And stroked by earlobe's furry down,
Until my blood came boiling up
As though I'd drunk from Bacchus' cup.

About the path her slim heels fled,
But through the gloom, her pale limbs shone
Beside a tree, against a stone.

or all the poems of the type now called Spoon River poems,
such as Maya Angelou's "Child Dead in Old Seas" (from *Oh
Pray My Wings Are Gonna Fit Me Well,* Bantam Books, 1977)
in which the child now half-mystical sea-creature, speaks:

Father,
I wait for you in oceans
tides washing pyramids high
above my head.
Waves, undulating
corn rows around my
black feet.

My ear
listens. You whisper
on the watery passage.

Father.
I wait for you
wrapped in
the entrails of
whales.

or even the personification/metaphor of Edna Meudt's "Wood"
(in *No One Sings Face Down*, Wisconsin House, 1970):

I house you still
useful for beam and cabin door
as handle and cradle and coffin shell.
I bear you table fare, and you asleep.

Charged with tomorrow's forest,
and the tree that brightens December
I witness for one born to die in my arms
I am immortal.

One important difference from personification is that it is spoken
from inside; the poet is the thing she is speaking about rather
than looking at it in the third person.

In writing persona, the poet should remember that both
the mood of the speaker and the historic and cultural referents
determine language—whether formal, passionate, colloquial,
or metaphysical—and that these together should influence
or determine form. Details must be both vivid and correct
to the location, time and mood of the poem. Since the poem
works better in concentration, hinting at plot rather than employing extended narrative, it is important that details be few
and allusion or connotation used as effectively as possible.
Familiar or typical characters, places, events may be helpful.
Titles may serve to identify the speaker so that information need
not be included in the body of the poem.

In my own lament, "Iseult at Carhaix" (*A Sonnet Sampler*,
Spoon River Poetry Press, 1979), the language is formal and

archaic and the form a sonnet:

> Now all our hope and our despair is done,
> The guiltless guilt and the unswerving joy,
> The cup of fire and ice that made us one,
> Unwitting victims Brangwyn must destroy.
> Ended the pain of Mark's deserving love
> That both must trespass howsoe'er we wish,
> The endless trials we were master of
> And honeyed suppers from the common dish.
> From Yseut White Hands' jealousy, the cure
> Of black and silken sail has rung our knell,
> Though having known me long, you should be sure
> I'd come at call to Brittany—or Hell.
>   Together now where union cannot end,
>   I follow you to death, my love, my friend.

In another persona, "Serenata for Six Strings," (published in Cyclo Flame) with the character a young Spaniard speaking of a mysterious love/initiation incident, I employ free verse but make use of parallel structure and euphonious word-choices as an echo to the music mentioned in the poem. So:

> Voice and guitar
>   ancient magic
>   through the midnight barrio
> lead me back in time not space
> to a city
>   where wine blessed
>   and music chastised
>   my adolescent dreams.
> Forbidden and beautiful alike
>   the cantina
>   and the Cathedral
> where wrongs and rites guaranteed
>   I would not grow up
>   ignorant of the world's sorrow.
> I confused the singer's hair
> with the Madonna's veil
>   and loved
>   or made love to
>   the wrong one.

Yet another persona is that of a ten-year-old girl, in a poem that evolves into a feminist theme, called "Kite Time" (*Golden Asterisk in Time,* Verse Writers' Guild of Ohio, 1978):

> I'd like to fly my kite
> down by the football field
> where there's lots of room
> and no trees to snag it.
> I'd LIKE to.
> But the boys are there
> with their kites
> war-kites
> with ground glass on the strings
> fighting,
> cutting each other's kites loose.
>
> And they won't let a girl
> fly a kite there.

Other personae delineate wind, animals, a watch, a traffic light; in each, the speaker is the new personality the poet wishes to explore. For that one moment, if no other, she is the other mind.

Persona is an equally good exercise for the beginning or advanced poet, and is in fact very useful for workshop situations with writers at varying levels of accomplishment. An interesting persona even imperfectly presented may have enough life and emotional force to transcend technical flaws. It becomes easy to believe in the persona as a real person, no matter how different from the actual creator. Besides being deeply satisfying poems to read aloud, the immediacy of first-person presentation makes them frequent winners of contests and very popular with magazine editors. Surely that is reason enough to try one's mask.

CARNIVORE (Picasso sculpture, Chicago)

> Gigantic matriarch
> more vulture than mother hen
> crouches above her chicks
> watching from cyclops eye

our impotent flutterings.
Like some obscene jest
the color of drying blood
she muddies our horizon,
omnipresent static Nemesis.
We pursue our regulated
and quietly decent lives
in the shadow of Ptera-something;
we know and cannot tell
that the monster herself
is our own creation,
science-fiction Baal, to whom
we owe no sacrifice.

Amy Jo Zook

THE MOON IS MY TUTOR

All shining, flowing things,
those that reflect light
and those that make their own light
are my songs:
haiku of firefly,
candle-sonnet, bonfire-ballad,
or epic of constellation.
I learn my alphabets
from mothwings, daisies,
and night-blown clouds.
Yucca exclamation-point
and phlox parentheses
encompass my orthography.
And having learned to see
all pale and lovely things
illumined by the moon,
I turn to you. . .

Amy Jo Zook

BIBLIOGRAPHY

Poems published in *Encore, New Laurel Review, Spoon River Quarterly,*

Cornfield Review, Gryphon, Bluegrass Literary Review, Pivot, Pteranodon, Kentucky Poetry Review, Voices International, Cumberlands, The Lyric, Great Lake Review and others. Three published books: *Echoes of England,* 1975, *A Sonnet Sampler,* Spoon River Poetry Press, 1979, and *A New Page,* 1979. All reviewed by *Ohioana Quarterly.*

QUATRAIN

donnafred

The Quatrain is said to be the oldest and most popular verse form in English versification. Poetry anthologies and the collected poems of many well-known poets are filled with quatrains. You will have little trouble finding material for study and enjoyment.

The Quatrain has four lines per stanza with various rhyme schemes. Usually abab, abba, abcb. (*New World Dictionary.*)

To put a complete thought into four lines, one must use great economy of words, crisp and trenchant, concise, and laconic. Remove all excess baggage such as flowery adjectives and redundancies. Whittle it down to its bare bones. Above all, use the right word; the explicit word to express the meaning you have in mind; be sure to say something that needs to be said. The shorter the poem the more necessary it is to have something significant to say in it. Avoid the easy trite word or phrase. I suggest *Roget's Thesaurus* to aid you in your word hunt. There are others but I have found *Roget's* the most complete and easy to use.

Once in awhile the stanza seems to be right the very first time. More often I find it takes two or three drafts before it suits me. It helps to sleep on it, giving the subconscious a chance to come up with some special word or thought that solves the problem. Check your rhythm; reject limping meter; verify your facts; clarify the meaning; hone the humor. Be sure your rhymes are perfect, or if not perfect rhyme, then good examples of near-rhyme such as:

want	mouth	strong	steady	anger	say
haunt	youth	young	lady	hunger	I

ad infinitum. Near rhyme is the technical way to avoid trite, overused rhyme endings.

About ninety percent of Emily Dickinson's poems are quatrains; lazy ones at that with rhymes to end the second and fourth lines only, and those near rhymes more often than not.

THE BUSTLE IN A HOUSE

> The bustle in a house
> The morning after death
> is solemnest of industries
> Enacted upon earth.
>
> The sweeping up the heart
> And putting love away
> We shall not want to use again
> Until eternity.

Emily Dickinson, *Collected Works*

Emily Dickinson's poems are serious in intent and content, while Dorothy Parker's may have serious undertones but are lightened with humor and make the human situation a little easier to bear. She is a superb exponent of light verse and the quatrain form.

PARTIAL COMFORT

> Whose love is given overwell
> May look on Helen's face in hell
> Whilst they whose love is thin and wise
> May view John Knox in Paradise.

Dorothy Parker, *Collected Poems*

I suggest that using quatrain to build a longer poem does

not take quite the skill or finesse that is required to complete an entire thought or poem in one quatrain. Edna St. Vincent Millay's "Moriturus," (seven pages in length) is an excellent example. I shall quote only the last four stanzas:

Withstanding Death
    Till life be gone
I shall treasure my breath,
    I shall linger on.

I shall bolt the door
    With a bolt and a cable;
I shall block my door
    With a bureau and a table.

With all my might
    My door shall be barred.
I shall put up a fight,
    I shall take it hard.

With his hand on my mouth
    He shall bring me forth,
Shrieking to the south
    And clutching at the north.

Edna St. Vincent Millay, *The Buck in the Snow*

The *metric* foot you choose for your quatrain is important. Follow it strictly and be consistent. In a stanza as short and tight as a quatrain, there is no room or need for variation as is permitted, for instance, in a sonnet.

One should also take into account the line length. The old ballad line length of seven feet is too long for our modern format, and would have to be broken into two lines, thus destroying one's quatrain form. Two, three, four and five feet are best.

There are many possible rhyme schemes for the quatrain. Here are samples from my own verse. All except the last two are from my book, *Pocket Piece:*

VENGEANCE

a	Though every jar of ointment
b	has a fly in it
a	control your disappointment
b	he will die in it.

THIS PLACE

a	Never again will I dare
b	to look on this place
a	where Beauty and I stood bare
b	and face to face.

EPITAPH NOT TO BE CARVED

a	I have loved, I have wept, I have sinned.
b	Now that my day is done,
b	Let my bones bask in the sun;
a	Let my dust drift with the wind.

TETHER

a	However unpleasant
b	one never
b	can sever
a	his past from the present.

Couplet-wise:

HOOK, LINE, SINKER

a	You're the one my line was baited for;
a	You're the one whose kiss I waited for.
b	Though the fish in the sea are myriad
b	you're the one. Period.

Last quatrain is an example of shortening the last line for emphasis or surprise.

OUTNUMBERED

a   Of all the doors to heaven
a   I've counted less than seven
b   But the ways I've found to hell
b   are more than I dare tell.

Two examples of the *lazy* quatrain with second and fourth lines rhymed:

COLLECTOR'S ITEM

a   On a polished sky the moon
b   slides down from the meridian
c   like a golden drop of honey
b   in a bowl of black obsidian.

DAZZLED

a   You were a comet flashing
b   through my world's dark night.
c   I am forever blinded
b   to any lesser light.

There is also the four-line stanza with no rhyme, but it must be called a quatrain.

TRIPLE TROUBLE

a   In the market of Life
b   Love keeps his thumb on the scales
c   Fate puts her foot in the aisle
d   and Time will short-change you.

BLUE PLATE SPECIAL

a   The yellow moon
b   in its white cloud
c   is an egg fried sunnyside up
d   and served on night's blue plate.

A rhyme scheme which I have not seen elsewhere:

ENGRAVED ON A SILVER CANDLE SNUFFER

a	Never the glow
a	should burn low;
a	let it go
a	quickly—so!

DUST OF OBLIVION

a	Because one time and long ago I sinned
a	is it right that my spirit still be pinned
a	to the wailing wall, my pulsing passions thinned
a	and the dust of oblivion blowing in the wind?

donnafred, *Love Runs Naked*

SCORE

a	I've had my outings and I've had my innings
a	a few sad endings and some new beginnings.
a	I've tallied my losses and totalled my winnings
a	but Lord don't count my sinnings.

donnafred

A few rhyme schemes that I have not as yet employed are abbc, abcc and aaba, the rhyme scheme of "The Rubaiyat of Omar Khayyaim."

In summary; first of all have something important to say; keep it concise; use the explicit word, correct rhyme, a set meter, and polish it well.

I find that a rhyming dictionary is invaluable help in finding rhyme endings I have never considered. My sources are Clement Wood's *The Complete Rhyming Dictionary,* and an unabridged dictionary for exact word meanings.

BIBLIOGRAPHY

Emily Dickinson *Collected Works,* Hallmark; *Not So Deep as a Well* (Dorothy Parker poems), Viking Press; Edna St. Vincent Millays's *The Buck in the Snow,* Harpers; *Pocket Piece* by donnafred, Marizona Press; *Love Runs Naked* by donnafred, Word Weavers Press; "Score" published by *Arizona Sunday Magazine*

THE QUINTAIN

Lois Carden

The Quintain is so little known as a verse form, it is not even listed in most dictionaries. The simplest definition says: "Quintain: A stanza or verse group of five lines." That seems to be the only definition given by anyone. A special form as a complete poem is the cinquain.[1]

The quintain was, perhaps, perfected in the fifteenth century when it was used in romantic poetry, often as a short verse or as a stanza in a longer poem. It was sometimes used as a chorus or to add emphasis.

The quintain is not fixed by meter entirely. Poets seldom observe a strict line length in writing a quintain. They often shorten or lengthen alternate lines to achieve the desired effect.

Emily Dickinson gives us a good example of this in her quintain:

TO MAKE A PRAIRIE

> To make a prairie it takes a clover or a bee,
> One clover and a bee,
> and revery.
>
> And revery alone will do,
> If bees are few.[2]

Any time you have a *tercet* and a *couplet* in any combination, you have a *quintain.* They are found with rhyme schemes of aaabb, aabbb, abcbc, or any other scheme one can devise, or with no rhyme scheme at all.

Some poets have used the *alexandrine* line for effectiveness. Edmund Waller's poem, "Go, Lovely Rose," is a good example of such use.

Modern poets have taken liberties, even with the most sacrosanct of verse forms, the sonnet, each one vying with others trying to invent a new form of sonnet; so why would they not take liberties with a simple, flexible poetic form as the quintain, which lends itself admirably to experimentation?

It is not a rigid verse form with but one or two possible rhyme schemes, and an inflexible number of syllables. It has the economy of the finest Japanese poetry, but it is viable and rhythmical. It does not lend itself merely to humorous short poetry, as does the limerick, nor to the taut stanza with a shocking ending.

The quintain can capture mood changes, harmony, can paint fantastic word pictures; and even though it is brief, it can project exquisite sensitiveness and beauty, becoming a gem in pristine loveliness.

Modern poets were not the first to experiment with the quintain, nor did the fifteenth century poets invent it.

King Solomon gave us, perhaps, the most exquisite quintain ever penned when he wrote to his beloved the beautiful poem containing the five-line quintain ending with the line, "And the voice of the turtle (dove) is heard in the land" (Songs of Solomon 2:11-12). And this quintain has no rhyme scheme at all.

Anacreon, in the sixth century B.C., in Asia Minor, reveals his hectic love life and his perpetual striving for youth in a long quintain sequence. He inspired generations of Hellenistic poets who came to be called the Anacre-

onic Tradition. His quintain sequence, "Old Age," reveals his unconventional life style, as well as his craftmanship
as a poet.[3]

Everyone is familiar with Shelley's "To a Skylark." It is
perhaps the best known of all quintains, and a perfect example
of the form.

The quintain is a satisfactory vehicle for the ode. Edgar
Allen Poe's "To Helen" is a marvelous source for the study
of the quintain.

The cinquain, as stated before, is a form of the quintain.
It was invented by Adelaide Crapsey, 1874-1914. The cinquain
contains five lines in iambic pentameter, in a rigid pattern of
twenty-two syllables; the lines arranged in 2, 4, 6, 8 and 2
syllables. It is an excellent form for condensing much in a
few syllables. The following cinquain illustrates this form:

YOUNG LOVE

> Softly
> And radiantly,
> Cornsilk hair veiled in white
> The bride comes down the aisle to love—
> And life!

The Poets Guild, Summer 1874

Limericks are another form of quintain. They are usually
humorous, or outrageous puns, as in my:

MOONLIGHTING

> They sent us off to the moon,
> Each dressed up like a cocoon.
> We hurtled through space
> At a terrible pace;
> Now, we're moonlighting on the moon!

The Archer, Summer 1970

The quintain may be serious as well as humorous. The serious and exquisite quintains are as numerous as limericks, whether as stanzas in a long poem, or as individual poems.

A quintain may contain a profound truth in what may seem to be a frivolous verse form, as in:

ATOMIZER

> Man was determined to make an atomic bomb.
> Now all mankind lives in fear,
> Afraid of destruction of all we hold dear,
> Of proliferation we cannot forestall—
> The atom may yet, atomize us all!

Or a quintain may be as exquisite as a morning in spring, or young love:

LOVE

> Morning dawned serene and golden,
> Across our valley wide.
> My heart sang with the song of the dove,
> And the laughter of the incoming tide
> For today, you became my own, my love!

The quintain is a verse form well worth experimenting with—and perfecting.

FOOTNOTES

[1] Joseph Shipley and T. Wadell Shipley. *Dictionary of World Literary Terms.* (Boston: The Writer, Inc.).

[2] Thomas E. Sanders. *The Discovery of Poetry.* (Glenview: Scott Foresman and Co.)

[3] Robert Warnock and George K. Anderson. *The World in Literature.* (Chicago: Scott Foresman and Co., 1950), p. 306.

THE RONDEAU

Marel Brown

There are a dozen or more poem-patterns among the group called the French forms. Their use, in France, dates from the thirteenth century. For a poem-pattern to last that long and still be a popular outlet far into the twentieth century proves it to be a form worth knowing.

Also, for the fixed French forms to have been borrowed— or filched—from the cultural elite of France says something for the astute learning ability of English-speaking poets. French forms have been used by top-ranking poets in England as far back as Chaucer. Later English poets possibly adopted them for their unusual appeal, and to give variety to their poetical experience. Knowing how to use any of the French forms can be a plus in any poet's stature.

High in popularity among French forms is the Rondeau. It is widely used, and poems in that form are easily quoted. The fixed formula for a Rondeau is this: Use iambic measure in four-foot lines. The first two feet of the opening line becomes the repetition, or refrain.

The first stanza has five lines; the second stanza four lines, with a closing line the refrain; followed by a six-line stanza, with the refrain as the last line. Only two rhyme words are used throughout the poem, so care should be taken in choosing each rhyme word. The rhyme-pattern is A A B B A, A A B C, A A B B A C—C being the refrain.

My Rondeau "Weep Not For Me," from my first book, *Red Hills,* is an example of the placement of rhyming lines:

WEEP NOT FOR ME

Weep not for me when I must go
Beyond horizons, close and low,
    That limit earth. Life has been good,
    Its every hour like patterned wood
Through which brave winds or shadows blow.

My heart has never ceased to know
The joy of change; if fast or slow
Somehow I always understood—
    Weep not for me.

I hold no grief, I beg no woe
On circumstance, or luck, or foe.
    When death brings me a new-style hood
    I'll wear it proudly—as I should—
My final word—may it be so—
    Weep not for me.

As if "Weep Not For Me" the theme of a Rondeau may be serious. Frequently it is a light exposé of some immediate and joyful experience. "This Vagrant Wind," in *Hearth-Fire,* reveals the universal lure in spring-time, with its tendency to forsake a duty succumbing to "Gypsy thoughts." A Rondeau may be a playful game on some aspect of life.

THIS VAGRANT WIND

This vagrant wind is a subtle spy.
With furtive glance it passes by
    And learns the weakness of my will,
    The secret gypsy thoughts that fill
My heart; attracts my roaming eye.

There is no peace. If I should try
To work, intent, who could deny
    The power inherent in such skill?—
    This vagrant wind!

Its weapon is the April sky,
Its lure is clover, grain stacked high,
    The essence that the orchards spill,
    The promise of each fresh-ploughed hill.
I yield. No wisdom could defy
    This vagrant wind.

Some poets who decry using a French form, even saying

they would not be able to recognize one, are nevertheless familiar with the well-known "In Flanders Field" where the poppies blow. That is a correct Rondeau. But, as it should be in all French forms, the theme overshadows the form.

Maybe it isn't out of place to suggest a study of French forms to all who have shied away from them. To quote a familiar cliche expression, "Try it—you'll like it!"

RONDEAU: AFTER THE CONCERT

I heard you play. Your eloquent
melody roused this instrument
silent too long. Now answering
it vibrates each remembered string
with all the air mellifluent.

How could I dream that you would bring
new breath to life diminishing?
Within my heart, wherever I went,
I heard you play.

Forgotten voices woke to sing
along with you, in sudden spring.
The wasted hours, the winter spent
without sweet sound, I shall repent.
All clocks turned back that evening
I heard you play.

Anne Marx, from *A Time to Mend*

RONDEAU FOR A FRIEND WITH AN UNALTERABLE SCHEDULE

You are my friend. You justify
your absence like a butterfly
so busy dipping down all day,
you find no time to stop, to stay
a while without some alibi.

When I am here, please, tell me why
we rarely meet, fond eye to eye,
though letters tell me, far away,

you are my friend?

All time runs out for all who die.
This season, let us satisfy
our need for touching, to convey
warmth of these words without delay:
You are my friend.

Anne Marx

RONDEAU: AFTER THE HURRICANE

I came alive. My peace, hard-won,
shattered, by sudden storm undone,
its center force uprooting me.
I trembled toward my destiny,
longing for quick oblivion.

Well-anchored in security,
how could I fall so readily?
Kissing the earth, touched by late sun,
I came alive.

How frail I was, a sap-starved tree!
Now, prone to death, new energy
surged as if life had just begun—
a hurricane phenomenon
to find when terror tore me free,
I came alive.

Anne Marx, first published in *Poet Lore,* included in author's book, *By Way of People,* 1970

RHYMED VERSE

Clovita Rice

Since Walt Whitman startled the world of letters in the mid

1800's with the reminder that rhyme is not a necessary part of poetry, whether to rhyme or not to rhyme has been a major point of contention.

Poetry, like language itself, is a living vehicle of creative expression and will continue to be in a stage of evolution. Twentieth century poetry shows definite decline in use of rhyme, with greater stress being put on the individuality of expression, a more casual vocabulary and the natural cadence of the English language.

However, many poets, critics and creative writing teachers agree that a certain concentration on the academics of established poetry patterns and efforts to write within these various limitations offer good discipline for the beginning or practicing poet. Any internship with the basic structures and devices helps develop not only an appreciation for old and contemporary major poets, but also helps develop a feel for the power of language, helps keen the ear to the music of poetic phrasing as opposed to prose, and helps the lay poet discover a style or technique with which he is comfortable.

Rhyme, defined loosely as the repetition of exact or similar sounds, has long been one of the expected and pleasurable aspects of poetry for many poets and readers. Whether its origin is Arabic, Celtic or Oriental is still debatable, but it is found in early Latin church hymns and was probably first used in English around 1200.

Besides a tonal effect of involving the reader or listener emotionally, with the sounds combining to create music or rhythm to the ear, rhyme is useful. It can partition a poem into stanzas, can strengthen the cohesiveness within a stanza or entire poem, can determine length of stanzas, and can establish parallel construction of stanzas. For many poets, it is easier and safer to have this sort of pattern, and it is also a challenge to create a poem to meet specific requirements.

Most rhymed poetry is also written in measured lines which contain set numbers of poetic feet, named and divided according to stressed and unstressed syllables. Poets long ago discovered that the bulk of English words is iambic, an unstressed syllable followed by a stressed one. And perhaps due to the popularity of the sonnet and blank verse, iambic pentameter (five iambic feet) has long remained the most popular measured line in poetry, rhymed or unrhymed.

The following poem is basically iambic pentameter and illustrates the predominate stanza form, the quatrain with alternate lines rhyming. The first two stanzas show parallel construction, while the last two lines form a couplet or pair of rhyming lines. It is quite common to close a poem composed of four line stanzas with a couplet, perhaps for greater impact:

BURNT UMBER

> An orange fall is coming! Smell the smoke
> That floats above the coral maple leaves.
> They're raked and piled with those from stately oak
> And gone by fire, but no one really grieves.
>
> We see how yellow tempers out the red.
> Hills soar high beside their narrow valleys.
> And just as tired workers need a bed
> Excited streets deserve their quiet alleys.
>
> The sprightliness of May, mellow December
> Seem compromised in sweetly swift September.

Sharon Younggren

From the very early rhyme of words at the beginning and end of lines, poets have invented new kinds of rhyme, but end rhyme remains the most used and is divided into two categories: masculine rhyme which has the rhyme occurring on one stressed syllable as in the words *mind* and *find* or *obey* and *away*; and feminine rhyme which contains two or more rhyming syllables as in *shaking* and *making* or *remember* and *December*. Examples of both masculine and feminine rhymes are seen in this poem:

PICKING UP THE PIECES

> Scalded, I go. Crisp hands winging
> My way along, paper thin, clinging

To the icy green day. Bright splashes
Of fire flaring among the ashes.
I smother each thought of him. Good-bye. Good-bye.
A million things to do. A vast glittering sky
Where noon clocks wind down. White sheets flutter.
The sun mellow and yellow warm like butter
Begins to melt. I hold together fast.
The hard quartz splinters of the day go past.

Ellen Jackson

Notice that except for the end rhyme, the poem is free verse, with no regular meter or line length. Notice also the use of internal rhyme (rhyme within a line or adjoining lines), with the words *mellow* and *yellow* in the eighth line.

In addition to straight or normal rhymes, perhaps due to the scarcity of rhyming words in English and the monotony of using the same combinations over and over, many poets employ what is called imperfect rhyme, with a slight change in the vowel sounds as heard in the words *scent* and *tint*, the difference being primarily in the amount of stress given the vowel in pronunciation.

Identical rhyme, with the same word used instead of a matching rhyme sound, is also often used. The poem that follows has two examples of imperfect rhyme and ends with repeating the same sound of the fifth line, though the words differ, to make identical rhyme. Notice also that this poem, other than the rhyme, is free form. To say that free verse never rhymes is a misstatement:

HOW TO MAKE A POEM WITHOUT ADJECTIVES OR ADVERBS

After you pen a poem,
pare.
Remove the skin, the hair.
Strip it to meat and bone. . .
and leave it.
The poem will have shown
the truth.
Believe it.

Marnelle Robertson

Other more indirect repetitions of sounds are employed. Assonance, the similar sound of vowels in accented syllables in the same line or two or more lines, can add much to the musical tone of poetry. Read the following poem aloud and notice the repetition of the same sounds of the i's in the first two words throughout the entire poem:

WINTER BRAKE

Twin winter trees
in a winter brake;
soft curious light;
I have seen it so
only in winter when the time goes slow
and the skies are mist.

This is the picture framed in gold
hung over the mantel which warms my soul.

Was it winter I wonder for both of us then?
Were the margins shallow
and our lives ice-rimmed?
It's hard to remember.

Whatever the state of our spirits then,
It's strange to see winter
and then think "friend!"

Betty Gosnell

Alliteration (words beginning with the same letter as in *sea* and *soon*) and Dissonance (with the consonants before and after the vowel repeated as in *hat* and *hit*) are other rhyming devices. Too much alliteration soon detracts while dissonance may often be totally missed unless the poem is read aloud with stress being given those words.

Using several rhyming techniques, the next poem is especially delightful when read aloud. Notice the *ou* vowel sound repeated in the first stanza, the several samples of alliteration, the parallel stanza construction with the fourth and eighth lines rhyming, and the repetition of *ing* words:

ADVENT

> Love came bound*ing*
> into my youth-years,
> gift*ing* with promises
> wonder endowed;
> etch*ing* a now-time
> out of the may-be,
> rid*ing* the maelstrom
> crest of a cloud.
>
> Love sped swiftly
> down all my hallways,
> out of my gardens,
> into my rooms;
> soothing the hurt-full
> rape of my wonder;
> lighting the dark-shade
> depth of my glooms.
>
> Love stepped gently
> over the shadows,
> reaching to comfort,
> ready to heed
> cries of my pent-up
> longing to salvage
> some of the let-down
> press of my need.

                              S. Ricarda McGuire, RSM

Still another kind of rhyme is slant or oblique rhyme, as in the words *stone* and *home*. Here the sounds resemble but do not match exactly. This is a method used in many song lyrics. The following poem has several lines paired with slant rhyme ends:

SEPTEMBER MORNING

> Mist of midnight, warmed by the sun,
> Burns its frail heart upon the lawn,
> Lifts, and is gone to the river.

Rising there, it touches the trees
Where yellow leaves drowse away
The mellow end of summer
In quiet sighs of slumber.
As if the world were sleeping cold
And restlessly stirs awake—
Reaching for blankets of gold,
Day breaks.

Sue Scalf

Hopefully the novice poet will learn quickly to establish his values in writing poetry. While rhyme can be a great complement to the poem, the trick is in keeping it natural and uncontrived. The chief focus must be on saying something new that wants to be remembered and not just writing another chorus of birthday verse. It is not the craftsman who can fit rhyming together perfectly within precise framework who is the poet, but rather the writer who can spell the words of a striking and haunting new idea in musical language which may or may not rhyme. The real poet can describe anew and in few words an old worn out subject, as Virginia Scott Miner shows in this poem:

AUTUMN

The time of year
when high
in sky
the killdeer
cry.

All poems used as illustrations have been selected from *Voices International*, edited by Clovita Rice.

THE BIG QUESTION

So they tell us now
that man came from the water
and carries suitcased in what
we call human flesh
a three-fourths content of water. . .
so be it. . .at least our bones,

deprived too long of their river bed home,
begin to ache and seem eager
to part company with that other part. . .

The big question
is about the other part:
from what seabed does it arise
to what shore does it return?

I stand, a child at the river's edge,
tossing questions across the water,
hoping they will skip or bounce
and splash answers. . .

                                        Clovita Rice

IF YOU CAN'T FIND ME

"A thought went up my mind"
sprouting like a bean
and leafing green
and leaning toward the sun
with words tendrilling
into lines and vining
around ideas. . .
And I like Jack
must climb the stalk
to find
    where it is going. . .

                                        Clovita Rice

HUNTED

Winter is always ominous. . .
Hungry, I cannot hide,
am forced from cover
to look for sustenance.
I hop from day to day
leaving tracks
in the cold white snow
for whatever will
to follow. . .

                                        Clovita Rice

SECRETS OF THE SESTINA

Anne Marx

An ancient unrhymed verse form, the sestina has had a surprising revival in modern times. While it is definitely a fixed form of demanding regularity and, therefore, a welcome proving ground for the traditionalist, it also enjoys wide acceptance among those who spurn other traditional forms. Because the sestina does not rhyme, they accept it without conceding that they use a very old and disciplined pattern. The sestina is an admirable teaching tool, as it reaches for the right and unforced sequence of lines without imposing rhyme.

The word *sestina* derives from the Latin word sextus (six), which immediately tells us that we deal with a combination of this number. As a matter of fact, the sestina consists of six times six units, i.e. six stanzas of six lines each. These thirty-six lines are followed by an *envoy* of three lines, making a poem of a total thirty-nine lines. *Envoy* means "the closing lines of a poem, a short stanza concluding certain archaic metrical forms." It is derived from the word "envoyer" (to send) in Old French. This leads us to a new clue, namely that the sestina originated in France. Arnaut Daniel, a Provencal troubadour, invented it in the 13th century. However, it was less popular in France than in Italy, Spain and Portugal. Dante and Petrarch liked and popularized it. The original rules still apply in part; other rules have been modified in modern usage. One rule which still stands is the characterisitic six-stanza form, each of six lines of the same length, with a concluding three-line stanza. Each stanza repeats the end words of the lines of the first stanza, but in different order, the envoy using the six words again— three in the middle of the lines and three at the end. So far then, it should be easy to write a sestina whenever the mood seizes the poet.

The difficulty arises when it comes to the prescibed order of words, changing in each stanza according to a set formula. Every Poet's Craft Book consulted offers this familiar column of figures representing the end words, to be copied or memorized mechanically:

1st stanza	1, 2, 3, 4, 5, 6
2nd stanza	6, 1, 5, 2, 4, 3
3rd stanza	3, 6, 4, 1, 2, 5
4th stanza	5, 3, 2, 6, 1, 4
5th stanza	4, 5, 1, 3, 6, 2
6th stanza	2, 4, 6, 5, 3, 1

One of the best poets' handbooks is by Babette Deutsch, but this is all she supplies:

> The sestina is an elaborate form usually unrhymed but the end words of the first stanza impose a pattern analogous to a rhyme scheme, since they are all repeated in the succeeding stanzas in strict order that varies with each stanza and they recur in the tercet. With the numbers 1, 2, 3, 4, 5, 6 representing a stanza, the theme may be set down thus. . .

and off she goes presenting the same arbitrary column of figures.

Because the sestina is one of my favorite forms, I need to find a way to write it spontaneously. After extensive research, I found only the familiar complicated graphs of numbered terminal words, seemingly arranged without logic and almost impossible to learn by heart. Typically, the latest edition of Clement Wood's *The Complete Formbook for Poets* claims that "there is no explanation of this original arrangement." Elsewhere, the author asserts: "Clearly, in writing the sestina, after the first stanza has been completed, the next task is to write down the terminals for all the lines of the next five stanzas."

How could poets slavishly accept such a verdict for so long? I was absolutely sure of the existence of some simple formula from which the first sestina evolved. Now we may forget about memorizing those unrelated numerals. Now we can develop the pattern ourselves.

Our concern is with the required order of end words. So—put down your own first stanza of six lines with your own chosen end words expressing your essential thought. This first stanza, its end words represented by the numbers 1, 2, 3, 4, 5, 6 is followed by the second stanza, its end words represented by the numbers 6, 1, 5, 2, 4, 3. And this is the only sequence you need to understand and remember! The simple pattern evolves by reversing the order of the last three end words and inserting them on top and in the first two spaces between the original numbers. They will now occupy the former positions 1, 3 and 5. The original first three end words are automatically moved into new places and will now occupy original positions 2, 4 and 6. I think of this counter-movement as a kind of dance between two groups approaching each other, suggestive of the sestina's Provencal origin in the 13th century.

Now comes the main difference between my method and previous instructions. We must never go back to the first stanza as our starting point because it results in those incomprehensible graphs. No, we must derive our third stanza from the second one in exactly the same way as outlined above. It is always your preceding stanza, never the first one, which sets the pattern for the next one. This is continued right down to the sixth stanza. 6, 1, 5, 2, 4, 3—it is all you need for writing thirty-six lines from memory, followed by an envoy, the half-stanza which may be written in several easily remembered patterns.

The envoy, also called a tornado, consists of a tercet or triplet, in which all the former end words must be used, either at the start or in the middle of the lines. It is the climactic summary of our sestina requiring great care to have the words fall naturally without apparent straining. This concluding half-stanza may begin with the first, third and fifth words somewhere at the beginning of the lines, but not necessarily as the first word. The words may even be used at the half-line, i. e. internally, which gives the tercet added flexibility. Of course, the remaining second, fourth and fifth words will be used at the end. This arrangement is easily remembered graphically:

1st line	1, 2
2nd line	3, 4
3rd line	5, 6

The original Provencal arrangement is an interesting variety, using the even numbers in a descending line, the uneven ones in a parallel ascending one:

1st line	2, 5
2nd line	4, 3
3rd line	6, 1

Now that we have a fool-proof method of evolving our own sestina stanzas, let us replace the numbers with words. There is still something too mechanical about these numbers. Why not go through the same process with words—eventually your own words—to be off on the exploration of your own sestina, perhaps to become inspired and carried along by those words? It is a sound way of writing a poem, any poem. Here, however, for the sake of clarity, I have selected the simplest group of words. Let us suppose we have written our first stanza, ending with the following words:

> Stanza 1   child
>   school
>   home
>   tree
>   milk
>   spring

For the next stanza, we begin with the last word; then the first; then the next to the last; then the next to the first; i. e. the second; then the third to the last, and finally the original third word. Now we have our key arrangement, easily visualized geometrically as a zig-zag pattern, as follows:

> Stanza 2   spring
>   child
>   milk
>   school
>   tree
>   home

For the third stanza, we do exactly the same, beginning with the last word of the *preceding* stanza:

> Stanza 3   home
>   spring
>   tree
>   child

school
milk

And again, continuing to the final stanza, we always derive the pattern from the preceding stanza:

Stanza 4	milk	Stanza 5	tree	Stanza 6	school
	home		milk		tree
	school		child		spring
	spring		home		milk
	child		spring		home
	tree		school		child

Finally, we add one of the variations of the envoy, either using:

child. .	school		school.	milk
home. .	tree	or	tree. .	home
milk. .	spring		spring. .	child

Now that we have mastered the classical sestina form without graphs, let us speak of some variations which have surfaced during usage. Originally, the rules specified that the lines were to end with the same six words which were not allowed to rhyme with each other. Besides, originally only two-syllabled nouns were permitted. Both these rules have been altered. Modern usage permits words to rhyme. The lines may end on accented syllables, and by no means exclusively on two-syllabled nounds. French, Spanish and Italian, we know, afford more double rhymes than English.

In English, Swinburne has experimented much with the sestina, writing the form in alternate rhymes and creating his own sequence patterns. Kipling, too, in earlier times, has availed himself of the form. One rule persists throughout: the six terminal words must be repeated, with no change in sound or spelling, through each succeeding stanza. In modern times Auden wrote an unconventional variation, with the end words appearing in an arbitrary order in the final tercet (3, 5, 1 in the middle of the lines, ending with 4, 2, 6).

Much freedom is apparent in so-called sestinas that have lately come to our attention. Is that a contradiction of the above assertion, that certain requirements immutable? Not at all! The same goes for the villanelle, the sonnet, etc. If a modern poet chooses to write his own version, who is to prevent him or her? The poet knows he is not writing a classical sestina, perhaps using only the outer thirty-nine line form but taking liberties with the words and their sequences, even changing the spelling of the end words. However, the difference must be understood, to be properly appeciated as an unconventional variation.

This leads me to the gist of writing any kind of poetry. If this particular form had not required dwelling at length upon technique, I certainly would have spent less time and emphasis on it. Now let us talk about the poem per se, which happens to take the form of a sestina. Here is the crux of it all: it must be a poem first, a sestina second. This is where the true artistry comes in. It must stand up under the bombardment of repetition. It must progress in each stanza toward an ultimate conclusion or climax. It must not be an exercise in words alone, but a highlighting of ideas from various vantage points with a definite viewpoint. The end words must be so subtly placed, with enjambments freely used, that the speech appears natural, never forced. And, if you wish to write a sestina according to the rules, you must adhere to them strictly.

One more bit of advice may prove valuable. Put your essential thought or statement down in your first stanza of six lines. Then get the feel of the end words you have chosen. Are they flexible, i.e. can they be used in different ways such as a noun which is also a verb like the word "part," or "change"? Or, do they lend themselves to different meanings such as the word "leaves"? Some of your end words may be rather static but essential to your meaning, and that is quite workable along with the more flexible words chosen at this point. By alternating the static and flexible words, you can bring enough variety to your sestina. Remember, right now is the best chance to make adjustments. Later you will be locked into a lot more advanced work, harder to give up. Most poets find it painful to be ruthless with work already brought into a definite mold.

Occasionally, we all write a poem, including a sestina, that flows effortlessly, requiring little change, given to the poet from that mysterious source that cannot be explained.

One of my sestinas that practically wrote itself last year is *To a Granddaughter Maturing*.   It was accepted immediately and appeared in *The Croton Review*. It flows naturally and easily; the theme suits the form.   It happens to be one of a group of family poems in the sestina pattern included in my most recent book:

TO A GRANDDAUGHTER, MATURING

A beach bestirred morning waves beginning
to strive past boundaries, you reach the end
of childhood calm. These days, you are a new
strong current touching me, your thrust inherent
in my own yet independent of my lead:
girl on the verge of storms about to start.

How well I recall my fitful start,
that search along the shore of my beginning
no longer blindly confident to lead
a carefree life; the pang that games must end;
the wonder that my body held inherent
powers of cycles surging strange and new.

You live in casual times and yet this new
process remains a mystery to start
you off on waves to womanhood inherent
in your changing shape, a surf beginning
to churn with restlessness which will not end
until you fill your role. Where will it lead?

I see myself in you but cannot lead
life over again, though briefly I renew
my image standing at the opposite end
of our ocean. Looking across, I start
once more; within, I know the slow beginning
of undertows, a pull with death inherent.

But life-affirming tides run deep-inherent
in both of us. The secret life you lead,
the solitude you seek, the thoughts beginning
to disturb you, strange urges still too new
for comfort, all these are awkward at the start.

Trust that they will enhance you in the end.

Today I watch the sea and view my end
becalmed. There is a certainty inherent
in my blood, my being, that every start
of every wave will ultimately lead
unto a tranquil shore from where a new
bright wave will make another brave beginning.

In you, where the beginning brings an end,
the cycle starts anew. In death inherent
is life. Now take the lead. I share your start.

Anne Marx
from *Face Lifts for All Seasons*, Golden Quill Press, 1980

I am going to share with you a sestina I entered in a major contest. It happened to be conducted at a university where the students made comments which were communicated to the prize-winning poets who had submitted entries. My poem was called *Sestina for Tommy at Forty*. The idea seemed particularly suited for a sestina, juxtaposing this milestone in my son's life with my own vivid recollections at the age of forty. In a way, the concluding sestet presented itself beforehand, a final summing up of a familiar and shared experience.

The first verse practically wrote itself. I realized that I had set myself a difficult task with such complicated words as "foresaw" and "undeterred." However, I knew that I could use the syllable "saw" which would be less obtrusive, and I trusted my ingenuity about varying the word "part." Mostly, I depended on a run-over line to take the emphasis away from the end words, rarely finishing a line with them. Yet these devices were mostly used without conscious effort:

SESTINA FOR TOMMY AT FORTY

Today you are the son I tried to raise,
a man moored firmly in his family,
tender yet strong; thoughtful yet undeterred—
you now at forty all I once foresaw
when I was forty in your spring-time years,

our rhythms uneven, needs too far apart.

At forty, I had not yet learned to part
with my own past, relied on words to raise
a teen-age son straight into adult years;
in retrospect, close-ups of family
relationships you had, the love you saw,
sustained you later, instincts undeterred.

Forty years old, I was still undeterred
from training you for life, a leading part
that featured all the dormant gifts I saw
in you. Was this my sole mistake to raise
your goals too high? You blamed the family
pride, stiff-necked, and shunned our world for years.

At last, you freed your view. Past fog-filled years
you found your path, followed it undeterred
fulfilling every promise. Our family
surrounding you with pride became a part
of you, no longer needed now to raise
your self-esteem, man that my vision saw.

Hard to convince, I never clearly saw
the truth, a wisdom unacknowledged years
ago that mothers are not fit to raise
their teen-age sons. Boys should grow undeterred
by women into manhood. As they depart,
they find their way back to the family.

At forty, you have spread the family
tree by three new branches. Changes we saw
begin in ourselves were due in part
to the diminished gap between our years.
As I observe you functioning undeterred,
what ghosts from my own forties should I raise?

You now raise girls, a strong-willed family.
Their views are undeterred by what you saw
and learned from years, a male, my counterpart.

from *Face Lifts for All Seasons,* Golden Quill Press, 1980

THE SEVENELLE

Virginia Noble

The Sevenelle is a challenging and delightful newer form whose author is Virginia Noble of Sacramento, California. The poet is active in a poetry group that encourages its members to write new forms; to be creatively conscious that the twentieth century poets, especially women, need to be renowned and recorded in the making of current and future history. The Sevenelle was born the summer of 1970.

The Sevenelle consists of no less than two seven-line stanzas in either iambic tetrameter or iambic pentameter. (The tetrameter is used in the example poem.) There is no limit to number of stanzas. The last two lines of each stanza is the refrain and is repeated as the last two lines of all stanzas. Sevenelles may use either masculine or feminine ending. The author uses the rhyme scheme of aa, bbb, cc in *The Poet's Awakening.* Employed in this poem a couplet, triplet and the second couplet:

THE POET'S AWAKENING

In dreams he asked strange gods to give
To him one poem that would live.
Then clamor and confusion stirred
And charged at him like some wild herd
Until a kind voice said, "Absurd.
Those who love God as He loves them
May write a pure immortal gem."

He slept and dreamed again that night.
The angels smiled with sweet delight
When he awoke and wrote great things
To please all souls from babes to kings.
Now to the world this song he sings:
"Those who love God as He loves them
May write a pure immortal gem."

Virginia Noble

THE BEYMORLIN SONNET

Wauneta Hackleman

As the title of the Beymorlin Sonnet suggests, the form was given birth by three prize winning poets of the Alabama State Poetry Society.

The members of ASPS had met in the home of Carl Morton for a monthly meeting and workshop period. Following the meeting a few poets stayed, as poets do, to discuss poetry.

Morton, Richard Beyer and Marjorie Lees Linn sat around the dining room table and as Mr. Morton reveals, they were slacking their thirst with beer, and discussing poetry in general and traditional poetry in particular. It was their opinion that traditional poetry was suffering. Mr. Morton suggested that possibly, the writers of traditional poetry needed a challenge. The others agreed and decided they would attempt to do something about it. So on that night in the spring of 1977 the trio wrote the first Beymorlin sonnet, using elements from the two most loved forms, Shakepearean and Petrarchan. After Miss Linn's death it was decided the form should be a memorial to her. The title was taken from the first three letters of each poet's last name, *Bey*er, *Mor*ton, *Lin*n, thus *Beyermorlin*. Since then it has been accepted and included in the annual national contests of the National Federation of State Poetry Societies, Inc.

It is a challenging form. The rhyme scheme can be either Shakepearean or Petrarchan (Italian) in end rhyme. It must also rhyme within the first two syllables of the beginning of the lines, also with the same rhyme scheme as end lines.

Example:

THE POET CONVERSES WITH A MOUSE

> I *know* that I will have to move your cage
> To *some* room far beyond me for a time;
> Or *go* myself, and take with me my page

And *come* when I have finished with the rhyme.
For *you* must stretch and eat and run your wheel,
And *run* and run and finally stop to stare
From *two* red searching eyes. . .yet do not feel
Un*done* for never getting anywhere.
So, *kindly* I will leave you, quite unstirred;
Your *face* cannot look in upon my cell
Re*mind*ing me that searching for a word
Is *rac*ing too. . .and maybe not so well!
    Could *you* please stop looking up at me?
    I *do* not want some power to set me free.

                    Carlee Swann, Lebanon, South Dakota

The poet used the second syllable for her rhyme in her beginning lines.

GLORIONIC SONNET

Gloria Martin

The Glorionic Sonnet was born within a month of conception. Date of birth: Thursday, March 11, 1976. I brought it into the world, not because I felt motherly, but because a contest called for an original sonnet rhyme scheme. A challenge faced me. The seed was planted.

The Glorionic sonnet grew out of desire to compete with competitors. The rhyme scheme took shape first. The body followed. Selecting a name was the most painful part of the delivery. Being a single parent, that which I created would be named after me. Gloria Ann. Somehow. . . .

I considered Glorianic. That reminded me of an ocean, but sounded like a phobia. I paced the floor. I heated some milk, and drank it myself. My tastebuds rebelled. More from the thought than the taste. It was then that Clement Wood came to my rescue.

Through him, my helpmate in times of creative distress, I was led to the Index of sonnets in his 1940 edition of *Poets' Handbook*.   There, I became reacquainted with the Miltonic Sonnet.   That was it.   Glorionic.   Ann had always sounded foreign to me anyway!   It sounded good to someone else, but not me.   And not my child.   I blanketed my daughter and set her aside, safe, warm and christened.

I had a deadline to meet.

The contest that I earlier referred to was sponsored by the Iowa Poetry Day Association.   The rules read: "Special Contest: American Sonnet: Create an original Rhyme Scheme, 14 lines, 5 feet per line.   Content suitable to the sonnet form."

I complied.   The Glorionic Sonnet was born; in iambic pentameter.   And like all newborns, she was original!   I dressed her in a rhyme scheme of 1, 1, 2, 2, 2, 3, 3, 3, 4, 4, 5, 4, 5 ,5, though I find it more desirable to say A, A, B, B, B, C, C, C, D, D, E, D, E, E.   It sounds so much more feminine!

In getting to know her, it took me awhile to actually love her.   I found her difficult at times, not in her octave, but in her sestet.   The interrupted tercets gave me some sleepless nights.

I titled my first model "Break, Bubble, Break."   That Glorionic sonnet was my entry to the "American Sonnet" contest.   It was awarded Honorable Mention by poetry judge Daniel Smythe of Bradley University, Peoria, Illinois.

The poem was published in Iowa Poetry Day Association's Bicentennial 1976 *Brochure of Poems,* page 25:

BREAK, BUBBLE, BREAK

> I sometimes fear the frosty thought of death,
> The rattle of a throaty gurgling breath,
> The unknown foe that finite man must face
> Within the realm of mental time and space;
> The stalking shadow of a cold embrace
> That snuffs the candle of a mortal dream
> And strips the ripples from the flowing stream

Of earthly life. The bubble of a beam.
But what is death but birth beyond the veil—
A thousand throbbings of a nightingale
Who knows the tunes that angels sing at dawn!
There lies a world born of a fairy-tale
From which a breath of beauty can be drawn;
O give me death—that I might travel on.

Gloria A. Martin

The Glorionic sonnet has a rigid rhyme scheme. The rhyme-body is comprised of a couplet and two tercets, followed by what could be called terza rima lines, 9-14 (4, 4, 5, 4, 5, 5). The poem as a whole is a one-stanza pattern in five-foot iambs. A pause between the octave and the sestet is optional, rather than mandatory. Internal rhyme is also optional; to be employed only with expertise. Poetic devices, those tools of a poet's trade, should be exercised.

The first promotion of the Glorionic sonnet took place in 1977, through a contest that I sponsored and judged. The contest was publicized in *Parnassus*, Spring 1977, Monica Boyce, editor. The announcement was brief and direct: "GLORIONIC SONNET CONTEST: The Glorionic Sonnet is a new American sonnet poetry pattern, originated by Gloria Martin in 1976. Iambic pentameter lines. Rhyme scheme: 1, 1, 2, 2, 2, 3, 3, 3, 4, 4, 5, 4, 5, 5." Entry rules followed.

Thelma Murphy of Minneapolis, MN was the winner of that contest. Her entry was titled "The Silent Harp." Mary B. Finn of Iowa placed second, and Francine Burke of California third. The winning poems were published in the Fall 1977 *Parnassus*.

Thelma Murphy's "The Silent Harp" was a delicately crafted poem, despite an identity rhyme, lines 11, 13 (which she later corrected.) Her revised poem is herewith used as a sample of the Glorionic sonnet.

A second Glorionic sonnet contest followed in 1978; a national contest. I did not see the winning poems until three years later, when I ordered a copy of the Prize Poems anthology. To my distress, the judge of that contest had given a poem containing an incorrect rhyme scheme the first place award! My sonnet child learned early that life is a series of growth born of mistakes. Still, she continued to thrive.

A little older, a little wiser, and somewhat steadier on her feet, the Glorionic sonnet journeyed throughout the United States and Canada; well on her way to unlimited planes. Apron strings had been loosened and guidance given. Success was to depend upon those poets who knew her by name.

My Glorionic Sonnet is five years old. It is the sonneteers who must love her, nurture her, rear her as their own. And someday she will say, "Thank you, poets, for giving me your songs."

THE SILENT HARP

The strings within the perfect frame are still
And unheard songs of leaf and daffodil
Float up the frame to blend with each carved bloom.
The harp stands in the silent music room
Beside unfinished tapestry on loom.
The harp is strong of frame, the curves are grand
With silver chased to flaunt a wonderland;
The silent strings are waiting where they stand
And beauty is but second to the sound
In custody, from lay to hymn profound,
Like bluebell chimes, or secrets brooks reveal,
Like crash of waves, or leaves along the ground.
The tapestry, undone, makes its appeal:
Where are the hands that made the music real?

Thelma Murphy, *Parnassus*, Fall 1977

THE MASON SONNET

Jeanne Bonnette

The word 'sonnet' almost always brings to mind one of two forms: the Shakespearean or the Italian (Petrarchan). The truth is that the sonnet has lived through many abberations, changes, alterations worked on by poets of all ages, and yet the two above-mentioned are still the Gibraltars of the form.

A challenge has arisen, however, by a well known poet of New York: namely Madeline Mason, who has retained the iambic pentameter five-meter fourteen-line form. What she has done to fashion a form of her own is to change the rhyme scheme to *abc abc cbd badda*. It is a difficult pattern for most poets who have long been accustomed to the old rhyme schemes falling easily into place. The Mason Sonnet, a title to which recognition is now given, must be worked on with increased effort and skill, and fitting its message into this rhyme scheme sometimes reminds me of trying to get a foot into a shoe one size too small.

The sonnet was first invented, or formed, by Giacomo da Lentino in Palermo in the thirteenth century in Sicily, we are told. It went through many changes of rhyme scheme, especially in the sestet. It is likely that da Lentino adapted the sonnet from a Sicilian folk song which had four couplets, *ab ab ab ab* with a six-line sequel, *cde cde*. This pattern he later changed to *cd cd cd*. Dante, the first great poet to use the sonnet, wrote *Vita Nuova,* a sonnet sequence of the story of a tender love. There are twenty-nine sonnets, some not in perfect form, some in two parts (i.e., two sonnets designated, for instance, 3 a and b) translated by Dante Gabriel Rosetti.

Francesco Petrarca (Petrarch) wrote a sonnet sequence of seven poems entitled *Visions*, translated by Edmund Spenser. These are in strict Shakespearean form, surprisingly enough, excepting 7, which has this rhyme scheme: *abab bcbc cdcd ee*. However, he has many sonnets in the Italian form also, which upholds tradition, as we look back. Even Petrarch did some experimenting!

Milton's famous sonnet, *On His Blindness,* is, as every poet or poetry lover knows, in the Italian or Petrarchan form. Thus one poet learns from another, and our language styles become enriched. These few references are chosen from many poets and hundreds of sonnets.

Let me remind you of Spenser's *Amoretti,* a sequence of three sonnets in the following rhyme pattern: *abab bcbc cdcd ee.* Thus we see that countless poets have played with the form and tried their skills at the form. Many such efforts have died gloriously unsung (i.e.); Madeline Mason has managed to win out. I quote from her 'Notes on the Sonnet,' in a foreword of her collection entitled *Sonnets in a New Form* (Part 4):

> This new sonnet of mine was not worked out intellectually in advance. . . . After some hours and days had lengthened into weeks and months, greatly to my surprise, and entirely unpremeditated by me. . . . even undesired. . . . it became clear that what was in the making was a whole chain of sonnets, all in the same exceedingly strict and difficult form. There are fourteen lines of pentameter, predominantly iambic, as is normal; the difference lies in the rhyme arrangement: *abc abc cbd bad da.* That is the way I finally taught the pattern to myself, in sets of three, though it could be equally well divided into 2's, 4's, 5's or otherwise.

Two of Mason's books, *Sonnets in a New Form,* 1971, and *The Challengers,* 1975, prove that she has achieved a deserved and recognized state. She was awarded the $1,000 Prize in the International Who's Who of Poetry, 1974-75.

Among poets known for their excellent sonnets mentioned here are John Donne, Edward Arlington Robinson, Prudhomme, Goethe, Pasternak, Elizabeth Barrett Browning, Keats, Auden, Dylan Thomas, Wylie, Millay, and others. What they might have done with the Mason form provokes interesting thought.

A quote from the foreword of *The Challengers,* published by Kay, Sons & Daughter Ltd., written by Ernest Kay states:

> Madeline Mason invented the Mason Sonnet which has become accepted throughout the world as a new sonnet form and in

April 1956 the Library of Congress in Washington D. C. invited her to give a reading, under the auspices of the Gertrude Clarke Whittall Poetry and Literature Fund. She was the first American poet to give the Festival Address and read her own poems before the Scottish Association for the Speaking of Verse at the Edinburgh Festival in 1953. She was awarded the $1,000 First Prize by the International Who's Who in Poetry.

Madeline Mason's original manuscripts, page proofs and first editions are now a permanent part of the Harvard University Library Collections. Other libraries in the United States and in the United Kingdom house her books and recordings, including Yale, Columbia, Buffalo and the Library of Congress in the United States; and University College of the University of London and the Keats Memorial Library in England.

There is a paragraph in *Notes on the Sonnet* in Miss Mason's book, *Sonnets in a New Form,* which seems to me to apply to much of the young writing of today. I quote:

Then the inevitable happened, and hordes of imitators who lacked Petrarch's spirit copied the weaker elements of his art. . . . they reduced writing to an extravagant search for originality, for the violent metaphor, the juxtaposition of words of contradictory meaning in startling contrasts.

Manner became everything. This is what happens in every age of declining spiritual impulse. In sixteenth century Italy the over-emphasis on the intellectual to the neglect of the spiritual in the education of youth had its demoralizing effect. Among the poets there was a growing insistence on the colloquial and the ordinary, and a contempt for what had been noble in style, such as Petrarch's, to whom elevation of thought and the music of the verse had been all-important.

It seems that the preceeding quotation could teach a great deal to today's young poets. We know we must say the old things in new ways, but in doing so the aesthetic value, the music, the respect for tradition must not be sacrificed.

The following is an example of a Mason Sonnet:

A GOSSAMER WAS SPUN

> With young, untarnished hope we saw the years
> That would become tomorrow as a stream
> Flowing forever silver, and to no sea
> Of vast oblivion. The misted tears
> Were those of joy, and so we dreamed the dream
> That children have of heaven. Eternity
> Was not too long for youth, for there would be
> Such great abundancy that life would seem
> A shining path of time that once begun
> Would have no turning and no end. A scheme
> Devised by innocence. The darker fears
> That soon might dim the glory of our sun
> Were yet unknown. A gossamer was spun
> With thread that glows and fades. . . and disappears.

Helen Cheney Defenbaugh
Winner of Honorable Mention, Louisiana Poetry Society, 1980
Helena Defenbaugh, a resident of Albuquerque, has won many state and
national awards, and is widely published.

There are Mason Sonnets in my own notebooks which will
likely not change the world, but there is one which was deemed
worthy of a First Award from the Poetry Society of Virginia
in 1971 ($50) which I quote from my book, *Leaf Change*
(1979):

I AM THE ANCIENT ONE

> I am the Ancient One who has seen the birth
> of mountain, mesa, valley, butte and lake;
> have heard the shrill metallic scream of pain
> as out of heaven, out of hell and earth
> the lava spilled to scrape like a giant rake
> the ground where once green grass and weeds drank rain.
> Now like bones across the sunburned plain
> the hardened lava strewn by shuddering quake
> covers the slopes like playthings of a child
> who leaves his blocks all tumbled in his wake,
> and the arroyo, once a sparkling firth,
> cuts the valley floor with curving wild

convolutions rocks have reconciled,
dormant below Me at the mountains' girth

Jeannette Bonnette

BIBLIOGRAPHY

An Anthology of World Poetry, by Mark van Doren, 1928; "Notes on the Sonnet," foreword, by Madeline Mason, 1971; *The Challengers,* foreword by Ernest Kay, 1975; *Sonnets in a New Form,* foreword by Cornel Lengyl, 1971; *Strophes,* April 1977

PETRARCHAN SONNET

Guanetta Gordon

Sonnets have ever spoken deep emotions of the heart with a sort of magic that touches the secret soul.

Francesco Petrarch, Italian poet and scholar (1304-74) wrote some of the greatest love sonnets inspired by his passion for one named Laura. Critics claim that his sentiments came from the discord between the senses and the soul, the flesh and the spirit, the sensuality of love and a mystic acceptance of its spirituality.

The Petrarchan, or Italian Sonnet as it is sometimes called, like any sonnet is a fixed pattern of fourteen lines of iambic pentameter rhythm, that is , fourteen iambic five-foot lines. Rhythm is the flow of accented and unaccented syllables. An iambic foot is a short syllable followed by an accented syllable. (désire, ā mán, or a combination of two words where one sound triumphs over the other such as wīld geése.) Thus the rhythm of a sonnet is fourteen lines of: -/-/-/-/-/ with true accent on words and the end word in each line a rhyme word.

The Petrarchan Sonnet sets itself apart by its rhyme pattern: abba, abba, cde, cde. The sestet, or last six lines, may differ as: cd cd cd. The first eight lines of the sonnet are called the octave which consists of only two rhymes (4 "a rhymes" and 4 "b rhymes") thus the poet must strive to find fresh rhyming words to avoid triteness. It is not permitted to break or vary the octave pattern and rhyme scheme, and the sestet usually conforms to one of the two endings mentioned above.

The first quatrain should introduce the theme, the second quatrain is a development of theme. The sestet leaves room for contrast, contemplation, and conclusion. The conclusion often includes a sense of the mystic or visionary or philosophic element.

Most sonnets are lyric in that the poet speaks his own moods, thoughts, and aspirations in an intensely personal manner, relying on imagery and expressed through metaphors and similies. A good sonnet must always be an emotional response, a captured mood, not a mere intellectual recognition:

FIRST LOVE

The hour I first met you my world became
the poignant splendid thing I vowed to hold
against my heart for always, sharp and bold
in daring prophecy to fortune's claim.
You took my hand, a stranger's, spoke my name.
At first, your dark appraising eyes were cold
and then a swift caressing glance foretold
of love that took quick spark from hidden flame.

A bud considers not analysis,
or reasons why it reaches toward strange rays,
depends by faith on fragile mystic bond.
So like the gift of April's sun-warm kiss,
this understanding sweet response to praise
that binds our hearts through life and time beyond.

Guanetta Gordon
American Bard, Under the Rainbow Arch, Windfall Press

RED ARE THE EMBERS, To Lynell

The night we met, a new dimension cast	a
its spell like comet sparks that dropped on plain	b
of winter grass, to fire our dreams, attain	b
completion, knowing love would always last.	a
Then suddenly. . . our life was almost past	a
and we, as earth and sea in mystic rain,	b
as stars grown old, then dangle from the chain	b
of memory as cherished dreams held fast.	a
We traveled valleys where we could but feel	c
our way across the realm of faith, unwind	d
the vines of doubt on tangled paths that led	e
to peaks of destined fate, beneath a wheel	c
of burning stars that fused the heart and mind	d
so long ago. . .yet embers still are red.	e

Guanetta Gordon
Stella Crowder Miller Memorial (3rd) award
from *Red Are the Embers,* Golden Quill Press

SHAKESPEAREAN SONNET

Catharine N. Fieleke

Evaluation of Shakespeare's Sonnet 116

This famous and often quoted poem runs as follows:

Let me not to the marriage of true minds
Admit impediments. Love is not love
Which alters when it alteration finds,
Or bends with the remover to remove:
O, no! it is an ever fixed mark,
That looks on tempests and is never shaken;
It is the star to every wandering bark,
Whose worth's unknown, although his height be taken.

Love's not Time's fool, though rosy lips and cheeks
Within his bending sickle's compass come;
Love alters not with his brief hours and weeks,
But bears it out even to the edge of doom.
   If this be error, and upon me proved,
   I never writ, nor no man ever loved.

As this poem illustrates, the Shakespearean sonnet typically consists of three quatrains and a couplet in iambic pentameter, with alternate lines of the quatrains rhyming, and an additional rhyme introduced in the couplet; to-wit: abab, cdcd, efef, gg.

Slight variations of the form in meter or rhyme traditionally are allowed—for instance, beginning a line with a trochee and balancing that with an anapest; using an occasional imperfect rhyme such as "love. . .remove," or a feminine rhyme such as "shaken. . .taken"; treating "even" as if it were a one-syllable word; or employing a run-on line if needed to finish expressing a thought.

These are minor indulgences. In the making of a first-rate sonnet, craft and intellect must combine to present a complete, coherent statement within fourteen prescriptively rhymed tropes. The sonneteer needs to determine precisely what he wants to say; in addition he needs an uncanny knack for words that will rhyme, scan, and communicate—artistically!—within the limits of the form. Certain learned critics have opined that Shakepeare who had comparatively little formal education, many times should have pruned or refined his works. Yet it is said that in his sonnets he "went to confessional," and revealed himself as an individual. Considering the rigidity of the form, this seems a superlative tribute.

He opens sonnet 116 with a run-on line in which, with winning courtesy, he asserts his proposition: that *true love never changes.* In the body of the poem, he describes and discusses love as he conceives it to be. He closes with the flat statement that if anybody can be found who loves or has loved in this way, nobody has yet truly loved! The concluding couplet of a Shakespearean sonnet must be a summing up. Here, the author turns it into a challenge.

Like much of his other poetry, sonnet 116 has a profusion of imagery. In the first and last quatrains, Love is personified. In the middle quatrain, love becomes a star. Mercifully, the last two lines of the first quatrain manage to suggest a compass from which we pass rather easily to consideration of stars, specifically the reliable pole star. As we move through the second quatrain, the Star becomes personified, bridging to the last quatrain, in which the poet gives similar treatment to both Love and Time.

Some might object to this heaped imagery, and indeed, this is not technically so perfect a sonnet as, for instance, Robert Frost's, "The Tent," in which a single sentence is made to build a single perfect image, without digression from or interruption of the train of thought. But to me, Shakespeare's 116 seems unmistakably genius at work; and as compared to his dramas, possibly genius at play.

For the diction of the poem is on the whole rather simple. It is not a show-off poem. Poetic devices are organic, including *alliteration*-"marriage...minds...(impedi)ments"; *assonance*-"star.. wandering...bark"; *imperfect rhyme*-"come...doom...proved... loved"; and repetition within lines which is not true *internal rhyme* but suggests it-"alters...alteration, love...love." The *run-on's* in lines one, two, and nine break up the basic iambic pattern, as do the *caesuras* in lines two, five, eight, nine, thirteen, and fourteen. No boring sing-song here. Especially valuable in this respect are the exclamation, "O, no!" in line five, and the opening phrase of line nine, "Love's not Time's fool." The latter approaches the spondaic, requiring almost equal reading stress on all words. But by whatever means, throughout the poem Shakespeare seems concerned with one objective, a concise, exact description of romantic love as he sees it, and the wonderful part he feels it can play in human life.

In his day, as now, love was written about in many different ways: with more conceit and hyperbole, true, and less over-all frankness; yet, as now, presenting samples of light, lewd, mocking, or lustful approaches, along with the serious or exalted. It has been averred that Shakepeare's sonnets were mainly addressed to an aristocratic gentleman friend and/or patron, and that therefore the first line of 116 refers to Platonic friendship or even to homosexual attachment. To me, the mention of "rosy lips and cheeks" indicates that either the poet was dealing with man-woman love or at least included both aspects. The sphere of women in the Elizabethan age was very narrow. For the most part, men shared bed, board, and children, or bed and frivolities, with women; while cultivated men shared all other aspects of life with friends of the same sex. In such a milieu, relationships between men might have developed a depth and warmth not now prevalent; Platonic, but not sexual. Be this as it may, I construe sonnet 116 as presenting instruction and affirmation for heterosexual lovers, together with lasting inspiration for poets through the manner in which Shakespeare unites means with meaning within the limits of a challenging form.

Edna St. Vincent Millay (1892-1950), one of America's finest lyricists, handled the sonnet form with elegance and ease. We may not agree with all her sentiments, but we must admire the skill with which she expresses them:

ON HEARING A SYMPHONY OF BEETHOVEN

> Sweet sounds, oh, beautiful music, do not cease!
> Reject me not into the world again.
> With you alone is excellence and peace,
> Mankind made plausible, his purpose plain.
> Enchanted in your air benign and shrewd,
> With limbs a-sprawl and empty faces pale,
> The spiteful and the stingy and the rude
> Sleep like the scullions in the fairy-tale.
> This moment is the best the world can give:
> The tranquil blossom on the tortured stem.
> Reject me not, sweet sounds! oh, let me live,
> Till Doom espy my towers and scatter them,
> A city spell-bound under the aging sun,
> Music my rampart, and my only one.

Edna St. Vincent Millay

THE SONNET, PURE, SEVERE

When first I met the sonnet—pure, severe,
For discipline of poet's pulse designed—
It roused in me a feeling close to fear,
I looked for argument to hide behind.
What? Hobble Pegasus—him pull and plod,
Chasten him like a naughty child at school?
Never! His right—to life above the sod,
Free of invented, arbitrary rule!
Then, as it happened, Bach came by to teach
How, given eight small notes, he, shepherd, friend,
Found no good thing beyond his patient reach.
Allotted fourteen lines, I would amend,
Be tractable as he, as sea or star.
How limitless the mastered limits are!

Catharine N. Fieleke

TERZA RIMA

Ruth Van Ness Blair

Most poets, particularly contemporary ones, prefer a less restrictive form of poetry than the terza rima. Stanzas of three lines have never been popular with English writers, especially if the stanzas employ the terza rima pattern of interlinking rhymes, that is: a b a, b c b, c d c, d e d, etc. In other words, if the end words of the first three lines are love, sweet, dove; the first and third line of the next stanza must end with a word that rhymes with sweet. And at the end of the second line a new word must be introduced that rhymes with the first and third line of the third stanza. For example: love, sweet, dove; meet, dear, complete; here, life, fear. The most famous example of the terza rima form is Dante's *Divina Commedia* which is continuous, not divided in stanzas.

Almost six hundred years after Dante's masterpiece was written, Robert Browning, in his narrative poem, "The Statue and the Bust," employed the terza rima pattern. His poem is composed of eighty-three tercets and a final quatrain. Most of the stanzas are in exact rhyme. Take, for example, the opening two tercets:

> There's a palace in Florence the world knows well.
> And a statue watches it from the square.
> And this story of both do our townsmen tell.

> Ages ago, a lady there
> At the farthest window facing East,
> Asked, "Who rides with the royal air?"

In the eighty-two stanzas that follow I can find only fifteen pairs of rhymes that are not exact. Among these are eye-rhymes (words that rhyme eye to eye, but not the ear) such as love, alcove; south, youth; above, remove; lost, ghost; etc. Other approximate rhymes are bronze, once; sigh, infallibly; etc. Since Browning employed more end-stopped lines than contemporary poets, the reader is more conscious of the rhyme scheme of the poem.

I find the terza rima pattern fascinating as a good cross word puzzle or a double acrostic. I consider it an adventure in words. What a challenge it is to employ this highly restrictive form and develop a poem that flows so beautifully that one is not aware of its rhyme scheme.

My poem, "A Message From Dante," is a dramatic poem of fifteen lines divided into an eight line stanza and one of seven lines. This is a variation from the standard form. However, if one draws a line from a to a, b to b, c to c, etc., one can see the interlinking pattern of the terza rima—like the links of a chain:

For centuries my patient bones have lain	a
here in Ravenna. I who climbed from hell	b
to heaven, and endured the patriot's pain	a
of exile; I who knew Earth's sorrow well,	b
am but a skeleton who cannot rise and go	c
to Florence *paradiso*. None will tell	b
so sad a tale as mine. No man can know	c
my loss, my city, and my Beatrice.	d

But she has heard my cry, and bending low,   c
my dearest one has left a cobweb kiss   d
upon my fleshless brow. The gods relent   e
and we are one, my love and I, in this   d
eternal world. And though my bones were meant   e
to lie forever in Ravenna's soil,   f
I am at peace. My spirit is content.   e

In this poem, the rhymes are exact. But if it is read properly, one is not aware of rhyme because of enjambment (run-ons) where the end of the line does not coincide with a speech pause, but carries over into the next line to complete its meaning; and because of caesuras (pauses within the lines.)

Often a poet will write a long poem divided in several parts, using different poetry forms for each part. Muriel Rukeyser does this in her "Adventures, Midnight." Part II is terza rima:

With these two I went driving in the dark
out from our town in a borrowed car whose light
ate forests as we drove deeper into the park.

Beloved, spoke the sweet equivocal night—
those two stood clapped, each breast warmly on breast,
I stood apart to remove them from my sight:

The creased brook ran in continual unrest,
rising to seastorm in the rioting mind.
Here night and they and I—and who was merriest?

He turned his face away refusing, and so signed
for her to stop who too was comfortless
and equally needy, as tender and as blind.

On the road to the city stood the hedge whose darkness
had covered me months ago with that tall stranger
as foreign to me as this loneliness,

as enemy to me as tonight's anger
of grief in the country, shut with those two in the park:
this crying, frantic at removal, the dark, the sorrowful
    danger.

In the last tercet, danger and anger are not exact rhymes;
but stranger, from the verse preceeding, does rhyme with danger.

An example of a short poem containing different forms
of stanzas, but keeping for the most part the terza rima pattern,
is Edna St. Vincent Millay's "Dirge." The first two stanzas are
triplets, the third, a quatrain, and the last, a couplet composed of
the first and third lines of the first triplet:

> Boys and girls that hold her dear,
> Do your weeping now;
> All you loved of her lies here.
>
> Brought to earth the arrogant brow,
> And the withering tongue
> Chastened; do your weeping now.
>
> Sing whatever songs are sung,
> Wind whatever wreath,
> For a playmate perished young,
> For a spirit spent in death.
>
> Boys and girls that hold her dear,
> All you loved of her is here.

Babette Deutsch's part IV of "At the Green Grocer" is
an interesting example of terza rima in five tercets, ending in
a quatrain, almost in the manner of a villanelle. Although
she does not repeat the first and last lines of the first stanza
alternately as the last line of the following four stanzas, she
does repeat variations of its lines in the concluding quatrain:

> A large whitecheeked old woman smiling:
> The homely solidity, the beauty of
> The cauliflower is vulgar and beguiling.
>
> Cauliflower, branched broccoli above,
> And leafy sprouts below, all grown to please,
> What share have they in the quality of love?
>
> Nothing on earth is unromantic as these
> But turnip lumps. The cauliflower's white

Florets, broccoli's green, are coarse as frieze.

The kale is blowsy. New cabbage, curled tight
As an embryo, the red, purply as cheap stained glass,
Are commoners, too obvious to delight.

Yet even the festive, rare asparagus
Does not take the eye like the simplicity
Of this vegetable that its neighbors here surpass

In voluptuous curves, color, delicacy.
There is a quality better than beguiling
In the cauliflower's homely solidity,
Like a large, whitecheeked old woman smiling.

She uses an interesting mixture of feminine rhymes (smiling, beguiling) and masculine (these, frieze.) Also note the change from metaphor, first stanza; to simile, last stanza; from the cauliflower is a "..whitecheeked old woman smiling" to the cauliflower "Like a whitecheeked old woman, smiling." This poem abounds in caesuras and enjambments.

As an unusual example of rhyme in terza rima, I would like to include Sylvia Plath's "Man In Black":

Where the three magenta
Breakwaters take the shove
And suck of the grey sea

To the left, and the wave
Unfists against the dun
Barb-wired headland of

The Deer-Island prison
With its trim piggeries,
Hen huts and cattle green

To the right, and March ice
Glazes the rock pools yet,
Snuff-coloured sand cliffs rise

Over a great stone spit

Bared by each falling tide,
And you, across those white

Stones, strode out in your dead
Black coat, black shoes, and your
Black hair, till there you stood,

Fixed vortex on the far
Tip, riveting stones, air,
All of it together.

As you have perhaps observed by now, this poem is one long sentence. It has the terza rima form, but if you look for exact rhyme you will not find it. According to J. D. McClatchy in an essay included in the book *Sylvia Plath, New Views in Poetry*, "Man in Black" is written in slanted terza rima. Cleanth Brooks and Robert Penn Warren in their book *Understanding Poetry*, say that slant rhymes approximate rhymes. Ice-rise, prison-green, would be such rhymes.

Babette Deutsch, in her excellent *Poetry Handbook* says, "Near rhyme includes the more or less radical substitutes for full rhyme and its variants. These substitutes have also been called paraphones, approximate, embryonic, half, imperfect, and slant rhyme. Among the kinds of near rhyme now admired, is assonance, where the stressed vowels in the words agree, but the consonants do not." According to Deutsch, "Consonance is the pairing of words in which the final consonants of the stressed syllables agree but the vowels differ."

A terza rima may be formed of four three line stanzas with a couplet. This makes a fourteen line poem. If the content is appropriate, it is sometimes called a terza rima sonnet. The following poem for children, "If I Could Rub Aladdin's Lamp," is a fourteen line terza rima, but has neither the shape or the content of a traditional sonnet:

If I could rub Aladdin's lamp I'd say
(to whatever Genie popped out its spout),
"What do I wish? I wish a perfect day

for every child on earth. A day without

a drop of rain. A day when April trees
sprout baby leaves, and daffodils spread out

across the grass like sunshine. 'If you please,'
I'd ask the Genie, 'Will you kindly bring
some lemonade and cake and bread and cheese

for every child on earth?'" Then we would sing,
and eat our lunch in some delightful spot,
and celebrate a perfect day in spring.

A picnic for the world? Is that a lot
to ask a Genie for? Of course it's not.

There are many examples of enjambment in this little poem.

The best way to write a terza rima is to arrange its pattern at the end of your proposed lines before you begin to write, thus:

```
- - - - - - - - - - - - - - - - - - - - a
- - - - - - - - - - - - - - - - - - - - b
- - - - - - - - - - - - - - - - - - - - a

- - - - - - - - - - - - - - - - - - - - b
- - - - - - - - - - - - - - - - - - - - c
- - - - - - - - - - - - - - - - - - - - b          and so forth.
```

If the resulting poem seems mechanical, try enjambment. Search for the best word and the most colorful metaphor. Use an occasional near rhyme. In the end, you may find you have written a truly lovely terza rima.

BIBLIOGRAPHY

Blair, Ruth Van Ness. "A Message From Dante," to be published in *The Pen Woman*. 1st prize, dramatic poetry, Virginia State Poetry Society national contest, 1980.

Brook, Cleanth and Robert Penn Warren. *Understanding Poetry*. New York: Holt Rinehart and Winston, Inc., 1963.

Deutsch, Babette. Part IV, "At the Green Grocer's," *The Collected Poems of Babette Deutsch,* New York: Doubleday and Company, Inc., 1969. p. 139.

Deutsch, Babette. *Poetry Handbook.* New York: Funk and Wagnall's, 1957.

Jerome, Judson. *The Poet and the Poem.* Cincinnati: Writer's Digest Press, 1963.

Lane, Gary, ed. *Sylvia Plath, New Views in Poetry.* Baltimore: Johns Hopkins University Press, 1979.

Millay, Edna St. Vincent. "Dirge," *The Collected Poems of Edna St. Vincent Millay.* New York: Harper and Row Publishers, 1956, p. 121.

Miller, Arthur. *Creative Writing of Verse.* New York: American Book Company, 1932.

Rukeyser, Muriel. Part II, "Adventures, Midnight," *The Collected Poems of Muriel Rukeyser.* New York: McGraw Hill Book Co., 1978, p. 120.

Watt, Homer and William. *Handbook of English Literature.* New York: Barnes, Noble & Co., 1959.

Wood, Clement. *Poet't Handbook.* Cleveland: World Publishing Co., 1946.

THE TRIOLET

Marel Brown

Among the French forms the Triolet is one of the most popular, for English-speaking people. Not because the form is short, nor because it looks easy. The Triolet can be serious or humorous, subtle or explanatory. Frequently it is like the exclamation point saluting an extremely joyous moment of time.

Any lesson on the Triolet will tell you: A Triolet is written in eight short lines. The first line is repeated in the fourth line;

the first and second lines become the final two lines of the poem. The rhyme scheme—using only three rhyme words—is A B d A d B A B.

But that simple pattern does not suggest or explain how the Triolet can be a delightful and lyrical outpouring of enthusiasm or praise for a sudden sight or sound or taste or feeling that overwhelms the poet until it must be expressed—then explained—then expressed again. A Triolet is frequently a paean of praise.

A Triolet can be written in three-foot lines, or four-foot lines. What is being said determines the length. Line length is not the primary edging of the Triolet form. Its exclamation-point outpouring is its chief charm.

As an example—from inspiration to completed Triolet—my "Triolet For Spring" came this way: Early one spring morning my husband and I drove to our country acres, after a season of late winter rain. We got out of the car, and behold! Outspread before us on the meadow grass that led to our spring area was a carpet of bluets. Nearly two acres of bluets! It looked like a jillion of them had suddenly pushed back winter's blanket and were shouting to us: "Spring is here!"

We stood still, in meditation and wonder at such a beautiful promise. He soon went to get his tools for winter-clean-up work we planned to do. I got pad and pencil and wrote the beginning of what became, with some revision, the first two lines. I did not know I was going to "find" a poem that morning. Nor did I know, when I jotted down feelings, it would result in a Triolet.

But as I was raking leaves from my rock garden on the banks of the spring stream, and kept mulling over those exulting "feelings," they seemed to "say themselves" in the Triolet form. Years before I had learned how to write a Triolet, so former study presented the appropriate form. My study had prepared me to be ready when the Triolet seemed to say, "Use me."

This is how I used it. *Georgia Magazine* quickly bought it for next spring's issue:

TRIOLET FOR SPRING

> When bluets have captured the blue of the sky
> And carpet my field with a velvet sheen
> My mind awakes and hope leaps high.
> When bluets have captured the blue of the sky
> My heart responds with the ageless cry:
> "Spring is here!" Its Promise is seen
> For bluets have captured the blue of the sky
> And carpet my field with a velvet sheen.

Sometimes a Triolet can have a somber tone. "The Song of the Sea," in my *Hearth-Fire*, was written during World War II. No mention is made of any war, but word and metaphor let the reader know it has to do with a war, one late enough in time that a torpedo could be used.

By use of imagery and metaphor in the lines, "Listen to the song of the sea/in the curve of this beautiful shell," there is contrast of the joyful song to the sound of "torpedoes hissing hell." The reader knows that the poet is denouncing war, something deeply felt that could be enclosed in eight short lines:

THE SONG OF THE SEA

> Listen to the song of the sea
> In the curve of this beautiful shell.
> Always the children's plea:
> "Listen to the song of the sea."
> Now I fear that its theme will be
> Of torpedoes hissing hell
> If I listen to the song of the sea
> In the curve of this beautiful shell.

Don't try to write a Triolet if your poem involves a lengthy narrative thought about a serious subject. But if it is for some "gem of a moment's revelation," whether a joyous or a somber theme, the Triolet can serve you well.

THE TRIPLET AND THE TERCET

Margaret Honton

Following the rules for the couplet, triplet, tercet, or any other poetic form is rather like following architectural blueprints: the concepts and specifications are at hand, but much depends on the materials used, the skills of craft, and an artistic flair. Following the rules, however, often helps poets to (a) economize with words, making careful word choices according to root meanings; (b) tighten lines, relying on verbs and nouns for structural strength; (c) discover hidden resources in themselves and in the collective unconscious; (d) consider, and develop, meanings on multiple levels; and (e) embody emotions, using appeals to our five chief senses and to the sense of time, balance, humor, and so forth.

When writing triplets, observe the same precautions as when writing couplets. (See pages 38-48.) When writing tercets, you will undoubtedly have greater freedom of expression; enjoy it, and make the most of it.

The triplet—three successive lines with the same rhyme and usually the same rhythm—developed as a variation on the couplet, to extend the idea contained and/or to relieve the monotony of pattern.

Katherine Philips, speaking in the 17th century "Against Love," uses a 4-foot line (tetrameter) in the triplets and a 5-foot line (pentameter) in the couplets, in an alternating design.[1]

AGAINST LOVE

Hence Cupid! with your cheating toys,	4a
Your real griefs, and painted joys,	4a
Your pleasure which itself destroys.	4a
Lovers like men in fevers burn and rave,	5b
And only want what will injure them to crave.	5b
Men's weakness makes love so severe,	4c
They give him* power by their fear,	4c
And make the shackles which they wear.	4c

Who to another does his heart submit,	5d
Makes his own idol, and then worships it.	5d
Him whose heart is all his own,	4e
Peace and liberty does crown,	4e
He apprehends no killing frown.	4e
He feels no raptures which are joys diseased,	5f
And is not much transported, but still pleased.	5f

(*him-Cupid, romantic love)

The kind of love that Philips rails against is romantic, imitative, idolatrous (blindly worshipping), possessive of the loved one, injurious to the lover, and constraining to everyone. The aphorism in lines 9 and 10 remains true, centuries later.

Lady Mary Wortley Montagu, the 18th century poet, in her impassioned lament, "Saturday: The Small Pox," relieves her couplet pattern with occasional triplets, for example: despise/prize followed by bore/wore/more, and forsook/look by betrayed/delayed/played.[2] The poet's using verbs as end-rhymes gives power to Flavia's lament, as does Montagu's varying in 8 ways the refrain, "Beauty is fled, and spirit is no more!"

Of the 19th century "Battle Hymn of the Republic," the first two stanzas are familiar to most Americans.[3] Very few people, however, realize that its composer was the feminist Julia Ward Howe, an advocate of world peace, or that the message is an indictment of physical warfare, not a glorification of it. Each of the five stanzas is a triplet followed by the one-line refrain. Howe, writing about moral warfare, voices a warning against self-righteousness, noting that men "of a hundred circling camps" all claim that God is on their side, and that their enemies, therefore, are God's "contemners." For a fuller understanding of the last three stanzas, take note that the quotation is a paraphrase of an Old Testament prophecy in which Yahweh is the speaker, and that the "Hero born of woman" is not a military man but the promised Redeemer who inaugurated a New Testament of love:

I have read a fiery gospel, writ in burnished rows of steel:	8c
"As ye deal with my contemners, so with you my grace shall deal;	8c
Let the Hero, born of woman, crush the serpent with his heel,	8c

Since God is marching on."   refrain

He has sounded forth the trumpet that shall never call retreat;   8d
He is sifting out the hearts of men before his judgment seat.   8d
Oh! be swift, my soul, to answer Him! be jubilant, my feet!   8d
    Our God is marching on.   refrain

In the beauty of the lilies Christ was born across the sea,   8e
With a glory in his bosom that transfigures you and me;   8e
As he died to make men holy, let us die to make men free,   8e
    While God is marching on.   refrain

The 20th century poet Isabella Gardner, in a quiet, mournful lyric, "Cock-a-Doodle-Done," addresses one highly personal aspect of war.[4]   Her ten short lines, alternating triplets with couplets, are filled with verbal puns, religious and sexual allusions, vocabulary and poetic techniques that resonate through several centuries, and underscore the historical fact of almost continuous fighting among men and the still terrible, contemporary and universal problem of war:

COCK-A-DOODLE-DONE

How struts my love my cavalier   4a
How crows he like a chanticleer   4a
How softly I am spurred my dear;   4a
Our bed is feathered with desire   4b
And this yard safe from fox and fire.   4b
But spurless on the dunghill, dead,   4c
The soldier's blood is rooster red,   4c
His seed is spent and no hen fed,   4c
Alas no chick of this sweet cock   4d
Will speak for Christ at dawn o'clock.   4d

These two stanzas are before- and after-pictures of what war does to young lovers.   The first portrays the cocky, boastful soldier, whose gallantry intensifies sexual desire, and his sweetheart or wife, able to make love away from foxholes and shellfire.   The second portrays the soldier weaponless, dead, lying on a "dunghill" (the battlefield, a heap of corpses).   He and his sweetheart will never have a child; there is no regeneration, physically or spiritually, from his participation in war.

Elizabeth Bishop, using a more contemporary idiom in her poem, "Roosters," develops extensively and with startling juxtapositions the themes of "unwanted love, conceit, and war," of "raging heroism," of fidelity and forgiveness.[5] In a virtuoso performance of 44 triplets, Bishop varies the line-lengths (her pattern generally is a 2-foot, 3-foot, and 4-foot line in each triplet) and uses an abundance of unexpected rhymes and off-rhymes, as exemplified by Peter's/flares/officers and preamble/marble/inaudible.

Not all poems in triplets contain such weighty thoughts, or embody such strong feelings, as the preceding three, but the form does lend itself to their expression.

The tercet, a freer stanza form than the triplet, does not require three successive end-rhymes or the same length and rhythm in each line. *The first line of the tercet can be unrhymed, producing an* x a a *pattern.* Josephine Miles, in "Purchase of a Blue, Green, or Orange Ode," using colloquial speech and an x-line at the beginning of each tercet, creates a free-flowing poem suggestive of free verse.[6] The speaker, saying that Jake's store displays odes in dusty glass, gradually reveals the metaphor: sticky candy, suckers, and jawbreakers are like odes—sweet with memories of less complicated times when pleasures were simple. Here are the concluding lines:

A suck of human victory out of a crowd,	5d
Sugared, colored, out of a jar, an ode.	5d

If the good old days were not all that wonderful, nostalgia will have them so.

The same poet, Josephine Miles, in her poem "Desert," demonstrates how *the first lines of all the tercets can rhyme with each other.*[7] The pattern that evolves is: a b b, a c c, a d d.

The tercet is adaptable to any theme or subject, and to a variety of tones. In grouping examples from my writing, I have chosen lines from love poems. Herein, *an unrhymed line can occur in the middle of the tercet:*

What makes me sit in judgment and condemn   5a
myself, consuming graham crackers and milk   5x
at the kitchen counter at 3a.m.?   4a

from "Battling the Dawn of a Personal Doomsday"[8]

or at the end of the tercet:

There's nothing up my sleeve   3a
when I offer love.   3a
Join me in magic-making.   3x

      ***

With a flourishing of words—   3e
abracadabra! songbirds!   3e
Hear the mating call.   3x

from "Legerdemain"[9]

The interior line of a tercet may have a delayed rhyme in the next tercet:

Let chickadees' dotted shadows   4a
be musical notations   3b
jotted on the staff-lined snow.   4a

Let the canary indoors sing   4c
with incremental repetitions: 4b
love, lover, loving.   3c

from "Fifth Anniversary Song"[10]

This pattern when developed at length becomes the terza rima. (See pages 191-198.)

The final line in one tercet may be rhymed in the final line of the following tercet, as in the next poem which was suggested by the list of ingredients on a box of herbal tea:[11]

ZINGER

I savor your lips	2a
like a tea of rose hips	2a
or syrup grenadine,	3b
stripped lemon grass	2c
or sassafras,	2c
or tingling wintergreen.	3b
I sniff flesh revealed	3d
like orange peel	2d
or bark of wild cherry,	3e
so pour your citrus	2f
like hibiscus—	2f
you're my cup of tea.	3e

Moreover, *all three end-words of one tercet may be rhymed in the next,* as in these stanzas:

Like the prince and fox we meet,	3h
with your approach at an appointed time,	4i
to explore poetry	3j
—words, life—abstract, concrete.	4h
Each step, like music, calls to a springtime	4i
of reciprocity.	3j
The eager fox could say	3k
that joy was in the anticipation	4l
of new discovery.	3m
Is it all that way	3k
for you? Is there some exhilaration,	4l
my prince, in taming me?	3m

from "Fox to Prince"[12]

I hope you discover form and feeling in this falling-out-of-love poem:[13]

CLASSIFIED: LOST & FOUND

Something's still missing. I'm unable to trace
the clues, though Holmes would probably say,
"My dear, it's elementary. . ."

I'm vermicelli instead of straight lace.
Paisanos would counsel me, "Just pray
to good Saint Anthony."

Mother says, "Calm down, and think.
Why all this fuss? You aren't hard up.
There are other men you needn't forego."

Dad shrugs as if love were a lost cufflink,
"Down cellar behind the axe in a teacup."
How could he possibly know?

There my heart is—pending doom,
cowering, hiding from attacks,
hoping not to cause a scandal.

The cellar is a pitched-night room.
I'm as afraid of the teacup as of the axe
flying off its handle.

FOOTNOTES

[1] Ann Stanford, *The Women Poets in English* (New York: A Herder and Herder Book, McGraw Hill Book Company, 1972), pp. 82-84.

[2] Katherine Philips, *Philips' Poems* (London: Printed by J. M. for *H. Herringman* at the Sign of the *Blew Anchor* in the Lower Walk of the New Exchange, 1667), p. 143.

[3] *In Patriotic Heart Songs* (New York: Grosset and Dunlap, by arrangement with Chapel Publishing Company), p. 6.

[4] Isabella Gardner, *That Was Then* (Brockport, New York, 14420, Boa Publishers, 1980), earlier publishes under the title "Cock-a-Hoop" in *West of Childhood: Poems 1950-1965* (Boston: Houghton Mifflin, 1965), by permission of Isabella Gardner.

[5] Elizabeth Bishop, *The Complete Poems of Elizabeth Bishop* (New York: Straus & Giroux, 1970), pp. 39-45.

[6] Josephine Miles, Poems *1930-1960* (Bloomington: Indiana Univer-

sity Press, 1960), p. 44.

[7]Josephine Miles, p. 15.

[8]Margaret Honton, *Take Fire* (New Wilmington, PA, 16142, Dawn Valley Press, 1980), p. 31.

[9]Margaret Honton, in *Driftwood East,* Winter 1978.

[10]Margaret Honton, *Take Fire,* p. 19.

[11]Margaret Honton, *Above Making Waves* (Columbus, Ohio, Woodwinds Impress, 1978, available from author), p. 6.

[12]Margaret Honton, *Above Making Waves,* pp. 24-25.

[13]Margaret Honton, *Take Fire,* p. 11.

TUANORTSA

Guanetta Gordon

In 1966 World Poetry Day Contest sponsored a new form of poetry, originated by Penn Laurel Poets. A Tuanortsa (spell it backward and you get astronaut) must be readable both upward and downward, with the title at the top and bottom, which may, but need not be, exactly alike, but both of which are read as part of the poem. It may be rhymed or unrhymed, 24 lines or less.

Once the subject matter is chosen and the thought development completed, begin by working three lines that will read downward and upward, then line by line, continue until the poem is completed. The Poet is free to choose his own rhythm pattern and to create his own poetic mood.

A tuanortsa is a challenge and flexes the brain cells to apply our technique, remembering that after we have mastered a technique that learning and creativity really begin.

SOMEONE SOMEWHERE

> can you feel my longing, my need to touch
> the treasured things of life which man calls freedom,
> just walking the streets with my own people, to hold
> my beloved in my arms at night, while I consider
> tomorrow's mundane routine with heart-weary numbness,
> the advance through the jungle, and death always bartering
> this giving of my all, though valued so little
> by all the world. Can you grasp the despair,
> hungering for home and feeling forgotten
> with other captives of war, through endless days,
> existing behind a barbed wire prison camp,
> praying through blackest night. . .remember me,
> > Someone, Somewhere

> > > Guanetta Gordon, The Sandcutters, Poet International
> > > *Shadow Within the Flame,* Golden Quill Press

ONCE HERALDED, NOW UNWANTED

> three years of torture when hope despaired
> in an oriental land of slant eyed gods,
> where war, blood, and putrid marsh blend
> strong hot winds of destiny. . .
> then freedom. . . whose outstretched arms embraced
> tomorrow, when metal wings lifted
> across the ocean where I dreamed
> heartbreak and loneliness lay in the past
> once again a hero before a microphone. . .
> words briefly said unmasking hunger. . .
> yet never conveying what I really meant,
> of wanting to pick up the pieces of value
> to let each day reveal itself
> as a page of life flipped over by winds
> against fortune. Today strolling along with my love,
> my wife who waited out years of emptiness. . .
> now I walk the streets, remembering
> that accolades are over; there's bitterness,
> a brine fills my mouth as employers say

> we are out of touch, veterans not needed,
>> Once Heralded, Now unwanted.

Guanetta Gordon, Poet International
Red Are the Embers, Golden Quill Press

TODAY, SOMEWHERE

> A butterfly is leaving
> the cocoon.
> A bud defies the frost,
> fresh petals bloom.
> The sun is warming
> a chilled and darkened earth
> New, ancient songs are sung,
> the joy of birth.
> The treasures of
> a touch, a smile, a friend
> with love to share,
> a gift we can all send
> Today, Somewhere.

LaNita Moses, West Palm Beach, Florida
The poet's first poem on this form

VILLANELLE

Emma S. McLaughlin

"Oh I could never write a poem using a French Form. They are all too difficult, with too many repetitive lines." This is the response I often get when French Forms are mentioned in poetry workshops. Yet I find it fascinating and very challenging to spend time experimenting with such forms, and I am often pleasantly surprised with the results. One of my favorite forms for this experimentation is the Villanelle.

Poets, for centuries, have always sung as their fancy pleased them, with rhythm and rhyme, using whatever form seemed the most appropriate, the most suited to the emotion they wished to convey. For this reason we find the Villanelle in many of our anthologies of poetry, and written by some of our most famous poets.

In its early form the Villanelle, for four centuries, was a kind of shepherd's song, used for pastoral subjects, or to convey light and fanciful thoughts. Still there have been several excellent examples of serious content or religious significance. "The House on the Hill," by Edwin Arlington Robinson, and "The Waking," by Theodore Roethke fall in this category.

Though at first glance this form might appear simplistic, we find the simplicity to be very artificial. The most generally accepted form of the Villanelle uses the following rhyme scheme, (aba, aba, aba, aba, aba, abaa). There are five stanzas of three lines each, and a final stanza of four lines. Only the two rhyme sounds are permitted throughout. The first and third lines in the first stanza are the refrain lines. Line one appears at the end of the second and fourth stanzas and as the third line in the sixth stanza; line three reappears at the end of the third, fifth and sixth stanzas. Meter and line length varies, from anapestic trimeter to iambic pentameter, determined by the poet and the theme of the poem. Refrain lines should remain exact. Modern poets have, at times, made slight variations to suit their purpose. Roethke, in "The Waking," changes the third line of the first stanza slightly when it reappears in the third and fifth stanzas, returning to the original lines when it reappears in the last stanza.

If you aspire to the writing of good free verse, you should first have the discipline of form and structure. As one does not give a piano concert without first having learned and practiced the basic scales, so also poets should become familiar with all manner of poetic forms. Time spent in the practice of French Forms is never wasted. You will be delighted with the results of such efforts.

(Parts of the above are from a revised editions of the *New Rhyming Dictionary and Poets' Handbook,* Burges Johnson, Litt., D., and *The Forms of Poetry,* Louis Untermeyer.)

Example poems:

AT THE BALLET

a   How gracefully they move upon the stage,
b   Like sunset clouds adrift on cosmic seas.
a   My mind does arabesques, decrying age.

a   I need not have the wisdom of a sage
b   To be aware of my arthritic knees;
a   My mind does arabesques, decrying age.

a   She leaps, he catches her and they engage
b   Their bodies like two slender twining trees.
a   How gracefully they move upon the stage.

a   I seethe inside with an unholy rage,
b   For once I danced like floss upon the breeze.
a   My mind does arabesques, decrying age.

a   Time holds me in an unrelenting cage;
b   Beyond the bars youth taunts with memories.
a   How gracefully they move upon the stage;
a   My mind does arabesques, decrying age.

                                        Emma S. McLaughlin

REMEMBERING MY APPLE UNCLE

          My apple uncle spoke soft, spoke low—
          Kept bees in the orchard where his apple grew;
          He tapped a tambourine on his knee, just so!

          His fat second wife had a face like dough
          And the querulous voice of a natural shrew;
          My apple uncle spoke soft, spoke low.

          He farmed in season, but his tempo was slow,
          So his wife complained and his girls made do;
          He tapped a tambourine on his knee, just so!

          On Sunday he shaved and prepared to go

In his dark serge suit to the family pew;
My apple uncle spoke soft, spoke low.

His friends were loyal, and he had no foe;
When my step-aunt died, he wed Alma Drew;
He tapped his tambourine on his knee, just so!

Memory reclaims odd things, we know—
And of all his doings I recall but few;
My apple uncle spoke soft, spoke low;
He tapped a tambourine on his knee, just so!

Katharine Larsen, Fair Oaks, California
from prize winning 1976 NFSPS Anthology

RIVER OF KNOWLEDGE

"Scoop only from the surface dear," she said;
She loathed the dark, decaying things below,
I was not one who could be strictly led.

Bright solar pigment stained the water red;
I squinted eyes to probe the ruddy flow.
"Scoop only from the surface, dear," she said.

Without a sense of wonder, man is dead;
Why yoke a life to one so staid and slow?
I was not one who could be strictly led.

I had to touch the river's pebbled bed,
Explore as far as childhood dared to go;
"Scoop only from the surface, dear," she said.

My eager hand plunged down. Her warning fled.
She would have stifled all desire to grow;
I was not one who could be easily led.

In cupped hands dripping light a new world spread.
She never dared the deeps to find it so.
"Scoop only from the top, dear," she said;
I was not one who could be strictly led.

Emma S. McLaughlin

SYLLABIC FORMS

THE ANNA

Anna Nash Yarbrough

The creator of the Anna form is James R. Gray of California. The Anna is a syllable pattern with seven lines. Syllable count is 4, 6, 8, 10, 8, 6, 4. The meter is iambic. The theme is love. This form was introduced to honor Anna Nash Yarbrough of Arkansas. The sample poem is by the creator, James R. Gray:

HOMECOMING

> The sun has set,
> Pale twilight fills the air
> Like woodsmoke from a supper fire,
> And lampglow beckons through the window panes,
> As I draw near my cabin door
> Where someone waits for me
> With open arms.

Published in *Benton Courier*, Benton, Arkansas

CAMEO

Anna Nash Yarbrough

The creator of the Cameo is Alice Maud Spokes of Arkansas. The Cameo is a one-sentence, seven-line poem with syllable count 2, 5, 8, 3, 8, 7, 2. Lines are unrhymed, and each line should end with a strong word. The Cameo presents a picture:

BALLET OF SHADOWS

> Moonlight;
> mysterious winds
> and maple trees collaborate creating
> scandalous interpretations
> of nude leaves gliding across
> my bed.

Verna Lee Hinegardner

CINQUETIN

Anna Nash Yarbrough

The Cinquetin form was introduced by E. Ernest Murrell in the mid-twentieth century. It is a syllabic form using forty syllables with syllable count of 8, 6, 10, 6, 8, 2. The rhyme scheme differs from most short poems. Line one rhymes with line four, and line three with line six. Lines two and five are unrhymed:

NIGHT IN FAIRYLAND
(view of New York from a helicopter)

> Giant blue and white bird lifts its
> Eager revolving wings
> Into the magic panoramic glow
> Of the city, and flits
> Over Lilliputian playground
> Below.

Viola Jacobson Berg, from *Pathways for the Poet*

CINQUO

Anna Nash Yarbrough

The Cinquo is a half-cinquain. Unrhymed. Syllable count is 1-2-3-4-1. Author is unknown. Example:

ALONG THE HIGHWAY

> Dry
> Sedge-grass,
> Like ghosts, dance
> In the wintry
> Wind.

Ann Nash Yarbrough

THE DIAMANTE

Cecilia Parsons Miller

This small syllabic form is used as an exercise in the lower elementary schools to teach the parts of speech. The spelling was checked in *Etymology of the English Language* and stems from the word "adamant" hence a diamond is of inpenetrable hardness as imagined by some. (*Webster Dictionary*, 1921.)

The Diamante is described in *Elementary English*, (46 May 1969, page 588) as a seven-line poem arranged in the shape of a diamond; the end word is a noun and is the opposite of the subject (love-hate-peace-war, friend-enemy, prison-cathedral.)

Noun

Two adjectives

Three participles -ing, -ed

Four words (noun related to the subject)

Three participles

Two adjectives

Noun

Example poem:

Peace

Sweet calm

Smiling, laughing, loved

Dream   of   the   world

Frowning, crying, hated

Bitter violent

War

Forms initiated by someone other than the poet require encapsulated feelings, precise language and a unified arrangement of the parts. One factor is different—the molds have already been made. With knowledge and practice, children may have new ways to convey their feelings, experiences and ideas.

"Knowledge of the economy of words is not only basic for all kinds of writing but may help a child save and use his substance more wisely. . .Artfully controlling emotions. . . the challenge. . .the poet's joy in a well-fashioned product." *Poetic Composition,* Robert A. Wolsch, pages 156-158.

My friend Inge Moser, fourth grade teacher in Centre County, introduced me to this form some six years ago. She guided me to the material sources I found in Pattee Library, Pennsylvania State University.

In the various examples given, syllable count is observed only in the first and last lines.

The restriction given above regarding love-hate, the use of the opposed two nouns, seems to be disregarded. The example I first saw used adverbs in lines two and six instead of adjectives. In line four three nouns were used, spaced so as to lengthen the line to the extent needed to shape a diamond. Since the textbooks do not agree, one is tempted to conclude that there is a wide variation in handling the diamante, or that teachers feel free to make substitutions that fit a particular classroom.

It is plain that the form does not lend itself easily to a true poem, but the challenge is there, not only for elementary pupils, but adult writers as well.

The interest shown in this project by Carol A. Roberts, well-known Pennsylvania poet and a Harrisburg area first grade teacher, has prompted me to come up with my third original example in syllable count form. The third line is of course a sly reference to other forms of poetry treated in this text-book. Example:

STIR
Softly, subtly
Misting, burgeoning, greening
Garden   fragrance   dogwood
Glowing, glistening, growing
Hesitantly, headily
Spring

WATCH
Steadily methodically
Ticking moving swinging
Work   recreating   sleep
Assuring befriending counting
Faithfully musically
Time

In the next example, syllable count has been observed, matching the number of words in the lines:

DIAMANTE FOR CAROL ROBERTS
Words
Chosen measured

Studying scavening researching
Villanelle   clerihew   sestina
Deciding selecting whittling
Polished joyful
Song

Cecilia Parsons Miller

BIBLIOGRAPHY

Webster's Dictionary, 1921; *Elementary English,* May 1969, p. 588; *Poetic Composition,* Robert A. Wolsch, Teachers College Press, Columbia University, 1970, pp. 156-158.

ERCIL

Anna Nash Yarbrough

The creator of this form is James Gray.   He honors an outstanding poet of Arkansas, Ercil Brown   The syllable count is 4, 6, 8, 10, 4, 6, 8, 10, 6, 6. The form has ten iambic lines with rhyme scheme of A, B, A, B, C, D, C, D, E, E. Example:
THE LITTLE HOUSE NEXT DOOR

You'd think they planned
To live there more than just
A part of spring. With airs so grand
They even scrutinized the roof, and fussed
In early dawn
About the tiny door,
Then ate a picnic on the lawn
While synchronizing songs I'd heard before.
They caught me spying too;
And whoosh, away they flew.

Verna Lee Hinegardner, Hot Springs, Arkansas

ETHEREE

Jaye Giammarino

The Etheree is a form poem originated by Mrs. Etheree

Armstrong, poet of Malvern, Alabama. Believing "That in the heart of every heart, a candle of yearning burns to create something immortal before his or her time to rest," and feeling the need for a pattern of poetry that would embrace both Form and Free Verse, she was inspired to create the Etheree.

The Etheree is a poem of ten lines, unrhymed, and of a serious nature. The form is not written in meter, but in syllable count. (fifty five syllables) The syllable count for each line must correspond to the number of that line.

> Line 1—contains a one syllable word.
> Line 2—contains a total of two syllables.
> Line 3—contains three syllables, etc.

with each line progressing one syllable until a 10 line poem has been created, the 10th line containing 10 syllables. The rules are strict and there can be no deviations.

The Etheree is not as simple to write as it may seem. As when writing any form of poetry, the poet must be conscious to some degree, of all the principles of poetry, of inspiration, intuition and imagination, otherwise only technique remains, and the form only a shell. A shell can never be poetry.

The poem must have meaning to carry the undertone of second meaning, and be very rich in imagery, painting a picture with words or feelings. The challenge comes in the selection of the exact word to express the idea, and also to contain the correct number of syllables for the line.

In 1967, Etheree Armstrong gave the pattern her name and introduced it to the Armed Forces Writers League Inc. Within three short months it was widely accepted by Writers, Editors, and Publishers over six continents. This ready acceptance, never dreamed of by the author, has made the form popular among poets willing to be challenged, and to write in forms different from those written by the majority of poets. The pattern is included in many poetry workshops, and appears frequently among the categories in poetry competitions. Examples of Etheree by Etheree Armstrong:

> THE PRICE TAG OF PERMANENCE
> At
> ninety

he plants a
tree and smiles, for
a small boy needs a
tree-house, better termed a
Fort, where independence is
a personal tool-constructing
character! Conceived in Liberty
where justice is a part within the Whole.
The
neighbors
shake their heads
knowing he will
not be around when
the tree matures, but just
a short time ago, in his
childhood 'Fort' came the reasoning
that all must build! The young and the old,
to preserve, and promote our Heritage.

This Etheree is written in a sequence of two; was the first written
and first introduced.

SUSAN
    She
    walks cloud
    high in love,
    shawled in Rainbows;
    her star. . . third finger
    left hand. And I, wiser,
    cannot tell her that Stars fall;
    that Rainbows ascend to Heaven
    and powder-puff clouds turn black with storm.
    I know too. . .the strength of a Band of Gold.

TOLERANCE
    We
    were not
    given the
    understanding
    of other people,
    neighbor, sister or son—
    for how could this be so, when
    we cannot plumb the fathoms of

our own Souls? The key is acceptance
for what we are, or aspire to become.

Examples by Jaye Giammarino:
SEEDS OF LOVE
Man
has a
natural
affinity
for his fellow-man;
and when he can root out
his prejudice like a weed,
and plant the seeds of Brotherhood;
then like the flower that growing splits
the rock, hatred can blossom into love.

from *Poetidings,* January 1972

AUTUMN LONELINESS
When
falling
autumn leaves
cover the path
with carpet of brown
and roses too are gone,
then like the bird nest, my heart
is empty too, for in the woods
the melancholy silence grows deep;
but loud as winter wind, are thoughts of you.

2nd prize, Arkansas Poets Roundtable 1979 contest

THE FANTASY

Cecilia Parsons Miller

The Fantasy is a syllabic form of poetry having ninety two syllables and three stanzas.
Stanza one-seven lines; rhyme scheme abccaba
Stanza two-six lines; rhyme scheme deffed
Stanza three-seven lines; rhyme scheme gghhiii

Each line has four syllables, except the third line in each

stanza which has eight syllables. Stanzas one and two follow a fixed indented pattern (see example poem); the third stanza keeps to the left margin of the first line of the poem.

The fantasy bears a marked relationship to the French forms. It lends itself to humor and/or satire. Subject matter may range from the romantic to diatribe; even to the extent of borderline ribaldry.

The creator of the fantasy form is Irene Gramling of Miami, Florida. She is a widely published poet and active in numerous poetry societies in America. She originated the form in the 1960s.

Example:
HEAVEN AND EARTH
My dreams of love
   are exquisite
      although you're snoozing unaware
      slouched in your chair.
   Bright stars above
   are requisite
for dreams of love.

I dream champagne
   and evening dress
      but there you sit with open shirt
      your form inert.
   Oh, well, I guess
it looks like rain.

My dreams were sweet
A gay conceit;
Like bubbles popping in a glass
They too will pass.
I'll take instead
Fond words unsaid
And so to bed.

Jessie Ruhl Miller, Carlisle, Pennsylvania
from Maybe It's Upside Down

GRAYETTE

Anna Nash Yarbrough

The creator of this form is James R. Gray of Commerce, California. It is iambic and varies in line length which results in a good patterned poem. Lines in feet are: 1, 2, 4, 4, 2, 1, 1, 2, 4, 4, 2, 1. Syllabic in form, it has a syllable count of 2, 4, 8, 8, 4, 2, 2, 4, 8, 8, 4, 2. The rhyme scheme is varied in that lines 1, 5, 7, and 11 do not rhyme. Line 2 rhymes with line 4; line 3 with line 6; line 8 with line 10 and line 9 with line 12. The sample poem is by the creator of the Grayette form:

BLACKBIRD

> I claim
> him as a friend
> and like to think we share a bond.
> He comes each year with summer's end
> to visit at
> my pond.
> He brings
> his family,
> and scores of other feathered kin
> to brighten lazy hours for me
> as fall's crisp days
> begin.

James R. Gray, published in *Latchstrings*, Little Rock, Arkansas

HEXADUAD

Anna Nash Yarbrough

The Hexaduad was introduced by Gee Kaye. It has twelve lines with sixty syllables. The syllable count is 2, 6, 8, 4, 6, 4, 4, 6, 4, 8, 6, 2. The syllable count of the last six lines is the reverse of the first six lines. The first two lines are transposed for the last two lines creating an interesting conversion effect and bringing the thought of the poem full circle. It is rhymed in couplets.

The example poem is so craftily written that it can be read from top to bottom and from bottom to top. This technique is not required but the sample poem is a challenge to the writer of this form. Example:

TO WRITE A BOOK

> To write
> A book is a delight,
> To bless the ones who share the word
> That he has heard,
> The songs he wants to sing,
> That he might bring
> The essence of
> His heart, his soul, his love,
> And make it real
> To those who laugh, and cry, and feel.
> A book is a delight
> To write.

Viola Jacobson Berg
from *Pathways for the Poet*, published by Mott Media

KERF

Anna Nash Yarbrough

Pattern, syllabic line count is 6-7-10-6-7-10-6-7-10-6-7-10. Total number of syllables, ninety two. The rhyme scheme is a, b, c, a, b, c, d, e, f, d, e, f. Example by Anna Nash Yarbrough:

LAKE COTTAGE

> It is a place for rhyme
> With love of life without care
> With rooms for spoken grief and rooms for joy.
> All guests choose their own time
> The old and the young are there,
> The happy father with look-alike son.
> Beauty is always seen
> Across the flower-decked yard
> To where a tall rockwall holds back the lake,
> For me, when grass is green,
> I go as a harassed bard
> And I court the muse for pure pleasure's sake.

KYRIELLE

Anna Nash Yarbrough

All lines have eight syllables. Rhyme pattern, a, a, b, B, c, c, b, B, d, d, b, B. Capitals show refrains (repeated lines):

THE LADY IN THE OLD, OLD HOUSE
> The neighbor's kids called her a witch
> Because her voice had a high pitch.
> Often her hair was not quite neat,
> But homeless cats thought she was sweet.
> She was a woman, all alone,
> A little bit of skin and bone,
> She had a meager bit to eat,
> The homeless cats thought she was sweet.
> No neighbors wept while she lay dead,
> "A good riddance," most of them said,
> But cats sought her on saddened feet,
> The homeless cats thought she was sweet.

Anna Nash Yarbrough

LANTERNE

Gloria Martin

The late poet Lloyd Frank Merrell (1887-1971), of Michigan, originated the Lanterne poetry pattern in 1936. He defined the lanterne as "a medium of expression for a mood."

Encouraged by poet friends Lucia Trent, Ralph Cheyney and Clement Wood, Rev. LLoyd F. Merrell tirelessly worked on his as-then-unnamed poetry form. "This is only the voice of one crying in the wilderness of American art; for I feel that our young country is still in the youthful stage of song," he stated on March 27, 1937, in a letter to Ralph and Lucia Cheyney.

Earlier, Rev. Merrell experimented with various names for the form he invented. His first models lacked the lantern typography; at that time he coined the word "Cinquo." The shaped whimsey design took root approximately six months following the form's creation. "It looks like a plant that is growing. It looks like an evergreen tree," he commented in a letter dated July 21, 1936, to personal friends.

In a further attempt to name his creation, Rev. Merrell sponsored a contest. From the entries received, he selected the name Lantern. The typography, fashioned by centering each line, indeed looked like a Japanese lantern. But, preferring the French spelling of the word, he added an "e" and christened the form "Lanterne."

Horizons, the official organ of the Western Poetry League, with Lucia Trent and Ralph Cheyney, Editors, first publicized the Lanterne. The Summer 1937 issue contained Lloyd Frank Merrell's poem "Heart's Autumn": "Winds of love are swirling memory's pale leaves." It was followed by many more. Clement Wood was to later include the Lanterne poetry pattern in his 1940 textbook, *Poets' Handbook,* under the section "Poem Patterns." Here he states, "Lanterne, invented by Lloyd Frank Merrell, syllable count 1, 2, 3, 4, 1, arranged in form like a Japanese lantern: a shaped whimsey."

On the next page, however, we find a conflict, for under "Forms Invented by James Neill Northe," we find this listing: "Cinquo, 1, 2, 3, 4, 1, without Lanterne typography." In my correspondence with the Merrell's, while Lloyd Frank Merrell was still alive, I was informed that Rev. Merrell coined the word Cinquo. Interesting enough, in Margarette Ball Dickson's book *More Patterns for Poems* (1957), she states on page 13, "*Cinquo,* Lloyd Frank Merrell of Clayton, Michigan, is half a cinquain with 1-2-3-4-1 syllables to the line in its 5 lines." On page 24, under "Index by Creator of Form," we find, "Merrell, Lloyd Frank, Clayton, Michigan, Cinquo"; and on page 36, "The Cinquo. The Cinquo is a half cinquain having 5 lines of 1-2-3-4-1 syllables, respectively. It was originated by Lloyd Frank Merrell of Clayton, Michigan, whose first model was: *Healing. . . .*" The poem, "Grass of love, grow quickly over my heart's wound," had strict lefthand margins. The Cinquo was also listed under Ms. Dickson's "Index of Poems and Forms." Be that as it may, the Lanterne was invented by Lloyd

Frank Merrell, a Methodist Minister.

Rev. Merrell was in his 49th year when he invented the Lanterne poetry pattern. To him, the form was a "miniature drama with climax and terse ending." He incorporated both physical and human nature in his writings. Deep thought is evident in his poem "Humbled": "Rose, your calm unfolding rebukes my torn soul." (*Palm Beach Sun,* 1940.)

The Lanterne is a one-sentence poem consisting of five lines and eleven syllables (1-2-3-4-1 syllables, respectively.) The rules for writing lanternes were set by Lloyd Frank Merrell in a letter dated July 21, 1936, at which time he was still searching for a name for his new form—names which also included "Cina" and "1-2-3-4-1 Cinquain." He stressed that hyphenated words should not be split at the end of lines, that an article should not end a line nor form a line in its entirety (the same rule applies to prepositions and connectives); attempts to avoid abstractions should be made; and he suggested that a title not be an actual quotation from the poem; a one-word title was also suggested.

There is more to the Lanterne than its typography would suggest. In writing Lanternes, one should incorporate poetic devices; figurative language, alliteration, an underlying thought, a message; any device that makes a poem a poem. A lanterne must also be a grammatically-complete sentence. One will find few exceptions to this rule in Lloyd Frank Merrell's own lanterne poems. Rev. Merrell was a craftsman. "Put the sensory image on the lines, and the wider significance between them," he instructs. "Each line should be a unit with the exception of the last, which should be the cracker on the end of the whip."

In my research through scores of his lanterne manuscripts I did find a few exceptions to the rule, "Each line should be a unit." However, we can accept exceptions when one knows the rules. For example, I have come to the conclusion that line four need not end on a strong (content) word; as in Lloyd Frank Merrell's poem "Strange". . ., which I separate here, line by line, to illustrate my point: "Man/can hate/only those/whom his heart can/love." (*Flozari Rockwood's Notebook,*

1939.) I do agree, however, that choice lanternes do (or should) have strong line endings.

The Lanterne was designed for brevity. Its typography disciplines the poet to write a volume with but a thimbleful of words. While typography is a characteristic of the form, it is the content, the idea conveyed, that makes a lanterne a poem rather than a prose picture.

The majority of Rev. Merrell's lanternes had one-word titles. Here, brevity again enters the picture. "Don't waste space by using as a title an actual quotation from the poem," he instructs. Titles appear not to be mandatory.

Lanternes may be light and whimsical or contain deep thought with, preferably, no break in thought. They may imply. That "growth quality" so essential to haiku, is also desirable in lanternes; the more closely one reads, the more one sees. Rhyme is not a characteristic of the Lanterne.

In studying the lanterne form in depth, through research, through publishing, and through contests that I have sponsored and judged over the years, it has become clearly evident that whimsey is an important element of Lloyd Frank Merrell's Lanterne. Whimsey enhances; it adds that special twist so becoming to the form.

The Lanterne is complex in its simplicity. Rev. Merrell best expressed this as he labored to give birth to his poetry form. "I feel that American art is ready for a keen brevity of utterance," he said.

Throughout the years that I edited and published *Glowing Lanternes* (1969-76), I learned to be tolerant of those poets attempting to master the Lanterne; just as Lloyd Frank Merrell was tolerant in perfecting it.

Constantly bearing fruit, Lloyd Frank Merrell once wrote, "Man flies from his nest, trusting the sky of himself calling to his wings." (*Chelsea Standard Newspaper,* 1968) As a poet calling to fellow poets, he cried out, when introducing his Lanterne: "Take it, fellow craftsmen, for the enrichment of an art that can be effectively used in building the brotherhood of man!''

Sample poetry by Gloria Martin:

Sun
sensors
probe the deep
of my darkened
thoughts.

Glowing Lanternes, Bicentennial 1976

An
autumn
thunderstorm
rinses summer's
face.

Velvet Pillows of Perfume, 1971

FINALITY

We
wither
like roses
when severed from
love.

Glowing Lanternes, June-July, 1971

EVOLVEMENT

Love
blossoms
from small deeds
budded in warm
thoughts.

Lyrical Iowa, 1972

LAURETTE

Anna Nash Yarbrough

This pattern was introduced by Etta Caldwell Harris, to honor Laura Durham. Pattern line count, 4-4-6-4-4-6. Total, twenty eight syllables. Only the six syllable lines rhyme. Sample poem by Anna Nash Yarbrough:

ETERNAL YOUTH

The robins sing

their songs of love
when baby spring knows birth
and all the world
seems young again,
a kindergarten earth.

THE MANARDINA

Cecilia Parsons Miller

The manardina is a syllabic form having eighty syllables. It has twelve iambic lines with syllable count of 4, 8, 8, 8, 8. 4, 4, 8, 8, 8, 8, 4. It is a fixed form in that the first and last lines must rhyme. The third, fourth, ninth and tenth lines have the same rhyme; second, fifth, sixth, seventh, eighth and eleventh lines do not rhyme. Poem can be on any subject.

The author of the manardina is Nel Modglin of Davenport, Iowa. This form was introduced in the early '70s and has been accepted as a contest form.

Example poem is by Nel Modglin:
EARTHRISE
From earth's strong pull
Apollo 8 sailed out to touch
Infinity's untrampled rim.
One airman humbly quoted Him
while nations bowed, imploring help,
invoking love.
Thus magnified,
man severed ancient mental bonds;
he had not reached the moon by whim.
Now slowly exiting from dim
eons, he sips a heady cup,
untouched and full.

MINUTE

Anna Nash Yarbrough

The Minute is a sixty-syllable poetry form of twelve lines. It is iambic with syllable count 8, 4, 4, 4, 8, 4, 4, 4, 8, 4, 4, 4. The rhyme scheme is AABBCCDDEEFF. The Minute is punctuated like prose. It captures a momentary mood, or a moment in time. The creator of the form is Verna Lee Hinegardner of Hot Springs, Arkansas and it was originated in 1964. Example poems are those of the creator and Julia Hurd Strong:

INSOMNIA

When darkness drapes a wakeful night
and grants you sight
to stroll or zoom
about my room
in fragmentary memories,
I grasp to seize
the best of you
that filters through
my midnight melancholy skies.
And when my eyes
no longer weep,
I fall asleep.

Verna Lee Hinegardner

ONE GREEN LEAF

So long as I have one green leaf
and my belief
that sun and rain
will ease my pain,
so long as I can stand alone
where I have grown
and occupy
my piece of sky,
from roots to limbs I'll murmur praise
for other days
when, young and strong,
I sang my song.

Verna Lee Hinegardner

VICTIM

Awakened from deep slumber, I

am startled by
the sudden sound—
not *thud* nor *pound*,
but *crash* as sharp as shattered glass.
The moments pass. . .
Alert, I keep
pretending sleep,
not knowing what or where to flee.
Then suddenly
I am aware
a man is there. . .

Julia Hurd Strong, Houston Texas
Award winning poem from 1980 NFSPS Anthology

NEVILLE

Anna Nash Yarbrough

The creator of this form is James R. Gray of Commerce, California. The form is named for an Arkansan poet, Neville Taylor, for his contributions to the writing and furthering of poetry in the mid-South.

The Neville has seven lines, iambic with syllable count of 8, 6, 6, 8, 6, 6, 8. The rhyme scheme is A, B, B, A, C, C, A. Example poem:

CANDY MINTS
Sweet words of love are candy mints,
And nice to have around
Because with each nice sound
I smile and taste delightful hints.
Therefore, I truly try
To keep a fresh supply
To color days with candy tints.

Anna Nash Yarbrough, from *Syllabic Poetry Patterns*

TIMELESS PLACE
Two thousand years have now been blown,
Like dust, by winds of fate
Since Christ unlocked the gate
To that place where a great light shown,

A kingdom free of sin—
Yet people still go in
And worship there before the throne.

James R. Gray, Arkadelphia, Arkansas
published in The Siftings Herald, 1975

OCTAIN

Anna Nash Yarbrough

This pattern was introduced by Lillian Mathilda Swenson. The pattern syllable count in lines is 2-4-6-8-8-6-4-3. Total number of syllables is forty one. The rhyme scheme is a, b, c, d, b, c, d, a. The example poem is by Anna Nash Yarbrough:

NOCTURNAL PLEASURE

At night
I like to sit
on our long side porch and
watch the lights of boats on the lake
so like lightning bugs flare and flit.
and make a fairy land
in their bright wake
of late night.

OCTO

Anna Nash Yarbrough

The Octo was introduced by James Neille Northe. It is a syllabic form of eight lines of eight syllables each. The first three lines transposed become the last three lines of the poem. Lines four and five rhyme. The example poem by Anna Nash Yarbrough was published in *Syllabic Poetry Patterns:*

INTERIM: THE DAYS OF MAY

After the cold of winter snows,
After the wildhorse winds of March,
After April's wet rain and shine
I claim the days of May for me—

One small wedge of Eternity.
After April's wet rain and shine,
After the wildhorse winds of March,
After the cold of winter snows.

ONDA MEL

Anna Nash Yarbrough

The Onda Mel was introduced by Remelda Gibson. It is a syllabic form of forty eight syllables with syllable count of 8, 4, 4, 8, 8, 4, 4, 8. Its theme is love interest. The rhyme scheme is A, B, B, A, C, D, D, C. The example poem by Anna Nash Yarbrough is from *Syllabic Poetry Patterns:*

ADVICE TO THE YOUNG
Love is a temple bell that rings
at vesper time,
in measured rhyme,
much like the lonely nightbird sings.
And when the bell has rung for you,
if lad or maid—
be unafraid—
your heart will signal what to do.

ORIENTAL OCTET

Anna Nash Yarbrough

The creator of the Oriental Octet is James R. Gray of Commerce, California. It is a syllabic form with syllable count of 5, 7, 5, 7, 7, 5, 7, 5. It has eight unrhymed lines. Like the tanka, its theme is usually nature. The example poem:

BOYHOOD FRIENDS
I sometimes wonder
If that fieldlark still offers
His greeting to dawn,
And if that path still wanders
Down the hill where wild horses

Gave me their perfume.
I know these things will exist
Always in my heart.

James R. Gray
American Poetry League Magazine, Winter 1979

PENSEE

Anna Nash Yarbrough

The creator of the Pensee is Alice Maude Spokes. It is a five-line poem. Syllable count is 2, 4, 7, 8, 8. The poem should have unbroken phrasing and use strong end words. Content should be appealing. In the sample poem the last two lines rhyme. But this is not a rule of this form. The example poem is by Wauneta Hackleman:

HIDDEN WISDOM
Somewhere
Within this wealth
of books ideas entreat
to be inscribed by writer's pen,
to live beyond my mortal ken.

QUATERN

Anna Nash Yarbrough

The Quatern is in iambic tetrameter. There are four stanzas of four lines each. Eight syllables (four feet) in each line. The first line is repeated one line down in each stanza. The rhyme pattern is A, b, a, b-b, A, b, a, -a, b, A, b-b, a, b, A. The capital letters are for repeated lines. The example poem is by Anna Nash Yarbrough:

CONFESSIONS OF A POET
I like to ponder, that is true,
I like to write my thoughts in rhyme.
I try to give true worth its due
But Oh, I fail time after time.

My words grow tart like too-green lime,
I like to ponder what is true
But when I hear the church bells chime
I ask my God, "Send strength from You."

He answers me, "Your faith pursue."
I try to make my words sublime,
I like to ponder what is true,
But often words I write are mime.

I often see clean turn to slime,
And often weep when plans fall through
But if its never worth a dime,
I like to ponder, that is true.

RISPETTO

Anna Nash Yarbrough

The Rispetto is an Italian form consisting of two or more stanzas with inter-rhyming lines ranging from six to ten syllables per line. In the sample poem, the author uses ten syllables per line. The rhyme scheme is 1, 2, 1, 2, 3, 3, 4, 4. (ABAB CC DD) The Rispetto is rarely used in English. The example poem is by Viola Jacobson Berg:

THE CHANCE TO ERR

Our youth seemed doomed to join in common fate,
To doubt the lasting worth of parents' ways,
Their standards and their goals to tolerate,
Their attitudes consigned to "olden days."

Advice well-meant from kindly wiser tongue
Seems lost upon the sprouting greening young.
Sometimes they badly need the chance to err
To see how very right their parents were.

from *Pathways for the Poet*, published by Mott Media

BIBLIOGRAPHY: Clement Wood, *Rhyming Dictionary*, p. 89 and *Calkins Handbook*, p. 52.

SEPT

Anna Nash Yarbrough

The pattern was introduced by Etta Josephean Murfey. Pattern, syllabic line count is 1-2-3-4-3-2-1. The total number of syllables is sixteen. The example poem is by Anna Nash Yarbrough:

ETERNAL QUESTION
Words
are small
imps at play,
racing across
my page, but
which to
keep?

SEPTET

Anna Nash Yarbrough

The Septet was introduced by Mary Owen Lewis. It is a syllabic form with thirty-nine syllables and syllable count of 3, 5, 7, 9, 7, 5, 3. The example poem is by Wauneta Hackleman:

THIS TIME CALLED ADOLESCENCE
When love weaves
webs of tangled threads,
silkspunned dreams and strange desires
larvaed in primal cocoon, stitching
the green-lean years of growing—
ad infinitum
—so they think.

Browning, in the first stanza of "Misconceptions" employed rhyme in this form (ABABBAA). Thomas Traherne used rhyme scheme of ABBABCC in his "Eden." Variations of rhyme and no rhyme are permissible in this form.

SHADORMA

Anna Nash Yarbrough

The pattern was introduced by James Neill Northe. The syllable count in lines is 3-5-3-3-7-5. The total number of syllables is twenty-six. Use strong end words or phrases. The example poem is by Anna Nash Yarbrough:

LAST LIGHT SNOW
> This morning,
> I smiled a thank-you
> at the sight
> of bright blue
> hyacinths defying late
> February snow.

TANGO

Anna Nash Yarbrough

The pattern was introduced by Chiquita LoJuana Gonzolas Sills. The syllable count is 9-10-11-12 for a total of forty two syllables. The rhyme is a, b, c, b. The example poem is by Anna Nash Yarbrough:

THE JOY OF BEING YOUNG
> As light as steps upon a dance floor,
> the rain came down across the dimpled lake,
> And youngsters squealed in sharp delightfilled yelling,
> And I smiled at the fact: They yelled for youth's sweet sake.

TRIPOD

Anna Nash Yarbrough

The creator of the Tripod is Frances T. Brinkley and is used widely in workshops in Arkansas. The form has twenty-seven syllables, 3, 6, 9, 6, 3. It is not rhymed. The poem should deal

with man's relationship to man. The example poem is by Anna
Nash Yarbrough:

SWEET THIEVERY

In the green
clover pasture, gypsies
are camping tonight. Their festive songs
and tinkling tambourines
steal my heart.

POETIC TECHNIQUES

ALLITERATION IN POETRY

Virginia Bagliore

Poetry is a multi-dimensional language. Its primary purpose is communication of the highest form. Why is this so? Because poetry is the universal language of the soul. Poetry is the ultimate experience, since all emotions can be expressed through poetry in a constructive way. The art of poetry is to make use of language at its optimum. One can best do this by exploring sound. There are many variations one can use. Alliteration is one of them.

Long ago, man guessed that the heartbeat might be the source of our speech rhythms and the rhythm in poetry acts as a tonic. We can relate to poetry, since poetry is rhythm and movement—our breath is rhythm; our heartbeat is movement. When forming an image it is necessary for us to experience visualization, repetition and suggestion. This is another way we relate to poetry since poetry is all images—repetition and suggestion. Repetition at the beginning of words and syllables is called alliteration. Knowing this, we can make use of a valuable technique when writing poetry.

For example, the "r" and "l" are both called mellifluous sounds because they seem to roll off the tongue. Sounds that vibrate through the nasal passages are "m," "n," and "ng." When we use these three sounds: bam, ban, bang, we can feel the different vibrations in our mouth.

An "m" sound is probably more expressive than any other consonant used by itself. It has been noticed that "m" occurs in the word "mother" in many languages, presumably because this is the sound happy babies elicit. The reason for this is that the lips are used by babies for sucking and tasting. The "m" sound can be made without opening our lips; it can be hummed as a pleasant accompaniment when involved in kissing or consuming food. It is interesting to note that the Eastern "Om" emphasizing the "m" is a universal sound vibration. In our language, we recognize it as the I Am. It is a highly meditative sound vibration effectively used in meditation. Notice also that it is found in the word *home*. It is a wonderful discovery when we realize the healing power of words.

Words heal and words destroy. We can choose to align ourselves with positive sounds when writing poetry and know its benefits. It is important to educate ourselves to know the difference in sounds that create positive and negative effects.

The "n" sound amplifies the nasal tone as it is higher in range, more of a whine than a hum. We find this nasal quality in negative words such as "no," "non," and "nein." The importance here is to be made aware of all sounds, in order to know when to use them—why we use them, so that we can apply alliteration successfully as well as beneficially.

When it is necessary to use harsh sounds to be true to the poem, we should be willing to do so as long as we are aware of what we are doing; and why we are doing it. It is a good idea to rehearse the alliteration out loud. I find a valuable technique is to read the poem into a recorder and upon hearing it played back, make corrections.

The "w" and "y" are the most vowel-like of the consonants. "W" is double "u"—an oo sound. In the poem "Western Wind," the "w" alliteration is obvious in its opening line, "Western wind, when will thou blow." Another smooth alliteration is the vowel-like "w." Contrasting sounds are fricatives because they interfere with the natural airflow causing rasping of the breath when spoken. They include: "h," "f" and "v."

Another interesting alliteration can be made with the "f" sound. Coleridge demonstrates six "f's" in two lines, followed quickly by a seventh:

> The fair breeze blew, the white foam flew,
> The furrow followed free;
> We were the first that ever burst
> Into that silent sea.

Emily Dickinson favors "h's" and "t's" in her poem, "My

Life Closed Twice":

> My life closed twice before its close;
>   It yet remains to see
> If Immortality unveil
>   A third event to me,
> So huge, so hopeless to conceive,
>   As these that twice befell.
> Parting is all we know of heaven,
>   And all we need of hell.

Notice in this poem that Walter de la Mare has embroidered in his tapestry, as a masterpiece of alliteration, the "b's," "w's," "o's," and "r's":

> Very old are the woods;
>   And the buds that break
> Out of the Briar's Boughs,
>   When March winds wake
> So old with their beauty are,
>   And no man knows
> Through what wild centuries
>   Roves back the rose.

One of the challenges in poetry is to be innovative and experimental. Let yourself write a meditative poem with alliteration. Haiku is a highly meditative one breath verse and can be written with alliteration in mind. This would suggest repetition as well as cadence. It would be interesting to experiment with alliteration when writing Haiku to achieve two forms of meditation simultaneously. For example, my poem:

SUMMIT

> My true mind murmurs,
> Mountains can be moved. Move them,
> O Divine Milieu!

Explore different uses of alliteration to enhance the poem. We are not to over-use the technique, but, instead create harmonious rhythm to evoke positive images. The discipline is to hone the poem to create sensations that transform themselves into word paintings. One can realize that in writing poetry, a universal language is symbolically present accounting for the imaginary patterns in our dreams, myths and art. This is exciting knowing that we can apply this in our everyday life.

Another interesting exercise for alliteration is to write a list of words and choose six to ten of them with the same letter; then weave it into a poem with additional words. In doing this you fix the poem in your mind and spontaneously create alliteration.

In alliteration we can elaborate in the usage of sound vibration with letters of the *alpha*bet. In my experience as a poet I have made wonderful discoveries in the exploration of the alphabet. *Alpha* is the Greek word for beginning. It has the vowel *a* which is a high sound vibration in the Universe used in sacred books. In the Hebrew language the name Adam represents the first man, again symbolizing the beginning. This is no coincidence. As I previously stated the *a* is used in the beginning of the word *Alpha*. It is also used in the name Abraham which stands for faith in the invisible Power of the One God.

M, another beautiful letter, is used in the word *mayim*, the Hebrew word for water. Water throughout history is associated with healing. Within the word mayim is the vowel *yud* which symbolizes essence or spirit.

This essence that is within chosen word sound vibrations can be an enhancing factor in the alliteration of poetry. Our awareness of the constructive usage of symbolic letters can help us to achieve this effect. Further exploration in developing this technique will enable the poet to expand the consciousness of poetry.

BIBLIOGRAPHY

de la Mare, Walter. *Poetry*. Elizabeth Drew. New York: Dell Publishing Co., Inc., 1959.

Nims, John Frederick. *Western Wind*. New York: Random House Inc., 1954.

Perrine, Laurence. "My Life Closed Twice," by Emily Dickinson, from *Sound and Sense.* New York: Harcourt, Brace & World, Inc., 1963.

ASSONANCE-CONSONANCE

D. L. Rudy

Among the many auditory techniques employed by the skilled poet in crafting the finished poem are assonance and consonance. Assonance involves the use of vowels; consonance, consonants.

The use, for effect, of identical vowel sounds placed medially (i.e. not at the beginning of words) and in close proximity, but without the accompanying similarity of consonants that constitutes conventional rhyme, for example *frame, babe* (assonance); *frame, same* (rhyme), is called assonance. Once established, the assonantal vowel sounds may be used in a more scattered pattern throughout the poem so that the ear can pick up the tonal qualities the poet is using to gain effectiveness. Assonance is, because of its musical quality, sometimes called "vocalic rhyme." Obviously, as part of their musical effect, assonance and consonance are often combined with alliteration, or repetition for effect of the same initial sounds, i.e. sounds at the beginnings of words.

Consonance is the intentional use of consonants medially or terminally where identical consonants are used but without the similarity of vowel sounds that would produce strict or pure rhyme, for example, strident, undulating (consonance); kiss, miss (rhyme.)

The beautiful music sound can be easily observed in Michele Lalonde's "La Mere Patrie" (The Mother Country), where the poet says: "ne demandez ni mon nom ni la couleur de mon teint." Note the fine use of assonance in the first two words of the line, and also later the effect in combination with the internal rhyme of "mon" and "nom," along with the "m's" "n's" "l's" and "t's" as they provide sound effects through the use of consonance.

The very title of Dylan Thomas' famous villanelle "Do Not Go Gentle into That Good Night" is a perfect example of the harmonious use of sound, so much so that when the reader is given this line again as the first line of the poem and repeatedly throughout the villanelle, there is gradually a completely orchestrated emotional tone built upon the plosive "g's" and "d's," the alliteration of the "g's" and the consonance involving the "t's" and "n's."

As most lovers of Thomas know, he found much of his inspiration in the Bible, and a perusal of almost any of the psalms reminds the reader that these beautiful free verse poems are a rewarding source of aesthetic as well as spiritual beauty:

> I will declare thy name unto my brethren;
> In the midst of the congregation will I praise thee.

Note how the psalmist has constructed his song through the use of consonants: "l" "n" "m" "g" and the diphthong, "th." In addition the assonance of "i" (short vowel) and short "e" in "brethren" completes the musical effect.   Small wonder that so many modern practitioners of free verse have been influenced by the King James or the Rheims-Douai version of the Bible which offer the tonal values of Shakespeare's era along with the heritage of the original text.

In my own poetry I have worked very consciously with sound.   For example, in describing Kinkakuji Temple at Kyoto, from the poem of the same name, I described in an imagistic pattern my impression of the temple, which stands reflected in a small clear body of water as:

> Slumbering its glow
> into the pine framed
> lake of dusty jade—
> Kinkakuji—pavilion of gold,
> where once the mighty shogun
> contemplated ease.

Later in the same poem, I described the ever present, well-ordered group of Japanese children visiting this shrine as:

> ripples of silk-like laughter,
> so billowed below the surface of all calm,
> no sound distracts the soft near silence
> that slowly licks the very lap
> of the golden stairs.

Except for the name of the temple, with its incisive consonantal use of the fricative "k" the mood of repose I sought to convey is carried out by softer consonance, such as the "l's" of "slumbering" "glow" "pavilion" "gold" "contemplated" and later "ripples" "silk-like" "billowed" "below" "silence" "slowly" "golden" plus, of course, the same "l" sound initially. The conclusion of the poem, thus describes in tonal fashion, both the reflected image of the gold-leaf temple which was the refuge of the shogun turned philosopher, and the nearly quiet children streaming by as an almost mystical part of the picture. Similarly, "m" "n" "s" and "b" sounds were important in forming the auditory image of the poem. Finally, assonance, in terms of short "i" sounds, "o's" and soft "a" as in "all calm" is an aid in achieving the desired harmony of effect.

In a poem called "For Thirty Dollars a Day, As Long As…" my focus was on the miserably unhappy conditions prevailing in so many of our nursing homes. Here I wished to use sounds to suggest a lack of repose, an absence of beauty, a sharpness of despair:

> ganglions of purple
> and green
> flower the cheap
> plastic drapes.

The consonants used here are the plosives, "g's" "p's" and the hard "r" sound. Although consonance is also represented by the repetition of "n's" all sense of softness has been obliterated by the conscious emphasis on cacaphony. The long vowel "e" in combination with the harsh consonants adds unpleasantness "green" "cheap"; this use of assonance is intentionally unpleasant. The aim is to insure that long before the ironic last line, "We take care of our senior citizens," the reader will be ready with the same scorn for the situation that motivated the poem.

My latest collection, *Grace Notes to the Measure of the Heart,* is , in its very title, an example of the musicality of sound.   Although I was more concerned with the ample use of vowels rather than with assonance per se, it is obvious that consonance is used in this title in terms of "t" and "s" sounds. A poem in this collection, called "By the Edge of Darkness" employs sounds within a visual pattern to give the unity of all things in nature with the quiet vision of the heart.   Here I have utilized "t's" "l's" and "s" sounds to the fullest possible extent, along with "n" sounds to create consonance and to establish the emotional and the physical scene for the reader. Assonance is used in terms of the short "e" in *Edge* and *Darkness*; and short "a" sounds and short "i's" find their place in the poem:

BY THE EDGE OF DARKNESS

    Softly
        it is the little true
  waves
    licking
        gently
  waiting   at the stranded
  shore
    of heart.
all loveliness in this solitude.

In essence, as the examples shown illustrate, assonance and consonance are rhyming devices. Used with skill, they perform the same melodic function as rhyme, but in a somewhat freer form, one that appears less formal perhaps than conventional rhyme, but has its own inner discipline and offers the same tonal insights into the emotional and spiritual depths of the poem.   Although rhyming devices such as assonance and consonance are common to all poetry throughout the ages, going back certainly as far as classical Greek poetry and appearing regularly thereafter, it is particularly important to be aware of rhyming devices in the modern poem where so often end-rhymes have been dispensed with.   J. Isaacs, while noting that poetry is always contemporary in its own age, remarks that "In texture modern poetry is a poetry of nuances. In structure it is a balance of tensions and conflicts. . . . at its best it is a 'dome of many coloured glass, staining the white radiance of eternity'." Describing the use of sounds in achieving the total effect of the poem, Gilbert Highet in *The Powers of Poetry*, defines melody as "the music of vowels and consonants, syllables and words, which delights the hearer and emphasizes the meaning in a different way."

> There is a young girl
> a child, a woman
> She extends her arms
> slightly curved
> to cradle a child
> or to cast rainbows.
> Her name is:
> Astarte and silver stars
> fill her heart   D. L. Rudy

BIBLIOGRAPHY

Bergen Poets VII. Fall, 1980.

The Bible. (King James Version)

Europe. "Litterature de Québec," revue mensuelle Fev/Mar., 1966.

Highet, Gilbert. *The Powers of Poetry.* New York: Oxford University Press, 1960.

Isaacs, J. *The Background of Modern Poetry.* New York: E. P. Dutton and Co., 1952.

Rudy, D. L. *Grace Notes to the Measure of the Heart.* Cranford: Merging Media, 1979.

—. *Psyche Afoot.* Francistown: Golden Quill, 1979.

—. *Quality of Small.* American Poets Fellowship Society, 1971.

CADENCE IN POETRY

Dorothea Neale

Cadence in poetry is the flow of music through the poem, the heartbeat of the poem, its living pulse. Components of cadence are rhythm in its motion through language and its inter-relationship with form, stress, accent, timbre, patterns of sound including the integral silences or rest pauses that help to form the total structure, tonal expression, and varied inflectional qualities. Cadence is multi-dimensional and includes everything that contributes to the flow of sound as it impinges on the listening ear.

John Redfield in "Music, a Science and an Art" states that "the mother of music is rhythm." This is equally true with poetry as rhythm flows through language creating cadences. Along with cadence of which it is a part, rhythm is a shaper and a moulder, an element of living fire that surges through the poem. Meter is the channel through which they flow. In a chapter on rhythm in his book "Prisms: Studies in Modern Literature" Albert Cook describes a phase of the relationship as he writes of the poetic design and the "poetic instance" as he shows the impulse of language in action successfully varying to a degree from the structure of meter and form in which held, thus enriching the cadences.

Rhythm is the most constant factor in the universe, from the dance of the electrons to the orbits of the planets, and the motion of the stars. In describing the rhythms of nature and man's inner responses, Louis Untermeyer declares in his book *The Pursuit of Poetry* that we inherited poetry from the universe. Stanley Burnshaw in "The Seamless Web" brings out the close relationship between the creative artist and his art which he considers as the expression of the artist's total organism, a seamless web in which the two become one.

Cadence in poetry begins with the poet. It must be felt before it can be translated into words that make music, thereby poetry. When we are in tune with the universe and with ourselves we feel a sense of inner rhythm. Poems frequently come into being with this flow of rhythm which arrives even before any of the words, or even a theme. A phrase might sound over and over in the mind of the author, a thought might strike a spark, sometimes there is a "given line" or one, or two, or three, and the very impetus of that line or lines will carry the poem to its conclusion.

Amy Lowell, Walt Whitman, Ezra Pound were all exponents of loose cadence as used in free verse, Amy Lowell frequently referring to free verse as "cadenced verse." All three of these poets were masters of cadence as found in free verse. Ezra Pound told his contemporaries to "compose in the sequence of a musical phrase" not in the sequence of a "metronome." The Princeton Encyclopedia of Poetry and Poetics on cadence as used in free verse—the rhythm of accentual phrasal units, a looser concept than the rhythms of traditional meter. However, cadence belongs to all poetry, the nature of the cadence of a particular kind of poetry varying according to the type of poetry. The writer of free verse, not making use of the other devices of poetry, needs an ear especially sensitive to cadence. Cadence is defined in *A Handbook of Literature* as measured, rhythmical movement either in prose or in verse. . . . the recurrence of emphasis often accompanied by rising modulations of voice. Cadence is related to rhythm but exists usually in larger and looser units of syllables than the formal, metrical movement of regular verse. Nevertheless, whatever other devices are available, rhyme, meter, form, various uses of language, it is largely cadence that makes the poem. Language must find its music before it can become poetry.

As Walter Pater claims in his most quoted statement, "All art aspires to the condition of music." This is particularly true of poetry. Music makes use of varied tones of wider range than language can encompass, timbres and harmonies of greater range. Both musical and poetic meter are based on the same general principle, a short, easily recognizable pattern of time and accent as chosen for the basic unit which is then repeated with possible variations maintaining the general theme until it reaches a well-rounded closure. The repeated rhythm of the foot in poetry bears a close relationship to the musical bar or measure.

Both music and poetry are auditory arts. Cadence, whether in music or in poetry, must be heard. Even the silent reader must make use of an "inner listening ear." In music we are accustomed to the composer as the creator of the work of music; to the interpretive artist, a singer or instrumentalist, as performer of the composition; to the audience who is there to listen and appreciate. All of this is likewise present in poetry, starting with the poet, who having created the work must also "speak" the poem, whether silently to himself or aloud in reading to others, and in varying degrees in all readers and listeners. A printed poem is like a sheet of music that requires a performance, whether heard by one or many.

Dr. Jack Diamond, at his Institute of Behavioral Kineaiology in Valley Cottage, New York has proved, in scientific experiments that both music and poetry can contribute to the health, energy and well-being of the individual by balancing the two hemispheres of the brain. The reading of poetry aloud, when read expressively bringing out the rhythms and cadences is a dual-hemisphere activity combining the verbal skills of the left hemisphere with the musical and rhythmical qualities controlled by the right hemisphere, thereby balancing the brain of both reader and attentive listener, resulting in a greater flow of available energy.

Barbara Bernstein Smith has made an important contribution to poetry in her book *Poetic Closure*, a study of how poems end. Cadence as a musical term refers to the fall of the voice or instrument as it relates to the ending of a phrase or composition, in half cadence or full cadence, with cadenza giving a final flourish to the ending. Closure in poetry occurs when the concluding portion of the poem creates in the reader or listener a sense of appropriate cessation, as in the resolution of a chord by means of the grouping element rounding out and bringing the cadence to a sense of finality. As poetry is the music of language this is the reason our ears are less than satisfied with a weak ending in a poem. Successful poetry closure comes about through bringing together and rounding out the cadences into a sense of completeness—the harmonic ending. As in music, a poem needs to be brought to a graceful and effective completion.

Two poems representative of cadence in poetry:

SEA CALL

    The night is still, the stars are far,
    And far is the whispering sea;
    The winds are still, the night birds call,
    And I hear the call of the sea;
    Silent the night and distant the sea,
    But I hear the surging of far-off waves,
    And I see the entrance of deep sea caves,
    With the ocean pouring in.
    Always I hear the ocean song,
    And before me sea lanes beckon and throng,
    Whenever I walk on moonlit paths,
    When the stars are far and the sea is far,
    And the winds and the night are still.   Dorothea Neale

TELL ME WIND

    Wind song, wind song, what are the words that you say?
    Blowing into my garden from the far away,
    Do you bring a song of the sea and salt sea spray?

    Or do you come from mountain peaks where the high winds blow?
    Rambling down ravines with the drift of snow,
    Gathering in the scent of pines and bird song as you go?

    Winds, as you travel by, what do you say to me?
    As you make the little leaves dance on this flowering tree,
    Turning all that you may touch into new melody?   Dorothea Neale

BIBLIOGRAPHY

Bartlett, Phyllis. *Poems in Process.* New York: Oxford University Press.

Brown, Calvin S. *Music and Literature.* University of Georgia Press.

Burnshaw, Stanley. *The Seamless Web.* New York: Braziliar.

Cook, Albert. *Prisms, Studies in Modern Literature.* Indiana University Press.

Diamond, John, M. D. *BK Behavioral Kinesiology.* New York: Harper and Row.

Fussell, Paul, Jr. *Poetic Meter and Poetic Form.* New York: Random House.

Munro, Thomas. *The Arts & Their Inter-Relationships.* Press of Case Western University.

Music and Your Emotions. Prepared for the Music Research Foundation, Inc., New York: Livewright Publishing.

Preminger, Alex, editor. *Princeton Encyclopedia of Poetry and Poetics.* Princeton University Press.

Redfield, John. *Music, A Science and an Art.* New York: Tudor Publishing Co.

Stallman & Waters. *The Creative Reader.* New York: Ronald Press.

Turco, Lewis. *Book of Forms.* New York: E. P. Dutton.

Untermeyer, Louis. *Pursuit of Poetry.* New York: Simon & Schuster.

Wilkinson, Marquerite. *The Way of the Makers.* New York: MacMillan Company.

CLARITY

Verna Lee Hinegardner

Since communication is probably the most universal reason for writing, it is especially important to be understood. You and only you can say it like you mean it.

If you have trouble with your poetry being understood, it could be you don't know for sure what you are trying to tell or who is trying to tell it. If you find yourself floundering in disconnected thoughts, cliches, and horrible rhymes, you might just need to travel back to that old grade school grammar book.

What is your primary purpose for writing a particular poem? Write down your primary purpose—who are you, what you want to tell, and to whom you are telling it. Write down your primary purpose in plain language and in one sentence. For example: I am a snake and I want to tell people who fear me about my good points so they will not fear me. Then write down a little outline. (1) You fear me; (2) I have some good points; and (3) Please do not fear me. Now you have set your plot and your poem must move forward from "fear" to "do not fear." Do not deviate from your primary purpose sentence or your outline—or you'll bungle at the beginning, muddle the middle and expound the ending.

Back to the snake and the primary purpose and the outline we made. If you begin your poem with "Fear not those green snakes underfoot" you have bungled because you already decided the persona was the snake, and you as a snake would be telling of fear. So back to the drawing board and you might say, "I am the small green snake you fear." Now you are the snake and you have stuck to your outline. Now go on to the middle of the poem. If you should say, "Snakes eat the rodents you fear" then you have muddled the middle because you decided back in the outline to be the snake (not all snakes) so you might say something like "I eat the rodents which you fear." Then you go on and say some more good stuff but keep it in first person. Then to the ending. If you have an ending like "You learned to love dogs, so you can learn to love us" you've expounded the ending. You also introduced another animal and that cluttered the poem. You're telling the reader what the reader has to do. You're assuming all people have dogs and all people love dogs, and again you use the pronoun "us" speaking for all snakes. Don't be too presumptuous. One poem will not change the attitudes of all people. Keep your ending simple, direct, and never all-encompassing.

One of the most common poems I receive as editor is plotted in this way: Sorrow; God helped me overcome sorrow; God helps everybody overcome sorrow. This is an overworked, highly presumptuous subject, a bias subject. Beware of highly controversial subjects. True, you must, in poetry, take a stand. You are either for or against something. You can't sit on the fence and waver maybe it would be this way; but maybe on the other hand it might be that way. You must know, in poetry, for sure what you believe. If you are wavy about a particular subject, write a poem each way and let both sides come out—but in two different poems. Get down to basics. Tell what your problem is and how you overcame your problem. You can't wrap it all up by saying God will heal, time will heal, the world will be rosy again. Your reader wants to know why you are such an authority. What was your problem? How did you overcome it? If this comes clear, the reader can live the poem with you. Or if you have a problem and did not overcome it, say that.

One sure way to bungle the beginning is to use a junk opener. An example of a junk beginning in a letter might be, "In response to your request for information, I am writing this letter." An example of a junk opening in a poem is, "As I sit here with my pen in my hand remembering how it used to be." If you begin with junk, your reader is apt to think junk will follow. But if you begin with something important, the reader is more willing to listen to what you have to say. Rambling and unimportant beginnings can kill a poem. Poems are not reports. The reader seldom cares what prompted you to write the poem. You must get rid of dead wood for a tree to flourish. In poetry you must cut, cut, cut. Often you can start a poem in the middle, toss out the first two stanzas and the last stanza and have a better poem. When you write poetry, nothing is less important than a fact. It does not have to be the truth. Just because it happened does not make it work for the reader. Give the reader the gift of experience. Something in your own life may prompt a poem; but when you finish, you seldom recognize it because you let the poem have its way. I have people write and say "Please publish this. It really happened." As an editor I don't care whether it happened or not. What I am trying to find are poems to which the readers can relate, which they will enjoy enough to clip and share. Don't be hesitant to have your name appear as the by-line on a fictitious poem. Those who know you, know; those who do not know you, could not care less. You have to be brave to write about hating spring and loving broken marriages; but nothing is more precious than a fan letter consoling you on loss when you write about a fictitious death.

Make your poems believable. If you are writing a descriptive poem, let the reader know where you are as you make your observation—but let the reader know indirectly by what you see. If you are sitting in a porch swing on your front porch, it is highly improbable that you will see a winding road, for example. If you are in an airplane you might see the winding road, but you will not get the close-up view. You have to have some logic in your poetry; and leave the reader some room for logic too.

Poor punctuation is another enemy of clarity. Punctuation would not matter if you wrote only for yourself. Since you write for others, it matters a great deal. Punctuation is a code. It tells the reader how to read your sentences. It establishes the relationship between parts of a sentence and clarifies your use of words. In a very real sense, punctuation is a proxy for your voice. When you speak, your pauses and vocal inflections tell the listener how to interpret your words. When you write, you pause and inflect by punctuating. In many sentences, incorrect punctuation either obscures meaning or demands a second reading. We can easily write ourselves into a "throw mama from the train a kiss goodbye" situation. As a poetry editor, I receive many unpuncuated poems with this note, "I'm no good at punctuation. Please fix my poem." As an editor, I can't "fix" it. I don't know if the writer means "macaroni, salad and potatoes" or "macaroni salad and potatoes." Most poets recognize the end of a line automatically gives the reader a slight pause, and that they can be stingy with commas at line ends except for grammatical clausing. Don't punctuate helter-skelter by relying on an inner sense of sound, placing a comma here, a semicolon there, depending on how you feel at the moment. The hardest part of learning proper punctuation is overcoming inertia, and caring whether you communicate. Like an improperly tuned engine, your writing will sputter, jerk and backfire without the fine tuning that proper punctuation provides. Not caring about fine tuning can cost you both clarity and credibility. I have heard it said about punctuation "When in doubt, don't." I prefer, "When in doubt, study."

Miller Williams of the University of Arkansas at Fayetteville says, "How simple it can all be said." John Dryden said, "The first duty of a poet is to be understood." Robert Frost said, "I prefer to be in the class of poets who wish to be understood." One way to leave the reader room for logic, for using his own mind to understand, is to guard against information release by eliminating words the reader already knows, such as "metal" gas tank, the rain is falling "down," and climbing "up" steps. A certain amount of subtlety is desirable. Excess of words, lines without purpose, will muddle the poem. A poem is more than a playful romp with language. A poem needs a reason to be. Every word in a poem needs a reason to be. After we write a poem, we should underline every word we can possibly consider throwing away. Be suspicious of any word you have just learned, and are proud of knowing. Underline all of your articles, conjunctions, and adjectives. Then try different ways to turn each sentence around yet say the same thing. Let your verbs carry the action. Back to the snake again. Saying "The snake goes down the road and he wiggles as he goes" takes twelve words. "The snake goes down the road wiggling as he goes" takes ten words. "The snake wiggles down the road" takes only six words. Be just as economical as you can with words. Miller Williams says there has never been too short a poem. When you finish your poem, forget you wrote it. Read it aloud many times. See if there are any doubts left to the reader. Perhaps one of the things you meant to do was to leave a little doubt to the reader. Did you accomplish that goal? Does your poem sound like you are talking? It should. Writing a poem is talking on paper. Some writers tend to protect the understanding of their poem from people down at the bus stop. By overwrapping poems in literary finery, references and inferences, classical allusions, layers of meanings, technical terminology and ghostly ramblings, the so-called intellectual poet defeats common understanding.

After you complete a poem, type it up on good bond paper and display it prominently where it will be seen by yourself and others. Put a pen by the poem. If you can go three days without making a single change, your poem is ready to parade in public.

Coleridge said, "Prose consists of words in good order, and poetry—words in best order." When you put together a string of words they should add up to something sensible, some reason for existence. Remember always, you are a real person speaking to real people. Only you—can say it like you mean it.

POETRY IN THE CLASSROOM

Evelyn Amuedo Wade

Poetry throughout the ages has touched the spirit of man. From the days of Homer to the latest issue of *The Wall Street Journal,* the feats and foibles of man have been recorded in poetry. Rhyme and metrical patterns were developed as man became more sophisticated in his search for self expression, but the basic themes of human experience and emotion remain constant.

It is these themes—these emotions—that we, as poets, work with today and that students are seeking to develop when they register for a class in poetry.

Although no teacher can endow a student with a gift for writing, nor breathe a poet to life where none exists, with proper guidance and direction, latent talents can be awakened and budding rhymsters can be moulded into recognizable poets.

Poetry lies, sometimes deeply hidden, in all of us, and to pare away the layers of timidity and unawareness and uncover a talent that the student himself does not even know he possesses is a joy that excites the imagination of any poet teacher.

Teaching the writing of poetry is, however, a job demanding both sensitivity and skill. The beginning poet needs to be treated with the care we use when handling our most delicate crystal. Even under normal circumstances, the ego is fragile; when the poet's heart and soul have been poured into his first few attempts, even greater care must be taken. Criticism that is too harsh could turn a potentially good poet away from the art altogether. On the other hand, praise heaped too generously on a poem is suspect.

What I like to do when critiquing a poem (particularly before I have gotten to know the poet well) is to start with the positive. I discuss the good points—the texture of the poem, the emotion it arouses, the total experience the poem has attempted to describe. If the language is good, the imagery arresting, the feeling present, then I point out these elements. If not, then I seek for something else of worth. It is a rare poem that hasn't some good feature. But not until I have stressed the strengths in the poem do I begin to touch on the negative. By this time the poet's faith in himself (that somehow disappeared the moment he presented his poem for review) has been restored and he can accept suggestions for improvement.

Whether my classes in poetry encompass the regulation three-hour credit course in college or are part of a continuing education program, I treat them all in a similar manner, in that they are basically workshops with the more pedigogical elements coming in as needed. When a course consists of only eight or ten two-hour sessions, we don't have too much time to put into the specifics of terminology relating to poetry. Yet, unless we all use the vocabulary of the discipline, we can't communicate. I start off, therefore, with a handout defining such terms as alliteration, imagery, symbolism, pathetic fallacy, enjambment, and periphrasis.

Most beginning poets that I have worked with, often begin writing in free verse. Free verse , on the surface, seems easier to compose since no parameters are set and a poet may wander about at his own free will. The danger here lies in the student's failure to understand that self expression without poetic nuances isn't poetry. All too often much free verse by beginners is no more than prose set in varying line lengths that ignore such elements as symbolism and imagery, two of the basic components of good poetry. As we read the poems, and discuss them, I try to incorporate lessons that teach these ideas.

In addition, I believe that students should have at least a rudimentary understanding of the forms before they attempt to transcend them. Yet a discussion of metrical devices is too confusing to the student for me to overwhelm him with that area of poetry in his early stages of composition. As the need arises, however, (and it always does) I then produce another handout with definitions and examples of some of the more accepted forms such as the sonnet, the sestina, the triolet, and the haiku.

At this point, we move into what I like to call "experiments" rather than "assignments," the latter term being obviously too confining or reminiscent of the structured class room. The idea of the experiment opens up a whole new approach, and no one is ever "required" to try anything that doesn't appeal to him. There is hardly a student, however, who doesn't succumb to the haiku which, by its very nature, encourages the student to produce—and we now have the beginnings of discipline.

Now the student begins to understand the economy of words, the strictures of rhyme and rhythm, the parameters of form. This is the challenge. This is the difference between the knowledgeable, well-disciplined writer whose style is taut and spare, and the careless or negligent writer whose self-indulgence takes him into wearisome convoluted sentence structure, or possibly worse, into an overflow of adjectives, adverbs, and conjuctions.

By merely using a student's own poems with suggestions for striking out unnecessary words and phrases, I am able to let him see a new version of his own creation—sharpened, tight, emphatic. We have departed from theory, and a poet emerges with a whole new approach evident in his next attempts. In these, the poet has now become crisp and self-assured.

Gradually we work on other areas of poetic weaknesses, and again I give specific examples offering works of the students themselves to illustrate my points. In teaching how to avoid abstractions, for example, where the word "tree" is used, I often ask, "What kind of tree? If it's a sycamore, say so. If it's an oriole, just don't say bird. If it's Aunt Julia, then don't speak of my aunt." Thus, I avoid abstractions in my teaching.

And finally, we come to sound, probably the most basic element of poetry. Since the sound system is part of the design of the language, how the poet uses sound will help clarify meaning. When this is explained to a student, particularly in light of his own poems or those of his classmates, it is remarkable how easily he catches on and how readily he makes use of his new knowledge.

A poem whose intent is one of harmony is best served with the use of the more liquid consonants such as l, m, n, and r as well as the fricative sounds of f and v; when a more cacaphonous effect is desired, then what is called "stops"—b, d, g, k, p, and t—are used in combination with other sounds. Vowel sounds are pleasing as they are more musical than consonants, and the long vowels are still more pleasing than short vowels.

In working with sound, we must, of course, touch on alliteration, but I am always a little cautious not to bear down too hard on this element of poetry. Alliteration is so easy to achieve, a beginner often tends to overuse the technique and can possibly weaken an otherwise strong poem.

Over the years, I have worked with dozens of students eager to improve their poetic styles and to see their works in print. And over the years we have met with success in both endeavors. When a student calls me on the phone several weeks after the class has ended to announce that a poem of his has been accepted for publication, we both rejoice. Here is the real reward. For to teach poetry to students already caught up with the fever is as satisfying as any creative endeavor can be.

CONTEMPORARY VS. TRADITIONAL POETRY?

Anne Marx

All too often, contemporary and traditional poetry are separated in people's minds like enemy camps. The truth is that all forms of poetry are interrelated, grown out of each other, to be juxtaposed but never polarized.

The good poet practices all forms and disparages none. A concert pianist, who has practiced his scales for years and has mastered etudes and intricate sonatas, reaches his ultimate dexterity and versatility by incorporating all his experiences. In the Middle Ages, apprenticeship to a master was the accepted means of learning the visual arts but, as the years passed, the method fell into relative disuse. Today, master/apprentice programs appear to be staging a comeback, which is all to the good. So, instead of "versus," let us insert "and" between our two viewpoints.

As to the definitions themselves, both seem unsatisfactory. "Traditional" means adhering to strictly prescribed forms. However, the traditionalist is bound to advance by using his knowledge and experience as a stepping stone to venture into experimentation with traditional forms. We also hear traditional poetry referred to as "conventional." But what is convention if not the mode of a particular time, an accepted usage or practice?

The term "contemporary" is equally inadequate. Poems written in traditional forms can certainly be contemporary in mood and impact. "Contemporary" is merely a historical designation. The same applies to the term "modern." And the use of the terms "avant garde" or "free" (vers libre) does not do justice to those practitioners of non-traditional forms who are aware of form, and have absorbed and incorporated it into their style, profoundly aware that there is nothing "free" about their writing. For the sake of convenience, let us settle for the suggested terms "traditional" and "contemporary," always bearing in mind the above-mentioned reservations.

If poetry is life named, arranged and transfixed through art in language, then the poet must concern himself with the techniques which can best express his own unique experiences at any given time. We are each the product of what and where we are, what and where we have been in the past. Therefore, we come to poetry with certain attitudes and prejudices, with personal orientations and preferences, which will affect our choices.

Elizabeth Drew said, "Poetry comes from a two-fold source—a mysterious inner compulsion and a fully conscious discipline. Living and language mingle; meaning and method vary; form is an amalgamate of both." Yet an astounding attitude assumes that how we write is a complete matter of free choice. It is not simply an arbitrary decision to write in one or the other fashion. That we are the sum total of our background and experiences manifests itself in our earliest writing. Those of us who were steeped in the classical tradition, who studied Latin and Greek and absorbed the rhythms of the 19th century through our parentage, may lean toward traditional forms. The music of nursery rhymes to which we vibrated, great teachers' concepts we embraced, a certain decorum of the earliest environment we knew—all this undoubtedly influenced our first leanings. I say "leaning" toward traditional forms advisedly, since later changes are certainly not only possible but desirable.

In the beginning there was sound humans made for and with each other. Poetry probably started as magical chanting to accompany the dance. It will always exist as the very music and dance of words. Words which are diction in its simplest form are the foundation of any poem. All old English poetry is accentual, meaning that it contains a recurrent pattern of the number of accents. The syllabic line, meaning a recurrent pattern of the number of syllables in the line, is a modern discipline.

But the vast number of poems in English throughout the ages have been written in what has been traditionally called "meter," which is a recurrent number of accents and syllables in the line. For the most part, the unaccented and accented syllables alternate in a recurrent pattern.

Each age develops or invents (or thinks it invents) new sound effects from words, and, in the course of its history, poetry has named a boundless variety of its rhythmical patterns. With exception of free verse, these all differ from prose by their root in meter, meaning measure.

Traditional poetry means that, in writing his poem, the poet follows a predetermined pattern. These predetermined fixed forms in the tradition of English poetry stem from many sources. Certain hymns and folk songs which might be termed "folk forms," were passed by word of mouth from one generation to the other. The familiar ballad stanza is still alive in nursery rhymes and other simple verse-structures. Only the truly ignorant would identify such simple forms with all traditional poetry and therefore dismiss it. But it is also a fallacy to think only of the classical forms, those adopted from Italy and France, as traditional.

Syllable count has come to us from the Orient. Japanese poems such as the three-line *haiku* and the five-line *tanka* must be considered strict forms of a different tradition. The imagists imitated these forms.

Many of the more conventionally traditional forms came from the fertile background of French and Italian poetry. The most famous and probably the most maligned and misunderstood of all forms is the sonnet, as originally borrowed from the medieval Italian poets.

Experimentation with the sonnet has been tempting to poets in the past and present and will continue to be a challenging vehicle, with its fourteen lines placed in ever-shifting relationships to one another. It is the variation from the norm which makes for artistry. An illusion of spontaneity along with the perfection of craftsmanship is the ultimate achievement. It is, of course, equally true that a sonnet can have all the proverbial flaws. Somehow, the lack of poetic impulse becomes more glaring in a sonnet than in less strict forms. Free verse writers can fool you more easily at first reading. Ultimately, all counterfeit poems fall by the wayside, no matter what the form. Other highly structured verse forms attract many contemporary poets who try to overcome the obvious monotony of repetitions by letting them come so naturally and in such subtle varieties that we appreciate the poem *per se* rather than its form. The more original poets have made slight changes in the repetitions, altering the progression to expand the total impact. However, only one who has mastered the original forms can ever accomplish successful variations. A poet may eventually create his own forms and has done so through the ages, though aware that others may well have done so before him. The sonnet was singled out here only because it is usually the target of those who, having never attempted to write in traditional forms, dare claim that a modern poet must write exclusively in free verse. There exist, of course, innumerable other fixed forms which present their own intricacies and challenges, too many forms, in fact, to be listed in a conventional glossary. What a wealth of chance for exploration.

Stephen Spender said in "The Making of a Poem":

> "Today we lack very much a whole view of poetry and have instead many one-sided views of certain aspects of poetry which have been advertised as the only aims which poets should attempt. . . . What matters is integrity of purpose and ability to maintain the purpose without losing oneself no matter what technique is our preference."

This, then, seems to be the ideal—that a poet sometimes writes in one mode, sometimes in another. By taste and temperament, he may tend to an individual quality in the use of words and forms. He judges the work of others by standards of excellence which have nothing to do with fashion. Language is an infinitely versatile instrument, tuned to be played in ever-new variations.

An example of traditional poetry:

THE OLD POLITICIAN

In shirtsleeves, shoeless, he sits quietly
aware his followers will soon forget
past accolades, wipe out their unpaid debt
accrued in an old bank of loyalty.
Becalmed at last, smooth as a settled sea,
he has accepted change without regret,
conveys a statesman's willingness to let
another generation set him free.

Free from the undertow of public life,
safe from the suction of an avid press,
not running now, a private citizen
will drift toward home, cast anchor far from strife,
shall come at times from shorelines to address
that whirlpool world he left to younger men.

               Anne Marx, 1st Prize Petrarchan sonnet category
from *Face Lifts for All Seasons*, Golden Quill Press

An example of contemporary poetry:

VISION OF THE WIDOWER

Downtown-bound along Riverside Drive
idling my car at a long red light
I spied him remounting a bicycle,
alien conveyance for one I knew
behind his dull desk of duty by day
steering words into poems by night;
after the year of mourning still numb,
passive on subways early and late.

Hot, much disheveled but purposeful,
heading North thirty blocks away,
no longer awaited by her who held
the spokes of his days together so long,
who would have forbidden such laboring
in the swelter of any June-afternoon,
would have confined him to safer blocks,
would have admonished him to beware. . .

Forseeing a stroke (a sunstroke at least)
or getting struck down by strangers nearby
from menacing doorways along this route
(all scolding merely the hum of love
heard, understood by well-married men)
to culminate in a glass of cold tea,
the caring act of a cold-running bath,
the devotion laid out in fresh underwear.

None of that for this sweat-soaked man,
yet I was glad of his secret pursuit,
to witness his grip of the handlebars
toward the daytime demands, the nightly goal.
Lights turned to hope as he pedaled on
prolonging the ride of life in new ways,
facing traffic, oblivious to me,
intent on balance and forward thrust.

       Anne Marx, 2nd Prize, Contemporary (free) verse category
          from *Face Lifts for All Seasons*, Golden Quill Press

"I ENTER"

Alice Morrey Bailey

"Congratulations! You have won. . ." A contestant receiving a letter with this salutation takes off like a paper kite and floats in ether, never fully comes to earth again. "This is heady stuff," said one first-time poetry award winner. Heady stuff, it is, and instantly addictive. Who wouldn't want to receive more such letters? Better still, be at the awards banquet or luncheon and hear the winning entry read to peers. In order to feed this new appetite, one must

ENTER MORE CONTESTS. A few years ago (say forty), and uncounted awards (not less than 300), ye author was quick to board this exciting, slow-starting chariot of stars, literary contests. After one awards banquet, when I had been lucky enough to come off with eight awards, a friend (by then a semi-friend) rushed, green-eyed, to ask: "How do you win so many awards?"

"I enter," I replied, and these two words have brought me much local fame, hence the title of this article. I was not being flip or facetious, just stating a fact. It was well-known by all present that there had been few entries in each of the categories awarded that night. I was thinking of the talented writers there who might have toppled my entries if they had just entered the contests. There are still many of these. I make it a point to thank them for not entering. "It cuts my competition," I tell them. Nevertheless, I am a competitive person. I'd rather lose to someone whose name is Anne Marx, Edna M. Leiper, Alice Mackenzie Swain, or Vesta Pierce Crawford, among many others, than to win over an empty field. I look for these names among the winners of contests and am rarely disappointed. In order to enter contests the contestants must have

THE RULES. "Where do you get the rules for all these contests?" is the query. From many sources. You get them from the writing societies of which you are a member, the writing magazines to which you subscribe, occasionally from the media, not often. Maybe your local society or chapter gives information about upcoming contests in newsletters to members. These usually only list the contests and the chairmen to whom you may write, sending a SASE (Self-addressed, stamped envelope). Too often it is too late for such a round trip before the deadline, and the outlay in postage and stationery can mount up. For myself, I take a shortcut: I subscribe to *The Golden Eagle* (P.O. Box 1314, New Milford, CT 06776, you're welcome), edited by Tom Morris, an alert gentleman who not only lists the upcoming contests, but includes complete rules far in advance of deadlines, plus a handy calendar. He even sends postcards if an important contest has missed his last edition. The price of this publication may seem high (presently $7.50 for five issues), but the savings in time alone offset the price. Once you get them

READ THE RULES. Abide by them implicitly. While most specify unpublished work and have standard requirements, such as size of paper, entry fees, deadline dates, usually postmarked before midnight, and SASE for win-lists, there are variations. These are important to the contestant. Some require unawarded work, some do not, some, very few, allow published, some make no specification as to a work having received a previous award, or one exceeding a certain amount. Some require an entrance fee, usually $1/poem, others require none, but limit the number of entries. A few require very large entry fees, as $5.00 per poem. These usually are asked when the award at stake is larger than the usual $25, $15, $10 for first, second and third prizes. Some publish the winning entries, even the Honorable Mentions. Thus we come to

THE COST OF CONTESTING. Add to postage and fees the escalating cost of good paper, ribbons, carbon paper and all other equipment used by a writer, including typewriter upkeep. Does it pay? Besides being an art, writing is a business. A limited amount of success may qualify one to associate with other writers, the very elite of society, to my thinking, but the ambitious writer will want more. At the end of 1980 I took serious stock. During the calendar year I had won 45 awards, counting Honorable Mentions (and I count those), but too many had been H.M.'s, not enough cash prizes. I really wondered if I could go on financially. The ledger for January 1981 reads:

IBM Service Contract for one year	$103.95
Memberships: USPS $10; P.S. of Va. $7.50; Terre Haute $3	20.50
Entry Fees: USPS $20; PPS $3; P.S. of Va. $6	29.00
Rag bond 20 wt. $11; second sheets, 1 ream $4.50	15.50
Carbon paper, 100 sheets	11.00
Postage	20.00
Total expenditures	$199.95

The above outgo was offset by the following income:

World Order/Narrative Poetry, John Masefield Award	$100.00
Florida State Theodore Lindgren Award, First Prize	25.00
Florida State Russell Leavitt, Third Prize	10.00
Columbine Poets of Colo., Christmas theme, First Prize	20.00
Columbine Poets of Colo., Hannukah theme, Second Prize	10.00
Connecticut River Review, publication, 2 copies @ $2.50	5.00
Sterling Pegasus, First H.M., book award, approx.	5.00
Kansas Poetry Contest, First Prize	50.00
Total Income for Jan. 1981	$225.00

A net earning of $25.05 for sitting hunched over the typewriter for that whole dismal month? No way, you will say, but I say yes. It paid for my magic carpet, the biggest item being IBM service for that extension of my anatomy, my wonderful typewriter. Who knows that I won't write a bestseller or a successful play this year? Other items are recurring expenses. There is hardly any way to balance this ledger. The income for work done in previous months; without it I would have all outgo. There is no price tag on satisfaction and excitement. The ultimate of both these, of course, is in writing, finishing a piece of work which had to be done and saying all you wanted to say, no more, in the way you wanted to say it. Sales and awards and even fame are only frosting on the cake. You may never have done it except for contests, their lure and their deadlines. One must have a repertoire, a backlog of contest material. "How do you find enough poems to fill all the categories?" asked one colleague. Categories, categories for

CONTESTS, CONTESTS. Veteran writers remember with nostalgia the wonderful magazine markets for poetry that used to be, the really good poems *Saturday Evening Post* used to publish, the *Ladies' Home Journal,* the *Good Housekeeping.* They still pay $5/line, but no longer take long, or even good poems. The author's name does not appear in Table of Contents, and the poems are used as fillers.

Poets, however, are not shy, retiring violets; they have hides like elephants and will not be extinguished. Like germs putting spores against antibiotics, they have formed themselves into a formidable society. Almost every state has an official poetry society and these are banded together by The National Federation of State Poetry Societies (NFSPS). Almost every state and the national organization have on-going, annual contests. The National League of American Pen Women with its numerous chapters offers more, but in all the arts, not just writing, and many others not named. Members give freely of time and means, and unselfish donors pour out precious funds as prize money. "I just go down the list," I told my questioner. "If I don't have a poem to fit the category, I write one." He thought this pump--priming of a true poet a huge joke, he followed that route. Now you see the name Leroy Burke Meague someplace on almost every win-list. With this increasing number of poems, the contestant very soon comes to the necessity for a system of

FILING. Each one must find what works for oneself. The following works for me: I use loose-leaf notebooks for the master file, the titles separated alphabetically, and of course alphabet sheets are a must. A history of each poem may be kept on the back of the master copy, or in an alphabetized card file. This latter is a little more work, but is much more successful, considering the constant revisions possible with the master copy of the poem. Looseleaf notebooks multiply with need, so that it now takes two thick ones to contain my unpublished poems, one thick to hold my published poems. In addition, I have one for light verse and one to hold the rules. The rules are placed in order of date of deadline, with the nearest date uppermost as you open the book. Card files multiply to published and unpublished. I also keep a separate card file for current contests, contests won and contests lost. These help me to avoid duplication of entry for a given poem in the same category and contest. Add files and cards, looseleaf notebooks, etc. to the cost of being a writer. Now we come to

A MATTER OF MILEAGE. A good contestant is always at the bottom of the subconscious well, in need of new springs, new contest entries. It is possible to win more than one prize on a good entry. If the poem wins first or second time out you may have a repeater. Enter it in a contest which does not prohibit previous winners, and one which does not publish the winning entries. Some even publish non-winners if the poem appeals to the chairman of the sponsoring agency. This should be by permission, unless the rules cover it. Such a repeat winner is my:

DEATH OF A FARMER

"What a place to die!"
My father's form, bib-overalled, lay prone
In horse-tromped hay and weedy loam, his head
Lap-held by his child son, now suddenly
Grown man. "I closed his eyes," he said,
"And held his jaw."
　　　　My mother's cry
Was anguish, yet what fitter place for him:
On land he tilled for these last thirty years?
The stable where he housed his first young flock
Already ghosted by the move to town,
Rain-leached, wind-dried, his only meagre shade
The nests of sparrows in the willowed shed.
The cabin where he brought her as a bride
Is gone, the chicken coop, the river gate.
The well was here, the granary stood there,
The wood-pile and the axe—I see them now
Between the banks of orchard, ringed by fence
And poplar trees, since yielded to his plow.
His small-boned feet are shrivelled in his shoes,
His work-scarred hands relaxed, ungloved, soil-grimed
Still shovel-handle curved, his hat aside.
The tall form spare, his chiselled nostrils still—
Breathed in, breathed out, and not breathed in again
Between the water turn and the shocking wheat
In one convulsive, crucifying pain.

Death waives decorum, neither waits the bath
On Saturday, the Sunday shave, the tie,

But took him as he was,. . . and so do I.

To illustrate, my file card on this poem reads:

"Death of a Farmer," Composed, December 1970
Georgia SPS Jane Judge Mem. 5 Dec. 1980, Nothing, Revised
Utah SPS Pearle Madsen Olsen Character Portrait 1Feb-30 April 1971
    FIRST PRIZE   25.00
Page 71 of *Eden From an Appleseed,* unpublished ms.
(which won the Morgan-Pehrson Publication Award in USPS "Poet
of the Year Series for 1971, published and released Oct. 1971)
Sold to *The Ensign Magazine,* published Oct. 1971   10.00
Entered in The Crossroads Leroy Special (free-wheeling) 1978
FIRST PRIZE, published in their Dec. Newsletter 1978 $339.00
          Net earnings for this poem: $374.00

Another poem which has won four prizes: N. Y. Forum, Ozark Writers, League of Utah Writers, finally writing the $50 First Prize in Kansas, is in process of publication in their prize poems, has netted $120.00:

FLIM-FLAM MAN

Some come on angel wings and some by stork.
He came by Haley's comet, left the same,
Upset the status quo and pulled the cork
On merriment. A Sleight of hand with name
With tongue in cheek, an innocent abroad,
A river pilot toward a mark twain port,
The pen of Sixteen-One's ribaldous fraud,
A Yankee wizard in King Arthur's court.

And still he pricks our pompous small balloons,
Explodes our human foibles with his wit.
Although he mirrors all of us buffoons
We never seem to get enough of it.
We crave his flim-flam words till we are fed
As easily as jumping frogs eat lead.

Note that the above poems are simply stated. I do not risk "Arty" or oblique poems in contests. Consider

THE JUDGES, who may receive up to two or three hundred entries in a given category. They have no time for second readings or guessing games. They are chosen because they are erudite, but appeal to them if possible, first by a professional-looking manuscript, sharp, black print on white paper of a good grade. No onionskin, even for the second sheet. I use 20-lb weight for both, but of a cheaper grade for the second sheet if one is required, the copy, not the second page. If the poem runs to more than one page I number the pages "1 of 2" and "2 of 2," and so on, including all information requested on the face page, or page 1 of the ms. Center your poem top to bottom, side to side. Your brainchild deserves the best dress you can give it.

AFTER YOU HAVE WON IT be courteous enough to thank the sponsoring agency if possible, the donor of the prize. "I have contributed money for this category of yours," said one grateful donor, "and you are the first one who ever thanked me." This letter and the sometimes lovely replies can be your memento, along with the pretty award certificates. If you make a carbon copy for your own file it can be a record. I keep still another looseleaf notebook for this purpose, last date uppermost. At the end of each year I make a list of all winnings, including Honorable Mentions, and publications. It helps me to evaluate my efforts, and is a handy compilation in case your society needs it for publicity and newsletter purposes. Do not float overlong in that ether, but open your rules file and enter the next upcoming contest, and the next and the next. The professional writer does not sit on the front stoop waiting for the mailman, commits even the memory of what is out and where to the card files. That way it is always a delightful surprise to receive a wonderful letter which begins, "CONGRATULATIONS! YOU HAVE WON. . . ."

CONCRETE DICTION

Ida Fasel

First of all, let me distinguish concrete poetry and concrete diction, with which I am concerned. Concrete poetry belongs to the history of poetry; it has a long past but achieved prominence in our century—prominence being the ability to attract the most media attention—as a manifestation of something new and original in poetic form. I consider the visual breakdowns of concrete poetry a writer's game, a printer's feat, and though at its best a concrete poem may be witty and perceptive, at its usual it is a tinkering with words to a dead end. Words chosen for poems proceed linearly, take their shape organically, resound with feelings in time to set rhythms of thought, and convey to the reader intensely conceived experience.

The phrase "vague generalities" is no doubt the cliche of most practical criticism of poems, as "be more concrete" the most frequently noted suggestion on workshop products. Students are apt to go to extremes in efforts to say something new. Sytax is broken for a collage which, it is hoped, the reader will create a oneness of in his response. Breaking away from the expected order is at times effective. But grammar is the least hindrance a poet has, and structure and statement are helped to clarity and persuasion by regard for it. The art and force of the poem depend on the words that use all the senses to present what is there and reverberate the more that is there: words that are pictorially faithful, measurably accurate, resonant, making the poem complete, achieving wholeness, pure and simple, clear and strong, in the reader.

For the kind of concreteness I am talking about, the poet must look, smell, taste, touch, listen, tell by his own strengths. That is not to say we are not to use our legacy of tradition; that is our substance, our example. And acquaintance with contemporary poets has hidden benefits even if they are only negative ones. Reading another poet's words often puts us into the momentum of presenting our own. But under our ballpoints or from our typewriters they must be our way of perceiving the world.

Some say of the world, with Conrad's Kurtz, "the horror, the horror." But I do not, and I know others who do not. I make the abstractions I believe in—truth, beauty, good, honor, reverence, right, obedience, loyalty, love—speak in what Wordsworth called a "selection of the language of men" and trust they vibrate their higher inner reality from firm, clear sounds of the actual world perceived at large. Pity the superstars of *Rolling Stones* interviews who have only one descriptive word for everything on their mind and their mouth.

The weight of the times presses against the Judeo-Christian tradition that of all reaches for spirit has the most meaning for me and others like me. All the more reason we should avoid generalization after generalization in our writing. It is a dark age, but that, too, is a generalization. Some of us experience the side of light as well as hope for it. These, too, are facts of the human condition. Man is a creature of great limits but of great possibilities, too. The words we use to demonstrate this ambivalent truth are the familiar words of our usual vocabulary— and all of them have seen much use—but they must be the right words, in our own voice, not someone else's.

The choice of words in poetry has, of course, always been a concern of the poet. Precise, realistic words have been the backbone of the best poetic texts. Sometimes the detail went no farther than its phenomenal significance, as in Ulysses hacking off the suitors' genitals on his return to Ithaca. Biblical spirituality is marvelously concrete. Consider the union of Moses and God, specifically "face to face," through the sound and sight of another created object, the bush blazing with the religious ardor of achieved seeking. Over and over Milton gets this ardor through pictorial vividness, in complex and in simple language. One of the most moving passages in all the literature of our English language, and one of the most mystical, is his account of Adam's "face to face" with God upon his creation. We cannot write in Milton's style today, but we continue to prefer words that are honest, forceful and exact to those that are flabby, general, and mindlessly repetitive.

Browning's facility with concrete language becomes almost insensitive in its glibness. Frost continues to be enjoyed for his conversational ease of language. At times he depends on general words to make a strong impression on the universal theme of decision, as in "The Road Not Taken." More often, specific, homely words give him clout and create the tender toughness that is the hallmark of living language and living things.

One of my first poems to appear in print outside school publications was called "Farther Shore." It describes twilight coming on, the street lamps "blot-still" as their light merged with the increasing dark. To my surprise—and of course enlarged understanding— I received a letter from a well-known author, who made this comment (in part) on the poem: "It reverberates precisely because of its quietness and reticence. Partly because it is so exact, almost photographic, it is also mysterious, haunting. It makes me think again of Henry Thoreau's acute remark: 'A true account of the actual is the purest poetry.' "

I have been speaking about words, and "photographic" suggests the images words sometimes make when put together. Our attention was called to imagery in poetry by the theory and practice of certain early twentieth-century poets. But their ideas were not new, only their emphasis. D. H. Lawrence uses imagery not for its own sake or for social commentary but in relation to his total world-view. I like what he said in a letter: "The essence of poetry with us in this age of stark and unlovely actualities is a stark directness, without a shadow of a lie, or a shadow of deflection anywhere. Everything can go, but this stark, bare, rocky directness of statement, this alone makes poetry, to-day." (quoted in *Crisis in English Poetry 1880-1940* by Vivian de Sola Pinto.) That was written in 1916. It is as true now as it was then. But what he failed to say was what his poetry showed: the directness of statement he spoke of had more than barrenness, had a harmony within itself and with the universe which gave his particular kind of spirituality the sense of oneness with what he called "unknown modes of being," as in his splendid poem on the snake.

A poet needs to be in control of language, needs to love it, needs to feel its force, nuance, melody. To me words are one of the wonders of the world, and a moving use of them in the shape of a poem requires maturity of perception, accuracy of observation, alertness to correspondences, intellectual and emotional awareness, and, in the fierce optimism I uphold, a willingness to break free of confining ideologies and love-hate opposites that characterize so much of human experience into their transcendent and only possible resolution, love. Can a computer, a chimpanzee, a child do that?

But I should give an example, and I offer one of my own poems, knowing better what went into it during the process of writing than I do another's poem, though at the time I was not aware of it quite in the same way as I see it now, looking back, applying words of theory to words of poetry—quite a different thing:

GENUINE CATHAY

Gift of the Orient
at its best:
I stand on the threshold.
I keep my feet off.

Vases, and flowers for the vases,
vases and flowers bordered
in pattern blended to its dyes,
pattern and colors rightly wanted:
carpet I do not walk.

One day I centered myself in its sun.
I danced all the way
through vases shaded with flowers,
down zigzags and solids of inclosure,

first the risk, and then the risk.
And as I approached the edge
where the threads lay unraveled,
out beyond anywhere I had been
discovered they were knotted, and held.

The imagery and diction are common to experience. The newly purchased carpet is made visible, but for kinetic reasons the colors are kept down. The emphasis is upon the richness of texture, the velvety softness so tangible the feet ache to dance. The perilous ends, in appearance loose, prove sustaining.

Experience explored with clarity, skill, restraint, economy, and intensity can at the same time pulse with hidden connections beyond the knowledge of the senses. Whether read aloud or in silence, the tone of the words exists together with its over-tone as part of the wonder of everything around us, even the calamitous acts of nature and men. Howard Nemerov describes angels as "holding in their slow immeasurable gaze all the transactions/of all the particles, item by atom." We are human beings, but we can take direction from them.

This is my favorite poem:

HANDS

> Don't touch, don't touch.
> We were brought up with that.
> I unlearned a lifetime of that growing
> in a moment's moment,
> our hands in each other's
> rampant, under the impetus of life.
>
> What densities of warmth surprised,
> what vital effects in that small embrace.
> Over and over against dividing summer,
> it was a winter's strength of one.
>
> After the bitter changes, I touch
> the icy knob to turn. Suddenly
> I am in a room
> warm, present,
> capable beyond measure
> of infinite changes
> from my first disobedience.   *Religious Humanism*

HOLDING PATTERN

> Sometimes it's a relief to get down from the high raven
> and his prophetic Nevermore to get the accurate assessment
> of the immediate thing an inch up from the floor—
> like a cat, or something lower, an ant perhaps,
> feel the life of another kind God spoke kindly of.
> Sometimes it's a relief to get down on all fours
> from my 5'5 and watch the scrambling away—
> apocalypse only the stab of breath, the flick of head—
> providence permitted, coming back to claim what's
> retrievable and yours. The carpet stretches me out
> on the rack of dazzling shapes that dance me to the fringes

knotted from fall, as if the floor were not enough.
Distances may give the assembled perspective of a photograph:
the sun centered in a series of vases, the vases duly
organized and bordered. Face to face with nitty-gritty,
the blue and bronze blotches, the zigzag crossings,
the fire, the fire of the flower, down there
the near sight of incoherence and hurt teems with surprise.

Religious Humanism

IF YOU WRITE A POEM

Marel Brown

When poet Robert Louis Stevenson wrote these lines:

Bright is the ring of words
When the right man rings them

we feel sure he included all the women who would be writing poetry from his day to this.

And surely every poet can read behind the words of that affirmation to know that by "bright" he meant "the ring of words" must be expressed in good form.

Poetry is written by poets—either women or men. Poetry has no gender. There is no age limit for the writing. The chief criteria for a poem is: good form, good taste, viable words, and an understandable sharing of whatever emotion or feeling sparked the poem.

In this modern "do your own thing in your own way" era, there seems to have risen a status that a poem is merely saying or telling in whatever words first come to mind, in any kind of arrangement—frequently in a jig-saw effusion on the page.

Realistically, poetry has a hidden discipline that imposes the same requirements on the poet as for any other art. To be real art, each creative process in its expression conforms to accepted cultural norm.

That does not imply that poetry—nor any of the Arts—is a static, monotone, spiritless creation. Nor a dreary recital of facts in old-style verbiage. There can be wide and stimulating variety in the artist's finished product—a variety as diffuse as the individual creator's personal application to basic requirements through personal experience.

And that should not seem strange. The universe has rules and patterns we accept and live with all the time—day and night hot and cold, rain and sun, the seasons. Even the set patterns of the universe have some variations, but they keep to the Creator's original Plan when "the morning stars sang together." Just so, the poet should create on the underlying foundation for the Art of Poetry.

After the fundamentals become a part of an individual's innate creativity then the poet can launch into whatever variety the poem requires. However far out that variation may wander there will be subtle and unobtrusive evidence that the poem, in its words and variety, is built upon the knowledge of the basic pattern.

This book is a sharing of knowledge by contemporary women poets who have learned, and have practiced, what they feel a poem should be. All the way from lyrics, to sonnets, to French forms, through Ode and Narrative, in subjective or objective expression, each poet is sharing what she knows of a special form. Each writer gives good examples of that pattern; but not one of these poets writes all of her poems in the pattern she details.

There should be no need for shying from basic form in writing poetry. Knowing forms—and with some practice in them—is conducive to concise expression, to economy of words, to clarity, suspense, good diction and grammar. Such knowledge helps perfect the *implying,* instead of *telling,* that is the true measure of any poem.

Occasionally some person who hasn't the foggiest idea of any form or requirement may write a superb poem. That does not happen often. We know there are not many Grandma Moses in the world of painting. Anyway, who wants to wait until past seventy years, on a chance to succeed as a poet! The earlier poet—or any artist—puts mind as well as heart to work to learn the requirements on that Art, the surer will be an early success.

Even music has its discipline. First, there is the matter of notes and scales. The would-be musician has a need for mastering them, with much practice. Occassionally we find a pianist who "plays by ear." Quite well, too. But how many of that ilk are invited to perform at Carnegie Hall?

And how many composers of march music have "gotten away" with several bars in four-four time, then injecting a few three-four bars? March music must have every bar, from starting point to parade end, in four-four time or marchers will be out of step. A waltz must have every measure in three-four time or dancers will be floundering all over the dance floor.

Form and pattern are universal requirements in music, yet they allow for grace notes, whole or half notes, some pauses—many varieties—but all music conforms to the pattern of each composition. Poets need to accept the same disciplines for writing poems.

From grade-school years through high school and college, and in writing workshops, whenever poetry technique is part of the creative writing class, the study should include forms, patterns, rhythms, rhymes. Even Free Verse has requirements! It may look easy, but it is one of the most difficult forms—to write a real *poem*. Free Verse is based on imagery and cadence, and that depends on individual and undefined quality of creative perception. Many of us feel that Free Verse is the last form that should be tried.

Not all poetry forms need be studied at once; but continuous enough that each would-be poet eventually has an all-over knowledge that a poem is more than a lot of hastily assembled words explaining an experience, or describing a tree, a battle, or a love affair in a careless fashion.

The poem is the poet's deep thought, feeling, or emotion—

the inward experience that gripped and whispered, "Hey! I'm here!" before a word is put on paper. How those words communicate the poet's innermost feelings to the reader determines the success or effectiveness of that poem. *The poem* is behind the words, suggested by the words, the metaphor or simile used. Words on the page are the only vehicle by which the poet can share *the poem*.

The poem itself determines the form or pattern. As when a woman bakes a cake, she knows for what occasion the cake is to be used, so she pours her batter into the correct mold or pan. It may be for cup-cakes, sheet cake, bundt pan or tiered for birthday. The cake's reason-for-being decides the mold.

Before me is a letter written by a poetry-writing-course-teacher forty years ago. In her correspondence course when I reached the French forms she wrote: "It doesn't matter in what form a poem is done so long as it measures up to being *a poem*. The theme should be so well handled that the reader is not conscious of the pattern."

That teacher was saying: no matter how super-perfect a person is in putting words together in the most intricate form, that does not of itself make a poem. The poem is the subtle overtone (or undertone, if you prefer) that the well chosen words imply. The poet must first have a poem—and then must know how to say it.

What that teacher said to me has been the measuring device for me in all these years. I've let the "measuring" slip many times, but at least I had something valuable at which to aim.

Though each sharing in this book is for the writer, each chapter can also serve for the poetry reader, or the teacher of literature. Most people like to know *why* and *how* and for what purpose the creator has produced—whether it is painting, sculpture, symphony or an architecturally beautiful building. We may not plan to paint, or sculpt, or compose or build an edifice. We like to learn how an artist works, discover the counterpoints of a musical composition, the intricacies that produce a statue or a building. We like to know, just for the warm feeling and closeness to that creative pulse. It is something that goes beyond intellectual knowledge. We grow in spirit as we learn, whether participant or observer.

The wise and joyfully successful poets—and the ones whose poems could outlast this moment of time—will be the conscientious learners who recognize that "IF you write a poem" it should be "bright"—the best that heart and mind can produce.

This is not advice but a suggestion out of long experience: Write as you wish, but know *why* you wish!

IMAGISM

Alfarata Hansel

"Imagism," a movement in modern poetry promulgated by a small group of poets in London, England, flourished roughly between 1912 and 1917. These poets, including the American ex-patriate Ezra Pound, were influenced by the French "symbolistes" in reacting against old forms and stereotypes into which the Romantic movement of the 19th century had more or less degenerated. They found inspiration rather in classic Greek and Latin poetry and especially in traditional Japanese forms, haiku and tanka, with which they experimented at their weekly meetings in Soho cafes.

The amalgam of these various influences, plus the fresh talent of members of the group calling themselves "Imagists" was expressed in the following Credo: (1) To use the language of common speech, but to employ always the exact word. (2) To create new rhythms. We do not insist upon free verse as the only method of writing poetry. We fight for it as a principle of liberty. (3) To allow absolute freedom in choice of subject. (4) To present an image (hence the name Imagist). (5) To produce poetry that is hard and clear, never blurred or indefinite. (6) Finally, most of us believe that concentration is the very essence of poetry.

These tenets were brought to the United States chiefly through the efforts of Amy Lowell. She had become acquainted with the Imagist group through Ezra Pound upon a visit to England shortly after publication, in 1912, of her first volume "Dome of Many-Colored Glass." She ardently embraced the principles of the group and was largely responsible for bringing the movement into prominence. According to Jean Gould, "It is significant that the poetry renaissance, which started under the leadership of men in England, never amounted to much until it crossed the Atlantic; when it spread with joyful fecundity under the leadership of women, principally Amy Lowell, Harriet Monroe and Margaret Anderson." Monroe and Anderson, as editors respectively of *Poetry* and the *Little Review*, were in a position to bring Imagist poetry before their reading public, but it was Amy Lowell's volume, "Some Imagist Poets," brought out by Macmillan in 1917, and containing three poems by three British and three American poets, that had the greatest impact upon the literary world.

Miss Lowell, in addition to her critical and creative talents, possessed important assets of wealth, social position and intellectual prestige. The president of Harvard University, Abbott Lawrence Lowell, was her brother as was Percival Lowell, the famed astronomer. James Russell Lowell was an uncle. Ellery Sedgewick, editor of the *Atlantic Monthly*, which first published her poetry, was the husband of an old school friend. She had ample means to guarantee the financial success of any volume she wished published as well as academic connections which brought her lecture engagements and the opportunity to bring the ideals of the imagist poets before receptive audiences.

To many young poets of the period, these ideals were a liberating, vitalizing force, and though the "movement," as such, was short-lived, we are indebted to it for much that is fresh, vigorous and significant in American poetry of the past fifty years.

Greater attention to the use of language of common speech has helped weed out much that was contrived or merely pretty, while freedom to create new rhythms, rather than be bound by rigid conventional patterns has (where practiced by disciplined craftsmen) enriched our literature to a notable degree.

To speak of freedom of choice of subject may seem a reiteration of the obvious to poets today, but we have only to glance through the verse of a generation ago, comparing it to more current poetry, to realize the strength of the bonds of convention as to subject matter.

The fourth and fifth tenets—to present an image, and to produce poetry that is hard and clear—provide an excellent corrective to mushy sentiment and fuzzy thinking that is anathema to excellence in all poetry, whether it be cast in traditional patterns or in free verse.

The final statement on the importance of concentration, "the very essence of poetry," is as valid today as when set forth by the "Imagists," those young, aspiring poets, meeting in London in the second decade of this century.

Two poems by this writer which may help to illustrate the influence of the Imagist Credo are appended:

LOGO
>   My logo is a bandage
>   binding the splints
>   that hold bones in place
>   grimed with soil and
>   stained with seepage.
>
>   I wind fresh gauze
>   for decency
>   not daring to tear off
>   the inner bands
>   where a trickle warns
>   old wounds
>   still bleed.

LAS VEGAS CASINO
>   waves of fluid glitter
>   wash against mirrored walls
>
>   the lonely crowds
>   cluster about padded tables
>   or pay solitary tribute to

ubiquitous machines

rapt voiceless entities
swimming
bemused
in an electronic sea
of chance.   by Alfarata Hansel, from *Look Homeward*

HEAT

O wind, rend open the heat,
Cut apart the heat,
Slit it to tatters.

Fruit cannot drop
Through this thick air;
Fruit cannot fall into heat
That presses up and blunts
The points of pears,
And rounds grapes.

Cut the heat:
Plough through it,
Turning it on either side
Of your path.   H. D. (Hilda Doolittle)

SALUTATION

O generation of the thoroughly smug
    and thoroughly uncomfortable,
I have seen fishermen picnicking in the sun,
I have seen them with untidy families,
I have seen their smiles full of teeth
    and heard ungainly laughter.
And I am happier than you are,
And they are happier than I am;
And the fish swim in the lake
    and do not even own clothing.   Ezra Pound

PRELUDE

The winter evening settles down
With smells of steaks in passageways.
Six o'clock.
The burnt out ends of smoky days.

And now a gusty shower wraps
The grimy scraps
Of withered leaves about your feet
And newspapers from vacant lots;
The showers beat
On broken blinds and chimney-pots,
And at the corner of the street
A lonely cab-horse steams and stamps.
And then the lighting of the lamps.   T. S. Eliot

BIBLIOGRAPHY

Benet, William Rose and Conrad Aiken. *An Anthology of Famous English and American Poetry.* New York: Random House, Inc., 1945.

Coffman, Stanley K., Jr. *Imagism,* a chapter for the history of modern poetry. New York: Octagon Books, A Division of Farrar, Straus and Giroux, 1977.

Gould, Jean. *Amy. The World of Amy Lowell and the Imagist Movement.* New York: Dodd, Mead and Co., 1975.

Hansel, Alfarata. *Look Homeward.* Phoenix: Alpha Publishing Co., 1980.

Pratt, William Crouch. *The Imagist Poem.* New York: E. P. Dutton and Co., 1963.

Smith, Janet Adams. *The Living Stream.* London: Faber and Faber, 1969.

THE IMPORTANCE OF IMAGERY

Alice Briley

In a PBS-TV interview, poet May Sarton observed that when you have the metaphor, you have the poem and Robert Frost in his essay, "The Constant Symbol," makes a similar statement:

. . . (Poetry) is metaphor, saying one thing and meaning another, saying one thing in terms of another, the pleasure of ulteriority. Poetry is simply made of metaphor. So also is philosophy— and science, too, for that matter—Every poem is a new metaphor inside or it is nothing.[1]

When Aristotle wrote his *Poetics* in the 4th century, B. C., he formulated many of the principles which guide us to this day. Observe how similar his remarks about imagery are to those of Frost:

> Metaphor is the application of an alien name by transference either from genus to species, or from species to genus, or from species to species, or by analogy, that is, proportion. Thus from genus to species, as: "There lies my ship"; for lying at anchor is a species of lying. From species to genus, as: "Verily ten thousand noble deeds hath Odysseus wrought"; for ten thousand is a species of a large number, and is here used for a large number generally. From species to species, as: "With blade of bronze drew away his life," and "Cleft the water with the vessel of unyielding bronze." Here, *apvarai*, "to draw away," is used for *raueiv*, "to cleave," and *raueiv* again for *apvarai*—each being a species of taking away. Analogy or proportion is when the second term is to the first as the fourth to the third. We may then use the fourth for the second, or the second for the fourth. . . . as old age is to life, so is evening to day. Evening may therefore be called the "old age of the day," and old age, "the evening of life, . . ."[2]

Imagery, as our school textbooks taught us, includes many devices by which the writer attempts to convey his thoughts to the reader. A simile, as defined by Webster, is a figure of speech comparing two unlike things, that is often introduced by *like* or *as* (as in *cheeks like a rose*). A *metaphor* is a figure of speech in which a word or phrase literally denoting one kind of object or idea is used in place of another to suggest a likeness or analogy between them (as in *the ship plows the sea*). A *symbol* is a word that stands for or suggests something else by reason of relationship, association, convention, or accidental resemblance; esp. a visible sign of something invisible (as the lion is a symbol of courage).

Nowadays, less distinction is made between a simile and a

metaphor.   Again, this is not a new concept.   Our wise old Greek philospher had already anticipated us by noting that "simile was also metaphor; for there is very little difference." Each type of imagery—simile, metaphor and symbol—contains so many of the same elements they begin to intertwine.   Even a seemingly simple simile like, "She is as pure as a lily," involves assumptions other than the fact a lily is unblemished, white, etc.   In addition, it assumes that the reader believes in the historical association of the lily with the purity of the lily in Christian lore.   If someone said the lady was as pure as a geranium, it wouldn't mean the same thing at all.   It has none of the same associations.   The statement is more than a simile because it also involves metaphor and symbol.

Through imagery, the writer appeals to the reader's senses. The reader, in turn, can experience in his own imagination a part of what the poet felt.   It is not a simple transfer, however. The verbal comparisons of the poet can awaken in the reader a constellation of new asssociations.   The more vivid the poet's imagery, the more the reader's own imagination comes into play, so that the poet and reader become partners in this word play of the imagination.

The choice of words is paramount in the development of the image.   Concrete and specific words are the anchors which tie down intangibles.   As X. J. Kennedy observed in *An Introduction to Poetry*, an entire image may be inherent in a single word, as in Japanese haiku.[3]

The use of certain words to convey both visual and auditory images can be illustrated by a quotation from Edna Meudt's poem, "It's Only September":

> For days we heard the muezzin jay
> calling, calling the summer away.
> From the sky and minaret tree, over and over he cried,
> *Summer!   Summer!*   Time to pay!

By using "muezzin" and "minaret" as adjectives, the poet not only conveys the prophetic voice of coming winter but also manages to compare the tree to the oriental tower from which the muezzin calls.   Something of the splendour of the rich tapestries of autumn are associated with the use of an Eastern image. How much less color would lie in the use of the word "watchman" instead of "muezzin" and "tower" instead of "minaret," for instance.

The metaphor has assumed great importance in modern verse. Poets who rely chiefly on vague adjectives or surface images often fall into the use of imagery for decoration alone. They fail to explore the depths of meaning that the ambiguity of metaphor may produce. ("Ambiguity" being used in the sense of several possible meanings.) Again referring to May Sarton, I quote from her essay, "The School of Babylon":

> . . .A poem does not move us deeply, I believe, unless the central image is capable of stirring us below the level of consciousness, is, in fact, an archetype. For the metaphor holds the explosive power of the poem.[4]

The imagery in "Trembling Like a Woman Desired" by Anne Marx gains much of its power from the context—a young girl in a concentration camp hides a few drops of perfume as a shield against her tragic circumstances. It concludes:

> Before they herded her
> into the final gangway,
> she poured all the perfume
> between her budding breasts.
>
> Trembling like a woman desired,
> head held high, she stepped
> into the chamber of showers,
> oblivious to the smell of gas.

The sparse language, the bare statements, all contribute to the starkness of the horror surrounding the young victim so that the final stanza acquires the quality of high tragedy.

Symbols also, in my opinion, are actually metaphors assigned to a particular object. That is why symbolism should be discussed as part of imagery. Almost everyone knows the common symbols deriving from Christian legends and Biblical references. In some parts of the world where people are not familiar with Western literature these symbols would mean little. Our patriotic symbols, likewise, would hold no meaning. Symbols depend on familiar associations for their meaning to be clear. Poets of the symbolist school, however, created their own symbols to add new dimensions to their imagery.

Quoting again from Edna Meudt, I turn to her poem "Wood." In this piece, the poet describes a number of things wood could symbolize for her: hearth, home, wagon wheel, etc. and concludes:

> Charged with tomorrow's forest,
> and the tree that brightens December
> I witness for one born to die in my arms
> I am immortal.

The wood has finally become "tree," symbol of Christ's cruci fixion. When you read the entire poem, you can also see that the poet has used a number of metaphors in one poem. This requires skill because often times a poet of less ability inserts images which do not apply to the main image. Poets also may use only one metaphor in a poem to convey their meaning. This is particularly true in a short lyric.

Personification is ascribing human attributes to an abstraction. Earlier poets used this device frequently. Poets today use great care in the use of personification in order to avoid the "pathetic fallacy" so common in the past—when nature was assigned human emotions in sympathy with those of the poet. But used properly, personification can be effective as in these lines from Jeanne Bonnette's poem, "Town Crier":

> Are they telling who came today
> into our locked house?
> Death entered, with no key;
> spread white sheets over something we loved.

Sometimes I think that scholarly explications detract from the poet's creative joy as the magic dust of a butterfly's wings are damaged by too careless handling. Those of you who are poets know that many of your best poems "came to you" spontaneously as if by supernatural means. No wonder, the old poets called on their "muse" to help them. Personally, I'd rather think of T. S. Eliot with a curvaceous (if confused) maiden floating overhead, rather than a committee of scholars explaining poetics. But I am joking. The research of scholars has determined standards of excellence. Philosophers, scholars and poets themselves agree that one of the basic qualities of good poetry is skillful use of imagery.

The editor has suggested that I include one of my own poems, so I conclude with a little one which is both a personification and a metaphor:

FLOWER BEETLE
    Mighty am I
    For where I walk
    Horizons tremble
    On their stalk.

    The world is golden
    To its brink
    And I—and I—am god
    I think.

FOOTNOTES

[1] Elaine Barry, *Robert Frost on Writing* (New Brunswick, N. J., 1973), p. 129. Originally published as the preface to his 1946 Modern Language edition of his poems.

[2] *Aristotles Poetics,* translated by S. H. Butcher with an introduction by Francis Fergusson, (New York, 1961), p. 99.

[3] X. J. Kennedy, *An Introduction to Poetry* (Boston, 1966), p. 77.

[4] May Sarton, "The School of Babylon" from *The Moment in Poetry* ed. by Don Cameron Allen (Baltimore, Md., 1962), p. 38.

ACKNOWLEDGEMENTS

To Jeanne Bonnette for lines quoted from her book, *Leaf Change*. Golden Quill Press, Francetown, N. H. 1979; To Anne Marx for lines quoted from her book, *Face Lifts for All Seasons*, Golden Quill Press, Francestown, N.H., 1980; To Edna Meudt for lines quoted from her book, *No One Sings Face Down*, Wisconsin House, Madison, Wisconsin, 1970; To *Encore* Magazine, Albuquerque, N. M. for "Flower Beetle" in *Encore, Encore!* Anthology, Allegheny Press, California, Pa., 1976.

THE IMPORTANCE OF METAPHOR

Alfarata Hansel

The metaphor, and its more stilted cousin, the simile, are the very heart and essence of poetry. They are the means by which the language of everyday life is given wings, enabling it to soar to the loftiest reaches of which the mind is capable. According to Louis Untermeyer, "the power of each lies in the relationship of things wholly unlike each other, a comparison between two objects that are alike only in the point of comparison."

> My heart is *like* a singing bird. . .
> The heavens *declare* the glory of God. . .

The word metaphor comes from the Greek verb meaning "to transfer," and Babette Deutch in her *Poetry Handbook,* defines it as "language that implies a relationship of which similarity is a significant feature between two things and so changes our apprehension of either or both." Whereas a simile is always introduced by *like* or *as*, and specifically points out the comparison the poet wishes to make, the metaphor strikes directly giving an immediate flash of insight:

> The Lord is my shepherd; I shall not want.
> He maketh me to lie down in green pastures;
> He leadeth me beside the still waters. . .

Here, we have compressed, through metaphor, the whole concept of a powerful, but loving, caring and protective God.

In another mood, the Psalmist calls upon God in his extremity:

> My soul thirsteth for God. . .
> My tears have been my meat day and night. . .
> Deep calleth unto deep at the noise of thy
>   waterspouts;
> All thy waves and billows are gone over me. . .

and again:

> Therefore will we not fear, though the earth be
>   removed,
> And though the mountains be carried into the midst
>   of the sea;
> Though the waters thereof roar and be troubled. . .

Through these metaphors the Psalmist is not only able to deal with the spiritual and intangible, but to make his thoughts clear through appeal to our senses of sight, hearing, taste and touch.

Those great speeches in Shakespeare's plays which are the actor's delight, draw much of their effectiveness from metaphor. Macbeth's deep anguish of guilt:

> Methought I heard a voice cry, Sleep no more!
> Macbeth does murder sleep, the innocent sleep,
> Sleep that knits up the ravelled sleeve of care. . .
> Balm of hurt minds, great nature's second course,
> Chief nourisher in life's feast. . .

is revealed through the profound psychological insight of this series of metaphors. And again in the final tragic climax, where Macbeth learns of his wife's death and comes belatedly to the realization of the brevity of life and the vanity of ambition:

> Tomorrow, and tomorrow, and tomorrow,
> Creeps in this petty pace from day to day
> To the last syllable of recorded time;
> And all our yesterdays have lighted fools
> The way to dusty death. Out, out brief candle!
> Life's but a walking shadow, a poor player

> That struts and frets his hour upon the stage,
> And then is heard no more; it is a tale
> Told by an idiot, full of sound and fury,
> Signifying nothing.

it is the striking metaphors, even more than the sonority of the lines that have made this passage live.

Metaphor gives power and beauty to Cleopatra at the death of Antony:

> The crown o' the earth doth melt. My lord!
> O! withered is the garland of the war,
> The soldier's pole is fallen; young boys and girls
> Are level now with men; the odds is gone,
> And there is nothing left remarkable
> Beneath the visiting moon. . .

and metaphor makes memorable the words of Julius Caesar:

> There is a tide in the affairs of men,
> Which taken at the flood leads on to fortune;
> Omitted, all the voyage of their life
> Is bound in shallows and in miseries.

Metaphor does not need to be couched in the stately rhythms of the Psalms or Shakespeare. It is intrinsic in the compressed and vivid lines of Emily Dickinson:

> How still the bells in steeples stand
>   Till, swollen with the sky,
> They leap upon their silver feet
>   In frantic melody!

or:

> Hope is the thing with feathers
> That perches in the soul,
> And sings the tune without words. . .

or, in writing of a train:

> I like to see it lap the miles,
> And lick the valleys up,
> And stop to feed itself at tanks;
> And then, prodigious, step

Around a pile of mountains. . .

Simple, everyday things like church bells and trains are given a new and striking reality seen through the poet's eyes, while death's poignancy is unforgettably expressed in:

> The bustle in a house
> The morning after death
> Is solemnest of industries
> enacted upon earth—
>
> The sweeping up the heart,
> And putting away love
> We shall not want to use again
> Until eternity.

Robert Frost's colloquial style is rich in striking metaphors:

> You know Orion always comes up sideways,
> Throwing a leg up over our fence of mountains,
> And rising on his hands. . .

In this poem, "The Star-Splitter," the mythological reference to the constellation is made homely and suited to a New England setting by the picture created: *throwing a leg up over our fence.*

Again in "The Grindstone" the commonplace and inanimate takes on new life and meaning:

> For months it hasn't known the taste of steel,
> Washed down with rusty water in a tin.
> But standing outdoors hungry in the cold,
> Except in towns at night, is not a sin.

In Frost's "Hillside Thaw":

> To think to know the country and not know
> The hillside on the day the sun lets go
> Ten million silver lizards out of snow!

we have an entire poem of thirty-five lines brilliantly sustaining the metaphor of silver lizards to describe a hillside thaw, letting us see an ordinary country sight in a new aspect through the lively imagination of the poet.

Though it has been generally thought advisable to avoid the *mixed metaphor,* Babette Deutch reminds us that "the highly compressed language of much metaphysical and symbolic poetry results in what seem to be mixed metaphors, but may better be called *telescoped* ones." She cites as example Hart Cranes's lines:

> The calyx of death's bounty giving back
> A scattered chapter, livid hieroglyphs. . .

We are fortunate in having Crane's own interpretation of this passage; "it refers in a double ironic sense both to a cornucopia and the vortex made by a sinking vessel. As soon as the water has closed over a ship this whirlpool sends up broken spars, wreckage, etc. which can be alluded to as *livid hieroglyphs* making a scattered chapter so far as any complete record of the ship and her crew is concerned."

In breadth of concept, the poetry of Robinson Jeffers is outstanding among twentieth century American poets, and his use of metaphor enhances this quality of his work. Pondering man—"the bloody migrations, greed of power, clash of faiths"— he sees our planet as from above, from a vast distance:

> The Atlantic is a stormy moat; and the Mediterranean,
> The blue pool in the old garden,
> More than five thousand years has drunk sacrifice
> Of ships and blood. . .

and he speaks of the Pacific as:

> . . . .this dome this half-globe, this bulging
> Eyeball of water, arched over to Asia,
> Australia and white Antarctica; those are the eyelids
>   that never close; this is the staring unsleeping
> Eye of the earth; and what is watches is not our wars.

By such metaphors the mind is stretched to new capacities. Again, in the words of Robert Frost, "metaphors are creative, door-opening, expansive"—they are indeed the poet's most effective tool.

BIBLIOGRAPHY

Aristotle. *Poetics.* University of Michigan Press, 1967.

Barry, Elaine. *Robert Frost on Writing.* Rutgers University Press. 1975

The Complete Works of William Shakespeare. Oxford University Press, 1928.

Deutch, Babette. *Poetry Handbook.* New York: Funk and Wagnalls, 1974.

Frost, Robert. *New Hampshire.* New York: Henry Holt & Co., 1923.

The Holy Bible. (King James Version), James Potts & Co., 1901.

Jeffers, Robinson. *Selected Poems.* New York: Random House, 1965.

The Poems of Emily Dickinson, Boston: Little, Brown & Co., 1930.

Untermeyer, Louis. *Poetry, Its Appreciation and Enjoymen.* New York: Harcourt Brace & Co., 1934.

PARALLELISM IN POETRY

Wanda Allender Rider

Writers of prose for a long time have been aware of the importance of using the technique of parallelism in their writing. Poets, too, must strive for paralleled form and structure in their poetry to communicate their ideas more effectively.

According to *Webster's Third New International Dictionary,* parallelism is similarity of construction of adjacent word groups which are equivalent, complimentary or antithetic in sense especially for rhetorical effect or rhythm as in poetry. Poetry, the art form of the poet like the art form of the artist, must have balance to be pleasing.

Parallelism is balance in the development of structure, meaning, and phrasing; and balance adds beauty to the format, sound, and sense. This paralleled balance may be achieved through the matching of equal or corresponding constructions, and by giving these constructions paralleled placement. Balanced, paralleled lines emphasize the similarity or contrast between

constructions. The following poem, a cinquain, by Helen Thomas Allison[2] is a good example of paralleled, contrasting ideas in
poetic expression:

> Shadows
> Are never there
> On our dark, moonless nights.
> They lie across our golden days,
> Omens.

The format of a poem should be checked for paralleled indentions, capitalization, and punctuation. This consistency
dresses the poem for the reader's eye so that time will not be
lost checking and thinking about an exception that is not there
for a specific purpose. This does not mean that every poem
must follow one consistent style, or that creativity should be
stifled; it does suggest, however, that there be some consistency
amid all the inconsistencies. The poem, "Lawn Lore," by Inez
Elliott Andersen[3] is a striking example of paralleled indentions,
capitalizations, and punctuations as well as a portrayal of parallelism in form and thought:

> Children, children, rush the rakes;
> The leaves are on our lawn!
> Neighbors like it neat.
>> Scrunch, crunch, with vehement strokes
>> They ply the rasping scrapers,
>> Reducing rustling carpet
>> To piles for dank decay.
> Children, children, bring the brooms;
> The snow is on our lawn!
> Neighbors like it neat.
>> Swish, swash, with vehement vigor
>> They wield the sturdy sweepers,
>> Reducing ivory carpet
>> To piles of dirty slush.
> CHILDREN! CHILDREN! GET THE GUNS!
> There are grown-ups on our lawn!
> Neighbors who like it neat.

Repetition of words in paralleled form is used to gain
emphasis. This may appear as repetition of a word, a phrase,

or the repetition of a complete line. The following lines from another poem by Inez Elliott Andersen,[4] entitled "From a Southern Spoon River Anthology," provides an example of the use of repetition of a word for emphasis:

> I longed to say, "I love you," but I never could.
>   Why couldn't I? Why?
> Seeking answers, Mr. Masters,
>   I read your long Poem SILENCE.
> Like the critics, I found it "gravely moving,"
>   But I found no answers.
> So the ghosts of words unsaid
> Kept haunting me,
> Kept trooping to my door,
> Kept marching to my couch,
> Kept surrounding me with silence,
> Until they pushed me to this place
> To join the silent dead.
>   Here I lie.

At times the importance of structure development entices the poet to select words that fit the pattern, thereby neglecting the search for a word that conveys the specific meaning desired. Even though the rhyme and meter requirement can be satisfied by using a word, this is insufficient reason to use it; the correct word to use is that specific word that will provide an effective shade of meaning as well. Take note of the very careful choice of words in the following poem, "My Possessions," by Helen Thomas Allison:[5]

> I have a picture in shades of blue;
> And one of sky for outside, too.
> I own a footstool made of pine;
> A stump in the woods I claim as mine.
>
> And I have a house with rooms to sweep;
> All of the great outdoors to keep.
> I own a dog with a friendly bark;
> But I also claim a meadowlark.
>
> It's hard to sort my wealth apart.
> The things I touch are within my heart.

This poem is a series of comparisons and contrasts stated in paralleled form. It is appealing to the senses, and it paints a picture which carries a specific message in a brief and interesting manner.

The wise use of a synonym and antonym substitution can help one to avoid a gigantic pitfall in writing poetry. Often the word needed may not be in the vocabulary of the poet, or the poet may not be able to recall the exact word that is needed. In addition, words that appear very similar often have such varying shades of meaning that they can not be substituted for each other. For example, references to various types of trees have different connotative meanings. In "The Garden," a poem by Andrew Marvell,[6] reference is made to "the Palm, the Oke, or Bayes." A garland of palm was used to recognize military honor; a garland of oak was used for civic achievements; and a garland of bay was used to recognize literary distinction. The same shades of meaning exist in other word families like highway, road, freeway, interstate, expressway, street, avenue, and parkway. All of them have the same general meaning, but each has a very specific meaning that the poet should consider in his choice of words. For this reason, a poet should have ready access to a good, complete thesaurus.

Parallelism, through its requirement of balance, is used to gain the attention of the eye and the ear. In addition to being used to appeal to the senses, this technique is used to develop and convey more concise mental images, to elicit a response from the reader, and to avoid the formation of an awkward pattern for the reader to translate into meaning. Parallelism is often used to stir emotions. The famous "Gettysburg Address" by Abraham Lincoln[7] contains an excellent example near the end in the last sentence: "and that government of the people, by the people, for the people, shall not perish from the earth." The power in this expression comes from the repetition of paralleled phrase constructions.

The "Speech in the Virginia Convention" by Patrick Henry[8] is another example of literary effectiveness: "I know not what course others may take; but as for me give me liberty or give me death!" The effectiveness results from the use of paralleled structure of contrasting clauses and ideas.

The device of parallelism is frequently used in the Bible.[9]
The poetic expressions in the Psalms and Proverbs provide many
examples using comparison and contrast in parallelism such as
the following:

> The Lord is my shepherd;
> I shall not want.   Psalms 23:1

> My son, keep thy father's commandment, and
> forsake not the law of thy mother.   Proverbs 6:20

In addition, the well-known "Ten Commandments" are stated
with repetitions of words and paralleled form to gain emphasis.

Paralleled poetic constructions contain line elements of the
same grammatical function, rank, and form. For example, two
closely related ideas should be expressed by corresponding grammatical constructions; a word balances another word; a gerund
phrase is used with another gerund phrase; and a clause is paralleled with another clause. There may be a pairing of the iambic
foot with the anapestic foot, and the trochaic foot with the
dactylic foot. Whether it may be words, phrases, clauses, or
poetic feet used to express the ideas, ideas of equal importance
should be expressed by duplicate constructions of form.

The poet should practice using the following four rules
for developing paralleled structure. These rules will serve as
an aid in the more technical aspects of writing poetry:

Rule 1: Coordinating conjunctions (*and, but,* or *nor*) connect
ideas of equal importance which are expressed in the same form
and structure.
> Example: Incorrect: She likes *to write* and *painting.* (Not
> paralleled; infinitive use with gerund.)
> Correct: She likes *writing* and *painting.* (Paral-
> leled; gerund is balanced with another gerund.)

Rule 2: Repeat a word when necessary to make the meaning
clear.
> Example: Incorrect: *Jane's hair* was as beautiful as *Mary.*
> Correct: *Jane's hair* was as beautiful as *Mary's
> hair.*

Rule 3:   Use paralleled constructions to compare or contrast
ideas.
> Example: Incorrect: *To listen* carefully is as important
> as *speaking* correctly.
> Correct: *To listen* carefully is as important as
> *to speak* correctly.

Rule 4:   Check the placement of compound conjunctions:
They are: *both-and, either-or, neither-nor,* and *not only-but also.*
They should be placed just before the words that are
parallel.
> Example: Incorrect: The novelist *not only* must select
> the characters to use, *but also* the place for the
> setting.
> Correct: The novelist must select *not only* the
> characters to use, *but also* the place for the
> setting.

Parallelism is a cohesive element in the lines of a poem
that provides for clarity, coherence, conciseness, smoothness,
emphasis, and strength. Poets should make wise use of
this technique; it will increase the effectiveness of poetic expression.

FOOTNOTES

[1] *Webster's Third New International Dictionary.*

[2] Helen Thomas Allison. "Shadows," in *Portals,* ed. by Edna Purviance (Bellingham Washington, February, 1980)

[3] Inez Elliott Andersen. "Lawn Lore," in *Never Send to Know* (Kingsport, Tennessee: Kingsport Press, 1962), p. 81.

[4] Inez Elliott Andersen. "And Now I Have Told You," from *A Southern Spoon River Anthology* (Memphis Tennessee: Riverside Press, 1979),
p. 96.

[5] Helen Thomas Allison. "My Possessions," in *Springfield News,*
Springfield, MO., and in *Tennessee Voices* (Memphis, Tn.: The Poetry
Society of Tennessee, 1970)

[6] George Def. Lord, ed. *Andrew Marvell, Complete Poetry* (New York: Modern Library, 1968), pp. 48-50.

[7] Abraham Lincoln, "The Gettysburg Address," in *Freedom's Frontier,* ed. by Ray Compton (Chicago: Lyons and Carnahan, 1953), p. 85.

[8] Patrick Henry, "The Speech in the Virginia Convention," in *Literature of America,* ed. by J. N. Hook (New York: Ginn and Co., 1957), p. 59.

[9] *The Holy Bible* (King James Version)

PREPARING THE MANUSCRIPT

An Interview with Evelyn Allen Hammett by Grace Kirk Wofford

Grace: Miss Hammett, you have prepared many manuscripts in your time. What would you consider the most *important* things to know about the preparation of a manuscript for publication?

Evelyn: Good typing, neatness, correctness of *spelling,* (I have had poems published in anthologies with mis-spelled words in them), proper spacing. . .What do you think?

Grace: I believe that you are right about those things. Is it correct, in writing poetry, to submit it single-spaced or double-spaced?

Evelyn: The rule says double-spaced, but I have seen good manuscripts single-spaced, especially if you have stanzas. Then you have stanzas single-spaced, then double-spaced between one and the next.

Grace: That's logical. What would you say with regard to narrative poems?

Evelyn: Narrative poems would be double-spaced straight through.

Grace: Is a narrative poem written without a stanza at all, or could it have couplets inserted?

Evelyn: It could have anything the poet wants. It could have spaces for emphasis. It could do what the poet wants.

Grace: I believe I understand that. Now, in submitting a manuscript of poetry, does the poet's name and address go in the upper lefthand corner as it does in prose?

Evelyn: As far as I know, it does.

Grace: On every page?

Evelyn: No not necessarily on every page, but now that we all have these little name and address labels, it would be very little trouble to paste a label on each page.

Grace: What about the numbering of pages in a manuscript?

Evelyn: Usually, it's better to number at the bottom of the page. I have always used a dash and then the number and then another dash, in the center, at the bottom of the page. And, of course, at the end you need a 30 just as in prose.

Grace: In typing poems for a manuscript, one should use a separate sheet for each poem. . .Let me ask you this, too. What is your opinion about using poems of different types in the same volume?

Evelyn: Oh, certainly. .for variety. . .for interest. I think it is rather stupid for anyone to assign a certain theme that must be the theme of every poem in the volume. I had a letter from a "Vanity press," and they wanted every poem to be on, say, "love" or "family" or "friendship" or what-have-you. It would seem to me deadly dull.

Grace: It would not make for interesting reading, unless one were looking for a poem, or a few poems, to be used for some specific lecture or program on a given subject—or unless a person found himself in the mood to read and meditate on something like "death" or "the ultimate victory" or "daily living."

Evelyn: Now, you are speaking about poems of inspiration. You can't find better ones anywhere than those you will find in the Bible. But the Psalmist (whoever he was) used variety, both in subject and matter and in form.

Grace: How long do you think a Foreword should be?

Evelyn: Oh, very short. And in numbering pages for a manuscript, I would say number "one" would go on the first poem, rather than on any preceding pages. I believe I would prefer, say, a title page, and then, if you like, an introduction or a Foreword, the Index, and then start your numbering with your poems.

Grace: How many poems would you say a manuscript should contain?

Evelyn: I would say probably forty, not over sixty.

Grace: How does a poet go about selecting the artist who will design his dust jackets? Do you know whether the publisher prefers to make that selection, himself?

Evelyn: I have no idea.

Grace: How was it done with your book, *I, Priscilla?*

Evelyn: Oh, that's not poetry.

Grace: Yes, I know, but how was the selection made?

Evelyn: The jacket was left to Macmillan, the publisher. The illustrations were sent. If you have an artist friend you want to suggest, the dealing should be between the artist and the publisher.

Grace: In other words, the poet does the script and the artist does the art work, and each one deals separately with the publisher?

Evelyn: Yes, that is what I mean; otherwise, you might see the end of a beautiful friendship!

Grace: It is easy to understand how that might happen! There was something else I wanted to ask you. Oh yes. . .it's true, isn't it, that the manuscript should be submitted flat, in a box slightly larger than the size of a standard sheet of typing paper?

Evelyn: Yes, I guess so. Or it could be sent in a heavy manila envelope, and, of course, you have your SASE that goes with it.

Grace: Now, let me ask you another thing about submitting a manuscript, how much success have you had with submitting your own manuscript? Or have you used an agent?

Evelyn: I have never had an agent. I have always submitted my manuscripts directly to the publisher; but, then, I haven't published as much as I would like.

Grace: That's all right. What you have published is significant.

Evelyn: I've never had an agent. The poetry has gone to the publisher. Sometimes, you get a good letter back. For instance, I wrote a little thing called "Scrap" about an old flat-iron and sent it to Margaret Cousins at *Good Housekeeping*, and she wrote back, "I like this so much it might have been written on assignment." But I've never been able to hit that market any more!

Grace: You hit the "Slicks" once. Didn't you? And many of us never do that even once.

Evelyn: Poets are usually glad to get into print.

Grace: Even in newspapers.

Evelyn: Yes, but you may be surprised at what is re-printed. For instance I did a little thing called "Mourning becomes the Apostrophe." (Of course the title is from *Mourning becomes Electra*) And it was published free in the little book called *Word Study,* and then *Scholastic* asked for it and paid for it, and then Max Nurnberg, who used to write on words and punctuation and what-not, bought it and paid for it, and then he bought it again and paid for it; but I haven't had that luck with many of them. That was just submitted first; in fact, I did it after a visit to Merriam-Webster.

Grace: That brings us to an interesting point. Do you think it is to the writer's advantage if he can visit a publishing company and maybe talk with the Editors?

Evelyn: Yes, indeed. I don't believe that *I, Priscilla* would ever have made it if I had not been able to go. I was in New York for an interview, and the Editor happened to be a New England woman who was familiar with my story already.

Grace: For instance, if I wanted to submit my manuscript of poems to a publishing house in Nashville which does publish poetry, would I write them and ask for an interview, or would I just go by there?

Evelyn: Oh, you'd better ask for an interview.

Grace: And I would carry the manuscript and maybe a sample of the art work with me? That would be the way to go about it?

Evelyn: Yes.

Poems by Evelyn Allen Hammett:

GRACE BEFORE BOOKS
  Blessed be God
  For every magic pen
  That lures us on

To seacoasts of Bohemia
And peaks in Darien!

published in *Kaleidograph* and *Literary Digest*

CANA

My draught of life—
Insipid, pale—
Crystal nor silver could avail
To give it savor or bouquet.

And then you came,
O Exorcist,
And made of it
An aromatic vintage fit
For bacchanal or eucharist.

published in *Poet's Forum*, February 1933

CLOVER

"What riddling talk!"
Cried the pagan Celts.
"The man is daft!
What is the Trinity?
How can one be three?"

"Behold the shamrock,"
Saint Patrick said to them,
"Three equal leaves,
Sprung from a single stem—
Perfect one,
Yet very three—
Thus is the Trinity."

He might have added this
Moreover,
"God witnesseth Himself
Likewise in a four-leaf clover.
Three leaves—the Trinity;
The fourth is man,
United with the Holy Three
He maketh rare and perfect
Symmetry." published in Portland *Oregonian*

Reprinted in B D, magazine for Xavier Society, Blind and Deaf, in Braille

Poems by Grace Kirk Wofford:

LATE SPRING
> Something tells me there will be
> Another hour of ecstasy,
> Somehow, somewhere, beyond this pain
> Will bloom the daffodils again.
> Beneath this ice, these winter snows,
> A flickering spark of certainty
> Throbs and lives and grows.
>
> I could not bear this hour of grief,
> This heavy weight of pain,
> Unless I knew that God would bring
> The robins to my trees again!
>> published in Paul Flowers *Greenhouse*
>> *Commercial Appeal* and *Pen Woman*

CYNIC
> Seeking only coldness in the clear December night,
> Finding only glitter in the heart of every star,
> You would see the quicksands in a singing brook that winds
> And the rocks along a road that stretches far.
>
> Oh you who see a nothingness
> In things that are to be,
> I wonder. . .do you ever think to find the dreams in me?
>> published in *The Mountain Breeze*
>> *Anthology of American Verse, Book IV*

ACHIEVEMENT
> She stands there, wavering,
> Eyes round, mouth still rounder,
> The small button of her nose
> Tilted to match the curling top-knot of her hair.
> We kneel before her, hoping,
> (The shadows of ages of parents behind us)
> Afraid to breathe,
> Watching the hem of her pink-checked apron,
> The tense little knees, the scrubby toes of her shoes.
>
> And look! She did!
> She took a step!
> The very first of all her life.
>> published in *Toward the Stars*
>> and *The Muse*

PROSODY

Wilma W. Burton

The word *prosody* appears to have the same root as the word *prose* but both their meanings and roots are different. Webster's New Collegiate Dictionary (copyrighted by G. & C. Merriam Co.,) tells us that prose comes from the Latin word *prosus* and defines it under a first meaning, "the ordinary language of men in speaking or writing," or "a literary medium distinguished from poetry especially by its greater irregularity and variety of rhythm and its closer correspondence to the patterns of everyday speech."

Prosody has its root in the Latin *prosodia* meaning "accent of a syllable," and the Greek prosoida "song sung to instrumental music, accent" from *pros* plus *oida* or "from an ode." Webster gives as a first meaning, "the study of versification; especially: the systematic study of metrical structure."

Somewhere on the misty flats between prose and poetry we find the prose-poem written by writers seeking to express themselves in an individual manner above all costs, but not yielding to the strict demands of poetry per se. Such a writer according to many authorities, among them George Saintsbury (*History of English Prosody,* pub. 1910-12) is Whitman of whom Saintsbury writes of what he terms Whitman's "dithyrambic versicles":

> . . . there is, through no meter, a comparatively regular progression of a quasi-metrical kind, capable of several divisions, no doubt, but grouping easiest into something like three, four, and six or seven examples of the 'prose feet'—paeons, epitrites, or dochmiacs. . .

Whitman was a great revolutionist expressing himself in a rhapsodic writing that he deemed to call "poetry." We are grateful for his outstanding contribution to the English language, but as for prosody—the kind a poet must concern him or herself with—it is not exemplary, other than in the free verse or prose-poem category.

Ancient Greek and Latin verse were based on *quantitative meter* and when English verse is considered in the light of quantity verse or meter, the natural iambic accent of the language becomes dominant and we are forced to recognize poetry written in English as falling in two categories: *accentual* and *accentual syllabic* (or stress syllabic). Quantitative meter, based on feet by length of syllables, or the length of time required to pronounce them, does not lend itself well to the English language despite the fact several outstanding poets have chosen to write in this style (and quite successfully) because stress so dominates the English language that we do not clearly hear numbers of syllables. When quantitative meter has been written in English, it was good because it sounded like either accentual or accentual syllabic meter.

Native Anglo-Saxon poetry falls into accentual meter: its lines are measured by accented beats while the unaccented syllables are ignored. This form is often used by modern poets. The unaccented syllables, however, have a way of demanding stress accents depending upon the reader and the accent he decides to give them.

Chaucer wrote in accentual syllabic meter which is the form most poets writing in English have followed. In this form of meter, the length of the line is not determined by number of stresses alone nor yet by the number of syllables but by the combination of stress syllables and non-stress syllables known as feet. The names of the feet (iambic, trochaic, anapestic, etc.) originated in classical poetry, in which oddly they were based on quantity rather than accent. Chaucer was not confused by this dichotomy and probably tapped out his poetic feet with his quill. The iambic foot is basically ta DUM/ta DUM and it is thought that all other measures of feet are derivatives of the iambic foot.

This standard iambic foot can be tampered with under rules of prosody thusly: it can be reversed: TUM ta; an extra ta can be added: ta ta TUM; or a stress can be dropped: ta. Or a stress can be doubled: TUM TUM; and on occasion TUM can be used alone without the ta: TUM. When there are extra tas left over at the end of the line, no problem, these can be used and called "hyper-metrical" and ignored in the actual scansion of the feet.   Chaucer, Milton, Pope, Shakespeare, Browning, Frost, Yeats, Thomas, MacLeish and many other outstanding poets adapted these variations of the iambic foot in their poetry and for the most part employed few others.

In prosody, along with accent and stress, is another important consideration: *diction.*   Judson Jerome in his column in *Writer's Digest* (May, 1981) gives an illustration on the use of diction in the word *controversial.*   In ordinary conversation this word becomes con-tra-VER-shul.   But in accentual syllabic meter, it may become CON-tro-VER-si-AL, such as in:

> On Eve or Adam should we blame the fall?
> The question still is controversial.

Good poets such as Shakespeare or Yeats use such words when writing accentual syllabic meter as though each syllable were pronounced separately.

However, the flexibility of the language permits the ordinary conversational use when so desired in verse such as:

> One thing to avoid in writing a commercial
> Is the use of all topics controversial.

Here we see the two ending syllables slurred into the conversational "shul."

The natural rhythm of accentual syllabic verse readily falls into the longer form of polysyllables to produce a musical form of poetry peculiar to the English language.   This is distinct from the slurring of conversational usage in free verse or accentual meter.   The latter meter is used by many modern poets and often in monosyllabic or disyllabic diction which forms lend themselves to heavy stresses.   When free verse is written in a prose form—without the use of heavy stresses—it can fall flat on the page, and is really not poetry, but prose that borrows the line usage of poetry, so that it *appears* to be poetry on the page.

The 19th-century poets both in English and American such as Longfellow became so skilled in their prosody that their works had the effect of lullabies being sung to their readers—readers who have been shaken from their comfortable cradles by the truncated verse of Hopkins, Dickinson and the rhapsody of Whitman and other modern poets, who like the composers abandon the diatonic scale. Sometimes they write new rules of prosody along with their poems.

No modern poet, however, can write good free verse—no matter how free it may seem—without first understanding the rules of prosody and having mastered the traditional forms.

SALUTE TO THE SONNETEERS

Liboria Romano

From the early Sicilian, Giacomo da Lentini, who is said to have originated the sonnet, to the sonnet sequence of Sidney to "Amoretti," of Spenser to "Astrophel and Stella," and of Shakespeare to his dark mistress, men have sounded their lady's charms. But it is my desire to salute several lady sonneteers, mainly of Italian origin. Of course, there are many lady sonneteers of other origins.

The earliest known sonnet written by an Italian lady is signed merely, "Compiuta Donzella" (the Accomplished Damozel). She is the author of three sonnets revealing her heartaches. The accomplished damozel is of interest, too, because she may be (according to Ernest Hatch Wilkins' *History of Italian Literature*), the recipient of a letter from Fra Guittone, born about 1225, the first of the Tuscany poets, who addresses her as "Most Charming Lady: Almighty God has endowed you with such a marvelous perfection of excellence that you seem to be rather an angelic than a terrestrial being. We were indeed not worthy that so precious and marvelous a person should dwell on earth. But I believe that it pleased Him to set you among us in order that you might be a mirror, wherein we all might learn to shun vice and to attain virtue..."

This letter, according to Mr. Wilkins, probably had a determining influence on other and greater poets (Guinizelli, Dante,

Petrarch, etc.) in the idealization of their ladies.

A lady sonneteer of the fifteenth century was Vittoria Colonna who is memorialized by no less a poet and artist than Michelangelo. Among his sonnets is one entitled "To Vittoria Colonna." I use here a few lines in translation:

> The best of artists hath no thought to show
> Which the rough stone in its superfluous shell
> Does not include: to break a marble spell
> Is all the hand that serves the brain can do.

Michelangelo goes on to say that not all the art that he wields can move the adamant lady.

Vittoria Colonna's sonnets expressed longing for her dead husband. She wrote sacred and moral sonnets, and no doubt influenced the later Victorian lady sonneteers, such as Chistina Rossetti, sister of Dante Gabriel Rossetti.

In the sixteenth century, Gaspara Stampa poured her heart into the most passionate of sonnets chiding a disappearing lover. Thoroughly disillusioned, she later wrote sonnets asking God's forgiveness for her grave errors. Her life and love was brief and tragic (1523-1554), but Gaspara Stampa takes her place in the roster of Italian ladies of literature.

It is impossible to list all the female sonneteers, but two great Victorians rate mention: Elizabeth Barrett Browning (1806-1861) wrote as a wedding gift to ther husband, the poet Robert Browning, "Sonnets From the Portuguese," and Christina Georgina Rossetti, wrote a sonnet sequence "Monna Innominata" (Nameless Lady), which her brother said referred to herself and her love for scholarly recluse, Charles Cayley, whom she declined to marry because of his liberal religious views. Poor Miss Rossetti gave her life taking care of a sick father and mother. She died of cancer.

We salute those lovely lady poets of pre-woman's liberation days. We have many American and English beloved sonneteers in the twentieth century, to name a few: Elinor Wylie, Edna St. Vincent Millay, Dorothy Parker, etc., but we wished mainly to remind the newer generations of the lovely ladies who wrote sonnets centuries ago in Italy.

TRISTAN AND ISEULT

A time of times for courtly love again,
  As tides of dreams hurl crashing on the rocks;
  Did Lyonesse recede beneath the shocks
  That Arnold felt and nineteenth century men?
With Marguerite he watched the sea roll, then
  The tide went out and left the gray-parched flocks,
  For truth is twins white-handed in green frocks,
  And dreams may go, but fogs will shroud the glen.

Iseult of Brittany, Iseult of famed
  White hands, of Tennyson's "Last Tournament":
  Iseult of Ireland, Iseult that quaffed
A golden wine that ever more inflamed
  Red Swinburne as he sought with mad intent
  The rocks of Lyonesse where lovers laughed.
            Liboria Romano (A Petrarchan Sonnet)

ROBERT AND ELINOR FROST AT WEST-RUNNING BROOK

Say Love had kept a lease-hold there to count
Contraries and the kisses they exchanged;
Together two could flaunt the future, mount
The heights; no night-fall found them long estranged.
Our world defines immortal, names a list,
Some famous lovers who have earned renown:
So Petrarch and his Laura, co-exist
With Dante and his Beatrice. The crown
Adorns Aeneas, Dido, pyre-belle;
What child had they? And what had they to do
But sing of love, and only passion tell
That passes with each passing rendezvous.
How Elinor and Robert stood the test,
Shows each had helped the other do his best.
            Liboria Romano (A Shakespearean Sonnet)

TO MARKET, TO MARKET. . .

Frances Riemer Burt

Of course you want your work to be published. You are an accomplished poet, and have won some prizes. You know how to prepare a manuscript. Who will buy?

Some DON'TS are constructive. Don't expect writing and selling poetry to be your career. Poetry is a calling. You choose a career—a calling chooses you. No one makes a living entirely from selling poetry. There is a relatively small market for it, and poems are the most over-produced commodity in the world. Out of fifty poems in perpetual circulation, in a year's time you may figure at the most to place a dozen—and some of these will be in non-payment publications. The pressure of having economic need to sell your poetry may be a hindrance.

Don't use the scatter gun approach to submitting your work to the editors. Do your homeword, and study the market! Even if you do not find an actual *yardstick* you will get a notion of the general concerns of the editors, and their artistic standards. Collect all the publications you chance upon which use poetry, and file them according to type. Write to editors and request writer's brochures—most will supply them. Subscribe to a writer's magazine, and refer to current market listings. If you do not wish to invest in a writer's market publication, go to your library and copy current addresses from their sources.

Most editors advise trying small markets first. The competition is not so keen, and many of them use more poetry and light verse as filler material. You may aim for a prestigious magazine, but the standards of the smaller publications are high, and you stand a greater chance of acceptance.

Get acquainted with readership. Find out what *goes*. If you are trying to reach a children's market—read your poems to children, before you send them out. If you are aiming at housewives and homemakers—read the verses to women's groups. Watch their reactions. Do they laugh? Are they touched?

The response during a program at a women's club encouraged me to send out these two verses, which were accepted by a family type magazine—and another, to an inspirational monthly:

QUESTION

> What does more uselessly equip
> Than zippers which refuse to zip?

HOUSEWORK

> Although with apathy I treat it,
> And uncivilly I greet it,
> And there is little time I give it in a day;
> It is patient, uncomplaining,
> Its humility retaining,
> My indifference will not make it go away.

The same themes have been used since ancient times, by poets. It is not necessarily the theme that makes a poem marketable. It must have a special quality—a twist at the end, or an unusual perspective to give the editor the thrill he is looking for. It must fill an emotional need, and strike a responsive chord. My poem "Minutes" says something that has been said before—but the allegorical treatment made it different and made it marketable. It also won a prestigious prize:

MINUTES

> The meeting was called to order
> March 23, 1917.
> God presided.
> I was the only member present.
> He appointed me a committee of one
> To give life
> And love
> To the project of our organization.
>
> I never tried to resign the committee,
> But several times I moved
> To adjourn the meeting.
> There was no one to second the motion,
> And God refused to let it pass.
> Our agenda is years long, now.
> There is so much to do.

When all the new business has become old business,
And I report our project is self sustaining
Under God
Jesus will come to our meeting.
He will second my motion to adjourn.
Then, I can go Home.

Inspirational and religious markets are usually good ones to which you may submit your poetry. They use more than general publications, although their payment rate is not always as high. They want family oriented and humorous pieces, too. Do not send abstract or ambiguous poetry to these markets. Make a point. These verses were among those accepted to a religious magazine:

SIX YEARS OLD
Protectively, I take his hand to cross a busy street;
Such a little fellow, and so many wheels and feet—
But with first grade independence, he looks right and left
                                                          to see
If it is safe; quite confident that he is leading me!

EIGHT YEARS OLD
He likes to think that we must give
Him masculine prerogative
To stay up late and talk man rough
And demonstrate that he is tough—
But bedtime comes, to his annoyance,
And he reverts to little boyance.

Editors look for poetry that says something definite. Do not worry about inventing or using new forms. It is all right to experiment, but study the forms which are most often published. Form and structure must have a foundation which editors recognize immediately. Sometimes an idea grows into a poem that simply falls into form—whether it has been used before or not. This happend with "Ghost Town," and the editor liked it:

GHOST TOWN
Empty shells; buildings with
Rotten timbers
Mouldering curtains
Crumbling floors

Cobwebs, rush.
No one cares. Buildings
Return to dust.

Empty shells; people with
Distorted values
Selfish desires
Faithless souls
Apathy, scorn.
God cares. People
Can be reborn.

Consider the purpose of the magazine before you submit works. Send poems about cats and dogs to publications whose main thrust is cats and dogs. IF you have a poem about babies, send it to a publication for young mothers. Anything about women's interest will logically be sent to those markets. I placed a poem about Tamsen Donner, of the Donner Party, in a heritage monthly, and one on a cure for colds in a medical journal. An art periodical used this one:

RETROSPECT
If I could put a frame around
My roses,
A bit of cloud,
A merry face—
A secret place—
A crowd;
Anything that pleases,
Or is quaint—
I'd save a lot of paint.

Editors do not like untitled poems, or lengthy titles. Titles should fit the subject of the poem, for identification and extension of the idea. Sometimes a good title helps sell the poem. If a poem is returned to you time after time—and you have faith in it—try changing the title. Perhaps it should be more enigmatic, or make more sense.

Perhaps you would like to dump your output in the lap of an agent, and let him worry about the markets. Agents are not likely to handle poetry—it does not pay enough, and most agents are not equipped to judge and find a suitable market for poetry. As someone said, "You do not need a weatherman to tell which way the wind blows."

If you should submit a previously published poem to a new market, be sure to include where and when it originally appeared. It is best to always reserve book rights, in case you may wish to publish a book of your poems. What rights you have kept are important, too, in case you are asked to be included in an anthology.

Some poetry anthology publishers ask your permission to print a poem of yours, and at the same time ask you to pre-purchase a number of copies to "defray expenses." Do not fall for this, flattering as it seems. Legitimate anthologists are backed by authentic publishers. The flow of money should be from the anthologist to the author, not from the author to anthologist. Be sure to list prior publishers, if your poem is to be included in an anthology.

The fact remains that good magazines need good poems— and it is up to poets to supply the market.

TRANSLATION

Margaret T. Rudd

Cervantes, I believe, likened a translation to the wrong side of a tapestry. An unfortunate simile, but unfortunately the figure applies to many poetry translations. I question whether there can ever be a perfect translation of a poem from its original language to another; that could only be the right side of the tapestry, the original poem in the original language, be it good or bad. A translation may improve on the original (some are so reputed) and thereby fall short of perfection.

Change is inevitable when an idea, or sometimes even one word, is expressed in a different tongue. Take the Spanish word *ninos.* The poet, Myra Sklarew, translated that word as "little boys." (*Washington Post Magazine,* 3/29/81) *Ninos* also means *children*. Did Ms. Sklarew know which meaning Federico Garcia Lorca had in mind when he wrote the poem "Agosto"? A translator, then, must settle for less or more, than half a loaf, never a whole one.

Three main elements comprising a poem are content, form and feeling or emotion—what does the poem *say, how* is it said and what *feeling* does it convey? The translator's task is to preserve all three as nearly as possible. Granted that content, form and feeling are often inextricably interdependent. None-the-less, in the process of translation one may have to take precedence at the expense of another. This being the case, which of the three should be paramount?

My first consideration is content; what does the poem say? (Meaning is a question of interpretation which is the reader's prerogative.) To translate any writing, especially poetry, one must have a thorough, first-hand knowledge of both languages involved. A poet once told me he had translated a sonnet written by a sixteenth century Spanish poet. "Oh," I said, "I didn't know you spoke Spanish." "I don't," he responded, "I used a translation by . . ." My friend had not translated the poem; he poetized someone else's translation. The sonnet he showed me was a good one but it was not his translation. I was challenged to translate the sonnet myself. Following is the original Spanish with my translation:

SONNET 228 by Luis de Argote y Gongora (1561-1627)

Mientras por competir con tu cabello,	a
oro bruñido el Sol reumbra en vano;	b
mientras con menosprecio en medio el llano	b
mira a tu blanca frente el lilio bello;	a
mientras a cada labio, por cogello,	a
siguen más ojos que al clavel temprano,	b
y mientras triumfa con desdén lozano	b
del luciente cristal tu gentil cuello;	a
goza cuello, cabello, labio y frente,	c
antes que lo que fué en tu edad dorada	d
oro, lilio, clavel, cristal luciente,	c
no solo en plata o viola truncada	d
se vuelva, mas tú y ello juntamente	c
en tierra, en humo, en polvo, en nada.	d

SONNET 228

As long as Sun displays its burnished gold
in futile competition with your hair,
as long as on your pallid brow so fair
the desert lily looks with jealous, cold
disdain; while fresh carnation cannot hold
as many eyes as lips invite to share,
and while the crystal vase cannot compare
with nature's artless curve in human mould,
enjoy that throat, that hair, those lips, that brow
before what used to be in life's sweet spring
carnation, crystal, lily turn, somehow,
to toneless strumming on a broken string
and all that was, together, that and thou,
becomes as dust, as smoke, a shade, no thing.

Translated by Margaret T. Rudd

This is an Italian sonnet, as are most Spanish sonnets, Spain having been historically involved with Italy during the Renaissance. I was able to maintain the same rhyme scheme without altering the content. Before tackling the form, I had to study the poem to comprehend it fully. Though I learned Spanish as I learned English, sixteenth century Spanish differs from that of today even as Shakespearean English differs from today's English. Moreover, Gongora created the so-called "gongorism" in Spain which is a close parallel with "euphuism" which John Lily popularized in England during the same century— both terms indicating a superrefined, complicated manner of writing.

There must be many English versions of Gongora's famous sonnet. Three come to mind. Space limitation here prohibits quoting all three versions but I quote the last three lines of each to demonstrate inevitable differences in translations. All three refer to the poet's injunction to "enjoy that throat, those lips," etc. before they all:

1   become transmuted into baser stuff
       and sink, with you, to ashes, dust,
       earth mold, shadows, nothingness.

2   Shall fade and wither, darken and eclipse,

And you with it make one sad pilgrimage
To earth, to smoke, to dust, to shade, to night.

3   Before the change that time for all doth hold
Shall them and thee transmute to earth, to dust,
In nothingness and shadows to be lost.

Number 1 sacrifices form to content. Number 2 changes the rhyme scheme slightly as well as the content, which is also changed in the octet. Number 3 sacrifices the rhyme scheme only in the last line, and then slightly, since "hold" and "lost" make a close assonantal rhyme. Much Spanish poetry uses assonance, especially folk ballads, and if the translator is Spanish speaking, as his signature indicates, he could be forgiven.

There remains the element of feeling, emotion, perhaps the most elusive of the three elements under consideration, elusive because its relation to the other two, plus so much more: connotation of words and phrases in both languages and the *sound*, the *music*. Before man could write, the poet sang. Singing, is, I hold, the ultimate test of a poem. In her novel, *The Praise Singer*, Mary Renault describes a performance by the Greek poet, Simonides. She writes, "The sound works with the feeling, and seemed to come of itself." All singing is not rhymed and much modern poetry cannot even be measured (I use the term advisedly.) But somewhere inside, there must be music, at least for my ear. What is music for a westerner may not be music for the oriental, thus the two may not experience the same feeling, the same emotion to sounds. Here's the rub for the translator whose task is to let the author do his own singing; the translator is the instrument for anther's voice. With this in mind I wrote the following sonnet:

TRANSLATOR'S PRAYER
    If not the wine, the crystal blown to cup
    a golden potion of the poet's wine
    that tempts the cautious guest to tilt me up
    and taste elixir from a foreign vine.

    If not the form, the mirror that reflects
    a perfect image of the form I hold
    framed for the fleeting instant that projects

an alien grace in me made manifold.

If not the voice, an echo of the voice,
transcending features of a stranger's face
to pipe in measures of another's choice
the sounding symbol of a distant place.

Euterpe's instrument, I would transmute
lyrical essence on my human flute.
                    Margaret T. Rudd, from . . .*And Three Small Fishes*
                                    McClure Press, 1974

CHALLENGE—YOUR TINDER!

Vienna Ione Curtiss

You need not live with musty minds,
With persons unesthetic—
Imagination can be found
And intellects magnetic!

How stimulating to our own mental and esthetic projec-
tions are the searching minds and dynamic imagination revealed
in Emily Dickinson's succinct poems, Hans Uhlmann's sculpture
"Music" and Roloff Beny's painting "Prairie Lights." The impact of their genius and of our direct contact with outreaching
personal associates challenges each of us to see, mentally and
emotionally, as well as physically. In vigorously meeting the
challenge, we discover humor, beauty, profundity of which
we had been unaware.

The challenge, further, fires us to produce—through the
written word, color, music, dance or some other expressive
medium. We can intimately share our new-found observations
with other persons through deftly writing concise verse, for
every phrase or sentence has a rhythm, that compulsive part
of each human being which forms the ebb and flow of life.
If we write our verse in the first person, as did Emily Dickinson and Robert Frost, the reader feels the words to be his own;
if, like Miss Dickinson, we courageously slash away excess

words, we will go far toward achieving impact for our poems. Our word pearls become so precious to us, however, during the euphoric "flush of creation," that we resist craftsmanship's hard, hard work of perfecting our design.

Although each poem needs structure, few outstanding creative works are made strictly by formula or rule—a strong motivating force and mood are needed. (But, oh, let's forego the "widow's weep" or the esthetic binge.) Let a statement, an exclamation or a question form the first few lines of your verse; beat out the rhythm to see whether any correction is needed before proceeding with your poem. Before your creation is complete, many kinds of changes will surely be made. Because jottings are so important a preliminary step to a writer, I've included "Jottings" here, the verse to be analyzed for the strong and light beats that form its rhythm pattern:

Jottings are my unripened thoughts,	/ . . . . / . /
The most personal things I have,	. . / . . / . /
I don't want you to look at them—	/ . . . . / . /
They're my soul undressed.	. . / . /

You will enjoy beating out the strong rhythm of each of the following four poems. Read each verse aloud, for a poem is a song. Also analyze each product for its mood, motivating force, beauty, conciseness, adherance to its subject, and impact upon the reader. Now, write your own poems! From my personal experience, I assure you that your prose writing, also, will benefit greatly through the discipline of writing poetry and advertising copy, as well as the graphic designing of books and advertisements. Here are four brief verses for your pleasure, each with a different subject, or theme:

MY SKIN
A skin is a wonderful, wonderful thing
For it binds me altogether—
When I feel of the bones that lead out to my toes
Or the gristle that is just my nose,
I wonder just what of a man I would be
If I weren't collected within one skin
And my parts wracked about in the weather!

THE BAT IN THE BEDROOM
    Swi—sh, and click!
    Swi—sh, and click!
    Soaring through night then back with a click!

    "Squ—eak," and "eek!"
    "Squ—eak," and "eek!"
    Crying protest, a window to seek.

    Walls make a canyon, ceiling a cell,
    Floor gives an echo, clock has a bell.
    Persons are snoring, dreams they can't tell,
    Bedroom's a-groaning under the spell.

    Fly to a window, back again, crash!
    Rush through the dark, and then again, dash!
    Now for the curtain next to a breeze,
    Out through the window, do as I please!

    Sw—ish, and "eek!"
    Sw—ish, and "eek!"
    Crying for joy, with others to squeak!

    "Squ—eak," and "eek!"
    "Squ—eak," and "eek!"
    Flee from the moon, then dart again,—"Squeak!"

TO BE THE SILENTLY MOVING NIGHT
    To be the silently moving night
    In dark diaphanous gown,
    Trailing smoothly over all,
    Clandestinely gliding on!

    Enchanting presence, unseen but for
    A sparkling galaxy trail!
    Felt as whisper as she floats,
    Saluted by nightingale!

    Seductive siren she seems at times,
    Then cooling palliative,
    Harbor mother too is she.
    Enigma. Soft fugitive.

THE POET'S DILEMMA
> They chase me all about at night
> And chase me through the day,
> These haunting, rhyming bits of thought
> From verses I have wrought.
> They flutter 'round my ears
> And float before my eyes,
> Come back and nudge me, cudgel me,
> These cozy, winged, vixen lines!
>
> At first they seem so innocent,
> So dear and comforting,
> Enticing me with cadence sweet,
> Concordant thought in beat.
> Enslaving me! I grope
> For fleeting, errant line!
> Not finding it, I try in vain
> To shake this poem from my mind!

Poems from two books written, illustrated and designed by Vienna Ione Curtiss: *Life's Great Snow!* (poetry) and *Cappy—Rollicking Rancher Atop Arizona's Mighty Rim* (prose)

ONE OF THE HIDDEN UNICORNS IN POETRY: THERAPY

Wilma W. Burton

Studies in the early writings of mankind have shown that in a major number of cultures, poetry is thought to be the first form of writing to find its way into the language. It is true in the Judean-Hebraic culture. The Book of Job, thought by scholars to be the oldest book in the Old Testament, was written in poetry, the dramatic monologue.

The Creator-God writing through men's pens inspired them to write poetry. David's Psalms not only were spiritual healing for the young sheep herder, chosen to be king of Israel, hiding out from Saul in the lonely mountain caves, but they are still being used, as they have been through the centuries, as emotional therapy for all who read them.

How many dying have been comforted by the words of the 23rd Psalm, "The Lord is my shepherd. I shall not want. . .Yea, though I walk through the valley of the shadow of death I shall fear no evil"?

We are told that Thomas Merton thrashing on the wild sea of agnosticism, found an anchor for his mustard seed faith in the poetry of the metaphysical poets who had lived before him: Donne, Herbert, Blake, St. John of the Cross, and others. Inspired by their writings, Merton gave to the world many pages of inspirational writing both in prose and poetry.

Abraham Lincoln often bored his non-poetic friends by quoting poems he had memorized, or written himself. Time and again, in the great stresses of his life, he turned to poetry: when his beloved Anne Rutledge died; when his engagement to Mary Todd (who later reconsidered and married him) was broken; when he lost his son Todd, whom he adored, at an early age; when his was the awesome burden of the Civil War to bear with its unprecedented dying and suffering on the plains of America, turned by canon fire into battlefields.

Out of his close affinity for poetry, he penned one of the finest prose-poems the world has ever known, *The Gettysburg Address.* A literary gem written and delivered in a cemetary where the young men of a nation were buried in newly turned graves: "government of the people, by the people and for the people. . ."

In an article appearing in an issue of *Strophes,* the official publication of the National Federation of Poetry Societies, two books are recommended which advance the theory of poetry for mental health. One is a textbook for professionals entitled, *Poetry Therapy* by Dr. J. J. Leedy of the Cumberland Hospital's Mental Health Clinic in Brooklyn. Overly sentimental poetry verse that is preachy is not recommended by Dr. Leedy in the present posture, but poems written by such poets as Robert Frost, George Herbert, Gerard Manly Hopkins, William Blake, A. S. Housman, Emily Dickinson, Christina Rossetti, Edna St. Vincent Millay, the Brownings, to name a few, are on his list.

The second book recommended in *Strophes* is by the late

Dr. Smiley Blanton, *The Healing Power of Poetry.*

The Veteran's Administration has authorized the use of poetry as a therapy throughout its hospitals and is finding both the writing and reading of poetry an aid to the improved mental condition of the patients.

Patients in mental hospitals are being encouraged by doctors and nurses not only to read poetry, but to write it—and it is often surprising what good verse they produce. There is a poet in each of us. The language is jewelled with bright metaphors that spring from our picturesque thinking, spilling over into our vocabularies, enriched by the imagery in our poetry that enhances our heritage.

At an early age, small children are introduced to the magic of poetry. Tears are often dried and they go happily off to bed after the reading (by a parent) of Mother Goose rhymes. This is a prime example of poetry therapy. Children who are encouraged to write poetry surprise their teachers with their vivid expressions and inborn ability.

Regretfully, there is much depressed poetry being written that is too dark, too negative, to be useful in the field of poetry therapy. A. T. Baker writing in an issue of *Time* Magazine referred to "depressed or flattened" poetry. "The thing walks like a duck, its primaries are all in place, but what nobody seems to notice. . . is the bird does not fly. Oddly, it contains no phrases to be remembered." Even poetry written on sad subjects, when it is well written, will have an uplifting, soaring quality and it is in this very soaring essence that the depressed spirit of the reader can be aided.

Spain's leading poet, St. John of the Cross, imprisoned and kept in solitary confinement, must have found the forming of poetry an effective means of keeping his sanity. Without papyrus or a quill, he memorized his poetry—about two dozen prison poems in all—and upon his release, immediately requested writing instruments so that he could record his poems. Like the poetry of the Bible, his poetry is written on many levels so that it is understood by the simplest mind as well as by the higher intellectual.

One example of a simple poem rich in healing qualities is Robert Frost's "Stopping by a Woods on a Snowy Evening." It is one of his best known poems and Frost himself was surprised at the acceptance it received. He would be even more surprised were he to know it is now engraved on the circular edge of a brass tray in Indura Gandhi's reception room because her father, Jawrahal Nehru, had Frost's book open to this poem on a bedstand by his bed when he died. It is thought to be the last thing he read before death claimed him. Was he, in the midst of the many seemingly unsolvable problems of his prime ministery, seeking escape and healing for his stresses?

We live in a world where much has been written about *transcendental meditation* and the use of a *mantra* for the release of tensions of the mind. Far more effective can be the reading of words deep in richness of meaning, cadence, imagery, metaphor, which, of course, is what poetry really is.

I have been quoted in *The Writer* (June, 1980) with a definition of my own poetry, which I often use in workshops: "Poetry is finding new grace in the common place and expressing it in meter and metaphor." It is this new grace that has power to lift the mind of the reader and the imbue it with insight and courage. Good poetry reaches beyond the intellect of the reader to evoke his imagination, thus bringing him into a new revelation of life itself.

In finding "new grace in the common place," we must strive to avoid the trite, the rehashed, old forms of diction in favor of today's language, faded or dead metaphors (such as "teeth were pearls," "lips were rubies," etc.), and old imagery for the vitally new.

In the Lockwood Memorial Library of the University of Buffalo, there are over ten thousand books of poetry. This library is unique in that it contains numerous original manuscripts of the poets on which are evidenced the later changes. A study of these important pages reveals the many "hidden unicorns" that are a part of the ingenuous world of the poet. Rare is the original manuscript, although admittedly it sprung from the deep artesian well of the poet's Theta conscience, that has not had some words changed for the improvement of the poem. That is what the study of the craft can do, help the poet to make the proper distinctions in his craft, and to serve as his own editor.

The following is a sonnet typed as I wrote it in its original form and with the later changes I made in it before it was published in my book *Sidewalk Psalms*. I first titled it "Hidden Unicorns" and then changed the title to "Sonnet on Affliction":

> Did Milton in his blindness cry to you,
> O God, for healing? And when the light failed
> To return, no respecter You of Jew
> Nor Greek, did he assume your grace had paled
> Or that your garment hem was out of reach?
> Or can it be some arms are but too short
> To touch your robe? What tenet did you teach
> On prayer the poet failed to give import?
> True, other men, like Paul, have suffered thorns
> Of flesh you chose to leave to goad the will.
> What mystery, like hidden unicorns
> Exists in pain's dark human codicil?
> How often may we lift it to our lips—
> The grail of grace before it, empty, slips?

In this poem I had trouble with "hidden unicorns" because the unicorn is so much a part of Greek mythology and never can one mix mythology with Christian truth. However, the unicorn is definitely recognized in the Bible and therefore, although I had changed the line to "in patience duly borne," I decided to substantiate what Scripture has determined and therefore, I left the line or phrase "like hidden unicorns" in the final draft.

Much could be learned of the poet's thought processes by visiting the Lockwood Library and studying the original manuscripts which so clearly show the changes the poet made.

Psychologists tell us there are four levels of conscience: *Beta*—an awareness in which we converse and observe all that is around us. Two, *Alpha*—a quiet, relaxed state in which the proponents of biofeedback attempt to get us to live, and which state can be acquired by mental control, reading poetry and prayer. Three, *Theta*—the state in which artists, writers, poets, inventors are apt to do their creative work. And four, *Delta*— the state of sleeping.

Doctors are finding, and these facts can actually be proved on biofeedback machines, that the reading of poetry is valuable in treating depression, hypertension and other diseases brought on by stress.

Poetry has access to far places where other forms of writing cannot go. Among these far places, are the deep reservoirs of the mind that can be quietly reached by the poem and healed by the metered therapy.

We have only to read the poetic books of Scripture to realize that our Creator-God is a poet. We read his meter in all of the many phases of nature that surround us. God is a poet! His poetry, like the unicorn who laid its head in the young maiden's lap, is indeed a favor of grace to all who will receive it:

GOD IS A POET
We read His meter in the high hills
and low, and in the river's
winding path through the new
towns and old. We count
the spondee of His mountain
crests, the pyrrhic of His ocean
laps, the trochee of His dawn
the iambic quiet of His sun
yielding to sonnetry of star.

God is a Poet
whose imagery is meadowed
in yellow cowslip and buttercup
and in the brown cattails
soldiering the marsh.

God is a Poet
speaking in the dactyl
of the rain, the soliloquy
of snow. And on the pages

of the heart, He writes
the verse, disciplined, or free
He wants each daughter/son to know.

Wilma W. Burton, 1980

VARIATIONS IN RHYMING

Agnes Homan

Time was if it did not rhyme, I did not consider it a poem. I can remember Whitman in high school, and being moved by his magnificent lines, yet wondering if they were truly poetry. Since Whitman, many twentieth century poets have adopted the free verse forms, abandoning both meter and rhyme. However, rhyme is far from obsolete. Many moderns are moving from unrhymed to rhymed poetry by varying the position and the types of rhyme.

Full rhyme, placed in the position of the greatest prominence at the ends of lines is one of the most common forms of rhymed poetry, and the one with which we are the most familiar. Full rhyme at the ends of lines serve to make the poem more memorable, more musical, and more intense.

Internal rhyming began with a word in the middle of a line rhyming with the end word. Some notable examples are from Poe's "The Raven": "Ah, distinctly I remember, it was in the bleak December," or from Coleridge's "Rhyme of the Ancient Mariner": "Then all averred, I had killed the bird." Here the end word rhymed with a word in the middle serves to speed the movement of the poem while adding a strong even rhythm.

Edna St. Vincent Millay varied *internal* rhyming by rhyming the middle of one line with the middle of the following line in her poem, "Counting-Out Rhyme":

> Stripe of green in moosewood maple
> Color seen in leaf of apple.

The *full* rhymes, green and seen, within the lines, blended with the *slant* rhymes, maple and apple, at the ends of lines tend to slow the movement by placing the emphasis on the full *internal* rhyme instead of the *end* rhyme where the emphasis would normally occur.

Gerard Manley Hopkins places rhymes within the lines in his poem, "God's Grandeur":

> And all is seared with trade; bleared smeared with toil
> And wears man's sludge and shares man's smell, the toil—

In his poem, "The Windhover," he uses *adjacent* rhymes: "dapple-*dawn-drawn* Falcon" and "*Fall, gall* themselves and gash gold vermilion." In "Spring and Fall," he rhymes the end of one line with the beginning of the following line:

> Margaret, are you grieving
> Over Goldengrove unleaving
> Leaves, like things of man, you . . .

Richard Wilbur not only rhymes the end of one line with the middle of the following line, but also intersperses *inner* rhymes throughout his poem, "Statues":

> The children playing at statues *fill*
> The garden with their *shrill*ness, in a planned
> And planted grove, they *fling* from the *swing*er's hand
> Across the giddy grass, and then hold still.

Up until now we have been discussing *full* rhyme which has been the dominant form of rhyme in poetry in English. However, English is a rhyme-poor language, and although *imperfect* rhyme is generally thought of as a twentieth century invention, it has been around a long time. Remember Little Tommy *Tucker* singing for his *supper?* Emily Dickinson was a pioneer in the use of *slant* rhyme in serious poetry:

> I heard a Fly buzz—when I died
> The Stillness in the Room
> Was like the Stillness in the Air
> Between the Heaves of Storm.

Notice how the *slant* rhyme of Room and Storm creates a dissonance which is curiously in keeping with life in the twentieth century.

There are many variations of *slant* or *accidental* rhyme. For instance, *consonantal* rhyme occurs when the vowels differ, but the final consonants of the stressed syllable agree: faith/death, bitter/better. An example from Edna St. Vincent Millay's "Counting-Out Rhyme":

> Silver bark of beech, and sallow
> Bark of yellow birch and yellow
> Twig of willow.

Assonantal rhyme, on the other hand, pairs the vowel sounds without regard to the consonants. Examples are: neck/met, night/knife, bloom/brood. An example in verse is from the ballad, "Fair Annie":

> Bind up, bind up your yellow hair
> And tie it on your neck
> And see you look as maiden-like
> As the day that first we met.

Dylan Thomas uses assonance internally in his poem "After the Funeral":

> After the funeral mule praises, brays
> Windshake of sailshaped ears, muffle-teed tap
> Tap happily one peg in the thick
> Grave's foot, blinds down the lids, the teeth in black. . .

Here we have funeral/mule, praises/brays/shake/sailshaped/grave, tap/happily/black as example of *assonantal* rhyme.

Reversed or backward rhyme occurs where the vowel sounds are paired, but the consonants are reversed: mood/doom, toad/dote, speed/deeps. Consider this example from Edmund Wilson: "And resolved for a day to sidestep/My friends, their guests and their pets."

Eye-rhymes are rhymes whose endings are spelled the same,

but are pronounced differently: mind/wind, done/bone, though/
bough. An example from Emily Dickinson:

> The Birds rose smiling in their nests
> The gates indeed—were done—
> Alas, how heedless were the eyes
> On whom the summer shone!

Vowel rhyme in which any vowel is allowed to agree with
any other vowel was also used frequently by Emily Dickinson:

> Nature sometimes rears a sapling
> Sometimes scalps a tree—
> Her green people recollect it
> When they do not die—

Perhaps the most complicated rhymes schems is *analyzed*
rhyme. A notable example is this stanza from Auden which will
help in the explanation:

> That night when joy began
> Our narrowest veins to flush
> We waited for the flash
> Of morning's levelled gun.

The vowels of the end rhymes in the first and third lines are
identical: beg*a*n and fl*a*sh; the vowels in the second and fourth
lines are also identical: fl*u*sh and g*u*n. The ending consonants
of the first and fourth lines are identical: beg*an* and g*un* as well
as the consonants of the second and third lines: *flash* and *flush*.

Robert Frost speaks of sound in poetry as being 'the gold
in the ore.' Rhyme in all of its different variations is one of the
chief sources of sound. It might be fun for us who have been
writing free verse to experiment with some of these forms of
rhyme, and, perhaps, to devise some of our own. Playing with
words and sounds is one of the great delights in writing poetry.
I started writing the following with no definite idea in mind.
Just juggling the sounds to compliment or contend with each
other was so much fun that I had no clue as how the poem was
going to turn out. The ending came as a complete surprise:

A SOUND WINTER'S NIGHT
    Blue ice entraps the river
    White drifts conceal the meadow
    Winds whistle among the rafters
    Trees rattle against the window
    Wolf howls lonely from the mountain
    Owls hoot ghostly in the hollow
    And in her bed so cold and narrow
    The huddled widow hugs her pillow.

Nothing like taking one's own advice, I always say.

PLAY IT AGAIN SAM

    Now when you play that jazz, you play it sweet
    and soft with just a feeble hint of swing.
    We strain to hear that old familiar beat
    that could claim our breath and blood, and fling
    away the chains that held imprisoned feet.
    We stamped and stomped until the dawn would bring
    the daylight woes we danced all night to cheat
    nor did we think to count the reckoning.

    Just one more time take that horn and blow
    away the years that slow our breath and blood.
    O, blow that hot impassioned beat. We'll go
    into that dark with stomping feet, and should
    the daylight come before the dance is done
    we must not miss a beat, oh, Sam, play on.

QUICK REFERENCE INDEX

Preface

Wauneta Hackleman

Poets may have the inherent quality to write poetry or they may wish to enrich their ability to write good poetry. In either case, poets should master their craft. To do so, they need instruments with which to work.

This collection, or glossary of terms, is a new tool for writers of poetry at any stage in their literary career. It provides the readers with not only the words, names of poetry forms (many new ones included), but gives a finger-tip alphabetized explanation of the meaning of the words or the construction of the form. There are three hundred and sixty poetry terms in this quick reference index.

There have been occasions when all of us have sat under instructors and lecturers, or participated in workshops where poetry terms have been used that we did not understand. This index provides you, almost instantly, with the meaning of any poetry term used in the classroom, seminar, workshop, or for your individual use.

Abstract	an unrealistic or impractical idea which may become a concrete symbol, an example is the famed *Pegasus*, add wings to a horse and the mythological *Pegasus* emerges.
abstraction	Ex: Hannah Kahn's *Ride a Wild Horse*. . .Wings that can lift the mighty weight of a horse free your imagination from the *terra firma* of reality.
Acatalectic	prosody having the full number of syllables, especially in the final foot of the line, or verse; the unshortened line. Ex: W. H. Auden's "In Memory of W. B. Yeats": Let the Irish vessel lie *emptied of its poetry.*
Accent	stress given to a particular syllable in a word; emphasizing the syllable.
chromatic accent	created by vocal pitch which can be controlled. Ex: I love you/I love you/I love you.
emphatic accent	stress accent resulting in the amount of breath used in creating syllables. Ex: retire - rehire.
Accentual	employing the above, having rhythm based on stress rather than on the length of sounds.
Acrostic	a verse arrangement of words in which certain letters in each line, such as the first or last, when taken in order, spell out a word, motto or name; widely used in greeting card verse, especially at Christmas.
Alexandrine	an *iambic line* having six feet; *iambic hexameter.*
Allegory	in poetry, *allegory* is a poem in which people, things or happenings have a hidden or symbolic meaning; is depicted through *personification*. Ex: Chaucer's "Canterbury Tales" or the parable of the good seed (Matt. 13:24-30) "The kindgdom of heaven is likened unto a man which sowed good seed in his field."

Alliteration   is a repetition of consonant sound; it is the recurrence of the same consonant at short intervals in the poems; it is sometimes called *initial rhyme*; engages the reader and makes the poem flow; it can also occur in the middle of words. Ex: Amy Lowell's poem "Shooting the Sun":
> Four hori*z*ons *coz*en me
> To *d*istances I *d*imly see.

Very effective if not overused. Ex: *L*ove, we *l*inger by the *l*apping *l*ake.

Allusion   a reference to an historical event, place or person; an indirect reference to an actual individual; rich associations in poetry such as *Helen* with great *beauty*; Paris, a place, denotes high fashion.

Alveolars   are *sounds* executed by touching the tongue against the gum ridge behind the upper teeth; phonets: *t, d, s.*

Ambiguity   use of words, lines, or the poem having two or more meanings; *ambiguous,* meaning vague or indefinite; it is sometimes deliberately employed for *evasion;* lends its *usefulness* to *free verse;* Ex: Emily Dickinson's untitled poem:
> An altered look about the hills;
> a spider at his trade again;
> and Nicodemus' Mystery
> receives its annual reply.

Ambivalence   simultaneous conflicting feelings toward a person or thing such as *love* and *hate.* Ex:
> Parting is all we know of heaven
> And all we need of hell.   Emily Dickinson

Amphiboly   is misunderstood grammatical structure in the poem; Ex: Juliet's answer to her mother:
> "Indeed, I never shall be satisfied with Romeo, till I behold him-dead is my poor heart. . ." (read without the dash). . ."till I behold him dead. . ."

Anthesis   a state of fulfillment such as a flower in full bloom; the form *anthesis* is in triplets with no verse limitation;

it is monotonous if poem is too long. Ex:

> with giggles and yahoos and cartwheels in grass
> school kids grab books, and report cards marked
>   passed
> and run from the playground into Summer's forever.

Anti-climax

when the poem's best lines are up front or at the beginning of the poem. Ex: Edna St. Vincent Millay's "First Fig":

> First line: "My candle burns at both ends,
> Fourth line: It gives a lovely light.

Antipodes

anything diametrically opposite; the exact opposites such as "the *budding* and *falling* of leaves."

Antispastic

a variant foot in a scansioned line. Ex:

> Here flak/ing the/bright sun/to en/dure cold
> Gods plead/with men/and shake/the em/balmed
> earth.

Antistrophe

same metrical pattern as the strophe; first statement follows the strophe and answers the strophe. Ex: Shelley's poem, "To a Skylark":

> Hail to thee, blithe spirit!
> Bird thou never wert,

Antithesis

results when opposing ideas are placed in grammatical parallel such as *golden* locks will turn to *gray; andtithesis* invokes *sarcasm.*

Apostrophe

a direct address to an absent person or someone invisible; often addressed to dead persons in poetry such as:

> Sandburg, you should write
> a sequel about the mayor
> moving to the slums
> an act unsurpassed by any in high places.

The apostrophe is often used in spirituals, "Death ain't you gonna die sometime?"; can be used as abstract; the apostrophe gives *body* to the *indefinite.*

Apperception

referred to as the *sixth sense;* the fact of the mind

being *conscious* of its own *consciousness;* understanding the concepts of *soul, God, love;* the hand is an
example for it can *push, pull, squeeze, lift, hit,* yet
it can gently *touch* such as in *Romeo and Juliet* (Act
II, sc ii):
> See how she leans her cheek upon that hand
> O, that I were a glove upon that hand
> that I might touch that cheek.

Archetype

(Greek: "first molded"), which can mean the original
pattern; the perfect example of a type; a psychic organ
present in all of us; Carl Gustav Jung (1875-1961)
viewed archetype as a character, symbol or situation
that recurs again and again in literature, myths or
dreams. Examples to consider are the *White Goddess,
Beowulf,* the myth of *Perseus, Saint George and the
Dragon,* etc.

Architectonics

the form of the whole; along with *logopoeia, melopoeia,* and *phanapoeia* (according to Pound), comprise
the basis of all writing and emphatically that of the
most highly charged poetry.

Arsis

the unstressed part of a foot, esp. in quantitative verse;
later the accented syllable of a foot.

Ascending rhyme

rising of the rhyme-*the anapest* ($\smile\smile$/):
   As I ride,/as I ride (anapestic dimiter)
   And the sound/of a voice/that is still (anapestic tri-
meter)

Assonance

also called *vowel rhyme;* used in Provencal and old
French forms; George Eliot tried, unsuccessfully to
introduce it into English poetry; it is the repetition
of *vowel sounds,* especially in accented syllables;
vowels are paramount with no relationship to consonants such as in Ode to Evening by William Collins, "If *o*ught *o*f *o*aten stop or past*o*ral song."

Auditory

of hearing or the sense of hearing; hearing what is
in the poem; a part of the imagery in a poem such
Buson's Haiku:

The piercing chill I feel:
. . .dead wife's *comb,* in our bedroom
under my heel.
We can hear the breaking of the comb; this poem is
an excellent example of *visual* and *tactile imagery.*

Avalon — in Celtic legend—the isle of the dead; an island paradise; referred to as the society of poets, living and
dead, whose works have created an island of beauty; in
poetic sense, a *poet* is an *island.*

Avant garde — new or unconventional poetry; usually attributed to
modern writers of poetry; new ideas written in non-
traditional forms.

Bacchius — when a change of emotional tone is needed in the
poem, the bacchius (‿ ‿ ‿) permits an intrusion such as
"Thắt sweet mãn!"; this captures the attention of the
poet and reader and brings new awareness to the
poem.

Ballad — is a narrative poetry form with two categories: the
popular and *folk;* the *literary* or *art* ballad is an imitation of the *folk* ballad but is not to be sung; it ad-
heres to the strict observance of the ballad stanza
(iambic quatrain); Coleridge's "Rime of the Ancient
Mariner" is a famous *literary* ballad; "Frankie and
Johnnie" and "Barbara Allen" are good examples of
the folk ballad.

Ballad Stanza — is ordinarily, *iambic quatrian,* abcb, though any number of rhyming variations are possible; in the *folk*
ballad, the emotional response or the story is more
important than the metrics.

Ballade — should not be confused with the *ballad;* it originated
in France during the Middle Ages; revived during the
Renaissance and again in the twentieth century; it is
strict in its structure: three *octaves* and a *quatrain*
called an *envoy.*

Bathos — in poetry, it is the abrupt fall from the sublime to the trivial or incongruous; usually called anti-climax; line or lines of poetry that can bring laughter instead of tears.

Beat

the accent or stress in poetry.

Blank Verse

is a fixed form; *iambic pentameter*-unrhymed; the poet uses *alliteration, assonance, consonance* and various kinds of *accent* to establish *rhythm* and *echo* in the poem; poetic liberty to use anything but rhyme. Ex: see under form. (Some poets depart from the iambic.)

Cacaphony

discordant and harsh sounds; designed to irritate and annoy; related to *dissonance. Ex:*
   No cauldroned dirges were sung
   to strip the garments of Death.

Cadence

is rhythmic *flow of sound;* measured movement; repetition and variation blend into beautiful poetry; too much repetition produces monotony; *simple cadence* embraces one *metronomic beat; compound cadence* embraces more than one *beat;* triplex rhythm has *three syllables* per cadence; *duplex* rhythm has two to four syllables per cadence. Ex:
   Glory, glory, hallelujah
   Glory, glory, hallelujah.

Caesura

a pause within a line; usually occurs at a mark of punctuation; it is not necessary to punctuate if *Caesura is used; spacing between words* or phrases for breathing in the poem or to intensify thought; the Caesura is the rhythmical pause rather than the metrical pause; in Alexander Pope's, "The Rape of the Lock," we lift two example lines:
   Or strain her honor   or her new brocade
   forget her pray'rs   or miss a masquerade;

Cameo

syllabic form (see under form).

Canto

any of the main divisions of *long* poems. Ex: the 119th Psalm.

Carpe diem

literally means, seize the day or make the most of present opportunities; read Robert Herrick's poem,

"To the Virgins, To Make Much of Time":
> Gather ye rosebuds while ye may
> old Time is still a-flying;

it is an emotion of "eat, drink and be merry, for tomorrow we may die."

Catalexsis	the *truncating* or shortening of lines of a poem; dropping the *feminine* syllables from the end of the line. Ex: Shelley's "Music When Soft Voices Die": Music,//when soft/voices/die; Vibrates// in the/memory. (// Caesura)
Catharsis	the purifying of the emotions, or the relieving of emotional tensions; through fear and/or pity, the emotions are purged as in Richard Wilbur's poem, "The Death of a Toad," . . .the gutters of the banked and staring eyes. He lies as still as if he would return to stone. . . For poetic catharsis, read this poem of the frog caught in a power mower.
Chain Verse	any repetition of a rhyme, word, phrase, line or group of lines used to tie up a section of the poem with the succeeding section constitutes *chain verse*.
Chant	liturgical poem, song, Psalm; to say something repetitiously, or monotonously.
Chant Royal	is the longest and most dignified offspring of the ballade; has five stanzas of eleven lines each; usually rhymed 1, 2, 1, 2, 3, 3, 4, 4, 5, 4, 5R; sixty lines in all; the envoy has five lines, 4, 4, 5, 4, 5R; Seven (7) rhymes, ten (10) each of (1), (2), and (3), and eighteen separate rhymes for (4).
Chapbook	small book or pamphlet of poems, ballads or religious tracts.
Characterization	when personality or behavioral patterns are suggested or indicated in the poem; if they became the *pivot* essential to the poem, *characterization* results; Ex: Emily Dickinson's:

I cannot live without you
It would be Life
And Life is over there
Behind the shelf.

Chiasmus (Chiastic)	rhetoric inversion of the second of two parallel phrases; Ex: "She went to Paris; to New York went he."
Choriamb	a classical metrical foot of four syllables, the first and last are long (stressed) and the middle two are short (unstressed); pertains to a chorus.
Choric Ode	interlude in a drama; chanted to music as the *chorus* moves on the stage during the strophe, atistrophe and the epode.
Chorus	in poetry, it is the *refrain* following each verse; in *dramatic* poetry it can be the prologue or epilogue.
Chromatic Accent	is created by *pitch* of the *voice* which can be consciously controlled: *I* love you/I *love* you/I love *you.*
Cinquain	Adelaide Crapsey's form; stanza of *five* lines, syllable count of 2-4-6-8-2; 22 syllables/unrhymed; this form is preferred; another form of *Cinquain* is five lines of poetry with no demands of exactness in structure; the preferred form by Adelaide Crapsey is known for its delicacy and exactness.
Cinquetun	Poem with syllable count of 8-6-10-6-8-2; forty syllables; rhyme scheme a, y, b, a, y, b (y lines are unrhymed).
Cinquo	a *half cinquain;* syllable count of 1-2-3-4-1; eleven syllables.
Clerihew	poetic form named after its inventor, Edmund Clerihew Bentley (1875-1956); has four lines of varying length; is humorous and is quasi-biographical; the form was meant to gain popularity with the *Limerick* but did not succeed; Babette Deutsch liked form and used it.

Cliché	trite phrase; a type of poetry shorthand; should be shunned unless employed deliberately; Ex: Arthur Guiterman's poem, "Everything in its Place," final line, "The birds are in the bushes and the wolf is at the door."
Climax	is the *highest* point of interest in the poem; the climax should come at the end; in Helen Nenka's poem from her book *Island Seed,* the last two lines of an untitled poem: You need a heart with an impish elf that loves you when you hate yourself.
Coherence	is the cement holding the parts of a poem together to create unity; mixed metaphors lack coherence; logic is the basic ingredient of coherence.
Colloquial	casual conversation; impersonal language of educated persons; E. E. Cummings used colloquialism; Ex: Mrs. Jones need not call my windows dirty when its the gray of her curtains through which she looks.
Conceit	Noun conceit: the use of a noun in a way other than its ordinary part of speech; Ex: "the frets that porcupined our yesterday"; the noun *porcupine* is herein used as a verb; from Wilma Burton's "Sidewalks Psalms": Time was when morning was an apple tree, *wedding gowned,* betrothed to early Spring, *Apriled* with thread bouquet of twittery" *Wedding gowned* and *Apriled* are both nouns used as verbs, or *noun conceits*; also, nouns that symbolize or are defined such as, We've kept our mortal vows and have not *Cained* our sacrifice consumed on Abel's altar, we pause to sip the latter wine at Cana's feast before the trumpet summons from the East. lines from Wauneta Hackleman's sonnet "Racing the Wind"; *Cained* a symbol of *sinned.*
Concrete	concentrates upon the physical material from which the poem is made; *word imagery* which can result in

vague generalities; *concrete poetry* is referred to as a "writer's game and a printer's feat"; concrete poetry occupies an area somewhere between conventional poetry and visual art; Ex: (visual) would be Aram Saroyan's poem, (one word) "Oxygen" on an otherwise blank page; for good example read Dorth Charles (b. 1950) poem "Concrete Cat."

Confessional is written in *first person* although the poet may be speaking of someone else; usually speaks of the poet's sorrows, torments and problems; Sylvia Plath and Anne Sexton wrote confessionals; Ex: Elizabeth Barrett Browning's poem, "Dost Thou Love Me, my Beloved? III":

> Now I sit alone, alone
> And the hot tears break and burn,

Connotation overtones or suggestions of additional meaning; the word *pool* has connotations of a swimming pool, pool of blood, pool game, a small pond or a lottery.

Consonance harmony of final sounds such as mast, past; or up front of the words as in flash, flesh, flood, fled; it is the resemblance of consonants and is sometimes used for *end rhyme* as in III by W. H. Auden:

> Laugh warmly and turning shyly in the hall
> Or climb with bare knees the volcanic hill.

Consonant(s) study Clement Wood's *Rhyming Dictionary*, by Blue Ribbon Books, Inc., 1936; some examples of double consonants creating sound for one consonant are *KS* for *X*, *ZH* as in azure, or *KW* for *Qu.*

Contemporary modern; existing and/or happening in the same period of time; poetry may be traditional forms but contemporary in mood; it is set in an historical designation; what twentieth century poets regard as *NOW* poetry.

Contractions the shortening of a word or phrase by the omission of letters or sounds; Ex: aren't, 'twas; contractions are frowned upon on modern poetry.

Contraposition	placing opposite or over against; contrast; antithesis; Ex: "Blue skies will turn to gray."
Countermotion	a change of mood or tone within the construction of the poem to intensify or clarify the meaning of the poem; sometimes referred to as *pace*; Ex: T. S. Eliot's "The Love Song of J. Alfred Prufrock": In the room the women come and go talking of Michelangelo.
Counter-movement	a move made in opposition; see the form *Sestina*, by Anne Marx; the counter-movement of end words or lines in a fixed-form poem.
Countervoice	another voice speaking within the poem other than the poet's own voice.
Couplet	two lines, rhymed as when standing alone; in *couplet* sequence (poem of more than one couplet), the rhyme scheme is bb, cc, dd, etc.; it is the smallest poetic unit in Western poetry; two lines may be a complete couplet; see under form.
Dactyl	is a three-syllable foot accented on the first syllable ($-\,-\,\smile$). Ex: rēgŭlăr, sĭmĭlăr, and pŏpŭlŏŭs.
Denotation	all words have at least one denotation; an indication of another meaning for the word; a noun can be used as a verb or adjective; Ex: the word *field* (noun) denotes a piece of ground, sports arena, battle field; as an *adjective-* a field trip; as a verb- "he fielded a base hit."
Denouement	a tying up of loose ends; an explanation, or statement of outcome; often employed in a narrative; it is the *solution* of the poem.
Descending Rhyme	may be effected by the use of the trochee and dactyl; trochee ($/\,\smile$) dactyl ($/\,\smile\,\smile$). Example words: góĭng, stáyĭng are trochees; wávĕrĭng, múrmŭrĭng and mémŏrў are dactyls; various meters can be employed to effect descending rhyme such as trochaic dimeter, trochaic tetrameter, dactylic hexameter, etc.

Diaeresis	the break caused by the coincidence of the end of a metrical foot with the end of a word; also the separation of consecutive vowels, esp. in diphthong; the hyphen is used in words such as re-enter to show there are three syllables in this example word; in naive the mark (¨) may be placed over the second vowel to indicate it is a two-syllable word; in poetry a *bucolic diaerisis* is a diaeresis occurring in the fourth foot, especially in pastoral poetry.
Dialogue	conversation within the poem or an interchange of ideas; the hearing of other characters in the *Monolog;* in the "Search" by Wauneta Hackleman, the seeker's response to the whispered overture of a caring God:

God whispered: "Come walk with me"
Gladly I went
a steriled prey of a faithless way.

Diction	in poetry it is the choice of words; do not confuse with idiom; poetic diction is the body of words, phrases and the construction of them which is fitting to poetry; diction should be the best words for the subject at hand.
Didactic	poem that is morally instructive or means to be so; poet must take care not to be boringly pedantic (unnecessary stress on minor or trivial points); didactic poetry was popular in the eighteenth century.
Dimeter	the two-foot line or two measures; it is not too common in English-language poetry.
Dissonance	an inharmonious combination of sounds; incompatible or incomplete.
Distich	a couplet that stands alone as a complete poem; Ex: Couplet on a gravestone (Infant eighteen-months old):

Since I have been so quickly done for
I wonder what I was begun for.

Ditrochee	two trochees considered a compound foot.

Doggerel	cudgel verse; poorly constructed and usually written for burlesque or comedy; a jingle.
Double Ballade	consists of six stanzas of eight or ten lines each rhymed as other ballades; usually the *envoy* is omitted; Henley liked this form but always used the envoy; Ex: Henley's "Double Ballade of the Nothingness of Things," or Swinburne's "Ballade of Swimming."
Douzet	origin unknown; consists of twelve, five-foot, iambic lines, rhymed as follows; abba, cddc, abcd; this form introduces a novelty in the repeition of rhyme not encountered so far elsewhere; the concluding quatrain's rhyme scheme amounts to a summary of the rhyme-sounds in the poem.
Dramatic	usually written in monologue form; it differs from its narrative counterpart in its method of telling the story; in dramatic poetry, stage settings and directions are either stated or implied; read Amy Lowell's poem, "Patterns."
Duplex	Rhyme has two or four syllables per cadence.
Elegy	a poem of lament, usually for the dead; Ex: Shelley's "Adonais"; also Thomas Gray's "Elegy Written in a Country Churchyard."
Elision	the slurring of a vowel or syllable to preserve meter; leaving out the end vowel of a word preceding one starting with a vowel; Ex: "Th' evening slipped the sunset. . . ." or "Th' inevitable hour."
Ellipsis	the omission of words which are essential to the syntax of the sentence but which can be supplied by the careful reader; Ex: "Jane, this is John—Jane, John"; it is a major device in Haiku.
Emotion	specific feeling in the poem that arouses the reader to manifest love, hate, anger or fear, etc. Ex: Emily Dickinson's, "I heard a Fly buzz-when I died-The stillness in the room. . ."

End-rhymed

lines concluding in rhyme (end-rhymed); the repetition of metrical accent is comparable to the beat of music; this arouses expectation in the reader; Ex: Robert Louis Stevenson's "Good and Bad Children":
   Children, you are very little
   And your bones are very brittle;

End-stopped

if a line ends in a full pause or a thought is completed at the end of the line, it is called *end-stopped*; Ex: Theodore Roethke's poem: "Let seed be grass, and grass turn into hay; I'm a martyr to a motion not my own;"

Enjambment

is a thought not contained in one line but runs on into the next line; it is a pleasant experience for the reader if expertly done, and not overdone; Ex: Adelaide Crapsey's poem, "Song":
   I make my shroud, but no one knows—
   So shimmering fine it is and fair,
   With stitches set in even rows. . .

Envoy

a postscript to a poem, especially to the ballade; it is a *quatrain* following three octaves; is strict in it's ballade structure; the ballade rhyme scheme being *ababbcbc* throughout the octaves and the *envoy* is *bcbc;* the envoy is used with other fixed forms.

Epic

accent of national hero(s) as explanation for the beginnings of nations or races; Ex: "Hiawatha," "The Iliad," and the "Odyssey," and "Paradise Lost."

Epigram

a brief, witty, and penetrating statement, which denotes human weakness or ruins a hallowed idea; the Japanese used epigrams and called them senyru, written in Haiku form; Ex: Alexander Pope's "Epigram Engraved on the Collar of a Dog Which I Gave to His Royal Highness'—"I am his Highness' dog at Kew; Pray tell me, sir, whose dog are you?"

Epilogue

a short poem at the ending of a performance; providing further comment, interpretation or information; used by poets after writing a sequence of poems, then

writing the Epilogue; Edna Meudt's "Pattern of Wild Roses": I—"Wild Rose O'Neill, 1843-1920; II—"The Rose of Washington Square"; III—"To a Wild Rose"; her epilogue IV titled "Mere Sequence"—1906; the last two lines:
> If Time is a circle
> the forward thrust leads back.

Epitaph   a short composition written in verse as a tribute to a dead person; Ex: Read any of Edgar Lee Master's epitaphs in *Spoon River Anthology*.

Epode   a form of lyric poetry in which a short line follows a longer line; in the final stanza of the *Pindaric* (ancient Greed ode) it follows the strophe and anti-strophe; Ex: Shelley's "To a Skylark":
> Pourest thy full heart
> in profuse strains of unpremeditated art.

Ercil   syllable form; syllable count is 4-6-8-1-4-6-8-10-6-8; rhyme scheme is a, b, a, b, c, d c, e, e, e; ercil has ten iambic lines.

Etheree   poetry form authored by Ehteree Armstrong; pattern is syllabic, ten lines; syllable count is 1-2-3-4-5-6-7-8-9-10; is not rhymed. (see form)

Euphony   is the sound of words working together with meaning; it pleases both the mind and ear of the reader; Ex: Surrey's line "Calm is the sea, *the waves work less and less*."

Farewell   syllable form with seven lines; unrhymed; syllable count is 8-8-8-6-6-6-4; poem must suggest a farewell to someone or something.

Feet/Foot   Metric Feet: one foot-Monometer; two feet—Dimeter; three feet—Trimeter; four feet—Tetrameter; five feet—Pentameter; six feet—Hexameter; seven feet—Heptameter; eight feet—Octometer.

RHYTHMIC FEET	ACCENT SYMBOL	EXAMPLES
iamb	⌣ ´	one day, to love
trochee	´ ⌣	going, floating
anapest	⌣ ⌣ ´	entertain, in between
dactyl	´ ⌣ ⌣	wavering, tenderly
spondee	´ ´	blitzkrieg, empire
pyrrhic	⌣ ⌣	of the, as this
amphibrach	⌣ ´ ⌣	delighted, excited
amphimacer	´ ⌣ ´	hit the deck, come, my pet
pacan	´ ⌣ ⌣ ⌣	exquisitely, parentally

Feminine — feminine syllables are unaccented and weak in stress; they are scanned (marked) with a rocker (⌣); either the first or ending syllable may be feminine; in a three-syllable word the middle syllable may be feminine; Ex: first syllable: a-gree; middle: ac-ti-vate; ending: tender-ly.

Flashback — a recounting of events before the opening episode of the poem; or an interruption in the poem by the narration of an earlier event; Ex: Whittier's "Telling the Bees"; New England folklore tells us that New Englanders believed that bees left their hives for new homes if they were not told of a death in the family, and if their hives were not draped in black cloth; Whittier flashbacks in Stanzas 4 and 7 making it 13 months after the episode; then, he gives us the reason for the poem in the last line, "Mistress Mary is dead and gone."

Flowing — simply means rhythm; having smooth and pleasing continuity; Ex: Elizabeth Barrett Browning's Sonnet XLIII (Sonnets From the Portuguese):

How do I love thee? Let me count the ways
I love thee to the depth and breadth and height

Foreshadowed — suggested in advance in such a way that it is expected when it occurs; it is most effective in the final lines of the poem as in Richard LeGallienne's poem "I Meant To Do My Work Today," final lines:

And a rainbow held out its shining hand
So what could I do but laugh and go?

Free Verse
(Vers Libre)

the writer of free verse must discover strong words and subtle rhythms for the poet has no metrics to lean on; Robert Frost said, "writing free verse is like playing tennis without a net." See under form.

French Forms

ballade: strict in form; three octaves and quatrain called an envoy. See form.

chant royal: five stanzas of eleven lines each; usually rhymed 1, 2, 1, 2, 3, 3, 4, 4, 5, 4, 5R; envoy has five lines 4, 4, 5, 4, 5R. See form.

kyrielle: an invocation or reponse used in various Christian churches; a Psalm; a part of the Roman Catholic service after the *Introit* in the Mass.

lai: layman's response; short poem for singing; originally as by a medieval minstrel.

pantoum: verse made up of quatrains rhyming abab, bcbc, cdcd, etc. with other requirements of alternating lines. See under pantoum.

rondel: fourteen lines; two rhymes, etc. See under Rondel.

rondelet: short rondel; five or seven lines. See under Rondelet.

rondeau: thirteen lines; three stanzas; usually tetrameter; uses two rhymes and a refrain. See under Rondeau.

rondeau redouble: relative of the rondeau. See under Rondeau Redouble.

roundel: nine lines, two rhymes plus two brief refrain lines. See under Roundel.

roundelette: simple song in which a line or phrase is continually repeated; also called roundelay.

sestina: six stanzas, six lines each, ending with a tercet; strict rules of this form. See under Sestina and under article on the Sestina.

triolet: eight lines, iambic pentameter; rhyme scheme ABaAabAB, two rhymes. See under Triolet.

villanelle: six stanzas, two rhymes, five tercets and one quatrain. See under Villanelle.

viralai: jingle used as a refrain; short poem; short lines with two rhymes. See under Viralai.

Fricatives

voiced: *v* and *th, z s; th z s* as in pleasure

voiceless: *f* and *th*, *sh*; *f* in *soft*; *th* as in *th*in, *sh* as in *sh*op; sounds made by forcing the breath through the same mouth position.

Haiku

a Japanese verse form of three lines, 5-7-5 syllables, 17 total; usually on a nature subject; should portray a season; the form is becoming popular in America; the Haiku can have fewer syllables than seventeen; it is a very brief, concise form. See under form.

Heptameter

is a metric foot in poetry; it is seven feet per line; its length becomes wieldy such as in Riley's "When the Frost is on the Pumpkin":
"When the frost is on the pumpkin and the fodder's in the shock."

Heroic
verse couplet

because rhymed iambic pentameter was used for heroic (epic) poetry in English, it was called heroic verse; when the iambic pentameter lines were rhymed couplets, they were called heroic couplets; usually the first ending is a light pause, the second more heavily end-stopped. Ex: Pope's "The Duncaid":
Flow, Welsted, Flow! like thine inspirer, Beer:
Though stale, not ripe, though thin, yet never clear;

Hexaduad

newer poetry form; syllable count 2-2-6-6-8-8-4-4-6-6-4-4 couplet rhymes.

Hyperbole

exaggeration for effect; not to be taken literally; simply means overstatement. Ex: "The man is as strong as an ox."

Hypercatalectic

having one or more extra syllables in the regular measure of the line; it is called *galloping meter;* occurs in using extra feminine syllables such as -erring; usually employed by satirists and humorists.

Iamb

a metrical foot of two syllables; the first unaccented, the second accented; Ex: to seek, to find, to yield.

Ictus

metrical stress; rhythmical or accent.

Idiom	an expression that is contrary to the usual patterns of language; it creates a different impression than the literal meaning of the words. Ex: "to catch one's eye" or "the house burned up/the house burned down"; the literal meaning for both idioms is that *"fire destroyed the house."*
Image	suggests a thing seen; any sensory experience whether *visual, tactile* or *auditory;* like a picture, an image is worth more than a thousand words.
Imagery	literally mental pictures, voices or touches in the poem; *similes* and *metaphors* create images by establishing relationships; read article on subject in section on *Poetic Techniques.* Ex: Priscilla Farrington Schumacher's, "The Telephone Call":

His voice
plucked at the miles of singing wires
like fingers
unaccustomed to the twanging of guitar strings. . .

Introit	a Psalm or recitation, or song at the opening of a Christian service; a part of the Roman Catholic Mass.
Inversion	placement of words out of normal sentence order; it is discouraged in modern poetry. Ex:

Loved by someone
I must be. . .

Juxtaposition	combination of poetry forms having close meanings or connections; Juxtapose—to place beside.
Kennings	a figurative stock phrase used in Norse and Anglo-Saxon poetry, such as *"whale road"* for the sea; it has its equivalent in the stock epithet *"the wine-dark sea," "ox-eyed Hera,"* and the like—of the Greek epics; kenning of original hyphenated words can enrich poetry.
Kerf	syllable form; 12 lines; syllable count of 6-7-10-6-7-10-6-7-10-6-7-10; rhyme scheme is a, b, c, a, b, c, d, e, f, d, e, f.

Kyrielle

a French form; an invocation or response used in various Christian Churches; it is a part of the Roman Catholic service after the *Introit* in the Mass; a Psalm.

Labials

of the labia or lips; phonetic sounds formed with the lips such as *b*, *m* and *p*; labializing is to use the sounds excessively.

Lai

French form; a short poem, especially a narrative poem for singing; originally as by a medieval minstrel.

Lanterne

patterned in shape of a lantern; a shaped whimsey; eleven syllables; five lines; first line, one syllable, then two, three, four and back to one syllable in fifth line. See under form.

Laurette

syllable poem; six lines with syllable count of 4-4-6-4-4-6; lines must rhyme.

Light Rhyme

capricious or frivolous rhyme. See under *Rhyme*.

Limerick

a nonsense poem of five anapestic lines; now often bawdy; rhyme scheme is usually aabba, the first, second and fifth lines having three stresses, the third and fourth two stresses; the form was popularized by Edward Lear. Ex:

> There was a young lady named Harris,
> Whom nothing could ever embarrass
> Till the bath salts one day,
> In the tub where she lay
> Turned out to be plaster of Paris.

Litotes

a simple understatement for effect, in which something is expressed by the negation of the contrary. Ex: Thomas Hood's poem "Ruth":

> Sure, I said, Heav'n did not mean
> Where I reap thou shouldst but glean.

Ex: "now a few regrets."

Logopoeia

a term coined by Ezra Pound to distinguish a kind of poem in which neither the sound of the words nor the images they convey are as significant as the effect of unexpected usage; this use of language was credited to Jules Laforgue, a Frenchman, who greatly influenced T. S. Eliot; this "dance of the intellect among words" defies translation; *logopoeia* heightens the lingering quality of poetry; it can be used to proliferate new meaning, Ex. from Wilma Burton's poem "Thank You for a Friend's House":

the frets that *porcupined* our yesterday have lost their quills.

Here the noun *porcupine* becomes a verb and is an example of a *noun conceit* in logopoeia.

Lyric
a poem mainly expressing the poet's emotions and thoughts; sonnets, odes, elegies, and hymns are lyric poems. Ex: Edna St. Vincent Millay's poem "God's World":

O world, I cannot hold thee close enough!
Thy winds, thy wide, gray skies!

the last two lines:

My soul is all but out of me,—let fall
No burning leaf; prithee, let no bird call.

Masculine ending
lines ending on an *accented syllable* are said to have a masculine ending; there may be more than one masculine syllable in one word; it is scanned or marked with a dash (−); in a word that has two masculine syllables, there is a *primary* and *a secondary* accent; Ex: ac-ti-vate, di-a-tribe; another Ex: two syllable word with both being masculine: woodwind; typically appears at line ends, in verse of rising meter.

Melopoeia
Ezra Pound's term for the kind of poem in which some "musical property" inherent in the words is intrinsic to and governs their meaning; it can be appreciated by a reader ignorant of the sense of the words; if music is, in Dryden's phrase, "inarticulate poetry," *melopoeia* may be called "articulate music."

Metaphor
a comparison of two seemingly unlike things which do share comparable characteristics or qualities; the metaphor states that one thing is another such as "all the world's a stage"; it is the most useful figure of speech

in poetry; *Mixed metaphor:* to use two or more inconsistent metaphors in a single expression. Ex: "the storm of protest was nipped in the bud."

Metaphysical	very abstract; abstruse or subtle; beyond the material or physical; supernatural, or transcendental; English poets Donne, Crashaw and Cowley wrote *metaphysically.* Ex: John Donne's poem "Holy Sonnet XIV"; the total poem must be read to appreciate the ploy.
Metaphysical Conceit	Ex: Above poem—the human heart-walled town, the poet and the conquerer, Satan and the conqueror. etc. Samuel Johnson defines it as "that poetry wherein the most heterogeneous ideas are yoked together by violence."
Metathesis	transposition or interchange of sounds or letters in a word; usually a "slip of the tongue"; Ex: Minister to bridegroom: "It is now kisstomary to cuss the bride." See under Spoonerisms.
Meter	rhythm in verse, measured, patterned arrangement of syllables primarily according to feet, stress, or length (iambic and anapestic - rising meters); (trochaic and dactylic - falling meters), (accentual-stresses) and (quantitative-vowel length or sound).
Common Meter	another name sometimes given to the *ballad stanza* , especially when it occurs in hymns.
Metonomy	literally, name changing where the attribute or associated thing is substituted for the usual name of a thing; Examples: *blue* for the *sky*; the *White House* for the *President*; the *campus* for the *school*; the *Crown* for the *King*; the *devil* for *evil*; *finger* for *touch* and *hammer* for *pound*. Ex. by Frost:

    The buzz saw *snarled and rattled* in the yard
    And made *dust* and dropped *stove-length sticks of wood*
    Sweet-scented stuff when the *breeze* drew across it.

Metric	unit of length in, of the meter, in verse.
Metrical	of or composed in meter or verse; the reading and studying of Coleridge's poem, "Metrical Feed (lesson for a boy)" is excellent source of understanding metrical feet.
Metronome	the beat in a poem that results in regular tempo; the poet may use metronomic devices such as tapping the feet or fingers to count the stresses and syllables in the poem.
Minute	syllable poem; iambic; 12 lines; 60 syllables, rhyme aa bb, dd, ee, ff
Molossus	a fragment in poetry; a foot scanned " − − −." Ex: "That sweet man!"; it is defensible, but less interesting.
Monologue	a poem in which the voice of the poet addresses an unseen or imagined listener or audience.
Monometer	one foot; some poets have written monometer poem to delight and outwit the reader. Ex: Robert Herrick's "Upon His Departure Hence": Where tell I dwell. Farewell.
Monosyllabic	having only one syllable; they are called feet but contain no unaccented syllables. ( ) Ex: Yeats' "Who Goes With Fergus?": "And the *white breast* of the *dim sea,"* have the effect of hammering nails into a board; steady sound.
Narrative	a poem that tells a tale or story about a person, place or thing; narratives are not lyrical. Ex: *The Iliad,* and *The Odyssey;* and Longfellow's *Hiawatha;* the poet tells a story as if he had been a spectator.
Nasal	member of consonant family; nasals = *m n ng;* words ending in *ing* are normally sounded in the nasal passage - the nose. Ex: mor*ning.*

Near rhyme   same as slant rhyme; its use can be an asset, if properly used; Emily Dickison used it often. Ex: Poem: Presentiment - is that long - Shadow - on the lawn - Indicative that suns go down.

Neoclassic   a period in English literature called the Augustan age; dated from 1660 into the late 18th century; instead of saying "rats" a poet referred to them as "the whiskered vermin race."

Neville   seven line, iambic, syllable form/48 syllables; syllable count is 8-6-6-8-6-6-8/rhyme scheme is a, b, b, a, c, c, a. (See form.)

Noun conceit   See Conceit.

Objective
Correlative   study Eliot's *Preludes;* analyze each poem you write to see if you have developed *Objective Correlative;* is your object *despair, joy, ecstasy,* or *suffering?* Eliot's *Preludes* is a fine example of *showing* rather than *telling* in a poem.

Occidental   in reference to poetry it is relevant to Occidental or Western culture.

Octain   syllable form; syllable count is 2-4-6-8-8-6-4-2; rhyme scheme is a, b, c, d, b, c, d, a; forty syllables; see form.

Octameter   an eight metrical foot line; Poe's poem "The Raven" is a study in this meter; he used acatalectic octameter.

Octava Rima   is an Italian octave; Italian poets employed eleven syllables to the line; English poets preferred iambic pentameter; the octava rima is rhymed ababab cc.

Octava   eight lines rhymed as two quatrains fused; a couplet, a quatrain, and a couplet; two tercets and a couplet, etc.; the Spencerian stanza is an octave rhymed ababb cbc, plus the ninth *c.*

Octo   syllable form; eight lines of 8 syllables each; the first three lines transposed become the last three lines of the poem; lines 4 and 5 rhyme; sixty-four syllables. See form.

Octosyllabic	containing eight syllables in a line of verse.

Octosyllabic Couplet — two lines of verse containing eight syllables in each line; usually rhymed to form a unit. Ex:
Fill the cup and lift it high
and drink a toast to Captain Bley.

Ode — a poem written to be sung; a choral interlude in a play; Keats found it adaptable in his poem, "Ode to a Nightingale"; in modern use, it is a lyric poem, rhymed or unrhymed, typically addressed to some person or thing with dignified style, elaborate form, or lofty feeling.

Onda Mel — syllable form; eight lines; syllable count is 8-4-4-8-8-4-4-8; it is a love-interest poem; rhyme scheme is a, b, b, a, c, d, d, c, has forty-eight syllables. See form.

Onomatopoeia — literally *name making*; the naming of a thing or action by a vocal imitation of the sound associated with it such as *"buzz, hiss"*; the use of words whose sounds suggests the sense; Ex: *Swish* - a word which all but reproduces the sound it represents; Ex: *snap, crackle, pop* for cereal.

Ontithetic — in classical poetry, the existence of the accented syllable of a foot; in later poetry the unaccented foot due to a misunderstanding of the original Greek word.

Oriental — Eastern poetry; relating to the oriental people; their culture; familiar forms: Haiku, Senryu and Tanka.

Outrageous Rhyme — unrestrained rhyme; flagrant use of rhyme; employed by satirists or humorists; Ex: Ogden Nash's:
Many an infant that screams like a *calliope*
Could be soothed by a little attention to *its diope.*

Overstatement — hyperbole; exaggeration or magnification of a truth, facts, etc. Ex: "I've told you a thousand times."

Oxymoron   subtle contradictions are called oxymorons; Milton's description in *Paradise Lost* of Satan's first view of hell he recovers from his nine days' fall from Heaven contains oxymorons. Ex: *thunderous silence, sweet sorrow, cold fire.*

Pace   is the speed of motion and countermotion within the poem.

Padding   unnecessary words added to a poem to make it longer, or to effect a rhyme scheme.

Paean   epithet; a hymn or song of joy, praise and thanksgiving.

Paeon   a foot of three short syllables and one long; may occur in any order.

Palatals   sounds made with the front of the tongue by pressing the tongue on or near the soft and hard palate; certain sounds are *ch, j, sh,* or *zh;* sounds made with the rear of the tongue touching the palate are *ng, g, k.*

Pantoum   French form; verse made up of quatrains rhyming abab, bcbc, cdcd, etc. with the second and fourth lines of one quatrain recurring as the first and third of the next, and the first and third lines of the first quatrain recurring as the second and fourth lines of the last. See under form.

Parable   a brief narrative that usually teaches a moral; not always, but usually is allegorical.

Paradox   an assertion that seems to contradict itself, but which is the truth; used frequently in the Bible. Ex: Jesus said, "For whosoever will lose his life for my sake and the gospel's, the same shall save it."

Parallelism   the comparison of ideas, things, in order to show similarity or likeness, or find a counterpart for; also parallel structure in writing as a series of images causing a series of comparisons. Ex: Read Dorothy Parker's poem "Resume":

> Razors pain you;
> Rivers are damp, etc.

Paranomasia   the pun or play on words; Samuel Johnson was asked by a lady if he would define the difference between men and women; he replied, "I can't conceive, madam, can you?"

Paraphrase   putting into the poem what we understand the poem to say; sometimes it is a heartless thing to do to a poem as in Pope's line in the poem, "Duncaid":

> "And make night hidious - answer him, ye owls."

Slide *ye owls* together and you get *youls;* thus, Pope turns poor James Ralph's serenade into the nerve-wracking outcry of a cat.

Parody   imitation of another writer's style; nonsensical treatment of a serious subject by ridicule; one writer poking fun at another; Whitman, Eliot and T. E. Brown used it; Brown's poem, "My Garden":

> A garden is a lovesome thing
> God wot (knows)
> Rose plot.
> Fringed pool. . .

J. A. Lindon parodied it thus:

> A garden is a lovesome thing?
> What rot
> Weed plot,
> Scum pool. . .

Partial Rime   same as near, slant or off rime.

Pastoral   treating the rustic lives of shepherds; modern includes pastors, ministers rural people in simple and idyllic styles.

Pastorale   a poem about the simple and idyllic styles suggesting rural scenes; many times put to music for an opera or cantata.

Pattern　　　the arrangement of the poem on the page; the placing of words or lines of the poem on the page; when this technique is employed by the poet, it is sometimes called an *eye poem.*

Pauses　　　a rhythm break either by punctuation, caesura, hesitation in reading; any mark of punctuation; a pause puts poem under stress and gives it emphasis.

Pegasus　　　mythical winged horse that sprung from the body of Medusa (one of the three Gorgons slain by Perseus); a stamp of his hoof caused the fountain of the Muses (poets or other artists) to flow from Mt. Helicon, (in Greek mythology, the home of the Muses.)

Pensee　　　syllable form; five lines; 29 syllables; syllable count is 2-4-7-8-8; poem should have unbroken phrasing and use strong words. See form.

Pentameter　　　line of verse having five metrical feet or measures; a verse consisting of pentameters is called *heroic verse.* Ex: "He jests/at scars/who nev/er felt/a wound."

Perfect rhyme　　　repetition of the vowel and consonant which must be preceded by a different consonant; Ex: wall, tall, call, small; also called *right rhyme.*

Persona　　　poetry form in which the poet can enter into the personality and speak with the voice of someone else; *Persona* means mask. See form.

Personification　　　a figure of speech in which a thing, animal or an abstract term (truth, nature) is made human; personification is the attribution of human qualities to the inanimate. Ex: Emily Dickinson's:

> The Mountains stood in Haze - The Valleys stopped below
> and went or waited as they liked. . .

Petrarchan　　　a sonnet composed of a group of eight lines (octave) with two rhymes abba, abba, and a group of six lines (sestet) with various rhymes, typically cde, cde; cdc, or dcd or may be three couplets aa, bb, cc; sonnet form said to be authored by Francesco Petrarch, 1307-74, Italian poet and scholar. See form.

Phanapoeia   refers to the kind of poem which addresses itself to visual imagination, and which depends upon utter precision of word; it can be translated.

Pindar   Greek poet, a lyricist, 522-438 (?) B.C.

Pindaric (Ode)   in the style of Pindar; elaborate or regular in metrical structure; an ode in which the strophe and antistrophe have the same form in contrast to the epode, which was a different form; Noun: Pindaric ode.

Pivot   that point at which countermotion in the poem becomes obvious; marked $>$ in scansion; Ex: Emily Dickinson's poem:

> Beside the Autumn poets sing
> A few prosaic days. . .

last two lines, the pivot:

> Grant me, Oh Lord,
> a sunny mind—Thy windy will to bear!

Plosives   phonetic (sound) produced by the complete stoppage and sudden release of the breath, as the sounds of k, p and t when used initially; there are two divisions; *voiced plosives* = b, d, g; *voiceless plosives* = k, p, t.

Poetaster   a writer of mediocre verse; rhymester; a would-be poet.

Poetic-diction   a system of words refined from the grossness of domestic use, quote from Samuel Johnson's famous Dictionary 1755.

-license   the freedom to deviate from the strict usage of words and forms.

-truth   known as *verisimilitude* as applied to literary works;

the appearance or being truth; poetic truth has been referred to as the big lie that brings out the truth.

Poetry	the embodiment of emotions; structure, in verse form.
Precis	a summary; a shortcut or a brief; it is abstracted thought, reduced to the pithiest essence possible; practice to be used in reading poetry; employ the five steps of precis: (1) read the poem (2) reread the poem (3) decide which is the one central idea (4) paraphrase the cental idea; if more than one, place in logical order and (5) condense your paraphrase until it is as brief as possible; now you have a precis.
Projective verse	poem in which the poet's emotions and/or personality traits are thought to be projected on the page; for example, read Whitman's "When Lilacs Last in the Doorway Bloom'd'," note the indented lines using the same word (with) for emphasis; the Psalms are another example; Charles Olson employed projective verse; it is essentially a form to not only please the eye, but to aid the reader; it has a musical quality.
Prologue	the introduction to a poem; usually used in dramatic poetry; sets the tone of the dramatic poem.
Prose Poems	poems written in block form as in prose; the poet does not break a law by refusing to split thoughts into lines; does not worry about eye appeal or whether some of the rhythm may be lost in the formation of the poem on the page; Eliot, Shapiro, Duncan and Rimbaud wrote prosaically; Ex: see Shapiro's, "The Dirty Word."
Prosody	a study of the basic principles of verse structure; includes meter, rhythm and stanza form; a particular system of versification and metrical structure; also, in Greek, it means tone and accent in poetry.
Protest poetry	the word is self-explanatory; poetry in which the writer protests or speaks out against; used in political

poems, taxation, and national affairs; the Third World poets are employing it; conditions can be exposed through poetry that would not be permissible in prose; metaphors and similes are a must in protest poetry; Ex: Frost's "Fences" which he read in Moscow when accepting the Nobel Prize.

Psalm	quoting Robert Lowell, "supreme poems, written when their translators merely intended prose and were forced by the structure of their originals to write poetry."
Pyrrhic feet	a metrical foot of two short unstressed syllables.
Quantitative	Greek and Latin poetry is measured in long and short vowel sounds; an iamb in classical verse is one short vowel followed by a long vowel; meter constructed on the vowel sound is called *quantitative meter*.
Quatern	new form; iambic pentameter, four stanzas of four lines each; eight syllables (four feet) in each line; first line repeated one line down in each stanza, rhyme pattern is a, b, a, b-b A, b-b, a, b, A (capital letters are for repeated lines). See form.
Quatrain	poetry form; four lines, rhymed abab, abba, abcb, etc., couplets may be fused into quatrain, aabb; rhyme scheme remains constant in *quatrain sequence*.
Quintain	poem, five lines, rhymed aabbb, ababb, etc.; the combination of a couplet and a tercet.
Random rhyme	not uniform in rhyme scheme; inner rhyme, or one or more couplets may be used.
Refrain -incremental	a refrain whose words change slightly with each recurrence is called an incremental refrain. Ex: "Frankie and Johnnie."
-internal	a refrain that appears within a stanza, generally in a position that stays fixed throughout the poem. Ex: Yeats' "Long Legged Fly."

-terminal	a refrain that follows immediately after a stanza; Ex: "The Cruel Mother" (Anonymous), the second line is fixed in this Scottish folk ballad, "Fine flowers in the valley," appears as the second line in all seven stanzas; the fourth line is also fixed and is the fourth line in all seven stanzas.

Rhyme/Rime

end	as is indicated, comes at the end of line; even in run-over lines.
exact	sounds following vowels must be the same sounds in both rhymed words and phrases such as: fed-bled, walk-talk, passionless-fashionless.
eye	spelling of word looks alike but is pronounced differently; Ex: rough-dough; strictly speaking, eye rhyme is not rhyme.
double	two rhymes within the same line; Ex: same-lame, see-be.
initial	any identical or similar sound—not only vowel sounds; the consonant sounds that follow the vowel sounds are identical; Ex: prairie schooner-piano tuner.
internal	when a word within a line rhymes with another word in the line; does not have to be the end word; Ex: W. S. Gilbert's "Nightmare," "your pillow resigns and politely declines to remain at its usual angle."
feminine	a rhyme of two or more syllables; stress is on a syllable other than the last one. Ex: *care*ful-*ten*der, ef-*fect*-u-al.
light	capricious or frivolous rhyme. Ex: The female *shenanigans*/were performed with *fannykins*.
masculine	usually a rhyme of one word such as: mail-sail-rail; or if more than one syllable, the stress is on the final syllable such as: forGET-reGRET-aBRUPT; in a word that has three syllables, there is a primary and a secondary accent; Ex: *ac*-ti-*vate*, *di*-a-*tribe*.

near	also imperfect or half rhyme: different terms for words in which the final consonant sounds are the same but the vowel sounds are different such as: loved-moved, near-bear; often used by a poet to give the reader a jolt.
off	see near rhyme.
outrageous	usually used in satire or humorous poetry; poet distorts words to effect rhyming. Ex: The lady napped in the hammock under a canopy; she forgot her bikini was made of saranopy.
partial	see near rhyme.
perfect	repeats the vowel sound but must be preceded by a different consonant. Ex: wall-call-fall-ball.
random	not uniform in rhyme scheme; poet takes poetic license to use inner rhyme and/or more couplets within the poem; other than couplet rhymes may be used.
right	are not perfect rhymes, but have exactly the same sounds. Ex: write-right, sum-some, see-sea.
slant	same as near rhyme; sounds are similar but not exact; final consonant sounds are the same but vowel sounds are different. Ex: heaven-given, stone-gone.
uneven	not set pattern of rhyme; not considered good discipline for rhyming poetry.
Rhyme Royal	a poetry form; is iambic pentameter, rhymed ababbcc; used by Chaucer, Spenser and other English poets.
Rising meter	iambic and anapestic meters are called rising meters because their movement rises from unstressed syllable(s).
Rispetto	poetry form; is iambic tetrameter, rhyme scheme is a, b, a, b, c, c, d, d; usually eight lines.

Ritual

poem written for ceremonial rite, such as those used in Freemasonry, the Anglican churches and Eucharistic rites; otherwise referred to as the *liturgy*.

Rocker

a scansion mark in poetry ($\smile$); it is used for the unstressed.

Rondeau

French form of poetry; has thirteen lines; three stanzas, usually tetrameter; uses only two rhymes and a refrain; rhyme scheme is aabba, aab, aabba. See form.

Rondeau Redouble

a remote relative of the rondeau; it starts with a *quatrain* theme; followed by four additional quatrains in each of which successively lines one, two, three and four of the theme quatrain appear as terminal lines; the concluding stanza of four lines of regular length, and a one-line refrain containing the first half of line one theme; Ex: Cosmo Monkhouse's, "My soul is sick of nightingale and rose."

Rondel

French form, 14 lines; two rhymes, and the first two lines used as a refrain in the middle and at the end (the second line is occasionally omitted at the end); rhyme schemes is abb, aba, abba.

Rondelet

a short rondel, usually of five or seven lines in one stanza and a refrain made up of the opening words; rhyme scheme 7 lines, aba, abba. See form.

Roundel

French form having nine lines, two rhymes, plus two brief refrain lines rhyming with the second of the two rhymes; refrain is taken from the first word(s) of the poem and follows the first and third tercets; same as a roundelay.

Run-on

line of poetry that is completed in the succeeding line of verse; also called *enjambment*.

Sapphics

named for the poet Sappho, who is said to have used the form with great skill; a sapphic line consists of five equal beats; its central one of three syllables and the rest two each; the original *Greek sapphic stanza* consisted of three of these lines, followed by a shorter line called an *adonic*. Ex: Swinburne's sapphic lines.

Feet, the straining plumes of the doves that drew her,
looking, always looking with necks reverted,
Back to Lesbos, back to the hills whereunder
Shone Mitylene; (adonic line)

Satire

the use of ridicule, sarcasm, irony, etc., to expose, attack, or deride device or follies; irony evoked when mother offers caster oil to her son, saying, "you'll like this"; he replies, "*sure* I will." At its unsubtle level, irony becomes sarcasm, (cutting language which wounds); Jonathan Swift's "A Modest Proposal" is an excellent example of satire (starving Irish encouraged to breed children and sell them to the British landlords for food.)

Scansion

is analyzing verse into its rhythmic components; *dashes* and *rockers* are used in this technique; it is done by looking at and listening to the poem; scansion symbols are ⌣ or /⌣ ; half stress is (\\); see under feet (metric).

Sentimentality

the implied feeling of great emotion; usually results in a maudlin poem; Ex: Samuel Woodworth's "The Old Oaken Bucket,"

How sweet from the green, mossy brim to receive it,
As, poised on the curb, it inclined to my lips.

Sept

syllable form; seven line count is 1-2-3-4-3-2-1; no rhyme.

Septet

also called *heptet*; seven lines; stanza is a combination of couplets, tercets, quatrains and quintains; rhyming possibilities is endless; most popular is in iambic pentameter, rhymed ababbcc, called Rhyme Royal; used by Chaucer, Spenser and other English poets.

Sestet

five lines, rhymed ababab, abbabb, etc; two tercets may be fused, or a couplet and a quatrain; the rhyme scheme is numerous.

Sestina	poetry form having six six-line stanzas ending with a tercet; the end words of the first stanza are repeated with progressively changed order in the other five stanzas, and are included, medially and finally, in the tercet; it is a fixed form and a skilled writer of form can make the reader unaware of the strict rules of the form. Ex: read Anne Marx's poem "Sestina for Tommy at Forty." See form.
Sevenelle	consists of no less than two seven-line stanzas; no limit to number of stanzas; has four feet per line; the last two lines of any stanza becomes the refrain which is the last two lines of the first stanza; see under form.
Sextain	is a six-line stanza.
Shadorma	syllable form; has six lines, syllable count is 3-5-3-3-7-5; poem should have unity. See under forms.
Sibilant	sound having or making a *hissing* sound, such as s, z, sh, zh.
Simile	is a comparison likening two things that are, almost completely, dissimilar; expressed with words *like, as* or *than*. Ex: "Her lips are sweeter *than* honey" or "My love is *like* a red, red rose" or "She's *as* ugly as sin."
Slant rhyme	See under rhyme; same as near rhyme.
Soliloquy	a poem in which the poet reveals his/her thoughts to the reader, by speaking as if to himself/herself; Ex: read "Soliloquy of the Spanish Cloister," by Robert Browning.
Sonnet	a poem form, normally of fourteen lines in any of several fixed verse and rhyme schemes; typically in iambic pentameter; sonnets usually express a single theme or idea; the rhyme schemes for various sonnet forms are as follows:
Shakespearean	three quatrains and a couplet or an octave and a sestet; abab, cdcd, efef, gg.

Spencerian	same arrangement; rhyme scheme is abab, bcbc, cdcd, ee.
Petrarchan	(Italian); an octave and varying sestet; abba, abba, cde, cde (tercets); also cdc, cdc, cdc, ede; or cd, cd, cd; Petrarchan has two restrictions; cannot conclude with a couplet or no end rhyme beyond "e" is permitted.
Mason	(difficult rhyme scheme) abc, abc, cbd, badda.
Glorionic	is comprised of a couplet, two tercets, followed by terza rima lines; or another couplet and ending with a abaa quatrain; author's rhyme scheme is aa, bbb, ccc, ddedee.
Asian	(new) originated by Dr. Amado Yuzon; consists of two quintains and ends with a quatrain; rhyme scheme is abaab, cdccd, efef.
Spencerian Stanza	named for Edmund Spencer, English poet, (1552? - 1599) born in London; credited with raising a new standard of excellence in English poetry; died poverty stricken; was buried in Westminster Abbey; greatest non dramatic poet between Chaucer and Milton; the stanza is eight lines of iambic pentameter; a ninth of iambic hexameter (the alexandrine); Ex: Read Spencer's "The Faerie Queene."
Spondaic	adjective of spondee; spondaic line from Milton's *Paradise Lost,* "Here we may reign secure and in my choice."
Spondee	a metrical foot, consisting of two heavily accented syllables (English poetry); in Greek and Latin it is two long syllables.
Spoonerisms	are really "slips of the tongue" which are used effectively in humorous poetry; they get their name from Rev. William A. Spooner, for many years the warden of New College, Oxford; it began when the Reverend while marrying a couple told the groom, "It is now kisstomary to cuss the bride"; Harry Von Zell, radio

announcer slipped with: "We bring you the President of the United States, Mr. Hoobert Heever," and Panelist Lowell Thomas, who, in a wartime broadcast referred to British cabinet minister Sir Stafford Cripps as "Sir Stifford Crapps."

Stanza	is a group of lines comprising a poetic division; it may be as brief as a couplet (two lines) or extend to any length the poet chooses; typically has a regular pattern in the number of lines, and the arrangement of meter and rhyme.

Stanza patterns

couplet	2 lines with rhymed meter aa; couplets with more than one couplet meter is aa, bb, cc, dd, etc.
tercet or triplet	3 lines, rhymed aaa, bbb. (See chapter on *terza rima* for varied rhyme)
quatrain	4 lines with flexible rhyme schemes: abab, aabb, abba, abcb; somewhere in the quatrain two lines must rhyme.
quitain	5 lines, rhyme scheme, aabbb, ababb; quitain is a combination of the couplet and sestet.
sestet	6 lines, rhyme scheme of ababab, abbabb; a couplet and a quatrain; also, two tercets.
septec or heptet	rhyme schemes are many in this form; ababbcc, the iambic pentameter is most used and is called Rime Royal; couplets, tercets, quatrains and quintains may be combined as rhyming possibilities.
octave	8 lines; the octava rime is abababcc; Spencerian is ababbcbc rhyme; any combination of couplets, quatrains, tercets can be used.

Stanzaic	adjective of stanza; use of technique results in the poem being stanzaic.
Stress	the relative force with which a syllable is uttered according to the meter; the unaccented syllable; to em-

phasize; stressed syllable comes out slightly louder, higher in pitch, or longer in duration than other syllables; Ex: first syllable—*ea*gle, *sta*tue; second syllable—cig*ar*, pre*cise*.

Strophe
it applies to the Ode; originated in Greece; it is a turning or twisting; the movement of the chorus from right to left on the stage; the strophe is the first statement or verse, followed by the antistrophe (answer to the statement) and the epode then becomes the summary or application.

Structure
the building of the poem composed of its interrelated parts such as syntax, meter, rhythm, rhyme, alliteration, metaphors, similes, etc.; *expository* structure supports the poem with specific illustration and /or generality; Ex: Darylyn Neinkin's poem, "English Lesson,"

Nouns and verbs are quite complex
When the noun is a boy and the verb is "necks."

Style
is the poet herself; it encompasses ability, discipline, originality, craftsmanship and temperament; Dickinson would not have said,

I died for Vanity, but when buried in the tomb
I found the *scoundrel*
In the adjoining room.
(She died for *Beauty*- Truth was her companion in the adjoining room.

Surrealism
an attempt to portray or interpret the workings of the unconscious mind as in dreams; a declaration that higher reality exists which to mortal eyes looks absurd; surrealist poets are fond of bizarre objects such as soluble fish and angel-winged revolvers; foreign poets use this technque to criticise goverments and ways of life.

Syllable
a word or part of a word pronounced with a single, uninterrupted sounding of the voice; unit of pronunciation, consisting of a single sound of great sonority, (usually a vowel) and generally one or more sounds of

lesser sonority, (usually consonants); to show where the word can be broken. Ex: *"by a cinths de fy ing cold."*

Syllabic verse   is usually stanzaic, in which the poet uses a pattern of a certain number of syllables to a line; it has been used as an escape from the tyranny of the iamb; study the syllabic forms.

Syllepsis   a grammatic structure in which a single word is used to modify or govern syntactically two or more words in the same sentence of which at least one does not agree in number, case or gender.

Symbol   something that stands for or represents another thing; it not only signifies the actual object, but all the ideas, attitudes and responses associated with it; one symbol should create a larger idea, etc. Ex: Bonnie Elizabeth Parker's poem, "Beethoven,"
　　The waves come in implacably as gods,
　　Run out on little silver feet like girls,
causing the symphony to totally encompass the listener as the sea; another example is Poe's raven.

Symbolism   the use of symbols in the poem. Emily Dickinson employed the use of symbols in much of her poetry as in "The Lightning is a Yellow Fork/From Tables in the sky. Emily's poem about the *locomotive* is full of metaphors. . . . "I like to see it lap the miles-And lick the Valleys up-And stop to feed itself at Tanks-And then-Prodigious step/Around a Pile of mountains, etc."

Synechdoche   the use of a part of a thing to stand for the whole of it or vice versa; an individual for a class. Ex: Army for soldier, or copper for a penny; also to say "Lend a hand," means to lend the whole body, iron for golf club, pigskin for football.

Synonym   a word having the same or nearly the same meaning; poet needs to scrutinize the application of synonyms in the poem for the wrong synonym could change the meaning of the poem; a *faux pas* is often induced into the poem by poor choice of synonyms. Ex: words such as contemplate—syn., nurse, fragile—syn., slender.

Syntax	the arrangement of words as elements in a sentence to show their relationship to one another; to join, put together; proper grammatical arrangement of words; contemporary use of line arrangement in free verse.
Synthetic	the unified whole in which the opposites (thesis and antithesis) are reconciled; when the accented and unaccented syllables are placed together; the constructed parts of a poem either by techniques or ideas.
Tactile	type of imagery that touches; it may be an odor, or a taste, or body sensation such as pain, prickling as gooseflesh, or the quenching of thirst. Ex: Emily Dickinson's poem, "I should not dare to leave my friend," If I should stab the patient faith So sure I'd come—so sure I'd come—
Tango	syllable poem; syllable count 9-10-11-12; four lines; rhyme is abcb.
Tanka	is an Oriental form; also a free verse form; sometimes referred to as an extension of the Haiku; the last two lines are to enhance the Haiku, not to introduce a new theme; the Tanka has 31 syllables; count is 5, 7, 5, 7, 7; see under form.
Telescoping	condensing or shortening of the poem; either by lines, words, stanzas. See *elipsis*.
Tercet	is a three-line stanza; if rhymed, it usually keeps to one rime sound, aaa, bbb; if interlocking rhyme is used, employing the repetition of rhyme in a new stanza from a previous one, it becomes a terza rima; two rhymes are used if tercet has more than one stanza; Ex: Mother Goose—"Come, let's to bed/Says Sleepy-head/Tarry a while, says Slow. Put on the pot/Says Greedy-gut/We'll sup before we go.
Terminal refrain	the lines or refrain that follows immediately after a stanza. See under refrains.

Terza rima

form with interlocking rhyme with the repetition of rhyme in a new stanza from a previous one; Dante used the rime scheme of aba, bcb, cdc, ded, efe, etc. in his *Divine Comedy;* Shelly employed it with the use of slant rhyme, and couplets. See form for example.

Tetradine

syllable form; theme is usually light or fanciful; has twelve lines, syllable count is 2-4-6-8-10-10-10-10-8-6-4-2; the lines that have the same number of syllables rhyme. Ex: see under form.

Tetrameter

the four-foot line, the popular length for Villanelles, ballades, rondeaus and triolets; for examples, see under forms mentioned.

Theme

the central thought the poem as a whole conveys; does not have to be the subject matter; usually is inferred rather than told or shown; it is the attitude of the poet toward the subject; Ex: Emily Dickinson's poem about the locomotive, in this case could have been both theme and subject matter; trains in her day were a mechanical phenomenon; it appears that she enjoyed comparing the locomotive to a great, noisy beast which makes a great to-do but is firmly under man's control.

Thesis

in classical poetry, it is the accented syllable of a foot; in later poetry it is the unaccented syllable; this resulted from a misunderstanding of the original Greek word *thesis.*

Title

self-explanatory but of great importance to the poem; Ex: Adelaide Crapsey's poem, "Niagara"; instance was a night in November; consonant "n" has a cold sound as does the title and the month; the poem:
>How frail
>Above the bulk
>Of crashing water hangs
>Autumnal, evanescent, wan
>The moon.

"Frail, wan, evanescent," gives mood of weakness, loneliness; and "crashing" a feeling of violence, autumnal, the Fall of her life; all indicative of the dying woman, that she was.

Tone

the dominant quality of sound in a poem or a portion thereof; the poet chooses words to achieve the emotional attitude of the poem; Ex: word bell - if it rings, it is neutral in sound; it it peals, it is joyful; if it tolls, it connotates mourning.

Traditional

poetry handed down from the generations; conventional forms; immediately one thinks of the sonnet, or rhymed verse, but free verse, blank verse is also traditional since it has been written for centuries; the general assumption is that traditional verse is in a fixed or rigid form.

Transition

is passing from one point to another in the poem; it may be achieved by a word, phrase, a repetition or suggested association; the poet must be an expert in good transition for he cannot rely on such obvious words as however, next we will, first; poetry can be done by one image growing out of another image. Ex: Wordsworth's "Daffodils."

Translation

to put into words of a different language; Shakespeare has been translated from English into German; many Japanese poets works have been put into English; rephrasing or paraphrasing one language into another; St. James version of the Bible is a good example of translation; it has been translated several times since its original wording.

Trimeter

three feet or measures in a line of poetry; it is said the trimeter lends inself to melancholy.

Triolet

French form; it has eight lines, iambic pentameter; rhyme scheme is ABaAabAB, two rhymes only; lines 1, 4, 7 are identical but words may vary slightly; lines 2 and 8 are identical (B); lines 3 and 5 rhyme with 1, 4 and 7; line 6 rhymes with 2 and 8. Ex: Truth Mary Fowler's poem, "Ring of Mushrooms":

| I love to go Septembering | A |
| beneath a robin's egg-blue sky; | B |

to scuff dry leaves, remembering	a
we used to go Septembering	A
and once we found a fairy ring	a
we wished on where the grass grew high;	b
I love to go Septembering	A
beneath a robin's egg-blue sky.	B

Triple rhyme

the correspondence of sound is carried through three consecutive syllables. Ex: vict*orious*-merit*orious*-*glorious.*

Triplet

a group of three successive lines of poetry; three lines, rhymed aaa, bbb, aab, abb; does not have to rhyme; it can be unified in stanzas. Ex: Marianne Moore's poem, "Talisman" consists of four triplets, one enjambing into the next.

Triplex rhythm

has three syllables per cadence; see under cadence.

Tripod

syllable form; has 27 syllables, five lines, syllable count of 3-6-9-6-3; theme: must deal with man's relationship to man; See under form.

Trite phrase

the poet's real problem and danger in writing the poem; another name is cliche; a clever poet can employ them deliberately and effectively; it is a phrase that through repeated use has lost its freshness and impressive force. Ex: "like a bolt from the blue."

Trochaic

a metrical foot of two syllables, the first accented, the second unaccented. Ex:
    Peter, Peter, Pumpkin eater.

Truncate

when using iambs, it is the dropping of the feminine or the head of the iamb, and start with the masculine. Ex: "Oh Come, my Celia, let us prove while we can, the sports of love"; the "Oh" would be dropped and the line start with "Come"; lines from Ben Johnson's "Volpone"; truncate means simply to cut off or shorten; see catalexis; Ex: Gerard Manley Hopkins often truncated his lines of verse.

Trunk   when a poem is truncated, the masculine syllable at the start of the poem is the trunk.

Tuanortsa   originated in 1966 by the *Penn Laurel Poets;* spelled backwards it is *astronaut;* must be readable both upward and downward, with the title at the top and bottom; it may be rhymed or unrhymed, 24 lines or less. See under form.

Understatement   to express too weakly; in a style that is restrained and often makes use of irony or litotes. Ex: Robert Frost's line, "One could do worse than be a swinger of birches. . ."; Frost uses verbal irony in this line.

Verisimilitude   the believability of the poem; plausible or seeming to be true.

Verse   a sequence of words and/or lines arranged metrically in accordance with some form, rule or design; a poem or line of a poem.

Vers Libre   French term for Free Verse; term handed down from a 19th century anti-classist movement.

Vignette   a short literary poem; more like a sketch that depicts a lovely picture.

Villanelle   French form originated in 1660; has six stanzas; uses only two rhymes; five tercets and one (6th stanza) quatrain; nineteen lines in all; rhyme scheme is AbA, abA, abA, abA, abA, abAA; (capital A's rhyme; the b is the second rhyme); the first and third lines rhyme in the five tercets, and lines one, three and four rhyme in the quatrain; it originally was a round sung by farm laborers; it has become one of the most versatile of the French forms lending itself to both light and serious themes. Ex: Dylan Thomas's "Do Not Go Gently Into that Goodnight."

Viraley   French form (Viralai); jingle used as a refrain; short poems, consisting of short lines with two rhymes, and having two opening lines repeated at intervals; any similar verse form, especially poem with stanzas made up of alternating long and short lines; the short lines having one rhyme; the long lines the second rhyme; short lines must not be indented. Ex:

Hear the whipporwill
Sing his nightly trill—
O, say
Can he mean no ill
Though his codicil
Is gray?
Sing now, by the mill—
He will soon be still—
Come day.   Wilma Burton

Virgule   is the slant line (/) to separate words and/or lines when writing a poem; also to separate feet in the poem to show where each begins and ends. Ex:

And walk/ing ank/le-deep/ in water

Visual   imagery that induces sight in the poem; seeing what the poet is trying to say; Ex: Buson's Haiku, the second line is visual: "my dead wife's comb, in our bedroom."

Vulgate   vernacular or common speech; speech not affected by schooling. Ex: E. E. Cummings:

mr. youse needn't be so spry
concerning questions arty.

BIBLIOGRAPHY

The American People's Encyclopedia. Chicago: Spencer Press, Inc., 1953.

Harper's Dictionary of Contemporary Usage. New York: Haper and Row, 1975.

Kennedy, X. L. *An Introduction to Poetry,* 2nd Edition. Boston: Little Brown, 1971.

Sanders, T. E. *The Discovery of Poetry.* Glenview: Scott, Foresman, 1967.

Webster's New World Dictionary, 2nd College Edition. New York: Simon and Schuster, 1980.

Wood, Clement. *Rhyming Dictionary.* New York: Doubleday, 1936.

CONTRIBUTORS' NOTES

VIRGINIA BAGLIORE, poet and lecturer, is the Vice-President of Letters, National League of American Pen Women. She is the recipient of several awards including the Creative Service Award for "Poetry in Sterling" from World Poets Resource Center. Her poetry has appeared in *Poet Ocarina, Bitterroot, Modern Images, Southwest Times Record* and *The Shore Review.*

ALICE MORREY BAILEY is a poet, playwright, sculptor and musician. She has won many awards for her poetry including Utah's "Poet of the Year" in 1971 and the "Grand Prize" Award given by the National Federation of State Poetry Societies in 1979. She is also the recipient of the John Masefield Award and The World Order of Narrative Poetry Award. She has published in the *Ladies' Home Journal, Saturday Evening Post, Seven, Salt Lake Tribune, The Ensign Utah Magazine* and *Frontier Magazine.*

RUTH VAN NESS BLAIR graduated from the Seattle Pacific College and has taught in Everett, Washington. Her poetry, articles and stories have appeared in the *Athens Magazine, Music Journal, Writer's Digest, Christian Living, Cricket, The Pen Woman* and *Pegasus.* She has published children's books including *Paddle Duck, Bear Hibernate, Why Can't I?* and *Mary's Monster.*

JEANNE BONNETTE was educated at the University of Chicago, the Cosmopolitan School of Music and Dramatic Art and the Hazel Sharp School of Ballet. She received an Hon. D. Litt. from World University. She is the editor of the Southwest issue of *Poet.* She is the author of seven books of poetry and has published in *the Christian Science Monitor, Good Housekeeping, Poet Lore, Gryphon, Encore, New Laurel Review and Bitterroot.* Her poems have been translated in several world anthologies.

ALICE BRILEY received degrees in English and Biology from the University of New Mexico at Albuquerque. She is the editor of *Encore*, a quarterly of verse and poetic arts and also edits *Strophes*, the national bulletin of the National Federation of State Poetry Societies. She is the recipient of the book award of the New Mexico State Poetry Society for her book of verse, *From a Weaver's Shuttle*. Her poetry has appeared in the *Saturday Evening Post, Denver Post* and the *Wall Street Journal.*

MAREL BROWN is the author of four books of poetry: *Red Hills, Hearth-Fire, Fence Corners* and *The Shape of a Song*. She was awarded "Writer of the Year" by the Atlanta Writers Club and "Poet of the Year" by the Dixie Council of Authors and Journalists for *The Shape of a Song*. In 1980, she received a Special Award from the Dixie Council for "her contributions to literature and poetry in the South."

FRANCES RIEMER BURT is a graduate of Wisconsin Teacher's College and taught elementary school in Wisconsin. She has published a book of poems called *Random Rhymes* and is presently a columnist for the *Penwoman* magazine. She teaches art and writing in public schools and is a frequent speaker on art and poetry at civic and art organizations.

WILMA WICKLAND BURTON, Litt. D., was educated in Des Moines, Iowa. She is the national editor of *The Pen Woman,* the official magazine of the National League of American Pen Women. Her books of poetry include *I Need a Miracle Today, Lord* and *Sidewalk Psalms and Some from Country Lanes.* She has published two books of prose. Her latest prose book, *The Martyr's Child,* will appear in 1982.

LOIS MASTERSON ROQUEMORE CARDEN received her B.A. and M.S. degrees from New Mexico Highland University. She has published widely in magazines such as *Good Housekeeping, Better Homes and Gardens, Poet* and *Orphic Lute.* She is presently a teacher in the New Mexico Schools.

FRANCES T. CARTER received a B.S. degree in Home Economics Education from the University of Southern Mississippi, an M.S. in Home Economics from the University of Tennessee and an Ed.D. in Education from the University of of Illinois. In 1981 she received an award from the Alabama Writers Conclave for service and dedication. She is the author of four books published by Convention Press and Southern Baptist Home Mission Board. She has published in *Dimensions, Junior College Journal, Alpha Delta Kappan, Contempo, The Village Post, The Sampler* and *Author-Poet.*

JEAN HUMPHREY CHAILLIE is an instructor on the staff of the Maricopa County Community College, District of Arizona. She is a consultant to the Arizona Education Association on "How to Teach Poetry to Children." She is the recipient of the "Triton Gold Medal," presented by Triton College in 1975 and 1976 for American Indian poetry. She won the Franc-Johnson Newcomb Memorial Award for Indian Poetry in 1974. Her poetry has been published in *Arizona Highways Magazine, Poet Lore, Ideals, The Arizonian, Poet* and *New Times.*

VIENNA IONE CURTISS earned her doctorate at Columbia University and studied at Parsons School of Design. She is the recipient of the National League of American Pen Women's First Prize for Nonfiction Books. Her books include the award-winning *Pageant of Art: A Visual History of Western Culture, Cappy—Rollicking Rancher Atop Arizona's Mighty Rim* and *I Should Be Glad to Help You, Madame: Europe Minus One's Wardrobe.*

DONNAFRED has taught creative writing and oil painting at Gila Pueblo College in Globe, Arizona. She is the author of four books: *Daughter of Eve, Pocket Piece, Love Runs Naked and Hold Me, Earth.* She illustrates and lectures on subjects from poetry to petroglyphs.

IDA FASEL received her B.A. and M.A. from Boston University and her Ph.D. from the University of Denver. She is the founder of Campus Poetry Workshops. In 1980, she received the national first place book award for her book, *On the Meaning of Cleave.* She taught at the University of Denver from 1962-1977 where she was Professor of English Emeritus. She was awarded first place for lecture in 1980 from the National League of American Pen Women.

CATHERINE FIELEKE studied at Drury College, Olivet

College and the University of Chicago. She is the author of four books of poetry and is the national poetry editor of the *Pen Woman* magazine. She has published in *Pen Woman, Encore, Spoon River Quarterly, Looking Back, Bardic Echoes, The Virginia Quarterly Review* and *Voices International.*

TRUTH MARY FOWLER is a graduate of North Adams State Teachers College in Quincy, MA. She is an eager student of Oriental poetry and life and its influence on Western Culture. She is the author of four books: *Haiku For All Day, Come, Laugh With Me, Sing a Song of Cinquains* and *Glow From a Stone Lantern.*

DONNA DICKEY GUYER received a B.A. in Humanities from the University of Chicago. She is a member of the Advisory Council, the National Society of Arts and Letters. She is two-time winner of the Lyric Memorial Award. She has published in *the New York Times, New York Herald Tribune, Wall Street Journal, Reader's Digest, The Writer, The Writer's Digest, The Lyric, The Sign, McCalls'* and the *Ladies' Home Journal.*

JAYE GIAMMARINO is a graduate of City College, New York. She holds an Honorary Degree of Doctor of Humane Letters, LHD, from the International Academy of Hull, England. She is the author of four books: *The First Thaw, Wine in a Gold Cup, Sun of Reflection* and *A Certain Hunger.* She is the compiler and editor of two national anthologies, *Badge of Promise* and *Moon Age Poets.*

GUANETTA GORDON is the author of six books: *Songs of the Wind, Under the Rainbow Arch, Petals from the Moon, Shadow Within the Flame, Above Rubies, Women of the Bible* and *Red Are the Embers.* She is the recipient of numerous awards including the World Poetry Society Honor Award: Selected Poem Magna Cum Laude - Distinguished Service Citation for "The Dream Reaper." The University of Kansas maintains a depository of her work sheets and published works.

WAUNETA HACKLEMAN, distinguished editor of this volume, is the president of The National Federation of State Poetry Societies, Inc. (1981-1983) and former president of The National League of American Pen Women, Inc. (1978-

1980). She has won numerous prizes for her poetry, including two Arizona State Awards in 1976. Author of *How to Slay a Dragon, A Lump of Sugar and a Dash of Spice,* and *Soliloquies in Verse,* she taught creative writing at Yavapai Community College and the University of Panama. She is a life member of the Society of Literary Designates, Washington, D.C. She received an Honorary Doctorate in 1981 from University of Taipei.

EVELYN ALLEN HAMMETT received her B.A. and M.A. degrees from the University of Chicago. She is Professor Emeritus in English of Delta State University, where she taught for thirty two years. Her poems have appeared in *The English Journal, World Outlook, New York Herald Tribune* and *Good House-keeping.* Her juvenile fiction, *I, Priscilla,* published by Macmillan, has appeared in two German editions.

ALFARATA HANSEL received both B.A. and M.A. degrees in English Literature from Wellesley College. She was awarded a "Certificate of Merit for Distinguished Contributions to Poetry" in 1971 by the *International Who's Who in Poetry* of London, England. She has taught classes in poetic technique at Phoenix Community College and various other colleges. Her poems have been collected in two volumes: *Ribbons of Melody* and *Look Homeward.*

ETHEL EIKEL HARVEY, a native of New Orleans, is co-founder of the Louisiana State Poetry Society as well as a co-founder of the National Federation of State Poetry Societies, Inc. A workshop teacher and consistent contest winner for her poetry, she has been writing and publishing for many years.

VERNA LEE HINEGARDNER is the author of five books of poetry: *Magic Moments, The Ageless Heart, Mud and Music, One Green Leaf* and *Seven Ages of Golf.* She has edited a poetry column for fourteen years. She is the winner of the Arkansas Award of Merit and the Sybil Nash Abrams Award in 1973 and 1975. She is the Chancellor of the National Federation of State Poetry Societes, Inc., 1981-1983.

AGNES HOMAN is a graduate of the University of Miami. She writes a column, "The Poets Direction," for *Directions Magazine* and is also the poetry editor. She is vice-president of the

Florida State Poets Association and is a Founder-Fellow of the International Academy of Poets. She presently teaches poetry at the Highlands Art League and has also taught classes in writing poetry at Broward Community College in Hollywood, Florida.

MARGARET HONTON holds an M. S. degree from Ohio State University. She has edited three anthologies and is the author of *College Bound, Affinity Poems* and *Above Making Waves.* Her poems and articles have appeared in *Cornfield Review, Wild Iris, Wisconsin Review, Sojourner, James Joyce Quarterly* and *Journal of Women's Studies in Literature.* She has a new book entitled *Take Fire.*

JEAN JENKINS received B. A. and M. A. degrees from Brigham Young University and a Ph.D. from the University of Utah. She also received an L.L.D. from Lasalle University in Chicago. She was honored as "Poet of the Year" in South and West International and "Woman of the Year" by the American Association of University Women in 1977. She is the author of a textbook, *Voice, Diction and Interpretation* and a book of poetry, *The More for Loving.* She is presently Professor of Professional Speech at Brigham Young University.

DONNA SHRIVER JONES received a B. M. in Music from Stetson University and M. A. in English from Georgia Southern College. Her many awards include two First Place awards in the New Mexico contest and a First Place in New York Poetry Forum contest. Her work has been published in *Janus/SCTH, Fireflowers Modern Images, Modern Haiku, Nutmegger, Bardic Echoes, The Archer* and *Haiku West.* She is currently an instructor of English at Georgia Southern College.

FRONA LANE is a playwright, drama coach and book reviewer. She holds doctorate degrees in Literature and Cultural Humanities. Her many awards include the International Woman of Year to Hall of Fame. She is the author of twelve books of poetry. She taught in the Los Angeles City Schools and at Golden State University and Palomar College.

GLORIA MARTIN's books include *Memories of a Sod House, Velvet Pillows of Perfume* and *A Foreigner to Earth.* Her poetry has appeared in the *U. S. Congressional Record* and she has contributed to various periodicals, anthologies and books. She is a past editor of *Glowing Lanternes.* She is the inventor of the Glorionic Sonnet.

ANNE MARX is the author of nine books of poetry, her first a collection of German lyrics. Her other books include *A Time to Mend (Selected Poems 1960-1970), Hear of Israel and Other Poems, 40 Love Poems for 40 Years* and *Face Lifts for All Seasons.* A life member of The Poetry Society of America, she was on its Executive Board and a Vice President for eight consecutive years. For four years, she has been national poetry editor of *The Pen Woman.* She is co-editor of *The World's Love Poems* (Bantam Books) and *Pegasus in the Seventies.* Widely published in America and Europe, her work has been translated into six languages.

EMMA S. McLAUGHLIN is the winner of *Poet Lore's* Stephen Vincent Benet narrative award. She is the author of *Shining Fearless* and *Flying Proud.* Her articles and stories have been published widely in prose magazines. She appears frequently as a national prize winner in the National Federation of State Poetry Societies anthology.

EDNA MEUDT is the author of five volumes of poetry: *Round River Canticle, In No Strange Land, No One Sings Face Down, The Ineluctable Sea* and *Plain Chant For a Tree* and two plays. She is the President of the Wisconsin Fellowship Poets and past President of the National Federation of State Poetry Societies. Her honors include the Bard's chair and the Jade Ring from Wisconsin Regional Writers. She is the recipient of the Governor's Award for Creativity in the Arts.

VIVIAN M. MEYER received an A. A. in Humanities/Social Sciences from County College of Morris and a B. A. in Secondary English Education from Fairleigh Dickinson University. She is the founder of the New Jersey Poetry Society and editor of *Poetidings*, the NJPS newsletter. Her poetry has appeared in many literary magazines and poetry anthologies.

CECILIA PARSONS MILLER received a B.A. degree from Hillsdale College. She is the Charter President of the National Federation of State Poetry Societies, Inc. and was the first woman to become president of the Greater Harrisburg, PA Arts Council. She is the author of *Not Less Content, Peculiar Honors, Space Where Once a Husband Stood, To March to Terrible Music, Glow in the Sky* and *Stand at the Edge.*

DOROTHEA NEALE received a degree in English from the University of Maryland. She studied journalism at the University of Maryland and public relations at the New School in New York City. She is the founder, executive director and president of the New York Poetry Forum and vice-president of the Shelley Society of New York. Her many honors include a gold laurel crown and certificate as International Woman of 1975, silver laurel crown for "Leadership in Poetry," the 3rd World Congress of Poets.

VIOLETTE NEWTON is the author of five books of poetry: *Moses in Texas, The Proxy, Just My Size, A Cathedral Ringing* and *Poems of Guatemala.* Her awards include Poet Laureate of Texas in 1973 and the Medwick Award from the Poetry Society of America. Her work has appeared in *Literary Review, Forum, Fiction and Poetry by Texas Women* and in compilations such as *Emily Dickinson, Letters from the World.*

VIRGINIA NOBLE is an artist, composer and poet. She is a graduate of Famous Artists School and Hiram Johnson College. She is an associate editor for the American Poetry League. She studied poetry under a private tutor for two years. She is the creator of the Sevenelle and Orvillette forms. Her work has appeared in *the Christian Science Monitor, American Bard, American Poetry League* and *Aquarium Times.*

CLOVITA RICE received a B. A. degree from the University of Arkansas and M. S. E. from Arkansas State University. She is the editor of *Voices International*, a poetry quarterly, and the author of two books, *Blow Out the Sun* and *Red Balloons for the Major.* She judges national poetry contests and is a poetry consultant in the Little Rock, Arkansas area.

WANDA ALLENDER RIDER, a teacher of English and poetry, received a B. S. E. degree from Arkansas College and M. Ed. from Memphis State University. She also holds a Ph.D. from the University of Mississippi. She is Vice President of the Poetry Society of Tennessee. She is the recipient of the Golden Owl Award for Versatility in writing. Her articles have appreared in *the Arkansas Education Journal, The English Journal* and *Thrust for Educational Leadership.*

LIBORIA ROMANO holds a B. A. degree in Education and M. A. degree from Hunter College. She received an Honorary Doctorate for Philosophy in Literature from Arts and Science Institute in Florida. She is an Honorary Life member of World Poets Resource Center. Her numerous honors include the Third World Congress of Poets golden medallion for "Excellence in Poetry." She has published four books of poetry and her work has appeared in national and international magazines.

MARGARET THOMAS RUDD received a B. A. degree from the University of Richmond and M. A. degree from Columbia University. She taught Spanish for many years at the University of Richmond and was Dean at Blackstone College in Virginia. She served as president of the Virginia Chapter of the American Association of Teachers of Spanish. Her poetry has appeared in a number of anthologies including *Moon Age Poets.* Her articles have appeared in *Romance Notes, Journal of Inter-American Studies* and *Social Education.*

D. L. RUDY was educated at Queens College, Columbia University and Radcliffe. She is the author of three volumes of poetry. Her latest collection of poems appears in *Grace Notes to the Measure of the Heart.* She is currently Professor of English at Montclair State College where she specializes in creative writing and contemporary poetry. She is working on a series of biographical poems.

AMY JO SCHOONOVER (pen name, Amy Jo Zook) received a B. A. degree in English from Wittenburg University and M.A. in English from West Virginia University. She is the past President of Verse Writer's Guild of Ohio and editor of the poetry quarterly, *Dream Shop.* She is contest chairman for the National Federation of State Poetry Societies, Inc. Ms. Schoonover is currently working on her doctorate at West Virginia University.

ORA PATE STEWART has been writing poetry and composing songs since childhood. She also began performing her work at an early age. She has published twenty-five books, among them, *God Planted a Tree*, in its 27th edition. Her poetry book, *Gleanings*, is in its 7th edition. She has taught classes for the University of Utah and summer classes for Brigham Young University.

LIBBY STOPPLE has had seven books published: Red *Metal, Never Touch a Lilac, No Other Word, Singer in the Side, Peppermints, A Box of Peppermints* and *Song For All Seasons*. During 1975, she was Poet in Residence for two elementary schools. She has won awards for her poetry and appears in several anthologies. She is currently collaborating with Hal Shane, New York actor, composer and singer.

EVELYN AMUEDO WADE received a B. A. degree from American University and M. A. from George Washington University. Since 1976, she has been Director of the poetry workshop for Georgetown University's Writer Conference. Author of *Laughing It Off*, she has published poetry, short stories and articles in the *Saturday Evening Post, Wall Street Journal* and *Good Housekeeping*. She is currently Associate Professor of English at Northern Virginia Community College.

IRENE WARSAW, a native of Bay City Michigan, has had two volumes of poetry published by the Golden Quill Press, A *Word in Edgewise* and *Warily We Roll Along*. Her poetry has appeared in numerous national magazines and papers. In 1980, she was awarded the honorary degree of Doctor of Letters by Saginaw Valley State College. Frequently asked to act as judge for poetry contests, she lectures at schools, colleges and writers' conferences.

GRACE KIRK WOFFORD received her B. A. degree from Grenada Jr. College and pursued graduate studies at the University of Chicago. Her numerous awards include "Drew's Woman of Achievement." She has held national offices in Pen Woman and was Branch President of the NLAPW. Author of *Lyric Poems*, her articles and poetry have appeared in the *Mississippi Poetry Journal* and *The Pen Woman*.

ANNA NASH YARBROUGH is the director of the Arkansas Writer's Annual Conference and served as president of this organization for twenty-five years. She served as president, at both the branch and state levels, of the Arkansas Pen Women. She has been a newspaper columnist for many years. Author of *Flower of the Field, Building With Blocks, Poetry Patterns* and *Syllabic Poetry Patterns*, her poetry and fiction have appeared in magazines and newspapers.